HANDEL AS ORPHEUS

Handel as Orpheus

VOICE AND DESIRE IN THE CHAMBER CANTATAS

Ellen T. Harris

HARVARD UNIVERSITY PRESS

Cambridge, Massachusetts, and London, England · 2001

Copyright © 2001 by the President and Fellows of Harvard College
All rights reserved
Printed in the United States of America

Publication of this book has been supported through the generous
provisions of the Maurice and Lula Bradley Smith Memorial Fund
and by a grant from the Massachusetts Institute of Technology.

Library of Congress Cataloging-in-Publication Data
Harris, Ellen T.
    Handel as Orpheus : voice and desire in the chamber cantatas / Ellen T. Harris.
        p.   cm.
    Includes bibliographical references and index.
    ISBN 0-674-00617-8 (alk. paper)
        1. Handel, George Frideric, 1685–1759. Cantatas.   2. Cantata.   3. Homosexuality and music.
    I. Title.

ML410.H13 H283   2001
782.4'8'092—dc21   2001039075

For my husband, John

Contents

Acknowledgments

The preparation and writing of this book might be compared to a long journey with scenic diversions, detours and delays, and a destination I could not have imagined when I began. I have, over the many years of this journey, incurred more than a few debts, and I am grateful to a number of individuals and institutions without whom the research and writing would have been harder (and less fun) and the finished work weaker. With the risk of overlooking some, whose forgiveness I beg, I will try to acknowledge at least some of the help I have received.

Over the years I have benefited from research support. The National Endowment for the Humanities (summer stipend 1978, fellowship 1988–89), the American Council of Learned Societies (fellowship 1980–81), and a year (1995–96) at the Bunting Institute of Radcliffe College at Harvard University (generously supported by MIT) greatly aided my research on the cantatas at various stages. An MIT-supported leave in 1999–2000 gave me the time to write. I am extremely indebted to MIT in various ways, and I hope the Institute's support of humanistic scholarship is duly recognized by readers of this book.

The process of writing and revising has offered me a stronger, and more wonderful, experience of being a part of a large but interconnected academic community than at any point in my career. To the "gang of five" I am indebted for friendship and collegiality. Jessie Ann Owens (Brandeis University) was the only person I allowed to see my first drafts, and her combination of apt critique and specific enthusiasms spurred me forward more than once. At subsequent stages Kay Kaufman Shelemay (Harvard University) and Jane Bernstein (Tufts University) read entire drafts, helping me to sharpen and clarify my argument. Judith Tick (Northeastern University) offered sage advice and encouragement throughout the process.

I have also benefited enormously from specialist readers whose suggestions and corrections have improved and expanded the final work. I am very grateful for the help and friendship, sometimes newfound through this process of cri-

tique, of the classical scholars Richard Tarrant (Harvard University) and Robert
Ketterer (University of Iowa), the art historian and distinguished author in gay
and lesbian studies James Saslow (City University of New York), and the musi-
cologists Ellen Rosand (Yale University) and Jeffrey Kallberg (University of
Pennsylvania), as well as John Roberts (University of California, Berkeley), who
read a completed draft and carefully dictated his comments and concerns long-
distance over the phone, completing a trio of fellow American Handel Society
board members (Ketterer, Rosand, and Roberts) who lent me their expertise.
Anthony Hicks (London) critically read Appendix 1 on chronology, leading me
to a complete reorganization, and Daniele Benati (MIT) and Terence Best
(London) provided detailed commentary on the Italian orthography and English translations of Appendix 2.

A particular debt of gratitude belongs to Ruth Smith (Cambridge), who not
only read a complete draft but agreed to offer her professional skills as a copy
editor in addition to her detailed knowledge of Handel. An author who benefited previously from Dr. Smith's red pencil thanked her for saving him from
many a solecism. She has saved me from that and more.

I am honored to hold the Class of 1949 professorship at MIT, and I am very
grateful to the Class of 1949 for their support, which has aided the preparation
of this book in many ways. The research fund allowed me to benefit from the
work of three research assistants. Fleur de Vie Weinstock worked with me on
the issue of silence in music during my year at the Bunting Institute when she
was an undergraduate at Harvard, and John McKay worked with me on the
analysis of the instrumental cantatas during the summer of 1999 when he was
an undergraduate at MIT. I am particularly indebted to Minji Kim, a Ph.D.
candidate at Brandeis University, who assisted in preparing the footnotes and
bibliographical references, and whose help was both essential and excellent. I
look forward to welcoming her fully into the field of Handel studies.

The Class of 1949 professorship also supported the fine work of Hyunjung
Choi in preparing the musical examples and Marilyn Bliss in creating the index.
It also funded the acquisition of photographic reproductions for the book. I am
very grateful to the museums and collections (named in the figure captions
throughout the book) for granting permission to reproduce these images.

I am grateful for the help over the years of my cantata research to many li-
braries, three of which I need to single out. The British Library holds most of
Handel's autographs and is, for most Handel scholars, a magnetic attractor.
Whether studying a cantata manuscript or eighteenth-century trial records
from the Old Bailey, I typically found help and advice as valuable as the sources.
However, the book could not have been written without the resources of the
Harvard University and MIT libraries, which supported me on my home turf.
The MIT libraries in particular provided extraordinary service across a system

that takes pride in its support of scholars and scholarship; I would like especially to thank the MIT librarians in the Rosalind Denny Lewis Music Library, the Rotch Library (for Art and Architecture), the Humanities Library, and Interlibrary Borrowing (whose efforts gave me access to every book I needed).

I am very grateful to Peg Fulton, Mary Ellen Geer, and others at Harvard University Press for expertly and efficiently guiding me and the book through the publication process. I must also single out the help of my assistant, Elizabeth Connors. We have worked together for twelve years, and, increasingly, she has played a critical role in my scholarship, where I can benefit particularly from her musical skills and poetic talent. She is in addition a first-rate proofreader.

The one person who has participated in my work on the cantatas from the outset is my husband, John, who watched my beginning steps in manuscript studies, supported my diversion into administrative work, and encouraged me to continue my research as the content of the book evolved and changed. It is to him that this book is dedicated, with love.

Note on the Musical Examples

To date the only attempted complete edition of Handel's continuo cantatas is that of Friedrich Chrysander in the Händelgesellschaft edition dating from the end of the nineteenth century. Because this edition, although a monumental achievement, contains many errors, omissions, and corruptions, I have, whenever possible, based the examples directly on the autographs or a primary manuscript copy. Despite the overall fine quality of the new Hallische Händel-Ausgabe edition of the instrumental cantatas by Hans Joachim Marx, I have followed the same practice with examples from the instrumental cantatas, and the astute reader will note differences in detail, as in *Apollo e Dafne*, Example 4.4, where I omit the bassoon as well as the oboes from the rushing scales following Daphne's transformation, and *Echeggiate, festeggiate*, Example 5.13, where three measures before the end I interpret the bass as having a rest rather than the note *f*. However, these examples do not an edition make. They are deliberately spare, providing only what is required for the example. I often revert to short score, and instrumental lines are identified by shorthand. Bass figures are omitted throughout; the omission of instrumental accompaniments is always indicated. Editorial accidentals and ties are provided without comment.

HANDEL AS ORPHEUS

Prologue: "The Ways of the World"

I know there will be many . . . who will reprimand me for things for which I may perhaps be justly reproached. To [these] I say that it is possible that some things have been improperly included, and I will easily believe it, for it often happens that a writer is deceived not only by ignorance of the matter but by excessive love he has for his work. If I have done this, I am sorry, and I ask, for the glory of honorable studies, that wiser men tolerate with kindly spirit what has not been done properly. And if anyone has a charitable soul, let him correct what has been improperly written by adding to it or deleting and improve it so that the work will flourish for someone's benefit, rather than perish torn by the jaws of the malicious without being of service to anyone.

Boccaccio, *Concerning Famous Women*

I became interested in Handel's cantatas more than twenty-five years ago while writing my dissertation. Since that time I have pursued these sometimes elusive works through source studies, analyses, editing, and performance;[1] in addition, the research of other scholars has offered a rich fund of information to which I am deeply indebted.[2] In the course of my studies three milestones critically affected the outcome of this book. First, source studies demonstrated that cantata composition was limited in Handel's life to a specific period (1706–1723), which, I slowly realized, exactly matches the years during which Handel lived in the homes of his aristocratic patrons. Second, examination of this world of private patronage revealed a male-dominated social environment that both fostered and accepted the same-sex activities of many of these patrons. Third, translation of all the cantata texts and a close reading of them in terms of their literary heritage and social environment confirmed a persistent homoerotic subtext. The conflation of context and content then led me back to the music with a broader social and sexual perspective. Consequently, my original intention to write a monograph providing detailed source information, chronology, and descriptive analysis was superseded.

This book, which grows out of and fully engages the past thirty years of archival research and source studies, offers a contextual interpretation of the cantatas and their musical development during a discrete period of private patronage in Handel's life. It encompasses the political, religious, and sexual background of these works; any emphasis on the sexual aspects results from the erotic nature of the cantata texts themselves and the specific contexts in which they were written. Based on pastoral poetry and mythological stories descended from classical literary sources, these texts provide a critical pathway to interpretation. Handel, like his Italian contemporaries, composed the majority of his cantatas for solo voice with continuo accompaniment; this study offers, for the first time, complete translations of the 67 texts Handel set, sometimes more than once, for voice and continuo. Handel's instrumental cantatas comprise 28 works (or 29 if *Aci, Galatea e Polifemo* is included) for one or more voices with instrumental scoring, ranging from a single violin or recorder to full strings with various wind instruments, including oboe, flute, bassoon, and trumpet, added to the continuo. This book presents the first comprehensive study of all the cantatas, both continuo and instrumental, set within the parameters of private aristocratic patronage and the eighteenth-century context of same-sex love.

In this study, while tracing Handel's life as closely as possible, I have adopted a topical framework based on changing patterns in Handel's composition of cantatas. Chapter 1, "Code Names and Assumed Identities," focuses on an early cantata of 1707 whose text by Cardinal Pamphili specifically compares Handel to Orpheus. A rereading of the classical and early modern history of this legend, with special attention to the depiction in Ovid's *Metamorphoses,* illustrates that the image of Orpheus provided a double emblem of musician and homosexual, not just in the classical era but in the eighteenth century as well.

The next three chapters examine in turn each of the three types of cantatas that Handel composed in Italy: solo instrumental cantatas, solo continuo cantatas, and multi-voice instrumental cantatas. Chapter 2, "Women's Voices/Men's Voices," investigates the solo instrumental cantatas, dating largely from 1707. In many of these the singer has a specific identity, and in the earliest cantatas the representation of women's voices dominates. Descendants of Ovid's *Heroides,* Handel's women are condemned, abandoned, raped, suicidal, love-crazy, and celibate (Agrippina, Armida, Lucrezia, Hero, and Diana). Significantly, they speak through Handel's music in their own passionate voices, whereas the cantatas about individual men (Abdolonymus, Daedalus), who are often more concerned with fortune and ambition than with love, are narrated in the third person. Chapter 3, "Pastoral Lovers," studies the continuo cantatas in light of the tradition of pastoral poetry descended from Theocritus's *Idylls* and Virgil's *Eclogues,* examining textual codes and same-sex attraction as both a classical tradition and a contemporary one in the Arcadian Academy in 1707 and 1708. I explore the ways in which the voice representing a male persona, in contrast to that of an "abandoned" female, was controlled and constrained with artifice. Chapter 4, "Cantata Couples and Love Triangles," investigates the instrumental duet and trio cantatas and their revisions, most of which date from 1708, showing how their classical and mythological texts, with intermediate resonance from Petrarch's *Poems,* deal with transformation or sublimation of desire.

In Chapter 5, "Silence and Secrecy," I consider the pervasive references to silence and secrecy in the cantata texts, discuss the increasing use of silent pauses and disruptions in Handel's cantatas for Hanover and London after 1710, and examine this stylistic novelty in light of cultural and literary trends in the first half of the eighteenth century in England. *On the Sublime,* attributed to Longinus, offered classical authority for dramatic silence in literature, but Handel's cantatas more closely resemble Garrick's later, and controversial, use of silence in the theater. Chapter 6, "Culmination of the Private," offers allegorical interpretations, dependent in part on the *Idylls* of Theocritus, of the large-scale works performed for the Earl of Carnarvon in 1718 toward the end of the cantata period: *Acis and Galatea* and *Esther.*

The Epilogue looks at the revival and alteration of works by Handel from an earlier period in the decade of the 1730s, investigating the reasons for the changes. I continue here the discussion of assumed identities, examining in particular three related identities assigned to Handel in this decade. Appendix 1 presents a semi-tabular summary of the documentary evidence that underlies a chronological understanding of the cantatas. Appendix 2 provides complete texts and translations of the continuo cantatas in alphabetical order, but identified by date to facilitate reference to Appendix 1. Texts of the instrumental cantatas and translations by Terence Best have been published in the Hallische Händel–Ausgabe edition of the instrumental cantatas; I provide excerpts from these as necessary in my discussion of the instrumental cantatas.[3]

I was first drawn to Handel's cantatas by their music—music of great brilliance and genius that explores a wide range of emotions. "Senti, di te, ben mio" from *Nel dolce tempo,* for example, resounds in unambiguous major tonality and upbeat tempo; the alternation of cascading scales with repeated or sustained notes in the voice along with the oscillating and sequential motives in the bass depicts both a quickening of pulse and the fluttering of birds. The charm of this musical portrait cannot fail to bring a smile to the lips of the listener. In contrast, "Siete rose," from the cantata of the same name, begins hesitantly: tiny musical phrases, encompassing only a handful of notes separated by rests and marked by dotted rhythms, resist moving forward. Slowly the singer expands these phrases outward in range while embellishing them with increasingly elaborate musical turns, describing the transformation from wonder and disbelief to an affirmation of love touched with just a frisson of pleasure that sends chills down the spine. In "Dunque se il tanto piangere" from *Lungi n'andò Fileno* the minor tonality, the slowly rising chromatic line in the bass coupled with the insistent repetition of a four-square rhythmic motive, and the upward leaps in the voice of a tenth and an octave leading to an unresolved conclusion communi-

Example P.1 *Nel dolce tempo,* "Senti, di te."

Example P.2 *Silla,* "Senti, bel idol mio!"

cate a tortuous agony and cry of pain that is followed by despair and breaks the heart.

Although the cantatas remain the least known of all Handel's compositions, Handel himself never forgot them, and they remained throughout his life a personal treasure trove of invention. "Senti, di te, ben mio," for example, reappeared in his opera *Silla* (1713), as shown in Exx. P.1 and P.2. More than a decade later, in 1724, "Siete rose" returned as the aria in which Andronico first describes his love for Asteria in the opera *Tamerlano* (Exx. P.3 and P.4). In 1749, "Dunque se il tanto piangere" became the basis for "If guiltless blood be your intent" from the oratorio *Susanna* (Exx. P.5 and P.6).

However, neither their intrinsic beauty nor the force of Handel's imprimatur have been sufficient to recover these works from historical obscurity. A handful of the cantatas was printed in Samuel Arnold's edition of Handel's works in the late eighteenth century,[4] but the first attempt to publish all the cantatas was in the Händelgesellschaft edition, edited by Friedrich Chrysander, a century later.[5] Even after the Gesellschaft publication, the cantatas languished. In 1932, in one

Example P.3 *Siete rose,* "Siete rose."

Example P.4 *Tamerlano,* "Bella Asteria."

Example P.5 *Lungi n'andò Fileno,* "Dunque se il tanto piangere."

Example P.6 *Susanna,* "If guiltless blood be your intent."

of the first attempts to discuss these works, Walter Ford acknowledged the neglect of the cantatas in the scholarly community:

> Many besides myself, who have counted ourselves lovers of Handel, must have
> had twinges of conscience when their eyes fell upon the four volumes [of the
> complete works] which contain his cantatas.[6]

In 1954, Anthony Lewis contributed a chapter entitled "The Songs and Chamber Cantatas" in *Handel: A Symposium,* but like his predecessors, he was stymied
by knowing little or nothing about the origin or chronology of the cantatas.[7]

This situation changed in 1967 with the publication by Ursula Kirkendale of
documents from the archive of Prince Francesco Maria Ruspoli that not only
showed that many of Handel's cantatas were written for this Roman patron, but
provided an initial rough chronology based on the dates when they were first
copied.[8] Thereafter, additional discoveries of documentary and manuscript evidence contributed more information about the music Handel composed for a
number of his private patrons in Italy, Germany, and England:[9] the Medici
court in Florence,[10] Cardinal Ottoboni in Rome,[11] Cardinal Pamphili in
Rome,[12] the court of the elector, Georg Ludwig, at Hanover,[13] and the Cannons
estate of James Brydges, later the Duke of Chandos.[14] In the midst of these dis-

coveries, John Mayo in 1977 completed a dissertation that for the first time presented an overview of the cantatas.[15]

In parallel with the archival discoveries, an increased interest in source studies aided the development of a chronology of the cantatas. Identification and comparison of the watermarks in Handel's autographs has provided more and better information about the provenance and dating of individual works.[16] Identification and comparison of the scribal hands in manuscript copies clarified the process and the speed by which these works were prepared for performance, and provided additional evidence concerning dating and patronage.[17]

The application of archival research and source materials to Handel studies transformed our knowledge of the cantatas, offering a useful chronology, the evidence to associate certain works with specific locales, a better understanding of known manuscript sources, and the identification of new sources. The new edition of instrumental cantatas from the Hallische Händel–Ausgabe is one significant outgrowth of this research, providing good musical texts of the instrumentally accompanied cantatas for the first time.[18] From a historical point of view, however, the most important outcome has been the revelation that the cantatas were written during a clearly circumscribed period, bounded on the one side by Handel's departure from his German homeland in 1705 or 1706 and on the other by his moving in July 1723 into the London house that was to remain his residence for the rest of his life. The significance of these boundaries cannot be overestimated.

As has been repeatedly asserted, these years include the most critical period in Handel's development as a composer. Julian Herbage writes, "Handel's stay in Italy was undoubtedly the most formative period of his career";[19] Claude Palisca claims that "four years in Italy converted Handel almost entirely to the melodious Italian manner";[20] and Winton Dean states more specifically that "in Italy [Handel] assimilated the flexibility and eloquence of Scarlatti's vocal idiom, and the polished energy of the instrumental style of Corelli."[21] The cantatas offer insights into Handel's stylistic development not only during the Italian years but, more broadly, between the first opera he wrote, *Almira* (Hamburg, 1705), and his first opera for the Royal Academy of Music in London, *Radamisto* (1720). As opposed to his operas written sporadically between 1705 and 1720,[22] the cantatas, especially in Italy, were in almost continual production. However, it is only now, thanks to the establishment of a working chronology, that Handel's stylistic development over these years can be critically evaluated.[23]

The specific period during which the cantatas were composed, 1706 to 1723, not only encompasses critically important years in Handel's stylistic development; it is also, exactly, the only period in which Handel lived and worked as a guest in aristocratic homes. It is this living arrangement that marks the years of

Handel's regular composition of cantatas and serenatas as unique. After leaving aristocratic patronage, Handel rarely returned, and then only under special circumstances, to the genre of the Italian secular cantata.[24] Further, he never published any of his cantatas—the only genre in which he composed of which that can be said.[25] The reason certainly does not lie in lack of interest in published cantatas: many of his contemporary colleagues, including John Christopher Pepusch and Giovanni Bononcini, saw cantatas into print.[26] There is also no lack of quality, as Handel's own musical borrowings from this buried treasure attest; and even the borrowings themselves would hardly have prevented publication, as Handel also borrowed freely from published works of his own and others. The cantatas thus represent the clearest example of private music in the life of this quintessentially public composer. Understanding them demands a closer look at the aristocratic patrons in whose houses they were composed.

From 1706 to 1723, Handel passed through the Medici court and the palaces of the Roman cardinals Pamphili, Ottoboni, and Colonna and the Marquis Ruspoli—where he performed in private salons (or academies) as well as the larger Arcadian Academy hosted in these years by Ruspoli—and then to the court of the elector in Hanover, the house of Lord Burlington in London, and the villa in Cannons outside London owned by James Brydges. Among the distinguishing features of this patronage is the role of same-sex friendship, love, and desire. As illustrated more fully in the following chapters, the thread of male love can be documented in a range of sources stretching from clear archival evidence concerning the homosexual activities of the Medici princes, to the homosexual undertones of poetry written for the Arcadian Academy based on classical models, to the same-sex erotic atmosphere of Burlington House. Although not limited to this topic, Handel's private house music for these patrons cannot be understood without consideration of its context of same-sex love.

The issue of sexuality raises the critically important question of voice. In the cantatas, the voices and personae of men and women tend to be sharply differentiated. Typically, women are depicted as dangerous, and women's uncontrolled voices are heard as a threat to male power and artistic creation. As the traditional myths tell us, not only do Ariadne's threats and Diana's anger wreak havoc on Theseus and Actaeon, but it is only by drowning out his voice with their cacophony that the Thracian women are able to kill Orpheus (see Chapters 1 and 2). In contrast, the persona of the Arcadian shepherd, borrowed from classical literary sources, offers the requisite artifice and distance, as well as a same-sex model, for the expression of male love as opposed to unchecked (female) emotion. Throughout the cantatas, a progression away from passionate expression and formal irregularity toward more stylized and formally controlled rhetoric can be musically associated with a retreat from the uncontrolled female voice to the idealized male voice (see Chapter 3). The instrumental multi-voice cantatas offer a variety of personae, each of which presents a different point of view. The myth of Apollo and Daphne, for example, is not only a single story about two characters but also a double story about each character individually, and this multi-vocality, although not simultaneous as in a Mozart ensemble, is essential to its interpretation (see Chapter 4). The multiple voices in some of the larger cantatas point the way to a consideration of multi-vocality in all of them. That is, all of the cantatas potentially contain voices in addition to those of the imaginary characters—including author, composer, patron, and auditor (or all of the above)—raising the question of whose voice is heard, whose suppressed, whose disguised. In their assumed names, codes, and silences, Handel's cantatas epitomize the prevalence of hidden identities in the society of his time.

The eighteenth century was a playground of disguise. In social circles the physical use of masks lay at the heart of the Venetian carnival and the English masquerade (established in 1717 by Handel's colleague John Jacob Heidegger, the Swiss impresario) and enabled those who attended to overstep the boundaries of gender, age, and class, as well as normal social and behavioral constraints. Similarly, authors and artists used metaphorical masks when they published their works either anonymously or under a pseudonym. To take a single musical example, the composer Agostino Steffani, Handel's predecessor at Hanover, after assuming diplomatic responsibilities, adopted the name of his copyist Gregorio Piva for his musical compositions.[27] Literary instances are legion: among Handel's associates in London, disguised authorship was as much the norm as authentic attribution. The John Bull pamphlets of 1712, supposedly "printed from a manuscript found in the cabinet of the famous Sir Humphry Polesworth," are now comfortably attributed to John Arbuthnot, although many contemporaries (and scholars as late as 1925) attributed them to Jonathan Swift.[28] Together, Arbuthnot, Swift, Alexander Pope, and John Gay created the fictitious author Martin Scriblerus, and Swift's *Travels into Several Nations of the World*, published under the pseudonym of Lemuel Gulliver, probably developed out of the Scriblerus project.

In the Arcadian Academy of Rome, to which all of Handel's Roman patrons belonged and for which he composed, members adopted elaborate pastoral names—Cardinal Ottoboni, for example, was known as Crateo Ericino Pastore,[29] and Cardinal Pamphili as Fenicio Larisseo.[30] Members of the Academy often published under their pastoral names and could be referred to in texts by their assumed names as well, as happens in Handel's multi-voice cantata *Oh, come chiare* (1708) where one of the characters is Olinto [Arsenio], the Arcadian name of Handel's patron Ruspoli.[31] In part these so-called pastoral names were honorifics, signifying membership in the Academy, and, as such, the real identity of these shepherds was an open secret. In part, however, the assumed name, even though it was well known, provided license to assume an activity, such as publication, associated with a different station in life; Steffani's assumed name for composition served this purpose.

In contrast to the elaborate and individualized Arcadian identities, the conventional pastoral names of Tirsi and Aminta from the cantatas cannot typically be connected to specific individuals; however, these common names could serve as better disguises for personal expression than the thinly veiled Arcadian names. Not only does this fit the tradition of the pastoral—in his *Eclogues,* Virgil sometimes speaks in his own voice under the name Tityrus or Corydon, and, in his *Pastorals,* Pope identifies himself as the shepherd Alexis—but evidence for such a conclusion survives in a Roman manuscript of cantatas by Alessandro Scarlatti with watercolors by Pier Leone Ghezzi (see Figure 3.1). Here Tirsi and other pastoral lovers are surprisingly depicted with scenes of contemporary courtiers in and around Rome—the Arcadians of the Roman Academy rather than the idealized Arcadian shepherds of the texts—indicating the likelihood that the simple pastoral names concealed the passions of the aristocracy, perhaps in some cases with specific reference.[32]

Not only was assumed identity important to individuals in various settings and professions (whether at masquerades or clubs, or for authors and provocateurs), but authors and artists in pamphlet attacks and literary or pictorial allegories frequently assigned hidden or assumed identities to others. Readers and viewers looked for the covert meanings in published writings and paintings, and elaborate keys, often differing from one another, were frequently offered to the public—not, of course, by the original author or painter. The *Key* to the John Bull pamphlets ran to six editions, showing, to take one instance, that Lewis Baboon represented the Bourbon King Louis XIV of France.[33] Concerning *Gulliver's Travels,* John Gay wrote to Swift in Dublin that he should return to London "where you will have the pleasure of a variety of commentators, to explain the difficult passages to you."[34] It was generally agreed, for example, that Filmnap, the ill-natured Lord High Treasurer of Lilliput, represented Sir Robert Walpole.[35]

Assigned identities also flourished in private letters—in part, one assumes, to give an insider quality (akin to club membership) to the correspondence, but also to preserve an element of privacy in an era when letters might be intercepted and opened by government spies, servants employed by an enemy or snoops. Mary (Granville) Delany, who first met Handel at the age of ten and as an adult became one of his greatest fans, left a voluminous correspondence in which she assigns code names or nicknames to most of her family and closest friends.[36] Luckily she left a Key in her autobiography, which allows us to decipher most of her comments. These range from affectionate childhood names, such as Bunny for her brother Bernard Granville, to abbreviations, such as Dup for the Viscount Thomas Dupplin, to what one imagines are descriptive monikers, such as the Dragon for the Countess Grace Granville and Apollo's Imp for the Hon. Henry Hervey.[37]

Code names in correspondence were not, of course, always so innocent. Political upheaval over the British royal succession at the beginning of the century had spawned at least two clear factions: one that favored Protestant rule and so supported the Hanoverian Succession that would bring a German king to the throne of Great Britain in 1714, the other that favored Catholic rule or "rightful" succession above religion and so was willing to accept as king the Catholic James, son of James II and half-brother of Queen Anne, and to maintain the Stuart line. With the Act of Settlement in 1701 providing for an eventual Hanoverian succession, the opposition "Jacobites" needed to maintain the strictest secrecy to conceal their maneuverings and protect themselves from charges of treason. Around 1712, the code name for Lord Burlington, one of Handel's English patrons at the time, according to a Jacobite "key" for coded correspondence, was "Mr. Buck."[38]

As these examples indicate, the use of assumed and assigned names provided various combinations of secrecy, intimacy, and license: secrecy to protect or hide one's identity, as with the masqueraders or Lord Burlington; intimacy to create the sense of a special group, whether as formal as the Arcadian Academy or as informal as Mrs. Delany's group of correspondents; and license to say or do what could not otherwise be voiced or done, such as Steffani's continued composition after assuming a diplomatic position or Arbuthnot's and Swift's publication of political satire. As ever, at multiple levels ranging from personal gossip to national politics, activities preeminently related to the topics of politics, religion, and sex attracted and necessitated such pseudonyms.

Politics, religion, and sex also lie behind the texts of Handel's vocal music, providing, as in literature, art, and correspondence, the background for allegorical interpretations and metaphor. Overall, a large-scale division may arguably be made by genre. Political allegory dominates Baroque operas in general, deriving in part from the strong positions of royal and aristocratic operatic sponsors.[39] In Handel's oratorios, national religion and statehood defined by religion take pride of place, strongly affected not just by royal patronage but by the religious convictions of individual librettists. As Ruth Smith has ably demonstrated in her study of Handel's oratorio texts (and one could say the same about his operas), the allegories are frequently general rather than specific, and often loose enough to permit readings on both sides of the political argument.[40] In the Baroque cantata, by contrast, the primary focus is on passionate love. Of course, the connections between genre and allegorical subject are not absolute, and some works may have no allegory at all, but musical texts were no exception to the prevalence of codes and disguises in the early eighteenth century.

Despite this emphasis in Baroque opera, oratorio, and cantata on, respectively, the political, religious, and sexual background, the strong relations among these topics made the boundaries between them permeable. In the classical era, Theocritus and Virgil had used the mask of the pastoral to address all three topics, and Handel's cantata texts, direct descendants from classical pastoral poetry, do the same. Although the majority of cantata shepherds are intent on physical passion and love, a few, like Ruspoli in his Arcadian identity, are described as engaged in fighting the War of Spanish Succession, and some others are spiritual shepherds pursuing lost souls (in the metaphorical form of nymphs) or seeking sacred solitude. As with the related forms of love—*philadelphia, agape,* and *eros*—it is not always easy to distinguish among these allegorical pursuits that so closely mirror one another. The pursuit of love depicted in the cantatas may emphasize *eros,* but it encompasses politics (representing alliances as brotherly love, or *philadelphia*) and religion (*agape*).

In the cantatas, as in the classical pastoral, *eros* is both heterosexual and homosexual. Indeed, the pastoral—and classical literature more generally—represents one of three eighteenth-century models for theorizing homosexuality. These can be categorized loosely by their religious, sexual, or political undertones, and each offers male love as a metaphor for, respectively, sin, ideal love, or political threat. The religious view, based on biblical condemnation, saw homosexual acts as destructive of the basic fabric of society: the very word for bestial or anal intercourse, sodomy, was based on the biblical city of Sodom, destroyed for its sins. Taken over by the legal system, sodomy was understood not only as a sexual act, but as a sign of predisposition to overthrow natural and social law. Thus men accused of this crime were frequently condemned to death in order, so it was thought, to protect the state from internal destruction. In contrast, the classical tradition represented a largely positive authority for same-sex love. Such passionate male friendships as that between Achilles and Patroclus were not just sanctioned but encouraged as essential to a well-functioning society. Thus the classical heritage offered an idealized model, as well as a metaphorical screen behind which same-sex desire could flourish. By and large, the legal and classical models did not distinguish different types of relationships but rather characterized the same relationships differently.[41] The exotic or Orientalist view of homosexuality was only beginning to take root in this period, but there were already signs that same-sex practices were increasingly connected with an image of eastern culture as attractive but dangerous. An outgrowth of a determined British belief in the foreign origin of homosexuality, whether from Europe (Italy particularly) or the East, the exotic image adopted the allure of the classical model and transformed the implied danger to the state from the wages of sin (in the religious and legal view) into an external political threat. This study touches on all three of these eighteenth-century images of homosexuality, and I will engage them more fully in the Epilogue in relation to assigned identities for Handel. However, my focus, like that of Handel's cantata texts, is primarily on the classical tradition.

The inclusion of political or ideological context in musicological scholarship has often faced resistance. Susan McClary, for example, provides an amusing description of the reaction several years ago of some Bach scholars to contextual studies:

> As a scholar classified as a Baroque music specialist, I participated during 1985 in several Bach Year celebrations: panel discussions in which my contributions were modest attempts at resituating Bach in his social, political, ideological context. . . . I was told outright by prominent scholars that Bach (unlike "second-rate" composers such as Telemann) had *nothing* to do with his time or place, that he was "divinely inspired," that his music works in accordance with perfect, universal order and truth. One is permitted, in other words, to deal with music in its social context, but only if one agrees to leave figures such as Bach alone.[42]

Handel enthusiasts and scholars have sometimes reacted similarly, but it is specifically the addition of homosexuality to this contextual mix that has caused the strongest response. The composer Michael Linton put it this way in a 1997 editorial entitled "America's Messiah" in *First Things: A Monthly Journal of Religion and Public Life:*

> The cultural significance of Handel and his *Messiah* for American music cannot be overstated. But it is a significance not universally welcomed. For roughly a generation, there has been a movement among musicologists to de-Christianize Handel, a by-product of which would be the reduction of *Messiah* to just one more religious work by a composer who really knew better. In 1966, the biographer Paul Henry Lang felt compelled to invent a string of mistresses for Handel (thereby making him "normal"). In 1980, Winton Dean, while acknowledging the "sincerity" of Handel's Christian beliefs, concluded that he was really a pantheist and hedonist at heart. More recently, writers have argued for a homosexual Handel as part of a queer studies agenda for political and social revolution. Handel, a life-long bachelor, is proving to be fertile ground for a kind of airy scholarship that prefers virtuosic innuendo to unambiguous historic data.[43]

The assessment of any discussion linking homosexuality and Handel as "airy scholarship" and "innuendo" has not been limited to religious journals. However, it is only when same-sex love is brought up that sexual innuendo becomes off-bounds for Handel's biographers.

In the past, various sexual scenarios, ranging from Handel the lady-killer to Handel the avowed celibate, have been enthusiastically presented and accepted. Much emphasis has been placed, for example, on contemporary rumors of a relationship in Italy between Handel and the soprano Vittoria Tarquini, wife of the composer Jean-Baptiste Farinel, even though there is no confirming documentation.[44] Some biographers eagerly accept this affair and use it as a model for a multitude of additional possibilities (including most of Handel's female singers), none of which can be proved and few of which, if any, seem probable.[45] Others reject the possibility of a relationship with Tarquini on specious grounds, either because she is deemed too old for Handel[46] or because the composer is considered "a man of singular personal purity" who registered "disgust with . . . the sensuality that he saw rampant around him."[47] At the 1989 meeting of the American Musicological Society, Gary C. Thomas, a scholar of cultural studies and comparative literature, brought the question of homosexuality out of the closet by tentatively offering a positive response to the title question of his paper: "Was George Frideric Handel Gay?"[48] By and large the Handel community has resisted Thomas's work, but even before his paper, as Thomas himself points out, opposition had been raised to the nagging possibility of homosexuality in Handel's life. Jonathan Keates not only provides Handel with a long list of female conquests but asserts that "Handel was very well built and lacked nothing in manliness," which "more or less sums everything up. . . . The assumption that as a lifelong bachelor he must perforce have been homosexual is untenable in an eighteenth-century context."[49] Donald Burrows, whose biography appeared before Thomas's article was published, depends on a theory of celibacy, speculating that the death of Handel's father "was so traumatic for the 11-year-old that it produced a psychological insecurity that explains the apparent celibacy of his adulthood,"[50] and asserting that homosexual relations would be unlikely in "the life of someone who had probably received a fairly strict Lutheran upbringing in eighteenth-century Germany."[51] Although Handel's sexual activity, if any, remains private, an understanding of the "eighteenth-century context" clearly demonstrates that arguments opposing the possibility of homosexuality are themselves based on false assumptions. From the point of view of historical accuracy, these errors need to be addressed.

Same-sex intimacy between men was understood differently in the eighteenth century than it is today.[52] The word "homosexual" did not exist, nor, by and large, did a homosexual identity. An important shift from homosexual acts as an activity, to homosexuality as a more specific and limited identity, occurred only in the late nineteenth century and can be dated from the introduction of the concept of "homosexuality" as "contrary sexual sensation." However, this transformation was hardly instantaneous. The beginnings of an understanding of the homosexual as an individual type date from at least the eighteenth century, and Joseph Cady has argued that "the Renaissance had a definite recognition of a distinct homosexuality."[53] Nevertheless, the coining of the term "homosexual" marks a strong divide before which time a person who engaged in homosexual acts usually did so within a larger compass of sexual activity, whereas afterwards the action itself increasingly identified the person with reference to assumed behavior, personality, and upbringing.[54]

This important terminological and social distinction between eighteenth-century and modern understanding of homosexuality makes it impossible to draw conclusions about the earlier period in light of today's practice. However, it is not that homosexuality was less prevalent in the eighteenth century, but rather that the twentieth-century tendency toward an either/or identification of individuals as homosexual or heterosexual has obscured the sexual context of earlier periods when homosexual and heterosexual love or sexual activity were not considered mutually exclusive. The twentieth-century concept of bisexuality, although superficially helpful, also fails to describe eighteenth-century practice in its implication of two distinct types of sexuality, neither of which had as yet been so identified.

In discussing same-sex desire in the eighteenth century, it might be possible to avoid this 200-year terminological and conceptual divide by avoiding the word "homosexuality" altogether and following instead the eighteenth-century practice of using the term "sodomy," which word came commonly to mean homosexual acts between men, even though its formal definition includes hetero- or homosexual anal intercourse, as well as bestiality. However, the word "sodomy" is no longer normative in literary and legal prose, so that today it takes on different and narrower implications, which reverse the chronological, terminological quandary. Same-sex desire means more than sodomy,[55] and, more important, same-sex culture describes more than sex. Like heterosexuality, homosexuality encompasses various states of preference and desire, as well as sexual activity. Sodomitical acts were condemned and outlawed, but, of course, it was not illegal to have homosexual inclinations, and passionate same-sex relationships (both sexual and otherwise) were an integral part of the lives of many eighteenth-century men—whether or not they had heterosexual relationships. Although it is often difficult in eighteenth-century sources to distinguish between passionate friendship, on the one hand, and an intimate homosexual relationship, on the other (and it is clear that this difficulty is frequently intended),[56] it should be no more necessary to prove a sexual relationship in order to discuss the existence of homosexual desire than it is in order to discuss heterosexual desire (the extensive work on Beethoven's "Immortal Beloved" comes to mind as an example).[57] Rather than seeking a new word not associated with modern homosexuality or limiting myself to the word "sodomy," I have chosen to use "homosexuality" as a term that includes all states of same-sex desire and activity with the hope that the reader will be able to disassociate it from its modern meaning of an individual identity. I also freely use the related terms "homosocial" to describe activities that drew men together and "homoerotic" to describe the expression of same-sex passion.[58]

An understanding of Handel's possible association with same-sex love through his patrons demands recognition of the differences between eighteenth-century culture and our own. For example, Handel's rumored affair with Tarquini, or any affairs he might have had with other women, cannot be seen as an indication that he lacked experience of same-sex love and desire. The best-known aristocratic sodomites from the eighteenth century, including the Medici princes, were married, and Lords Hervey and Beckford were married with children. The same pattern was typical of the lower classes. In the early years of the century, for example, London witnessed a broadening base of homosexual activity in a network of clubs, called molly houses, where men could meet for homosexual encounters,[59] and this increasingly public activity resulted in a backlash. In 1699, 1707, and particularly in 1726, groups of men who visited the molly houses were rounded up for prosecution through the efforts of informers from groups such as the Society for the Reformation of Manners. Those arrested held such professions as milkman, upholsterer, woolen-draper, and church clerk.[60] In 1707, following one of the group arrests, an anonymous poem entitled "The Women-Hater's Lamentation" emphasized a commonly stated belief that such men were all effeminate and women-hating, stating outright: "Each vow'd a Batchelor."[61] The records prove this incorrect—about a third were married.[62] This truth seems to have been acknowledged only in the next century in a broadside published in 1813, *The Phoenix of Sodom or the Vere Street Coterie* by Robert Holloway, which states of those who use molly houses for homosexual activities: "It seems many of these wretches are married."[63]

Handel's apparent "manliness" also provides no indication of his sexuality, even though the stereotype of an effeminate homosexuality already existed in the eighteenth century. The very term "molly" implied effeminacy, and the many pamphlets on sodomy make a specific connection.[64] Further, the mollies took on assumed female names, such as Countess of Camomile and Black-eyed Leonara.[65] However, "the Maiden Names which the mollies assumed bore no relation," as Rictor Norton writes, "to any specific male-female role-playing in terms of sexual behaviour." The molly who called himself Fanny Murray "was 'an athletic Bargeman,' Lucy Cooper was 'an Herculean Coal-heaver,' and Kitty Fisher was 'a deaf tyre Smith.'"[66] These assumed identities of the mollies, like the Arcadians' use of pastoral names, offered a sense of group identity and license. The case of Isaac Bickerstaff, a leading London playwright and colleague of David Garrick, provides a specific example of the effeminate stereotype and its negation. In 1772 Bickerstaff was accused in the press of soliciting a soldier and bribing him not to disclose the event. Without attempting to answer the charge, he fled to France.[67] The revelation of Bickerstaff's alleged private behavior drew much commentary because of his public stature. As one contemporary put it, the playwright had not been suspected of sodomy "as the man had nothing effeminate in his manner."[68]

Typically, the aristocracy who engaged in homosexual acts were immune to prosecution. However, following the raids on the molly houses and the resultant wave of sodomy cases in London, publicly accused members of the aristocracy, including public figures such as Bickerstaff, were forced to flee the country, at least for a time, to avoid prosecution. In 1780, according to the eighteenth-century jurist Jeremy Bentham, who devoted much of his energy toward a written, but unpublished, justification of homosexuality, Sir William Meredith was "driven into exile and for no other cause than his having partaken of gratifications, the innoxiousness of which it is one main business of this work in question to demonstrate."[69] Meredith was a member of parliament from 1754 to 1780 and had served as lord of the admiralty and privy councilor. William Beckford, son of a Lord Mayor of London, fabulously wealthy and "at the pinnacle of society," was accused in 1784 of homosexual relations with a sixteen-year-old boy. Beckford, twenty-four and married, forfeited his political and social position and lived in exile for ten years, but he was not prosecuted.[70]

English perpetrators who chose exile were seen as "returning" to their origins, since the British did not view sodomy as a native (or Protestant) vice but rather as an imported one, usually from Catholic Italy or, more exotically, from Muslim Turkey or Persia. As Hester Thrale, friend of Samuel Johnson, wrote in 1786 during a journey to Italy celebrating her second marriage to the musician Gabriel Piozzi:

> Our *Beckfords* & *Bickerstaffs* too run away at least from the original Theatre of their Crimes, & do not keep their Male Mistresses in Triumph like the Roman Priests and Princes. This Italy is indeed a Sink of Sin; and whoever lives long in it, *must* be a little tainted.[71]

Louis Crompton traces the English accusation that sodomy was imported to England from Italy "back at least as far as the fourteenth century."[72] Certainly, the idea was common in the seventeenth and eighteenth centuries. A 1699 pamphlet entitled *The Tryal and Condemnation of Mervin, Lord Audley Earl of Castle-Haven* speaks of "this sin being now Translated from the Sadomitical [*sic*] Original, or from the *Turkish* and *Italian* copies into *English.*" In 1701 Defoe writes, "Lust chose the torrid zone of Italy, / Where blood ferments in rapes and sodomy."[73] *Plain Reasons for the Growth of Sodomy in England* (c. 1730) states that "this *Fashion* was brought over from *Italy*, (the *Mother* and *Nurse* of *Sodomy*); where the *Master* is oftner *Intriguing* with his *Page*, than a *fair Lady*."[74]

A prevalent attitude in England associated the notion that homosexuality was imported from Italy with the danger of Catholicism and popery, and the execution in 1631 of the Catholic Earl of Castlehaven for sodomy and other sexual crimes must be read in the context of virulent contemporary anti-Catholic sentiment.[75] However, Anglican priests and churchgoers were not exempt from homoerotic desire. For example, the Rev. John Wilson, vicar of Arlington in Sussex and married, confessed in 1643 to having "divers times attempted to commit buggery" with up to eighteen of his parishioners. He "hath professed that he made choice to commit that act with mankind rather than with women to avoid the shame and danger that oft ensueth in begetting bastards . . . and hath openly affirmed that buggery is no sin."[76] Handel's Lutheran upbringing likewise would have provided no shield against same-sex desires. Despite repeated assertions to the contrary, homosexuality was certainly not relegated to Catholic Italy or Muslim Persia, even if these locales were believed to be the font from which the practices sprang. Homosexuality flourished among the sturdy Protestants of England and Holland (where mass prosecutions similar to those in England occurred in 1730 and 1731).[77]

The persistent English association of homosexuality with Italy led to a related connection between the importation of Italian opera and the resultant decline of "manly" English music. The most significant link in this connection was the Italian castrato, who was compared to the eastern eunuch:

> For since the Introduction of ITALIAN OPERAS here, our Men are grown insensibly more and more *Effeminate;* and whereas they used to go from a good *Comedy,* warm'd with the Fire of Love; and from a good *Tragedy,* fir'd with a Spirit of Glory; they sit indolently and supine at an OPERA, and suffer their Souls to be Sung away by the Voices of *Italian Syrens.* . . . Rome likewise sank in Honour and Success, as it rose in *Luxury* and *Effeminacy;* they had Women Singers and Eunuch's from *Asia,* at a vast Price: which so softned [*sic*] their Youth, they quite lost the Spirit of Man-hood, and with it their Empire.[78]

Handel was not untouched by the association of opera and religious subterfuge. In 1733, a pamphlet was published entitled: *Do you know what you are about? Or, A Protestant Alarm to Great Britain: Proving our Late Theatric Squabble, a Type of the present Contest for the Crown of Poland; and that the Division between Handel and Senesino, has more in it than we imagine. Also that the latter is no Eunuch, but a Jesuit in Disguise; with other Particulars of the greatest Importance.*[79] The author claims that the aria "V'adoro pupille" from Handel's *Giulio Cesare* is actually a hymn to the Virgin accompanying a celebration of the Catholic Mass on stage. Although the arguments are silly at best (the English translation provided for "V'adoro pupille" bears no relation to the Italian text), the association in London of Italian opera with sexual excess and effeminacy, on the one hand, and political and religious sedition (through the undermining of native manliness), on the other, was a relative commonplace.

The idea that Handel might have engaged in homosexuality is hardly, as Keates writes, "untenable in an eighteenth-century context." The best example of the eighteenth-century attitude comes from Mrs. Delany, a model of good breeding and morals, friend of the court, and ardent supporter of Handel. Despite the actions of the Societies for the Reformation of Manners or the exaggerated claims concerning the importation of foreign vices, private homosexual acts were typically winked at. Delany writes to her sister on 29 December 1738 in a paragraph omitted from the published correspondence:

> I had almost forgot one piece of news of my Lady Bateman which you will be very glad to inform the Bishop of [—] I hope he has not already heard it that you may have the pleasure of telling him. First, my Lord you must know has some times been famous for a male seraglio, and tis said my Lady detected him in one of his amours, and finding she might be *spar'd* has chosen to retire and leave him unmolested. She might expose him to the Law, but I have not heard she designs it.[80]

No legal proceedings ensued, and Lady Bateman was given a "grace and favour" residence by George II.[81] Mrs. Delany's chatty mention of this affair and her expressed hope that her sister would be able to be the first to tell the Bishop are typical of the period.[82] Some years later, in describing David Garrick's play *Miss in her Teens,* in which the leading character, Fribble, mocks effeminate homosexuality, Mrs. Delany writes, again to her sister (29 January 1747):

> It is said [Garrick] mimics *eleven* men of fashion—Lord Bate—n, Ld Her—y, Felton Her—y, some others you don't know, and our friend Dicky Bate—n, I must own the latter is a *striking likeness;* but do not name to any body these people, for I don't love to spread such tattle, though I send it for your private amusement, and that you may not be ignorant of the ways of the world.[83]

Mrs. Delany's letter clearly illustrates that in order to gain a better understanding of Garrick's *Miss in her Teens,* which alludes to both homosexual and heterosexual love, it is necessary to appreciate the sexual atmosphere of the eighteenth century. The same is true of Handel's cantatas. Only by placing them in their proper context can we begin to understand them fully.

Contextual study is not, however, without its hazards. One of these is the essentialist argument that transfers the attributes of the artist or his surroundings to his work.[84] In a relatively benign example, music historians commonly assign composers of different nationalities "essentially" different styles. For Handel, whose travels complicate the issue, the question of essential nationalistic qualities continues to be debated today in terms of German, Italian, and English style; Lang wittily dubbed this "the Battle for the *Umlaut*" in reference to the English or German spelling of his name (Handel or Händel).[85] However, the issue already arose in Handel's lifetime. For example, in 1738 an English letter-writer argued that the English composer Maurice Greene should be selected rather than Handel to compose a national tune, explaining that "it is not from the least Distrust of Mr Handel's ability that I address myself preferably to Doctor Greene; but Mr Handel having the Advantage to be by Birth a German, might probably, even without intending it, mix some Modulations in his Composition, which might give a German tendency to the Mind and therefore greatly lessen the National Benefit."[86] That is, the letter-writer worried that Handel's music might have essentialist German qualities.

The issue of essentialism becomes more fraught in categories other than nationalism, such as those that have arisen in musicology more recently and more pointedly: black music, Jewish music, anti-Semitic music, women's music, and gay music.[87] The questions multiply seemingly endlessly. Is Schubert gay?[88] Can gayness be heard in his music?[89] Is Wagner's anti-Semitism embedded in his music, or can the man and his creative output be separated?[90] More to the point for this study, what is the relationship between Handel's cantatas and sexuality? Although I believe that the social and biographical context allows an association to be made between certain stylistic traits in the cantatas and same-sex desire, none of these is limited to composers known to be attracted to same-sex love, nor are such composers limited to these musical traits. That is, I find nothing "essential" to homosexuality in the analyses I present. Rather, the combination of context and text in some cases permits a same-sex reading, usually in addition to others.

Analogously, I do not believe that the cantatas offer a representation of Handel's emotions at the time of composition, nor that my readings reveal Handel's intentions.[91] As Wolfgang Hildesheimer has demonstrated so brilliantly in his biography, Mozart's moods rarely matched his compositions. At the times of his deepest sorrows, he often wrote his lightest and happiest music, and while composing his greatest works, his verbal statements not only are confined to prosaic routine but are also interspersed with an (often forced) silliness, which will astonish only those who think a genius must maintain and demonstrate in every statement and action the highest level of the spirit that singles him out from all others. Actually, it is more characteristic of the *would-be* genius to be continually expressing his awareness of his own importance.[92]

Such points of view are not uncommon, however, to Handel lore. The familiar anecdote that while composing the "Hallelujah chorus" Handel is said to have declared that he "did see all Heaven before me and the great God Himself" attributes divine inspiration to Handel and defined religious intent. The anecdote cannot be substantiated, but it offers validation to those who bring religious intention to the work, sometimes resulting in a "reverse-essentialist" stance, where the listener takes his reaction to the music (say, religious inspiration) and assigns it as an attribute of the composer.

That is, it is often more the intentions of the listener than those of the author that "determine" the meaning of a piece of music. I would argue not that the author is unimportant (and that the notes on the page are our only evidence), but rather that the goal to uncover the author's intention as the single authentic reading is unattainable and reductionist. In contrast, listener theory, which privileges the interpretation of the listener or listeners, and deconstructionism allow for flexible and changing meanings.[93] Great art is typified by layers of meanings and multiple possible interpretations, but this does not mean, I believe, that anything goes. While it is clear that the evaluation and interpretation of a composition change with the listener, with the context of performance, and over time, I would argue, conservatively, that interpretations still exist within a range of validity and need to be grounded in the work of art itself.

Finally, I do not offer, nor would I be capable of offering, a psychoanalytic reading that unites facts of biography with Handel's artistic output.[94] Since a composer's intentions cannot be definitively uncovered, even where composers leave more of a trail than Handel,[95] it is often tempting to offer an armchair psychological explanation for behavioral or compositional traits. This approach has also found its way into Handel scholarship. For example, a significant effort has been devoted to an understanding of the composer's use of preexisting material. At one stage, it was thought that Handel's borrowing only became an important part of his compositional process in the late 1730s around the time of his so-called "paralytick disorder." Basing his argument on this premise, Edward Dent proposed in 1934 that the illness precipitated this compositional gambit: "It is quite conceivable that his paralytic stroke affected his brain in such a way that he may sometimes have had a difficulty in starting a composition."[96]

However, the work of John Roberts and others has now shown definitively that Handel's borrowing was a fact of his composition from his earliest years, and that his illness (whether physical, psychological, or both) had little effect on the process.

More recently, Burrows, as quoted earlier, has suggested that Handel's presumed psychological trauma at the death of his father "explains the apparent celibacy of his adulthood," even though he acknowledges that Handel's father, who lost his own father at age fourteen, was "not inhibited [in] the development of his own relationships."[97] Looking for causes and connections is an essential part of the role of a historian, and I do not doubt that there is a wealth of material in Handel's life that would support psychoanalytic study.[98] Nevertheless, given my lack of expertise in this field, I have tried to avoid assigning psychological meanings to Handel's actions or decisions.

It is not the purpose of this book to "out" Handel but rather to broaden the interpretation of the cantata texts and music by placing them in the social context of the period. Most chapters begin with a discussion of an individual work that initiates an examination of the biographical, social, or political context, which in turn permits a broader analytic perspective on a specific class of cantatas. Some readers will find the analyses presented here tantamount to a conclusion on Handel's sexuality; others will be relieved that there is no absolute documentary evidence to confirm one specific reading. The absence of a definitive statement concerning Handel's personal life is deliberate on my part. On the one hand, it is an effort to let the music and other evidence speak for itself. On the other, it avoids the kind of imaginative specificity of earlier biographers who list women with whom Handel might have had affairs, a trap I have not wanted to fall into. Nevertheless, the evidence presented by the cantatas does indicate an important role for same-sex love both in Handel's social context and in his music, and the Epilogue provides what I believe to be specific references to homosexuality in his later life. Within the context of the eighteenth century, it would have been normal for Handel to share his creative and intellectual interests with men. Generally speaking, women were still not given the benefit of a serious education, so that the "marriage of true minds" could only occur between men—suggesting at least one possible reason the biblical David could say of his deceased friend Jonathan, "Thy love to me was wonderful, passing the love of women."[99] Thus it is not at all surprising that, as in Shakespeare and the Bible, male friendships in Handel's time were passionate in expression, whether or not there were sexual relations involved. Although Handel's love life remains veiled, the eighteenth-century context demonstrates, I believe, that a component of same-sex love and desire is far from untenable.

A model for this approach within Handel studies can be found in Smith's examination of Handel's oratorio texts in light of the historical context of an outpouring of tracts and sermons supporting Britain as both a religious and political entity.[100] As she writes of the oratorio librettos,

> We should not be inhibited in our readings of the librettos by a notion that Handel would not have set a text containing ideas to which he did not personally subscribe. Equally, we should not assume that Handel did not subscribe to the commonplace ideas of his time simply because he did not leave us authenticated verbal statements in support of them.[101]

The same is true of the cantata texts. That is, a sexual context permeates the cantatas, just as the national and religious context of England infuses the oratorios. However, the inclusion of sexual metaphors cannot directly answer the question of what Handel did or did not do, nor even whether Handel was always fully aware of the subtext.

The number of possible "voices" in Handel's musical works generally makes it difficult to determine which, if any, is Handel's own. A professed Lutheran, he wrote Catholic music in Italy and Anglican music in England. He set texts that supported both sides of the War of Spanish Succession. He wrote a Te Deum and Jubilate for Queen Anne to celebrate the peace of Utrecht, to which his employer, the Elector of Hanover, was opposed. And as Burrows writes, "Possibly the most curious aspect of Handel's biography is that, while the composer has always been identified, quite correctly, in England with the House of Hanover, many of his strongest patrons and collaborators were, like Charles Jennens, librettist of *Saul* and *Messiah,* supporters of the Old Succession (without necessarily being Jacobites)."[102] The texts of Handel's vocal music may speak variously with the voices of his librettists, patrons, or specific dramatic characters, but Handel's own voice is surely part of the mix. Just as his works do not present a single ideological position, it is unlikely that Handel himself was one-dimensional. Most likely he tried on, or assumed, various roles at various times.

Handel was certainly assigned multiple identities. Cardinal Pamphili compared him with Orpheus, which became a continual trope with at least dual meanings. Handel was also associated musically with Timotheus and Apollo. In contrast, Paolo Rolli, one of Handel's librettists, referred to Handel in correspondence by various negative code names ranging from The Man to The Savage or The Bear.[103] Handel's (formerly) close friend Joseph Goupy painted a vicious caricature of him as a fat boar, and his patron and friend James Harris referred to him as a Persian. Although clearly he was part opportunist, accepting commissions on any topic that might please his patrons, Handel was also just as clearly a complicated and multifaceted personality. It would be as wrong to force a single interpretation upon him and his actions as upon his music.

However much a scholar strives to maintain a dispassionate stance, historical research retains a personal component. Arguments presented about Handel or other historical figures often tell us more about the modern-day authors than about their historical subject, and they underscore not only how most scholarship is a form of advocacy but also how scholars consciously and unconsciously identify with their subjects. Lying just below the surface of such writing (or, in some cases, right on the surface) are the authors' prejudices, phobias, and practices. In 1966 Lang wrote with justice of the nationalist battle for Handel between German and English scholars: "Until recent times, Handelian musicography was not based on a scholarly and creative contemplation of the historical past; it was largely an echo of its own desires, beliefs, and musical-religious order, which it projected into the past."[104] The place of sexuality in musicology has raised issues at least as personally disturbing as those of national pride and identity. It is not surprising that some gay scholars have wanted to "out" historical figures who will by their identification affirm the societal role of homosexuals today, or that some in the heterosexual community have resisted what they see as the appropriation of "their" heroes. From one point of view, then, the different readings represent a battle for political and professional territory that concerns the role of sexuality in today's society and whether sexuality is an appropriate or acceptable subject in the historical study of music. From another point of view, however, the different readings simply derive from a deep-seated desire to identify personally with what one loves.

I will not pretend that my person is somehow absent from this book. Further, I declare openly that I am an unabashed advocate for Handel's music and that I believe the cantatas hold a multitude of untold (and unheard) glories that deserve to be better known. As a woman, however, I do not personally identify with Handel, and the issue of his sexuality is therefore somewhat distanced for me. Nevertheless, I must admit that as my research progressed I found myself more and more sympathetic to the attitude of Mrs. Delany. She writes to her sister of the male seraglio of Lord Bateman without alarm or condemnation, and she explains the homosexual impersonation that is part of Garrick's *Miss in her Teens* as a point of information. Indeed, a paraphrase of her final comment in this second instance could serve as appropriately for this book as for her letter: I do not write to spread tattle, but so "that you may not be ignorant of the ways of the world."

Code Names and Assumed Identities

In general, quantum mechanics does not predict a single definite result for an observation. Instead, it predicts a number of different possible outcomes and tells us how likely each of these is.

Stephen Hawking, *A Brief History of Time*

Among the most fascinating of Handel's cantatas is an early work with a text by Cardinal Pamphili about Handel himself: *Hendel, non può mia musa.*[1] John Mainwaring, Handel's first biographer, describes its origin:

> [Pamphili] had some talents for Poetry, and wrote the drama of IL TRIONFO DEL TEMPO, besides several other pieces, which HANDEL set at his desire, some in the compass of a single evening, and others extempore. One of these was in honour of HANDEL himself. He was compared to OR-PHEUS, and exalted above the rank of mortals. Whether his Eminence chose this subject as most likely to inspire him with fine conceptions, or with a view to discover how far so great an Artist was proof against the assaults of vanity, it is not material to determine. HANDEL's modesty was not however so excessive, as to hinder him from complying with the desire of his illustrious friend.[2]

Mainwaring's notion that some idea of exaggerated praise served as the stimulus for this cantata seems to be confirmed by Handel in an anecdote preserved by Charles Jennens, one of Handel's later librettists, in a marginal note to his copy of Mainwaring's text at the reference to this cantata: "Cantata the 19th in my collection. . . . Handel told me that the words of Il Trionfo &c. were written by Cardinal Pamphilii [*sic*], & added, 'an old Fool!' I ask'd 'why Fool? Because he wrote an Oratorio? Perhaps you will call *me* fool for the same reason!' He answer'd 'So I would, if you flatter'd me, as He did.'"[3]

Modern scholars largely follow Mainwaring's lead in placing flattery at the core of the cantata's meaning, although differences occur in the evaluation of both the extent of praise intended by the text and the level of music it inspired. Ursula Kirkendale, for example, imagines its actual performance at a musical gathering in Ruspoli's palace. Since Ruspoli kept the autograph and had copies made repeatedly (in August 1708, August 1709, and May 1711), she posits that this work originated under his patronage rather than Pamphili's. In Kirkendale's scenario:

> The cardinal was a frequent guest. Since Ruspoli apparently did not write poetry himself, he presented the composer with poems of his house poet or of his friends. . . . Pamphilj says that his muse cannot in a twinkling sing verses worthy of Handel's lyre, but feeling in himself such sweet harmony, he was impelled to sing like this (there follows the Orfeo aria, etc.). This was a reply, in a tone which shows a little resignation. In addition to the oratorio *Il Trionfo del Tempo* Pamphilj certainly had given Handel other texts. . . . [Handel] had approached his former patron for more poetry. Evidently Pamphilj's muse was just then somewhat tired, so that he wisely took refuge in this personal address, describing his situation. His use of the Orpheus metaphor should not be taken too seriously, as a monumental apotheosis of Handel, but rather as a nice compliment paid by the old gentleman to the young one.[4]

John Mayo takes the praise more seriously, but largely dismisses the music: "[Pamphili] supplied Handel with a fulsome text *Hendel non può mia musa*, in which the composer is likened to Orpheus. Handel was not greatly impressed by the flattery and provided some very routine music in this cantata."[5] In contrast, Donald Burrows in his edition of the work writes that "the composer was somewhat sceptical about the Cardinal's flattery; nevertheless, he did not skimp on musical matters when composing the cantata."[6] Despite their differences, all of these modern evaluations depend on an assumption that the Orphic symbolism can be narrowly equated with flattery. By first taking a closer look at the Orpheus legend and then examining the circumstances surrounding Handel's journey to Italy, I will place this cantata in a broader context, providing evidence for reconsidering the Jennens anecdote and reevaluating Handel's music.

The complete text and translation of the Orpheus cantata appear in Appendix 2; it can be summarized as follows:

> Handel, I cannot quickly improvise verses worthy of your song, but I feel such a sweet harmony within me that I am compelled to sing of your music thus: Orpheus was able to attract birds, wild beasts, trees and rocks, but he couldn't make them sing; so how much greater are you who have been able to force me into song after I had hung up my plectrum on a dry tree where it lay motionless; so now let everyone sing and, to the harmony of the new Orpheus, give motion to the hand and voice to the song as was never heard before, and in such pleasing sounds, let the soul be joyful and let the hours and the day pass happily.

The cantata follows the most typical pattern of two recitative-aria pairs. The recitatives contain rather straightforward declamation with no striking dissonances, disruptions, or disjunct motion. Both arias are in simple triple meter (the first in 3/4; the second in 3/8), largely syllabic and tuneful; neither has an opening ritornello. Indeed, they are more song than aria. The first aria begins with a repeated two-bar phrase with regular accents on beats one and two that set up a short-long rhythm over each bar: (1, 2— | 1, 2—), as shown in Ex. 1.1. To depict the birds and beasts stopping in mid-flight or mid-step, Handel then sets up a contrasting two-bar pattern that alternates the short-long rhythm with its reverse in a stepwise melody (Ex. 1.2), creating a striking sense of amazed suspension: (1, 2— | 1—, 3). At the repetition of this text he paints the stop-action *(fermar)* with rests throughout the musical fabric (Ex. 1.3).[7] In the B section of the aria, Handel maintains the two-bar hesitation step (the short-long long-short pattern), now using both disjunct motion (mm. 37–42) and the decoration of smaller, passing notes (mm. 33, 36) to indicate the movement of the trees and rocks (Ex. 1.4).

The second aria continues the syncopated, two-bar pattern, once again prefacing it with a repeated rhythm (here, for the first time, adhering to the long-short rhythmic pattern most typical of triple meter), as shown in Ex. 1.5. To depict the new motion of the hand ("alla destra il moto"), Handel leaps up a mi-

Example 1.1 *Hendel, non può mia musa,* "Poté Orfeo," mm. 1–4.

Example 1.2 *Hendel, non può mia musa,* "Poté Orfeo," mm. 5–12.

Example 1.3 *Hendel, non può mia musa,* "Poté Orfeo," mm. 21–24.

nor seventh (modified in its third iteration to a major sixth ending on a higher pitch) and elides the second first-beat accent with a tie over the barline, smoothing over the asymmetries (Ex. 1.6). Perhaps we glimpse Handel's famous sense of humor in his setting of the phrase "inspired by the harmony of the new Orpheus" with eight bars of a C pedal, producing a largely unmitigated C major harmony; or, in response to a text which deals more with reaction to Orpheus's song than with the song itself, the harmonic stasis may depict the awestruck

Example 1.4 *Hendel, non può mia musa,* "Poté Orfeo," mm. 33–44.

Example 1.5 *Hendel, non può mia musa,* "Ognun canti," mm. 1–4.

Example 1.6 *Hendel, non può mia musa,* "Ognun canti," mm. 5–16.

state of his audience (Ex. 1.7). In the B section, "whiling away the time" is depicted in the longest stretch of regular long-short patterns in the cantata and by an elongated phrase structure over eight bars connecting two four-bar phrases on the verb *passi* ("let it pass"), first by a rising octave leap and then with a tie in anticipation of the verb (Ex. 1.8).

The text and music of *Hendel, non può mia musa* differ from most musical renditions of the Orpheus myth in that the legend is only alluded to in the briefest terms, omitting any reference to Eurydice or to Orpheus's trip to the Underworld. Most important, Orpheus's own voice is never heard, and there is thus no attempt on Handel's part to represent Orpheus's music. This becomes

Example 1.7 *Hendel, non può mia musa,* "Ognun canti," mm. 20–28.

Example 1.8 *Hendel, non può mia musa,* "Ognun canti," mm. 52–67.

particularly clear when the music and text of this cantata are compared with those of *Del bel idolo mio,* a cantata probably also written in the spring of 1707, which tells an Orphic story of an anonymous lover descending into hell to rescue his beloved, Nice.[8] In *Del bel idolo mio,* the lover sings that he will descend to the gloomy lake of Acheronte, where his beloved will be his guiding light among the abysses. The first aria is addressed to the "formidable gondolier," from whom he asks passage. The second aria expresses his fear of not finding Nice, his grief and his hope: "I will weep, but my tears will be symbols of faith. When a strong soul cries, even in the kingdom of death, it hopes to find mercy." Both these arias from *Del bel idolo mio* are more typical of Handel's cantata idiom generally, and the musical settings represent an Orpheus-like figure using music to overcome death. The first aria with its extensive vocal figuration and pervasive dotted rhythms in the bass turns virtuosity into a weapon of attack (Ex. 1.9); the second uses short phrases, rests, and plangent chromaticism to move the listeners' emotions (Ex. 1.10), a style familiar from later arias, such as "Piangerò" in *Giulio Cesare,* where a similar despair is expressed. In a final aria,

Example 1.9 *Del bel idolo mio,* "Formidabil gondoliero."

Example 1.10 *Del bel idolo mio,* "Piangerò."

the lover reverts to the simplest musical means: an extended musical line in syllabic, even-note triple meter that feels like a long sigh states the direct demand—"I want Nice" (Ex. 1.11). Although many early cantatas can be distinguished by the use of a closing dance movement, much like a closing minuet in
a multi-movement overture or dance suite, its use here is clearly dramatic and
appropriate. "Su rendetemi," in its simple, syllabic setting and dance rhythm,
explains the goal of the first two elaborate and complex arias and offers effective
punctuation to the singer's mission and to the cantata.

By comparison to *Del bel idolo mio,* the "other" Orpheus cantata, *Hendel, non
può mia musa,* stands out more clearly. It is exclusively and specifically in
Pamphili's voice, thus creating the ironic situation of a composer's music being
praised in the music of that very composer without depicting what is being
praised (Orpheus's voice). Would that we could recreate the situation in which
it was written. Can we accept the text at its word that Pamphili was improvis-
ing? Was Handel's setting improvised on the spot? Is it possible that Handel
composed a simple setting meant for Pamphili himself to sing? Given the lack
of reference in the text to Orpheus's greatest musical achievement, that of conquering death by winning Eurydice back from the Underworld, Kirkendale
may be correct that the metaphor of flattery should not be taken too seriously—but the question of metaphor, therefore, needs further examination.

The Orpheus legend, of course, symbolizes the power of music, for Orpheus's song not only tames beasts and moves inanimate objects, but overcomes
the power of death.[9] The early operas of Jacopo Peri, Giulio Caccini, and
Claudio Monteverdi used the legend to assert opera's own power by depicting

Example 1.11 *Del bel idolo mio,* "Su rendetemi."

how the music of Orpheus gives life (to trees and stones) and restores life (to Eurydice). F. W. Sternfeld lists twenty Orpheus operas written between 1599 and 1698 alone, including works by Hidalgo, Schütz, Lully, and Keiser.[10] In the mid-eighteenth century, Gluck's so-called reform of opera returned to Orpheus to effect an operatic rebirth. Throughout much of the history of Western music, Orpheus and the power of music have remained frequent topics.[11]

The Orpheus story did not simply engender musical settings; individual composers (or patrons) were frequently honored with the title of Orpheus. Henry Purcell, for example, was known as Orpheus Britannicus, and Prince Ferdinand de' Medici, one of Handel's patrons, was described as the Orpheus of Princes. Not just in the Orpheus cantata, but throughout his life Handel was also equated with Orpheus. In England the practice originates with his very first opera, *Rinaldo* (1711), when his librettist Giacomo Rossi identifies him as "the Orpheus of our age."[12] He is compared to Orpheus in a poem of 1724 praising his operas *Flavio* and *Giulio Cesare*.[13] In a French magazine of 1735, he is again named "the Orpheus of his age,"[14] as he is in an English magazine of 1738.[15] The statue of Handel by Louis François Roubiliac placed in Vauxhall Gardens in 1738 was commonly understood to depict the composer as Orpheus,[16] and one surviving silver season ticket to Vauxhall shows the statue of Handel with the motto *blandius Orpheo* ("more enchanting than Orpheus"), taken from Horace.[17] By the 1740s Handel, succeeding Purcell, became known as the "British [or English] Orpheus."[18]

However, the myth of Orpheus is not simply about the power of music. In some readings music itself becomes a metaphor for power, intellect, or divinity. For example, the story has sometimes been viewed as a parable for the rise of humanism where the beasts represent uncivilized, and the stones untutored, mankind, and Orpheus leads them into peaceful community and rational learning.[19] The myth also initiated the theological doctrine of Orphism, where Orpheus was seen as a partly human, partly divine figure who descends into Hell, overcomes death, and redeems humanity.[20] By and large, these readings, like the contrived happy endings of most operas on this subject, overlook the fact that Orpheus ultimately fails in his quest to rescue Eurydice from the Underworld.[21] Indeed, the ending of the Orpheus story has been so often rewritten in versions dating from 1600 that the ending depicted in classical Greek and Latin works, as well as in Renaissance Italian versions, is today little known.

In the earliest known written version of the myth, the Hellenistic poet Phanocles from about 250 B.C. specifically relates that Orpheus was killed because after Eurydice's death he was "the first in Thrace to desire men and to disapprove the love of women,"[22] thus defining the Orpheus story as an origin myth of homosexuality.[23] Ovid repeats this claim in his *Metamorphoses,* calling Orpheus the originator (*auctor*) of male homosexuality.[24] Virgil's version in the Fourth *Georgic* avoids a definitive statement about Orpheus's sexuality, saying only that Orpheus rejected the interest and advances of women and was killed by women because he disdained them. Although this passage is frequently interpreted to mean only that Orpheus rejected other women because he remained faithful to the memory of Eurydice, such is not actually stated by Virgil as the reason for Orpheus's murder.[25] Implicit depictions of the homosexual motive date back to the fifth century B.C. in Greek vase paintings, where Orpheus is often shown surrounded by admiring men while women approach to attack him (Figure 1.1 shows the Thracian women attacking Orpheus with stones and other implements),[26] and explicit literary versions continue into the Renaissance. Poliziano's *Favola di Orfeo* is especially clear in this regard, having Orpheus end his lament for Eurydice with these words:

> Let the love of woman bind me no longer. . . . [Thus] Jove . . . scorns the sweet amorous tie that binds him and in heaven enjoys his beautiful Ganymede; and on earth Phoebus enjoyed Hyacinth. To this holy love Hercules surrenders, he who won the world and was won by fair Hylas. The married man I urge to seek divorce, and all to flee the company of women.[27]

Orpheus's homosexuality was known in the seventeenth and eighteenth centuries, particularly through Ovid, whose *Metamorphoses* formed the basis of

Figure 1.1 *Death of Orpheus* (red-figure vase, c. 480–470 B.C.). Cincinnati Art Museum (1079.9), John J. Emery, William W. Taylor, Robert S. Dechant, and Israel and Caroline Wilson Endowments.

many Baroque operatic and vocal works. The educated would have read Ovid
in Latin, but vernacular translations were also widely available that clearly rendered the original text. For example, Arthur Golding's English translation of the
Metamorphoses, first published in 1565–1567 and reprinted in 1575, 1587, 1603,
and 1612, was known and used by Shakespeare; it renders the pivotal lines that
follow Orpheus's failure:

> And *Orphye* (were it that his ill successe hee still did rew,
> Or that he vowed so too doo) did utterly eschew
> The womankynd. Yit many a one desyrous were too match
> With him, but he them with repulse did all alike dispatch.
> He also taught the *Thracian* folke a stewes of Males too make
> And of the flowring pryme of boayes the pleasure for too take.[28]

In 1626 George Sandys produced a new translation, which reached its eighth
edition in 1690. In 1717, a composite translation was published with contributions from John Dryden, Charles Addison, Alexander Pope, John Gay, and
many others; this translation continued to be reprinted well into the nineteenth
century. The section on Orpheus was translated by William Congreve, who
renders the homosexual motive so gently as to make it disappear.

> Whether his ill Success this Change had bred,
> Or binding Vows made to his former Bed;
> Whate'er the Cause, in vain the Nymphs context,
> With rival Eyes to warm his frozen Breast:
> For ev'ry Nymph with Love his Lays inspir'd,
> But ev'ry Nymph repuls'd, with Grief retir'd.[29]

Despite Congreve's obfuscation, the original text would have been well known
to this volume's illustrious group of translators, a number of whom were close
colleagues of Handel, and to most educated men. Certainly, the association of
Orpheus with homosexuality was not erased from public view.

In 1772, after the playwright Isaac Bickerstaff fled England, having been accused of soliciting sodomitical acts with a soldier, William Kenrick published a
mock "eclogue" accusing David Garrick of a relationship with Bickerstaff or, at
least, of harboring him as a known sodomite. It is no surprise that Kenrick
equates Bickerstaff with Orpheus.[30] By the end of the century, homosexuality
was even defined in terms of this myth in a travel book published in London as
"the passion contrary to nature which the Thracian dames avenged by the massacre of Orpheus, who had rendered himself odious by gratifying it,"[31] and a
suspicion of homosexuality likely lies behind a comparison of Lord Byron to

Orpheus in 1812 by a critic concerned with the misogynistic opening of *Childe Harold*: "Fie, my Lord! the lyre of Orpheus was divinely strung; your own boasts equal harmony, but, oh! remember, and beware that Poet's fate!"[32]

The association of Orpheus both with musical or poetic artistry and with homosexuality at the end of the eighteenth century leads one to ask whether both meanings could have played a part in other, earlier Orphic allusions. The question does not imply that such would be the case in every use of Orpheus's name; nor does it mean that, in any or all cases where this was intended, this reading would have been the general interpretation. One possibility is that the name of Orpheus openly referred to the highest musical attainment but at times took on a second, sometimes covert, meaning. Theatrical representations of Orpheus on the seventeenth-century English stage, for example, are distinctly unheroic, and Curtis Price suggests that in these plays homosexuality is among the character's attributes.[33] Perhaps some of the identifications of Handel as Orpheus, like the later ones of Bickerstaff and Byron, imply more than musical characteristics as well. An investigation of this possibility demands a closer look at Handel's journey to Italy and his patrons there.

Handel's interest in traveling to Italy grew from his earliest contact with music. His childhood composition teacher, Friedrich Wilhelm Zachow, had, between about 1693 and 1698 (when Handel was between eight and thirteen), made the boy study and copy works of German and Italian composers "to cultivate his imagination, and form his taste."[34] Then, during a trip to Berlin that Mainwaring places in 1698, the "king" (that is, Frederick, Elector of Brandenburg, who called himself "King in Prussia" only from 1701)[35] wished to take Handel into his service, having "conceived a design of cultivating [Handel's genius] at his own expence." He proposed to "send him to Italy, where he might be formed under the best masters, and have opportunities of hearing and seeing all that was excellent in the kind." Mainwaring, writing in 1760, relates that Handel's friends decided the young composer should not commit himself to a position that he would not be free to leave "whether he liked it, or not," and therefore "resolved that some excuse must be found" for declining the position. Nevertheless, it was Handel's "acquaintance with the eminent masters at Berlin [that] had opened his mind to new ideas of excellence, and shewn him in a more extended view the perfections of his art." As a result, "he never could endure the thought of staying long at home, either as a pupil or substitute to his old master ZACKAW." Mainwaring states that Handel resolved at this time to journey to Italy independently and, for the purpose of securing the necessary funds, determined "to consider of some place less distant, where he might employ his time to advantage, and be still improving in knowledge and experience."[36]

At the age of eighteen Handel moved to the city of Hamburg, a bustling commercial port and operatic center where Johann Mattheson, composer, singer, and theorist, became his close friend and colleague. Mattheson describes Handel's arrival:

> Handel came to Hamburg in the summer of 1703, rich in ability and good will. I was almost the first with whom he made acquaintance. . . . At first he played back-desk violin in the opera orchestra, and behaved as if he could not count to five, being naturally inclined to a dry humour.[37]

Handel immediately sought employment in Hamburg: "The first thing which he did on his arrival at Hamburgh, was to procure scholars, and obtain some employment in the orchestra."[38] In both areas he probably received help from Mattheson. It was apparently Mattheson who introduced Handel to the house of John Wych, the British Resident, whose son Cyril became Handel's pupil, and it was undoubtedly Mattheson who assisted Handel during his early rise in the orchestra. Mattheson's family also helped, for as Mattheson writes, "during that period he went most of the time for free meals at my late father's house."[39]

Mattheson's account of this period paints a very close friendship between the two young musicians (Mattheson was four years older than Handel). He describes how the two met in the organ loft of St. Mary Magdalene Church on 9 June 1703,[40] went on a water journey together on 15 July,[41] and on 30 July played the St. Mary Magdalene organ again. On 17 August they traveled together to Lübeck, where Mattheson had been invited to compete for the position there that was being vacated by Dietrich Buxtehude. A condition for taking Buxtehude's position was marriage with his daughter, and this was refused by both young men. As Mattheson writes, "However, it turned out that there was some marriage condition proposed in connection with the appointment, for which we neither of us felt the smallest inclination, so we said goodbye to the place, after having enjoyed ourselves extremely, and received many gratifying tributes of respect."[42]

During the course of 1704, Handel must have written his first two operas that were premiered early in 1705. Mattheson writes that Handel "used to bring me his first opera scene by scene, and every evening would take my opinion about it—and the trouble it cost him to conceal the pedant [in him]!"[43] He also says that when Handel arrived in Hamburg "he composed very long, long arias, and really interminable cantatas, which had neither the right kind of skill nor taste, though complete in harmony, but the lofty schooling of opera soon trimmed him into other fashions."[44] These cantatas do not survive. The only surviving composition that can tentatively be dated prior to his first opera is a sacred cantata for soprano, *Laudate pueri Dominum* (in F major).[45]

On 8 January 1705 Handel's first opera, *Almira*, premiered. His second, *Nero*, followed closely on 25 February. After this we lose sight of Handel for almost two years. The first definite mention of Handel again is in the account books of Cardinal Pamphili in Rome, where a payment for the copying of the cantata *Delirio amoroso* by Handel is recorded on 12 February 1707. Filling in this two-year gap requires some speculation based on evidence from various sources.

Mainwaring states that while at Hamburg, Handel was invited to Italy by "the Prince of Tuscany, brother to John Gaston de Medicis, Grand Duke."[46] This statement involves some unraveling. At the time of Handel's journey to Italy in 1706, the Grand Duke of Florence was Cosimo III, father to Ferdinand and Gian Gastone. Ferdinand (1663–1713) was the older son and heir, but he predeceased his father, and Gian Gastone (1671–1737) became the last Grand Duke of the Medici family in 1723. It was Prince Ferdinand who was renowned for his musicianship, who played various instruments and sang.[47] Keyboard instruments were his particular passion: the first pianoforte was built in Florence by Bartolomeo Cristofori under his patronage.[48] Ferdinand took active responsibility for the annual operatic performances during November at the Pratolino theater, and he also supported private and public operatic productions elsewhere in Florence and its environs.[49] His lengthy correspondence with Alessandro Scarlatti about musical details in Scarlatti's operas attests to his knowledge of music. Composers whose works were performed at the Pratolino included Giovanni Legrenzi (1685), Giovanni Pagliardi (1687, 1688, 1693), and Carlo Pollaroli (1696, 1699, 1700), as well as Alessandro Scarlatti (1702–1706) and Giacomo Perti (1700–1701, 1707–1710). In addition Ferdinand's "protection and assistance" extended over a number of others,[50] and still more composers, such as Benedetto Marcello, who resided for a time in Florence, were attracted to the city by the musical scene.[51]

Mainwaring's description of a shared interest in music between composer and prince seems further to identify Ferdinand as Handel's patron:

> "A sort of intimacy [grew up] betwixt them: they frequently discoursed together on the state of Music in general, and on the merits of Composers, Singers, and Performers in particular. The Prince would often lament that HANDEL was not acquainted with those of Italy; shewed him a large collection of Italian Music; and was very desirous he should return with him to Florence."[52]

The problem is in placing Ferdinand in Hamburg "at the time that ALMERIA [that is, *Almira*, 1705] and FLORINDA [*Florindo*, performed in Hamburg, 1708]" were performed or at any other time.[53] Further, a letter of 19 October 1707, following Handel's first sojourn in Rome, to Ferdinand's chamberlain formally requesting an audience with the prince for Handel, described as "a keyboard player," strongly implies that there was no earlier bond between the two.[54] In contrast, Prince Gian Gastone, Ferdinand's younger brother, was during this time living near Prague with his Bohemian wife, and he was certainly in Hamburg from October 1703 to as late as February 1704.[55] Although Gian Gastone was less accomplished in the arts than his brother, he was no less learned, having studied philosophy and being a "follower of Leibniz."[56] In fact, it seems likely, whether or not he had intense musical discussions with Prince Ferdinand, that Handel's invitation to Florence came from Gian Gastone.[57]

Handel apparently refused to accept financial assistance for his travels. As Mainwaring writes, "Handel, without intending to accept of the favour designed him, expressed his sense of the honour done him. For he resolved to go to Italy on his own bottom, as soon as he could make a purse for that occasion."[58] The time was propitious. Not only had Handel "made up a purse of 200 ducats" required for the journey,[59] but the situation at Hamburg had become increasingly unstable. Reinhard Keiser, the head composer and manager, had left Hamburg and the opera early in 1704. In March Handel wrote to Mattheson, who was on his way to England, reaching him in Amsterdam and entreating him to return, "for the time is coming when nothing can be done at the Opera in your absence."[60] Handel's first two operas (*Almira* and *Nero,* produced in January and February 1705) were the last two in which Mattheson performed as a singer, and after *Nero,* the opera house closed for Lent and did not reopen after Easter. There was no further production until Keiser's *Octavia* in August 1705, marking the older composer's return.

Mainwaring writes, "We left [Handel] just on the point of his removal to Italy; where he arrived soon after the Prince of Tuscany. FLORENCE, as it is natural to suppose, was his first destination."[61] Gian Gastone, having been summoned by his father the Grand Duke, arrived back in that city in June 1705.[62] If Handel stayed in Hamburg for Keiser's *Octavia,* he could have arrived in Florence "soon after" the prince in early autumn. Mattheson insists, however, that Handel remained in Hamburg until 1709. Although we know this not to be true (Handel certainly was in Italy by early 1707, when his presence in Rome can be documented), it does raise the possibility that Handel traveled between Germany and Italy more than once.[63] As John Roberts has suggested, Handel may, therefore, have been in Hamburg for the January 1708 performances of his *Florindo* and *Daphne* (a single opera telling the story of Apollo and Daphne that was divided on account of its length into two performances). Since Gian Gastone went back to Germany in the spring of 1707 (when Handel was definitely in Rome) and only returned permanently to Florence in 1708,[64] he might have been in Hamburg for these performances, as Mainwaring states.[65] However, Mainwaring incorrectly places *Florindo* between *Almira* and *Nero,* so his chronology is particularly problematic at this point.

Although a number of Handel's patrons and colleagues during his four years in Italy (1706–1710) can be associated with the homosexual culture of the period, the activities of the Medici are by far the best documented.[66] As was typical of the time, homosexual and heterosexual activities were not separated as mutually exclusive. Prince Ferdinand, for example, pursued both male and female conquests, but an early favorite was the "young and beautiful" castrato Petrillo, and his longest-standing lover, who wielded "great influence over him," was the Venetian castrato Cecchino.[67] Ferdinand died from syphilis, which he is said to have contracted during Carnival in 1696 from a Venetian lady named Bambagia "of noble family."[68] His marriage to the princess Violante Beatrice of Bavaria was without issue.[69] Prince Gian Gastone's unhappy marriage to princess Anna Maria Francesca, daughter of the Duke of Saxe-Lauenberg and widow of the Count Palantine, Philip of Neuberg,[70] was also childless, and Gian Gastone's most important long-term, intimate relationship was with his groom, Giuliano Dami (1683–1750).[71] It was with Dami that Gian Gastone traveled to Hamburg, and it was with Dami, not his wife, that Gian Gastone returned permanently to Florence in 1708.[72] Thereafter, Dami provided for the prince a coterie of mostly young boys called *ruspanti* after the coins they were paid for their services.[73] A strong influence in the lives of both Medici princes was their uncle, Cardinal Francesco Maria (1660–1711), only three years older than Ferdinand. His preference for pretty boys, who waited on him dressed as girls,[74] may have presaged Gian Gastone's *ruspanti*. In 1709 Francesco Maria's brother Cosimo III, the princes' father, forced the cardinal to relinquish his vows and marry, with the hope that this liaison would produce the Medici heir that was not forthcoming from his sons and their wives, but (not surprisingly) this marriage too was barren.[75]

Little research has been done on the sexual ambience of Hamburg at this time, but the existence of a homosexual coterie, such as existed in many urban centers, and especially in port cities, seems likely.[76] Indeed, it may have been such a social circle that attracted Gian Gastone and Dami to Hamburg. If this is the case, then Handel's opera *Nero* would certainly have appealed to them. Nero's bisexual excesses, repeatedly chronicled by classical authors, were widely known, but the emperor was particularly noted for his male lovers, including Sporus, Pythagorus, and Doryphorus, whom he married and called wife. Nero had his mother, Agrippina, murdered in 59 A.D., and his wife, Octavia, in 62. In the same year he married his mistress, Poppea, whom he killed in 65 A.D. by kicking her in the stomach while pregnant.

Because of his musical ability, Nero also became an important symbol for the relation of music and homosexuality. He particularly enjoyed singing. As Suetonius writes, "And he did actually appear in operatic tragedies, taking the parts of heroes and gods, sometimes even of heroines and goddesses, wearing masks either modeled on his own face, or on the face of whatever woman happened to be his current mistress. Among his performances were *Canace in Childbirth, Orestes the Matricide, Oedipus Blinded,* and *Distraught Hercules.*"⁷⁷ The use of Nero as an emblem for sodomy often embraced his musical reputation as well, as in the following example from 1711, the year of Handel's first London opera, *Rinaldo,* when John Dennis writes:

> The Ladies, with humblest Submission, seem to mistake their Interest a little in encouraging *Opera's;* for the more the Men are enervated and emasculated by the Softness of the *Italian* Musick, the less will they care for them, and the more for one another. There are some certain Pleasures which are mortal Enemies to their Pleasures, that past the *Alps* about the same time with the *Opera;* and if our [opera] Subscriptions go on, at the frantick rate that they have done, I make no doubt but we shall see one Beau take another for Better for Worse, as once an imperial harmonious Blockhead [Nero] did *Sporus.*⁷⁸

In Handel's *Nero,* sodomy actually plays an acknowledged role. The opera includes Handel's only openly homosexual character, the emperor's lover, Anicetus, described in the libretto as Nero's "Mignon oder Liebling." Historically, it is Anicetus who is credited with killing Nero's mother Agrippina and helping to free him of his wife Octavia by pretending to have an affair with her (he was exiled in luxury for this service while she suffered a terrible death).⁷⁹ In their discussion of this opera, Winton Dean and J. Merrill Knapp correctly refer to Anicetus as a catamite (the receptive partner in sodomitical relations) and express surprise at the prominence of his part.⁸⁰ Certainly Gian Gastone and Dami would have enjoyed and understood the personal implications of the story and the dominant role given to Anicetus. Although the situation with Nero's mother does not directly pertain to Gian Gastone's experience, since his mother had left Florence and her husband when he was four, the prince similarly rejected his wife, finally separating from her in 1708 when he returned to Florence with Dami, his groom.⁸¹

Because Gian Gastone had returned to Germany in May 1707 for about a year, the only opera by Handel that the prince might have heard in Italy is another Nero story, *Agrippina* (Venice, 1709).⁸² This libretto presents an unmarried Nero whose character seems less relevant to the life of the Medici prince, and the opera has no known connection with either Florence or Gian Gastone. Although Reinhard Strohm has suggested that the libretto contains a political allegory related to the War of Spanish Succession, recent appraisals have considered such a message unlikely,⁸³ especially given the opera's "amorality" that "contrasts strikingly with the high-toned seriousness of libretti" by contemporary librettists heard in Venice.⁸⁴ Nero's homosexuality is not overtly depicted, but neither is his first marriage to Octavia included, and his relationship with Poppea is deliberately obscured. In the final scene of Handel's opera, the emperor Claudius, Nero's stepfather, attempts to restore justice by giving Poppea to Nero in marriage and naming Otho his successor. Otho rejects the throne, wanting only Poppea, and Nero responds, "To take away the empire, and also make me marry, is double punishment." Claudius thereupon switches the rewards. Although there is no known connection between the libretto and Florence, Nero's state at the end of this opera—acquiring a kingdom and no wife—nicely matches what Gian Gastone might have envisioned for himself in returning to Florence with Dami in 1708, his older brother being very ill. What is perhaps even more significant, the sentiments expressed by Nero also must have paralleled exactly those of Cardinal Francesco Maria on being forced to renounce his ecclesiastical position in 1709 in order to marry, for him a double punishment indeed. When Handel's *Agrippina* was produced in Naples in 1713, it underwent extensive revision, including the elimination of Nero's line referring to marriage as a punishment. One reason for this may have been its homosexual implications.[85]

The Florentine court maintained close musical ties to the musical establishments of Handel's Roman patrons, the cardinals Pamphili, Colonna, and Ottoboni and the Marquis Ruspoli. They shared (or competed for) musicians, as might be inferred by the letter of 24 September 1707 from Prince Ferdinand's Roman correspondent Annibale Merlini describing a virtuoso archlute player who had performed at the palaces of both Ottoboni and Colonna and whose skill could be attested by "the famous Saxon,"[86] undoubtedly Handel, who would shortly be returning to Florence for the preparations for his opera *Rodrigo*.[87] This relationship seems to date back many years. As early as 1690 Pamphili had entered into correspondence with Cardinal Francesco Maria, and in 1693 he sent a book of cantatas elaborately bound in damask with gold leaf, including a *Lucrezia romana* written by himself and set by Alessandro Scarlatti.[88] During the years when Handel was in Italy, Ottoboni himself traveled to Florence in 1709 seeking and attaining the position of Protector of France, which Cardinal Francesco Maria had been forced to relinquish along with his religious office.[89] It is difficult to imagine that the Medici court did not provide Handel with introductions to these Roman patrons.

Cardinal Pietro Ottoboni (1689–1740) was one of the greatest artistic patrons and connoisseurs of the eighteenth century. His household included the painter Francesco Trevisani (see Figure 4.1), sculptor Angelo de' Rossi, architect and set designer Filippo Juvarra, and musicians Arcangelo Corelli and Alessandro Scarlatti.[90] That his moral character was not as highly esteemed as his patronage is clear in a particularly uncharitable description from 1740 by Charles De Brosses (1709–1777): "Ottoboni, doyen, nephew of [Pope] Alexander VIII, Venetian, protector of France, made cardinal at seventeen or eighteen years, without morals, without repute, debauched, decadent, lover of the arts, and a fine musician."[91] Certainly the cardinal did not maintain his vow of celibacy, if this is meant to imply abstaining from sexual relations rather than, as sometimes in this period, simply remaining unmarried. For about twenty years he maintained a relationship with Margherita Pio Zeno of Savoy (1670–1725), to whom his love letters survive.[92] Further, in 1701 it was rumored that Ottoboni would renounce his position in the College of Cardinals to marry the daughter of the Duchess Boncompagni of Sora, but nothing came of it.[93] Michael Ranft, an eighteenth-century biographer, wrote that the cardinal hung portraits in his bedroom of his mistresses portrayed as saints.[94] However, Ottoboni's constant companion was Andrea Adami (1663–1742), castrato, author, and from 1700 to 1714 *maestro di cappella* of the Sistine Chapel. According to Valesio, Adami was Ottoboni's "favoritissimo."[95] The cardinal nourished a particular affection for Adami, protected and recommended him on diverse occasions, and gave him a number of magnificent paintings.[96] At his death, Ottoboni left debts of more than 170,000 *scudi*, which forced his family to sell most of his enormous collection.[97] Ranft sums up Ottoboni's life: "He loved pomp, prodigality, and sensual pleasure, but was at the same time kind, ready to serve, and charitable."[98]

Cardinal Benedetto Pamphili (1653–1730), poet, librettist, and lover of music and art, maintained an elaborate musical establishment that for the months of January and February 1707, when Handel arrived in Rome, included five singers and more than ten instrumentalists.[99] Lina Montalto lists twenty-four dramatic libretti written by Pamphili between 1672 and 1712; one of the last, *Il trionfo del tempo e del disinganno,* was set by Handel, the copyist's bill being recorded in Pamphili's account books on 14 May 1707.[100] The first reference tentatively associated with Handel in Rome is the entry in the diary of Francesco Valesio for 14 January 1707 referring to "a German who is an excellent player of the harpsichord and composer" who "today . . . exhibited his prowess by playing the organ in the church of St. John [Lateran] to the admiration of everybody."[101] Although one could not automatically assume the "German" to be Handel, the likelihood increases in that the first specific reference to Handel occurs in the account books of Cardinal Pamphili as a payment on 12 February 1707 to the composer for a cantata, *Delirio amoroso,* based on a text by the cardinal; Pamphili had been named the archpriest of St. John Lateran in 1699.[102] Without such a high-placed patron, it would have been impossible for a Protestant German composer to have access to the organ of St. John Lateran, the pope's own sanctuary.[103] Although the older cardinal maintained more discretion in his personal life than Ottoboni, Ranft's summation of Pamphili's character is somewhat equivocal:

As to his character, he was a very learned, diplomatic and generous man who had many good attributes, which made him worthy enough to ascend the papal throne; what hindered him we cannot say given the lack of information. In his youth he was full of vanity, but, whenever possible, he always avoided injuring his good name with unpleasant excesses.[104]

The most revealing evidence of an erotic attraction in Pamphili's life may be the texts he wrote for Handel, especially the Orpheus cantata.

The known homosexual history of some of Handel's patrons, his setting of the Nero text in Hamburg (and its possible relation to Gian Gastone), and the connotations of the Orpheus legend itself necessarily raise questions about whether the parallel Pamphili draws between Handel and Orpheus is meant merely to depict the composer's compositional skills. If the text were to have both a musical and a sexual connotation, the latter, as would be typical of the period, is likely to have been subtly or amusingly disguised. In discussing eighteenth-century pornographic texts, Armando Marchi makes an important distinction between erotic and obscene literature by noting that whereas "an obscene text requires no act of interpretation," the erotic text in which sexual activities are euphemistically described requires "the reader's active participation."[105] None of Handel's texts are pornographic, nor would one expect them to be. Among the cantatas, however, there are certainly erotic, or suggestive, texts, like those dealing with Nero, where an understanding of the homosexual subtext permits multiple readings. The Orpheus trope fits into this pattern, having a public meaning on the surface while carrying the potential for a private, homoerotic reading.

The pervasive literary association of Orpheus throughout history with the origin of homosexuality, coupled with the lack of any reference in Pamphili's text to Orpheus's skills in the Underworld, encourages a reexamination of the cantata, and one need not struggle with esoteric meaning to uncover the sexual innuendo.[106] All the animate and inanimate objects that Pamphili lists as attracted to Orpheus—"bird," "wild beast," "tree trunk," and "rocks"—are familiar metaphors for the male sexual organs;[107] these symbolize the male sex generally, enabling Pamphili to claim that Orpheus attracted men and boys with his voice. The musical references also have sexual subtexts; specifically, the verb "to sing" can mean to have sexual relations.[108] Pamphili's own situation is rather graphically described with his image of the plectrum, which had previously hung unused and motionless on a dry tree. As a result of his "musical" awakening, he goes on to wish that everyone can "sing," calling on the hand to move and the voice to sing in a new way, and thus for the hours, and even the whole day, to pass pleasurably. Note that the phrase "again on the lyre" in Terence Best's translation (see Appendix 2) is not in the Italian, allowing for some interpretive ambiguity.

Metaphor is a commonplace in Handel's cantata texts. Sometimes it is explicit. For example, in *Da sete ardente,* the singer complains of intense thirst and imagines a stream that offers sweet and gentle relief. He then continues: "Lovers, behold, I reveal to you what is the burning I feel and what is the relief; the stream shapes the thought of my beloved and the thirst is the desire to see my idol." In *Clori, degli occhi miei,* the lover sings of a beautiful stream that breaks up its clear waters on a hard rock, later identifying "this rock [as] the heart of Clori." In *Nell'africane selve* (Naples, 1708), the lover describes a proud lion who when captured and caged loses his boldness and then reveals that he, proud and unfettered, passed his days like that lion until love wounded him and made him a prisoner. Even in cantatas where the metaphor is not made explicit, it remains obvious. A pair of cantatas by Handel possibly written for Cardinal Ottoboni in 1707, *Venne voglia* and *Vedendo Amor,* describe Cupid disguising himself as a birdcatcher. He builds a birdcage and puts Clori, Amarilli, Eurilla, Iole, and Filli (Phyllis) in it, using their "eyes, cheeks, lips and breasts" as his decoys, which ruse works so well that the birds cannot help "falling into his hidden nets." The singer of the cantata is lured and escapes, but finally is trapped and caged so that now night and day he sings. Here the "birds" clearly represent men, such as the singer, attracted to the sexual decoys, and their "falling" into the net surely represents sexual intercourse. Less clear, but also possible, is the use of singing to refer to sexual relations, here coupled with the idea that such passion, however compelling, turns a man into a caged animal: "I sing for love but more for rage."

If we look again at Pamphili's text for *Hendel, non può mia musa,* the metaphors become clearer. Orpheus's singing enchants, as in *Qualor crudele* where the lover states, "the enchantment of your singing torments and delights me, darling of the god of love, beautiful siren." It attracts birds, beasts, trees, and stones, and these objects—similar to the humanist reading of the Orpheus legend, where they symbolize uncivilized and untutored mankind—represent men as yet untamed by love (uncaged birds and beasts or hard-hearted stones), or, as in the case of the 54-year-old Pamphili specifically described, men who thought they were past love (a dry tree). However, the power of Orpheus's song is so great that even Pamphili is able to "sing" once more. The text, of course, says more about Pamphili than Handel, and it is less obvious whether this interpretation can be carried into the music. The syncopated rhythmic pattern that dominates both arias establishes a metric irregularity that is only overcome slowly with ties over the bar line, eliding the second downbeat and creating a progression through the cantata from the rather stilted physical movement of the trees and rocks to the smoother motion of the hand moving and the voice singing. Among other possibilities, this rhythmic progression could represent a physical progression (either sexual or musical) or a gradual freeing of an emotional or psychological hesitation.

The Orpheus cantata reveals, I believe, Pamphili's homoerotic attraction to Handel, and this desire can be found as well in his text of *Il trionfo del tempo,* which Handel also set in 1707.[109] The theme of the oratorio has Pleasure and Truth competing with each other for the soul of Beauty. In one scene, Pleasure describes his kingdom, which is represented exclusively by lovely youths sculpted in white marble, undoubtedly representing classical antiquity and, by extension, the homosexual love it celebrated in life and mythology. As Orpheus declares in Poliziano's version: Thus Jove enjoys his beautiful Ganymede, Phoebus (Apollo) enjoyed Hyacinth, and Hercules was won by fair Hylas.[110] Pamphili's cantata text describes some youths crowned with roses, one asleep with poppies and ivy woven into his flowing locks, and one smiling youth who is heroically slaying Old Sorrow. When Pleasure's narration is interrupted by the sound of an organ, Beauty asks for the origin of the heavenly tone. This living "youth," who stands out from and yet relates to the classically sculpted youths just depicted, doubtless refers to the 22-year-old Handel, who would have been at the keyboard playing the Organ Sonata. Pamphili's libretto describes him in these words:[111]

Pleasure:

Un leggiadro giovinetto,	A graceful youth,
Bel diletto	Awakens sweet delight
Desta in suono lusinghier.	With enticing tones.
E vuol far con nuovo invito	And with new allurements
Che l'udito	He would make listening
Abbia ancor il suo piacer.	Have its own pleasure.

Beauty:

Ha della destra l'ali,	His hand has wings,
Anzi fa con la mano	Or rather he makes with his hand
Opre più che mortali.	Music more than mortal.

Just as in the Orpheus cantata, Handel's music is described as arousing delight. Here Handel's physical attraction is emphasized as well (*un leggiadro giovinetto*—a handsome or graceful youth), and the movement of his hand (again invoked) is called more than mortal.

Given the apparent homosexual subtexts of *Nero,* the Orpheus cantata, and *Il trionfo del tempo,* their reception history takes on particular importance. Handel's *Nero* had only three performances and was never revived. Although it has been considered an artistic failure on those grounds,[112] the loss of the score prevents a modern evaluation. The libretto was criticized by contemporary German librettists, but Mattheson, who sang the role of Nero, recreating the opera-singing emperor, called it the "model of a tragic opera."[113] It is unnecessary to posit an intimate relationship between Handel and Mattheson, as has been suggested by Marion Ziegler, in order to consider their shared participation in a homoerotic circle.[114] In later years, Mattheson seemed to go out of his way to publicize their intimacy by hinting at escapades that only he and Handel could interpret. The private, coded nature of these is particularly clear in one instance:

> I know well that [Handel] will laugh to himself (for he rarely laughs outwardly) when he reads this. Especially if he remembers the pigeon-seller who travelled with us at that time in the post-chaise to Lübeck, or the pastry-cook's son who had to blow the bellows for us when we played the organ in St. Mary Magdalene Church. That was 30 July, and on the 15th we had been for a water-party, and hundreds of similar incidents come back to me as I write.[115]

Handel scholars have differed in their interpretation of this passage. Donald Burrows doubts its veracity, saying that Mattheson "seems to over-emphasize their [Handel and Mattheson's] personal familiarity," but Christopher Hogwood accepts it at face value, writing that it displays Mattheson's "tendency to treat his public writing as though it were private correspondence." Hogwood's comment is particularly striking in light of the very cool and disdainful attitude that Handel maintained toward Mattheson in later years. He responded with little enthusiasm to Mattheson's request for his thoughts on the modal system and refused, over a period of twenty years, to write an autobiography as requested.[116] Mattheson therefore wrote the biography himself for his collection published in 1740, but openly expresses his annoyance, saying that Handel has "broken his word."[117] His revelation of private details of their relationship may have been his peevish way of getting back at his former friend for not submitting his own biography. Handel was a consummately private man in an extremely public role, and Mattheson surely knew he would not relish any rumors or intimations of private affairs.

Handel's aversion to private revelations is clear in his revision of *Il trionfo del tempo* for London. In this 1737 version he surgically eliminates the reference to himself by recomposing the scene. Handel cuts the organ solo, originally the source of the heavenly music, substituting a violin solo, and, naturally, he also recomposes the following aria, "Un leggiadro giovinetto," for Pleasure so that its solo accompaniment is for violin rather than organ. In this version the heavenly sound now emanates from the solo violinist, without any possible reference to Handel as performer or composer. It is significant that this change results exclusively from a musical substitution; the words are not altered.

The conversation with Handel about *Hendel, non può mia musa* that Jennens reports in the margin of his copy of Handel's biography must have taken place around the same time as Mattheson's publication and the revision of *Il trionfo del tempo,* since Jennens's collection of cantatas was probably compiled in the 1730s. In light of the cantata's implicit homosexual connotation, this anecdote too demands closer scrutiny. As Handel's librettist, Jennens is notorious for making unflattering remarks about Handel, calling him lazy and criticizing his setting of *Messiah,* for which he wrote the libretto. He even took pride in hearing that Handel attributed his illness of 1743 partially to his criticisms,[118] writing later in the same year: "It is not [my home situation] that has made me quarrel with Handel, but his own Folly, (to say no worse), if that can be called a quarrel, where I only tell him the Truth; he knows it to be Truth, yet is so obstinate, he will not submit to it."[119] Given their relationship, Jennens's depiction of Handel approving his own lack of flattery may be more a self-serving comment than a significant insight into Handel. Of course, Handel could also have deliberately deceived Jennens by taking this pose even if his concern was otherwise. Handel might have blurted out that Pamphili was an "Old fool" for putting his emotions into words, thereby possibly identifying him as the object of homosexual desire.[120] In fact, the source of Jennens's copy of this cantata is something of a mystery. Contrary to his normal practice, Handel had not kept his autograph, which was preserved by Ruspoli; moreover, in the rare cases where Handel did not preserve a cantata autograph it is usually possible to identify an archival copy that he kept instead,[121] but no surviving copy of *Hendel, non può mia musa* can be identified as such.[122] Only six copies of this cantata survive: the autograph and a copy in Ruspoli's library, an independent copy in Venice, and three copies (one incomplete) made in England from an unknown source, including one for Jennens and one for Handel's friend and patron Bernard Granville.[123] For a man who seems to have been largely in control of his paper trail—carefully preserving musical manuscripts while discarding (or destroying) private papers—the appearance of this cantata in the hands of his none-too-friendly librettist might not have been welcome. Perhaps Handel destroyed his archival copy after seeing that it had been used by his circle of copyists as a source for Jennens's manuscript.[124]

The examination of Handel's Orpheus cantata and its context provides three tentative conclusions that will continue to be investigated throughout the remainder of this book. The first deals with literary codes. Not only are metaphor and simile intrinsic elements in the Italian poetry typical of cantata texts, but homosexuality is often signified specifically by the names of classical characters (historical or mythological) known for participating in same-sex activities. Two of the most important of these are also associated with music: Nero, the amateur musician, and Orpheus, the professional. Among other common code names are Ganymede (Jupiter's young lover), Hyacinth (Apollo's love), and Hylas (Hercules's love). Although homosexuality was widely accepted in the eighteenth century either between young men or between a dominant adult and a passive boy (such as Ganymede), the name of Sporus, Nero's castrated cata-mite, became an exclusively negative epithet for an effeminate, passive adult partner. In an era when homosexuality had no name, these codes were impor-tant for both participants in and critics of same-sex love. Although they wore their meaning on the surface, they remained ostensibly neutral as simple recre-ations of classical history or myth.

Second, in terms of sociological data, the identification and interpretation of a homosexual subtext are supported by evidence of the social context and com-munity of the main participants. The well-known and well-documented homo-sexual activities of the Medici princes provide a specific impetus for a homosex-ual reading of Handel's *Nero,* especially given the close biographical parallel between Nero and Anicetus, on the one hand, and Gian Gastone and Dami, on the other. This is not to say that a homosexual reading requires a known social context, but rather that the context often provides a key to such a reading. For example, the hothouse sexual atmosphere of eighteenth-century Rome, most clearly documented in the life of Ottoboni, opens the door to a homosexual in-terpretation of Pamphili's Orpheus cantata, but once examined in this way, the strongest evidence resides in the cantata text itself.

Finally, the personal behavior of an author or composer regarding his work often provides further evidence for a homosexual interpretation. In particular, the later alteration or obfuscation of passages that imply homosexuality suggests a protective and disguising motive. This seems most obvious in Handel's revi-sion of *Il trionfo del tempo* for London in 1737, but it may also apply to his possi-ble suppression of the Orpheus cantata. However, the alteration need not derive from the author himself. Targeted alterations by others point to the probable recognition of homosexual subtexts well beyond the immediate creative circle.

Women's Voices/Men's Voices

Man's love is of his life a thing apart,
    'Tis woman's whole existence; man may range
The court, camp, church, the vessel, and the mart,
    Sword, gown, gain, glory, offer in exchange
Pride, fame, ambition, to fill up his heart,
    And few there are whom these can not estrange;
Man has all these resources, we but one,
To love again, and be again undone.

Lord Byron, *Don Juan*

Handel's more than 100 cantatas can be divided into three groups on the basis of their performing forces: cantatas for solo voice with instrumental accompaniment, cantatas for solo voice with continuo accompaniment, and cantatas for two or more voices with instrumental accompaniment. In each of the next three chapters one of these groups will in turn dominate the discussion. In this chapter I examine the seventeen Italian solo cantatas with instruments, of which thirteen can be dated to 1707 or before.[1] Heavily rooted in Handel's earliest Italian period, the solo instrumental cantatas provide a good chronological introduction to his style.

Although the vast majority of the solo instrumental cantatas are for soprano (only two are not, and both are for bass: *Cuopre tal volta* and *Spande ancor*), the treble voice represented the voice of either a woman or a man, and men and women could equally perform roles of either sex. That is, both female (soprano) and male (castrato) singers performed roles written for either female or male characters. In this chapter I will distinguish singers from the characters they represent by naming the singers "male" and "female" and the characters "men" and "women." Chronologically, the subset of six works that present women's voices is largely clustered very early in Handel's Italian sojourn; five derive from Rome, 1707. Curiously, no solo instrumental cantata can be definitively placed in Rome, 1708; the three cantatas that can be dated to this year or later all derive from other centers of patronage. The only solo instrumental cantata representing a woman's voice that falls outside Handel's 1707 Roman period is *Agrippina condotta a morire,* probably written in northern Italy in 1709 following his second (and final) sojourn in Rome in 1708.

In order to include all of Handel's cantatas for specific women's voices it is necessary to add one continuo cantata—*O numi eterni* (*Lucrezia*)—to the group of cantatas under discussion. Like most of the instrumental cantatas for women, *Lucrezia* (by which title I will refer to the cantata) falls very early in Handel's Italian period, predating his first Roman residency. Further, in the closing ritornello of the *larghetto* "Alla salma infedel," it includes a treble instrumental line with the instruction *si suona* ("one plays"), presumably on the harpsichord. The use of an additional accompanimental line, which occurs in only one other continuo cantata, illustrates that Handel was pushing the boundaries of the genre and provides an additional reason, if one were needed, for considering *Lucrezia* with the other instrumentally accompanied cantatas for woman's voice. Using the chronology proposed by Hans Joachim Marx in the *Hallische Händel-Ausgabe* edition as a basis,[2] the solo instrumental cantatas, with *Lucrezia* added, can be divided between the voices of female and male characters as shown in Table 2.1.

Handel's cantatas about women differ strikingly from those written about men. The women, even when there is a brief narrative frame, speak in their own voices. The raped Lucrezia cries out for vengeance as she takes her own life. In *Delirio amoroso,* its text written by Cardinal Pamphili, Clori is rejected by Tirsi during his life and, delirious after his death, follows him in her dreams to the Underworld. *Diana cacciatrice* ("Alla caccia") celebrates the hunt in the voice of the goddess Diana and was probably composed for performance at Ruspoli's country estate in Vignanello, fifty miles north of Rome.[3] In *Tu fedel? tu costante?* an unnamed woman complains of the faithlessness of her lover Fileno and threatens to leave him. The sorceress Armida hurls threats at her departing lover Rinaldo in *Armida abbandonata,* but finds that her love leaves her powerless to harm him. In *Ero e Leandro* ("Qual ti riveggio"), the only cantata that can with any assurance be connected with the patronage of Cardinal Ottoboni, Hero finds Leander, her love, drowned on the shore, tears out her hair (symbol of her earthly beauty which had bound the heart of Leander) and then drowns herself.[4] In *Agrippina condotta a morire* Handel depicts the mental anguish of the former Roman empress immediately before her execution ordered by her son Nero.

Handel's men, by contrast, are distanced by a narrative structure. In *Abdolonymus* ("Figlio d'alte speranze"), for example, the changing fortunes of King Abdolonymus are described in the third person. Abdolonymus's voice is possibly heard only once, in an aria that expresses no emotion concerning his fall to the position of a gardener but rather makes a statement that the palm tree will

Table 2.1   Handel's Italian solo instrumental cantatas[1]

About Women	About Men
pre-Rome 1706/1707	
Lucrezia ("O numi eterni")	*Abdolonymus* ("Figlio d'alte speranze")
Rome 1707	
Delirio amoroso (12 February)	
	Nel dolce dell'oblio (April?)
	Notte placida (early? 1707)
Tu fedel? Tu costante? (16 May)[2]	
Diana cacciatrice (16 May)	
Armida abbandonata (30 June)	*Un alma innamorata* (30 June)
	Tra le fiamme (6 July)
Ero e Leandro ("Qual ti riveggio") (Sept?)[3]	*Ah! crudel* (Sept?)
	Spande ancor
	No se emenderá jamás (22 Sept)
Rome 1707/1708	
	Clori, mia bella Clori[4]
Naples 1708	
	Cuopre tal volta
northern Italy 1708/1709	
Agrippina condotta a morire	*Alpestre monte*

1. Although most of Handel's cantatas are identified by incipit, some also have titles. In those cantatas where the singing character is identified in the title, I have adopted that as the identification of choice, as with *Lucrezia*; with *Abdolonymus* I have extended this practice and assigned a title that is not contemporary with Handel.

2. Marx places this cantata in 1706 before Handel's arrival in Rome on the basis of the use of some sheets of paper he associates with Venice. The cantata is first listed in the Ruspoli documents on 16 May 1707, where I have placed it here. Watanabe ("Music-Paper," pp. 200 and 207) associates it with works written in Rome during spring 1707.

3. Marx places this cantata in April. Watanabe ("Music-Paper," pp. 200 and 206) also associates it with spring 1707.

4. Marx places this cantata in 1708 on the basis of watermark evidence and suggests that it represents the unnamed instrumental cantata in the Ruspoli accounts for 28 August 1708. Anthony Hicks suggests it was written in Rome in 1707 and apparently associates it with an unnamed cantata performed for Ruspoli on 26 June (CD liner notes: *G.F. Handel: Italian Secular Cantatas* [Collins Classics 15032, 1997], p. 7).

be his guide to greatness. Even this aria, however, could be heard as a quotation of Abdolonymus rather than direct address. *Tra le fiamme,* composed shortly after *Armida,* narrates (rather than dramatizes) the story of Daedalus and Icarus. In *Nel dolce dell'oblio* (also titled *Pensieri notturni di Filli*), the singer (representing a man's voice) describes Phyllis, his beloved, sleeping and dreaming, but not his own emotions. In *Notte placida* the (same?) man prays for sleep so that he can dream of Phyllis.[5] Although unusually in the first person, *Notte placida* barely explores the character's emotional state; the clearest musical image in this cantata is Handel's depiction of the "gentle zephyrs" that the singer calls upon to rock him to sleep.

Whereas the lamenting Clori, Armida, and Hero, like Byron's abandoned Donna Julia (quoted in the epigraph to this chapter), have placed love at the center of their being so that abandonment destabilizes them, the unnamed male lovers in *Nel dolce dell'oblio* and *Notte placida* seem to be able to hold love as a thing apart or, at least, to keep their emotions under rational control. Indeed, in many of Handel's cantatas about men the topic often turns away from love altogether and depicts the man's life in terms of fame and glory. The story of Abdolonymus concerns not love but position; the story of Icarus, ambition. In the only instrumental cantata to depict one of Handel's patrons explicitly, the multi-voice *Oh, come chiare*, Ruspoli is portrayed not as a lover but as a warrior. Under the pseudonym of his Arcadian name, Olinto, Ruspoli sings that he will exchange his pastoral bagpipe for the warlike trumpet.

Handel rarely depicts women who are not lamenting. The only two such instrumental cantatas appear together in the Ruspoli account books for 16 May 1707, and both depict women who have given up the company of men. In *Tu fedel? Tu costante?* an unnamed woman rails against the inconstancy of her fickle lover Fileno, but then decides either to find a new lover or to give up men entirely "to be free again, loveless as before." *Diana cacciatrice*, by contrast, depicts the virgin goddess Diana who summons her nymphs to banish love and join the hunt. Taking up the imagery of hunting, *Diana cacciatrice* is the only one of Handel's cantatas for women to use the trumpet. However, Diana does not thereby take on the mantle of glory (as does Handel's patron Ruspoli in *Oh, come chiare*); rather, like the lamenting women whose wild abandon(ment) and vengeful curses are dangerous to men, Diana represents a threat to male power.

According to myth, Diana was surprised while bathing by the mortal Actaeon; in retribution for his seeing her undressed, she changed him into a stag, whereupon he was killed by his own dogs. The manuscript of *Diana cacciatrice* contains an "arietta" in which the goddess sings a tribute to Melampus, one of Actaeon's dogs,[6] implicitly celebrating the death of Actaeon and emphasizing again the danger of women—a repeated theme in a number of early cantatas. This subtext of Actaeon's fate in the arietta shares a similar theme with a painting of Diana by Giovanni Battista Gaulli also entitled *Diana the Huntress* (or *Diana cacciatrice*) that was commissioned by Cardinal Ottoboni around 1690 (see Figure 2.1). In Gaulli's painting the goddess is portrayed with two clearly individualized dogs, one of which wears a collar with the Ottoboni armorial double-headed eagle.[7] The depiction of Ottoboni's dogs in Diana's possession suggests an interpretation that equates Ottoboni with Actaeon and implies that association with a woman could bring destruction. For the young

Figure 2.1 *Diana the Huntress* (Rome, 1690) by Giovanni Battista Gaulli (Baciccio) (1639–1709). The Minneapolis Institute of Arts.

cardinal, this might mean a death that was metaphorical, in terms of the spirit, or literal (since commerce with prostitutes frequently brought death, as to Ferdinand de' Medici, through syphilis). In his later relationships with women, Ottoboni was at least spared the latter fate, but in a meaningful gesture, the painting is one of a select group that Ottoboni gave to his male favorite, Andrea Adami, perhaps to underscore a preference for male love.[8] In their allusions to one of Actaeon's dogs and to Ottoboni's dogs, respectively, both Handel's cantata and Gaulli's portrait contain the insinuation that women, and even goddesses, represent a mortal danger to men.

The women in Handel's cantatas always express themselves directly and with vehemence; however, the strongest expression in first-person cantatas for men's voices comes not from direct emotion but from nature as a metaphor for emotion. *Ah! crudel,* composed for Ruspoli, probably late in 1707, reaches its emotional peak in an *accompagnato* describing lightning, a storm, and a clearing as a metaphor for the singer's hope that his sorrows will turn to joy. *Cuopre tal volta,* composed in Naples in 1708, uses a depiction of a storm for its entire text, saving only the last sestet to explain the metaphor. *Alpestre monte* depicts instead a "wild mountain and lonely forest, melancholy abode of horror, lair of wild beasts," to which abode the singer has come to seek death as his heart also is surrounded by "evil shadows and spectres." Although unpredictable and raging nature provides the men's cantatas with an equivalent to and a substitute for the uncontrolled woman's voice, the violent and disturbing natural images cannot match the power and emotion directly expressed by an abandoned woman. In *Armida,* and then again in *Agrippina,* written around the same time as *Alpestre monte,* storms are not external events, as they are for the men, but rather exist within the women and are sent by them as curses to overtake their betrayers. Indeed, in the cantatas for men, the storms are echoes of women's voices and represent a feminine disruption in the men's lives. However, the first-person, distraught voices of the women themselves bring to Handel's music a passion and emotional depth that are largely lacking in the cantatas for men.

The despair of Lucrezia, Clori, Armida, Hero, and Agrippina significantly affects their musical utterance, and Handel depicts their distress by tearing at the musical fabric with dissonance, disjunct motion, chromaticism, and rhythmic and formal irregularities. The normal structural pattern in Handel's cantatas, as well as his mature operas, is a succession of recitative-aria pairs, where the aria is typically in *da capo* form. The typical continuo cantata contains two such pairs, as, for example, in *Hendel, non può mia musa.* The instrumental cantatas likewise sometimes limit themselves to two pairs, as in *Nel dolce dell'oblio* and *Alpestre monte,* but it is also common to see the pattern extended to three pairs, as in *Abdolonymus* and *Cuopre tal volta,* or four pairs, as in *Notte placida* and *Clori, mia bella Clori.* All these examples, however, represent men's voices. The women's cantatas regularly break this formal pattern, being, like the women themselves, neither contained nor predictable. *Lucrezia,* for example, begins with two recitative-aria pairs, but it then dissolves into a unique sequence of recitative and arioso for an equivalent length of text; in places, individual and sequential lines of text are singled out for distinct treatment (*Furioso—Adagio—Larghetto*). In four of the six women's cantatas, the voice ends in recitative: *Lucrezia, Delirio amoroso* (for Clori, where the vocal recitative ending is followed by an instrumental minuet), *Ero e Leandro,* and *Agrippina.* All the cantatas for men's voices end with aria. That is, whereas the men's cantatas end with a complex and complete musical period, the women's cantatas tend to collapse into musical recitation.[9]

Just as the women's cantatas are more flexible in overall structure, they also exhibit more freedom in individual aria form. Of course, *da capo* form dominates in all the cantatas, and in the cantatas for men, there is only one aria not in this form: *Notte placida* ends with a free fugue for voice and instruments. The women's cantatas, however, offer more variation. *Diana* and *Delirio amoroso* both contain ariettas. *Tu fedel? tu costante?* ends with a binary dance movement. In contrast, the final movement of *Un'alma innamorata,* probably a male-voice cantata, expands the binary dance form into a *da capo.*

In instrumental cantatas generally, as in opera, recitatives are usually accompanied only by continuo—that is, *recitativo semplice.* Recitative with additional accompaniment, or *accompagnato,* tends to be used for particular heightening of emotion or description. Not surprisingly, accompanied recitatives in the women's and men's cantatas differ. In the men's cantatas such recitatives occur relatively rarely, in only three of ten cantatas: *Ah! crudel, Alpestre monte,* and *Notte placida.* In *Ah! crudel* the agitated *concitato* paints a storm; in *Alpestre monte* sustained chromatic chords depict the mystery of the "lonely forest, melancholy abode of horror"; and in *Notte placida* the sustained triads in the violins represent the peaceful state of sleep. Despite their enhanced expression, these accompanied recitatives continue to function as musical declamation, unchanged from simple recitative other than by the addition of instrumental support.

The situation is quite different in the women's cantatas. Here the *accompagnato* passages function less as recitative than as aria *manqué.* This "lost aria" concept is particularly strong in *Agrippina condotta a morire,* where the abandoned aria fragments metaphorically depict Agrippina's own abandonment. The former empress, condemned to death by her son Nero, expresses her vacillation and torment in an extended scene that forms the mid-point of the cantata. She begins as if in an *adagio* aria, saying that she cannot desire the death of one to whom she gave life. Then cutting herself off in recitative, she calls herself a madwoman for having such tender feelings and begins a *presto* aria calling for Nero's death. However, she is again unable to complete her "aria" thought, and falls back into recitative, moving to a complete recitative cadence in order, once again, to start afresh, this time with an aria fragment in 3/2 asking that death be hers alone. This pattern continues through yet another vengeful *allegro,* also abandoned. Agrippina now returns to her opening *adagio* and thereafter concludes the scene in simple recitative.

Lucrezia, in its use of continuo accompaniment, demonstrates that the stylistic issue cannot be reduced to accompanied versus simple recitative, but rather encompasses recitative and aria function. After two recitative-aria pairs of seething emotion, Lucrezia can no longer maintain this formal facade. The remainder of the cantata consists of recitative and aria fragments in one extended *scena* leading to her death: [recitativo semplice]-Furioso-Adagio-Larghetto-Sostenuto-Arioso-Furioso, ending in recitative. As in *Agrippina,* a dependence on musical declamation lends this cantata a stronger forward momentum than is possible in the more formal progression of successive recitative-aria pairs.

The differences in musical structure and idiom which distinguish Handel's

cantatas for women's voices from those for men's voices can be illustrated by a
direct comparison of *Lucrezia* and *Abdolonymus*, both of which, on the basis of
manuscript paper and handwriting studies, can be placed among the earliest
works Handel wrote in Italy. Whereas *Abdolonymus* is narrative, *Lucrezia* is a
first-person *scena*. *Abdolonymus* consists of three recitative-aria pairs, in contrast
to the flexible and fragmentary sequence in *Lucrezia*. Lucrezia's recitative is imbued throughout with dissonant and disjunct angularity expressive of her wild
passion and abandon; minor seconds, augmented fourths, diminished fifths,
and diminished sevenths abound in the vocal line and harmony (Ex. 2.1).

A voi, tremende Deità,	To you, fearful gods
Del abisso, mi volgo a voi s'aspetta	Of the abyss, I turn, [and] wait for you
Del tradito onor mio far la vendetta.	To avenge my betrayed honour.

In contrast, Abdolonymus's recitative comparing the king's calm to that of a
sailor amidst storms proceeds in a bland and formulaic setting. A diminished
seventh in the voice perhaps describes the dire extremity of the sailor (*nocchier*)

Example 2.1 *Lucrezia,* second recitative (ending).

Example 2.2 *Abdolonymus,* opening recitative.

Example 2.3 *Lucrezia,* "Già superbo."

in the metaphor, but the storm *(tempeste)* is depicted by a well-behaved and non-tempestuous, if expressive, cadence (Ex. 2.2).[10]

Lo spirto suo godere	See his spirit find contentment
tra disastri vedete,	amid disasters,
qual che posa nocchier	such as brings calm to the helmsman
fra le tempeste.	amid storms.

In its arias, *Lucrezia* emphasizes continual variation and asymmetry. The A section of the first aria depicts Tarquin as wicked and faithless at the moment of his departure. Handel captures the wonderfully liquid sound of the final word, *sleal* (faithless one), by following an apparently final cadence in the tonic key of F minor with a harmonic shift that passes through three different temporary harmonies before returning to the tonic (Fm-B♭m-C-A♭-Fm). Twice, the setting of *sleal* slips melodically out of its assumed key on the second syllable like an oily villain eluding one's grasp (Ex. 2.3).

Già superbo del mio affanno,	Already exulting in my suffering,
Traditor dell'onor mio,	The betrayer of my honour,
Parte l'empio, lo sleal.	Wicked and faithless, takes his leave.

Even the long vocal melismas in *Lucrezia* are angular and irregular, resisting any tendency to fall into patterns or sequences, as is clear in the settings of *infetti* in the second aria (Ex. 2.4).

Il suol(o) che preme, l'aura che spira	May the ground beneath his feet open up,
L'empio Romano, s'apra, s'infetti.	And the air the evil Roman breathes grow foul!

By comparison, in all three arias of *Abdolonymus* Handel chooses to depict not Abdolonymus's emotional state but fortune's wheel, giving each accompani-

Example 2.4 *Lucrezia,* "Il suol che preme."

Example 2.5 *Abdolonymus*, first aria, opening ritornello.

Example 2.6 *Abdolonymus*, second aria, opening ritornello.

Example 2.7 *Abdolonymus*, third aria, opening ritornello.

ment a set of distinct turning motives. In the first aria, Handel paints the wheel with two motives: by motion up and down an octave decorated with small melodic turns, and by a threefold repetition of a descending four-note pattern (Ex. 2.5). In the second aria Handel combines a turning figure with a descending chromatic bass, which is not, however, used as a ground (Ex. 2.6). The third aria combines a repeated-note figure with a turn (Ex. 2.7). Turning motives occur in the vocal line as well, leading to repetition, regularity, and sequence. Even on words like *tormento,* Handel maintains strict sequential patterning coupled with a circle-of-fifths motion in the harmony (diametrically opposite to his irregular setting of *infetti* from *Lucrezia*), as shown in Ex. 2.8.

e non è che tormento   and it is nothing but torment

Disjunct motion also occurs in sequence, as in the second aria when it seems to depict the potentially rocky path to greatness (Ex. 2.9).

Sia guida,   Let this alone
sia stella   be my star
quest'una   my guide
al décor.   to greatness.

Example 2.8 *Abdolonymus,* first aria, B section, mm. 41–44.

Example 2.9 *Abdolonymus,* second aria, mm. 14–18.

Lucrezia and *Abdolonymus* clearly illustrate the striking musical differences between Handel's cantatas for women's and men's voices. The underlying reasons for these differences reside in three central and closely related influences, each of which warrants separate discussion: (1) the distinctions in the texts themselves, which, however, can be shown not to be overriding; (2) an earlier musical style largely abandoned at the turn of the eighteenth century; and (3) a tradition of speaking metaphorically in the voice of abandoned and/or dangerous women.

The cantata texts featuring a historical or mythological woman (Lucrezia, Diana, Armida, Hero, and Agrippina), although anonymous, derive from a long tradition of cataloguing and impersonating celebrated women, and *Delirio amoroso,* a newly conceived story about Clori and her madness by Cardinal Pamphili, follows this pattern. The classical heritage of this tradition can be traced, as with the Orpheus story, to Ovid. In his *Heroides,* Ovid was the first poet to create a collection of women's voices by imagining letters that abandoned women might have sent to their beloveds.[11] These heroines include Hero (writing to Leander), whose voice is heard in one of Handel's cantatas, and women Handel depicted later in his career: Medea (*Teseo*), Ariadne (*Arianna*), and Dejanira (*Hercules*). The list also contains other popular operatic heroines such as Dido and Penelope. Through the writings of Giovanni Boccaccio and others, this tradition of heroic epistles was revived in medieval Europe. In his *Fiammetta* (1343–1344?), Boccaccio, like Ovid, took on a woman's voice; in his *De claris mulieribus* ("Concerning famous women," c. 1359) he initiated the parallel tradition of cataloguing celebrated women.[12] Boccaccio expresses his sur-

prise that, although ancient and modern authors (particularly his "master Plutarch") have composed brief lives of famous men, "women have had so little
attention from writers of this sort that they have gained no recognition in any
work devoted especially to them." He identifies famous women, whose portraits
he derives from classical mythology and history rather than from his own time,
not by their "virtue," but by their being "renowned to the world through any
sort of deed."[13] His list of 104 women reflects Ovid's *Heroides* and previews
Handel's cantatas and operas by including Medea, Dejanira, Penelope, Lucrezia,
Athaliah, Berenice, Cleopatra, and Agrippina. Boccaccio's path-breaking catalogue gave rise to other, similar works concerning women even as his own book
continued to be published in both Latin and the vernacular into the seventeenth century, at which time, as Wendy Heller demonstrates, the voices of
abandoned and celebrated women became inextricably associated with opera.[14]

The women in Handel's cantatas are familiar both from these catalogues and
from the literary works they spawned. Agrippina appears in a catalogue of forty-
five illustrious women, ancient and modern, of 1609,[15] and over the century became a favorite subject. In 1642, the year of Monteverdi's *L'incoronazione di
Poppea,* two dramatic histories also gave voice to Agrippina: Ferrante Pallavicino's *Le due Agripinne: La madre di Nerone* and Frederico Malipiero's
L'imperatrice ambiziosa.[16] Giovanni Francesco Busenello, the librettist for
Monteverdi's opera, also wrote a number of poetic laments of abandoned
women, including one for Agrippina.[17] Lucrezia can be found in 1633 in a catalogue of twelve women (as one of the four examples of chaste women, as opposed to the lascivious, on the one hand, and the saintly, on the other),[18] and in
1654, following in the tradition of Ovid, Giovanni Francesco Loredano published a series of imagined speeches of historical figures, including monologues
for both Lucrezia and Agrippina.[19]

There is also precedent in these seventeenth-century works for the man-
threatening Diana, who in Malipiero's *L'imperatrice ambiziosa* is compared to
Messalina, the first wife of Claudius. As empress, Messalina not only prostituted
herself but openly took two husbands. Malipiero proclaims of Messalina, "of
whom a historian cannot write anything either honest or good,"

I will say only that her unbridled libidinous sensuality induced her, like a new
Diana, to transform the emperor into an Actaeon.[20]

It seems to have made no difference to this comparison that Messalina was pro-
miscuous and Diana chaste; either one of these sexual attributes was viewed as
capable of destroying man's peace of mind, if not taking away his life.

Women's disruptive effect on men's lives was a repeated and particularly common element in classical stories of abandoned women. Catullus's Ariadne, de-

serted by Theseus on the island of Naxos, curses Theseus and asks the gods to make Theseus treat himself and his dearest love with the same carelessness he showed to her; the gods intervene, and Theseus's forgetfulness causes the death of his father.[21] Virgil's Dido, deserted by Aeneas, is even more vindictive, beginning with vile images and ending with the curse that is fulfilled:

> Why could I not have seized him, torn up his body and littered
> The sea with it? Finished his friends with the sword, finished his [son]
> Ascanius and served him up for his father to banquet on?
>
> . . . . .
>
> May he be harried in war by adventurous tribes, and exiled
> From his own land; may Ascanius be torn from his arms; may he have to
> Sue for aid, and see his own friends squalidly dying.
> Yes, and when he's accepted the terms of a harsh peace,
> Let him never enjoy his realm or the alloted span
> But fall before his time and lie on the sands, unburied.
> That is my last prayer. I pour it out with my lifeblood.[22]

As Heller points out, seventeenth-century abandoned women seem to follow this classical model only up to a point, and then, "with a curious schizophrenia," they immediately recant.[23] In Ottavio Rinuccini's 1608 libretto for Monteverdi's *Arianna* (1608), Ariadne calls forth the ocean and the winds to sink Theseus in the abyss, but then cries, "What am I saying, alas, what raving! Unhappy one, ah me, what am I asking for? O Theseus, O my Theseus, it is not I who spoke those wild words; it was my anguish that spoke."[24] In *L'incoronazione di Poppea* (1642), the lament that Busenello gives Octavia concerning Nero's abandonment of her follows the same pattern:

> O Jove, listen to me,
> If, to punish Nero
> You have no thunderbolts,
> I accuse you of impotence,
> I charge you with injustice.
> Ah, but I go too far, and I repent,
> I shall suppress and bury
> My torment in silent anguish.[25]

Although Heller identifies this change as a new adherence to the seventeenth-century female virtue of silence, her use of the term "schizophrenia" may be even more relevant.

Whereas in classical literature the abandoned woman was typically depicted as a disruption to others, in the seventeenth century she became internally disturbed as well. Unlike Catullus's Ariadne, Rinuccini's heroine does not ask, logically, that Theseus be made to show the same carelessness in regard to others as he has to her, but rather conjures up storms so that he will experience the external correlative of her inner torment: "O clouds, O whirlwinds, O gales, submerge him beneath the waves. Hurry sea ogres and whales, and with your foul bodies fill the deep abyss."[26] Moreover, she does not hold to her curse, as does her classical forebear, but with shifting emotions as volatile as the winds she addresses, immediately changes her mind. By the end of the seventeenth century, such "hysteria" was considered an ailment characteristic of the majority of women.[27] The symptoms were typified by "wavering and unsteady" judgment, whereby such women "resolve to do such an Action, a Moment after they alter their Purpose."[28] As one leading physician put it, "As to females, if we except those who lead a hard and hardy life, there is rarely one who is wholly free from it [hysteria]."[29]

Handel's abandoned women often voice their curses (and schizophrenia) in language that strikingly parallels the seventeenth-century models. Armida's curse (and recantation) echoes Rinuccini's Ariadne, first calling forth the winds and sea monsters, and then recanting:

O you dread monsters of the inconstant and stormy sea, come out from your deepest lairs to avenge me, and be merciless towards that cruel man. Yes, yes, let it be a proud boast for you and for your savagery that you tear apart a greater monster than yourselves. Waves, winds, what are you doing, that you do not engulf him? Ah, no! Stop! O winds, yes, stop, do not engulf him, no![30]

Agrippina, abandoned and condemned to die by her son Nero, also vacillates between revenge and forgiveness:

Immortal Jupiter, you who from the sky empty the quiver of wrath upon the head of the guilty . . ., avenge these tears . . .; thunder, immortal Jupiter, and let loose your lightning. May your cruel thunderbolt turn the tyrant to ashes, Jupiter in heaven, if you are just! . . . Yes, yes, let the traitor feel the mighty power of the great ruler; may it be his fate for his wicked heart to be torn apart, food for birds of prey, just to appease me; and then may the traveller gaze upon his entrails, scattered and quivering on the barren shores . . .; let my unworthy son die—ah! at that name I still remember that I am a mother, and my fury abates, I cannot say how.[31]

The emotional turmoil of these women distinguishes their texts from those for men and offers the opportunity for musical settings that are equally distinctive. However, Handel's choice to distinguish men's and women's voices not only results from opportunities presented by the texts but has an important chronological basis as well. That is, from a musico-historical point of view, Handel's cantatas for women strikingly adhere to an earlier, seventeenth-century concept of the cantata (and opera) as a recitative monologue (or dramatic recitation) interrupted by lyrical passages. In early opera and cantata, this form was especially favored in women's laments, and Ellen Rosand has identified the *locus classicus* of this style in Monteverdi's lament for the abandoned Ariadne. As she writes:

> The lament is self-contained, but it is not closed: it is not an aria. Arias, being fixed, predetermined musical structures, were inappropriate to the expression of the uncontrolled passion of a lament. . . . In writing their laments, librettists and composers in Venice were clearly responding to the model of *Arianna*. . . . Typically the texts are long . . . [and include] particularly vivid, often violent, imagery. . . . Finally, they all fall *Arianna*-like into multiple sections that mark the vicissitudes typical of a lamenting heroine in extremis.[32]

By the beginning of the eighteenth century, more regular structures had replaced the flexible and free forms of the seventeenth century. Textual and musical reform, most often discussed in terms of the development of *opera seria* in the librettos of Zeno and Metastasio, was fundamental to the mission of the Arcadian Academy of Rome as it sought to abolish the excesses of seventeenth-century poetry. This reform affected the cantata as well.

Malcolm Boyd has argued persuasively that 1697 represents a significant stylistic break in the style of Alessandro Scarlatti's cantatas.[33] The distinction he draws is familiar. The earlier style contains a diversity of forms, both very short and very long, including frequent ariosos and binary forms; although the style of aria and recitative is clearly differentiated, their alternation is not fixed and cantatas often end in recitative; the melodies use jagged intervallic structures, especially for musical symbolism. After 1697, Scarlatti cantatas illustrate the supremacy of the *da capo* aria, with other aria forms, ariosos, and recitative endings being discarded altogether and disjunct intervals being eliminated in favor of a "freer flow of sensuous melody." Josephine Wright dates a similar style shift in the cantatas of Francesco Mancini to 1700.[34] The style shift identified by Boyd and Wright can be documented in Handel's cantatas between 1707 and 1708.

The long, flexible form found in *Lucrezia* (1706) has parallels in the structures of a number of Handel's early works, including *Udite il mio consiglio* (Ruspoli, 1707; composed 1706?), whose large-scale structure follows the pattern recitative–fugal arioso–aria–recitative–aria–arioso. Cantatas that end in recitative or arioso can mostly be dated to 1707 or before; examples include *Udite il mio consiglio, Sarei troppo felice, Venne voglia,* and *Vedendo Amor.* By 1708, Handel's continuo cantatas generally fall into the strict pattern of two recitative-aria pairs, where the arias are both *da capo.* Arias in binary and other non–*da capo* forms typically date from the earlier period: examples can be found in *Aure soavi* (Ruspoli, 1707), *Menzognere speranze* (Ruspoli, 1707), and *Irene, idolo mio* (no date). Disjunct motion and nonsequential dissonant harmonies and melodies also tend to disappear in the later period. These stylistic features are so significant that they can be useful in dating otherwise undocumented cantatas. For example, *Figlio del mesto cor,* which has a recitative ending, is likely a work from 1707.

Handel has left clear evidence of his stylistic shift in six cantatas he composed in Italy and revised later in England. His revisions all work toward controlling the violence and exuberance of his earlier compositional style. He eliminates wide leaps, clarifies harmonies, removes redundancies, and generally tightens the formal structure; arioso endings of recitatives are typically replaced, and longer cantatas are reduced to the pattern of recitative-aria alternation.[35] A particularly good example may be found in *E partirai, mia vita?,* a cantata that depicts the voice of an abandoned lover (without identifying the sex of the singer or the beloved). Handel's first version reflects the tradition of women's passionate and unstable voices, while the later version depicts the same text more through rational artifice than passionate outburst. For example, as shown in Ex. 2.10, Handel reduced the disjunct motion and overall range of the first recitative. (See Appendix 2 for the full text and translation.) The arioso ending of the second recitative was replaced by a more "sharply declaimed" version (Ex. 2.11),[36] while the irregular bass and vocal lines of the second aria were made regular and sequential (Ex. 2.12).

With this chronological style shift, as witnessed in the cantatas of Scarlatti (1697), Mancini (1700), and Handel (1707), the seventeenth-century recitative frame that allowed for freer structures and recitative endings came to be seen as unformed, incomplete, and unfinished in comparison to the newer aria-dominated, recitative-aria building block. Handel's revisions illustrate his adoption of the newer idiom.

Given Handel's early use and later abandonment of freer formal and stylistic patterns in his continuo cantatas, one could simply conclude that in 1707 the young German composer had not yet caught up with style changes adopted earlier by contemporary Italian composers. Yet such structures occur among the instrumental cantatas only in those about abandoned women. From the outset, the cantatas for men are structurally simpler and more modern; based on the recitative-aria pair, they include, with the rarest exceptions, only *da capo* arias.

Example 2.10a *E partirai, mia vita?*, opening recitative: original version.

Not only do they all end with aria, but *Tra le fiamme* even builds an aria frame
with the repetition of the *da capo* from the opening aria to end the cantata. Although chronology explains some of these differences—the women's cantatas
are by and large earlier than the men's—the overall shift can only be understood
by examining both chronology and the use of gendered voices. That is, not just
in the composition of cantatas, but in rewriting *E partirai, mia vita?* and in the
evolution of his cantata style more generally, Handel largely gave up the voice of
a woman for the more controlled (masculine) voice of reason. On the one hand,
then, Handel clearly distinguished between the fragmented voices of disruptive,
lamenting women and the rational, controlled voices of men, but, on the other,
his style shifted away from the use of the "feminine voice" even in texts, like *E
partirai, mia vita?*, that would seem to call for it.

  A comparison of Handel with contemporary Italian composers illustrates
further these two trends: the earlier distinction between men's and women's
voices and the later shift away from the flexible female utterance even in texts
for women. For example, *Alpestre monte* (for man's voice) and *Lucrezia* (for
woman's voice) survive in settings by Italian contemporaries of Handel. Al-

Example 2.10b *E partirai, mia vita?*, opening recitative: revised version.

Example 2.11a *E partirai, mia vita?*, second recitative: original version.

Example 2.11b *E partirai, mia vita?*, second recitative: revised version.

Example 2.12a *E partirai, mia vita?,* second aria: original version.

though single comparisons in themselves cannot, of course, demonstrate a pro-
clivity or course of action, they provide specific evidence of interest and importance.

   Handel's male-voiced cantata *Alpestre monte,* perhaps the last solo instrumental cantata he wrote in Italy, was also set by the Neapolitan composer Francesco
Mancini (1672–1737); Mancini's cantata is undated.[37] It may be that Handel had
heard or seen a copy of Mancini's cantata (perhaps during his 1708 trip to Naples) and decided to set the text later himself. Both settings follow the pattern of
two recitative-aria pairs, and both respond similarly to the imagery of the text.
Although Mancini's cantata is for continuo accompaniment alone, it is possible
to make a direct comparison of the vocal settings (Ex. 2.13). The text begins as
follows:

Alpestre monte	Wild mountain
e solitaria selva,	and lonely forest,
tristro albergo d'orror,	melancholy abode of horror,
nido di fere . . .	lair of wild beast . . .[38]

Example 2.12b *E partirai, mia vita?,* second aria: revised version.

Example 2.13a *Alpestre monte,* first recitative: Mancini.

Example 2.13b *Alpestre monte,* first recitative: Handel (voice and bass only).

In the opening recitative, Handel's setting of *Alpestre monte* (wild mountain) by climbing up a major seventh is more rugged than Mancini's, which takes two efforts to propel itself up a major sixth (motive *x* in the example). Handel thereafter sustains the major-seventh harmony for the descent of the "solitary woods," while Mancini's similar descent is harmonized with a less dissonant dominant seventh (*y*). Handel stretches the following "melancholy abode of horror" melodically over a descending diminished octave, emphasizing the final falling interval of a diminished fourth on "horror" with a shift of an augmented fifth in the root from A-flat to E; Mancini moves chromatically (one could say he traverses an augmented unison) from *g* to *g♯*, also using a shift of an augmented fifth in the root from C to G♯ (*z*). In this recitative, Handel seems repeatedly to take Mancini's ideas and expand them into stronger and more striking images.

The arias also bear motivic comparison (Ex. 2.14). The opening phrase of Mancini's first aria has a pointillist character as it bounces syllabically between the tonic and dominant; Handel's more stealthy setting concentrates a similar musical idea into a repeated-note figure (*x*). Both arias then proceed to a sequential three-note pattern built from a rising second and falling third (*y*), which Handel extends into the cadential figure of the opening phrase, while Mancini instead opts for a thrice-repeated cadential jingle that is less motivically integrated.

Io so ben ch'il vostro orrore	I know well that your horror
è un'imago del mio core,	is an image of my heart,
è un'idea del mio pensiere.	and a reflection of my thoughts.

Both composers continue with repeated-note motives in the B section (*x*); both set the first appearance of the word *orride* with a similar tie across the barline leading to a dissonant clash on the downbeat (*y*); both on the repetition of the B text separate the words *ombre* and *larve* (shadows and spectres) into individual, disjunct exclamations over chromatic basses (*z*), as shown in Ex. 2.15.

Come in questo atro soggiorno,	As in this fearful dwelling
così stanno al core attorno	surround my heart
ombre, larve, orride e fiere.	shadows and spectres so horrible and evil.

In the second aria (Ex. 2.16), Handel seems to derive his falling dotted figure from a similar figure in Mancini's ritornello that continues as a bass motive and is later lifted into the vocal line (*x*). Handel also introduces the motive in his ritornello, but he integrates it more fully into his vocal line by making it the primary theme. Further, both composers arrive at their first cadential pause

Example 2.14a *Alpestre monte,* first aria, beginning: Mancini.

Example 2.14b *Alpestre monte,* first aria, beginning: Handel.

(Mancini on a half cadence, Handel on a full but passing cadence to the relative major) with a scale passage descending the interval of a seventh (*y*).

Almen dopo il fato mio	After my death
vieni a dar l'estremo addio	at least come and give the last farewell
alla fredda spoglia esangue.	to my pale cold body.

Example 2.15a *Alpestre monte,* first aria, B section: Mancini.

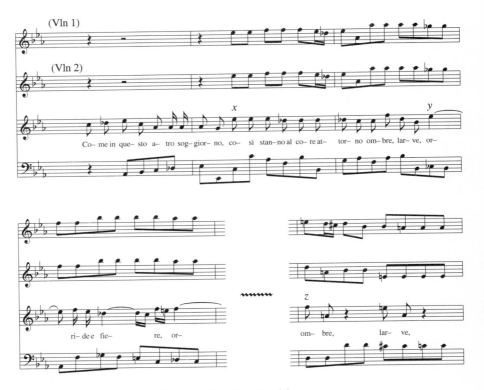

Example 2.15b *Alpestre monte,* first aria, B section: Handel.

The similarities between the two settings of this text by Handel and Mancini indicate a relationship between the cantatas, and it may be that Handel knew Mancini's composition. However, Handel's cantata is in every way the more expressive work. In addition to the advantage he gains from the string accompaniment, his musical images are stronger, more striking, and less repetitive. Never-

Example 2.16a *Alpestre monte,* second aria: Mancini.

Example 2.16b *Alpestre monte,* second aria: Handel.

theless, the two settings illustrate overall that Handel's formal approach to this male-voiced cantata in 1708 matches that taken by a contemporary Italian composer.

A parallel comparison of a female-voiced cantata is also possible, as the Venetian composer Benedetto Marcello (1686–1739) and Handel both set the same Lucrezia text.[39] Although neither cantata can be dated definitively, it is likely

Example 2.17a *Lucrezia,* final text: Marcello.

Example 2.17b *Lucrezia,* final text: Handel.

that the two cantatas were composed within a relatively close time frame. Un-like the parallel settings of Mancini's and Handel's *Alpestre monte,* however, Marcello's and Handel's settings of *Lucrezia* have very little in common, as has been demonstrated by Hellmuth Christian Wolff.[40] Handel's *Lucrezia* cantata, as we have seen earlier, follows a flexible large-scale structure using arioso and fragmented arias and ending in recitative style; Marcello's cantata, strikingly dif-ferent, is based on recitative-aria alternation and, using the same text, ends with a heightened arioso in aria style (Ex. 2.17).[41]

Nell'inferno farò la mia vendetta.	I will wreak my vengeance in the Underworld!

Handel's melodic line in both recitative and aria is notably disjunct, while Marcello's moves by step or consonant interval, as can be seen immediately by comparing the opening recitatives (Ex. 2.18).

O numi eterni! O stelle, stelle!	O eternal gods! O stars, stars!
Che fulminate empii tiranni,	You who strike down wicked tyrants,
Impugnate a' miei voti orridi strali.	Take up at my bidding your terrible darts.
Voi con fochi tonanti	With your thundering flames
Incenerite il reo Tarquinio e Roma;	Reduce to ashes the evil Tarquin and Rome itself;

Example 2.18a *Lucrezia,* opening recitative: Marcello.

Example 2.18b *Lucrezia,* opening recitative: Handel.

As Wolff points out, where Handel uses dissonant harmonies unattached to a harmonic sequence, Marcello uses chains of 7–6 suspensions, as in the first aria (Ex. 2.19).

Già superbo del mio affanno,	Already exulting in my suffering,
Traditor dell'onor mio,	The betrayer of my honour,
Parte l'empio, lo sleal.	Wicked and faithless, takes his leave.

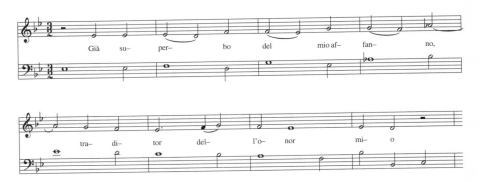

Example 2.19a *Lucrezia,* first aria opening: Marcello.

Example 2.19b *Lucrezia,* first aria opening: Handel.

In short, Marcello's style is less passionate, less irrational, and less abandoned. He and Handel clearly are following different compositional paradigms.

Handel's stronger and more striking imagery, compared to that of both Mancini and Marcello, can be attributed in part to unique personal style. Wolff also points to national differences resulting from native language, German being more strongly accented and inflected than Italian, and national musical idiom.[42] However, the comparison also shows that Handel's early use of the passionate voice of the abandoned woman in his *Lucrezia* cantata was not the only way of setting that text, nor even necessarily the preferred way for a contemporary Italian composer. Moreover, Handel's and Marcello's settings of Lucrezia's lament parallel the differences in Handel's two versions of the lament *E partirai, mia vita?,* suggesting that Handel altered his compositional practice under the influence of a more contemporary style. Only in Handel's earliest cantatas, which make use of freer formal structures, do women's voices dominate.

In his book *Abandoned Women and Poetic Tradition,* Lawrence Lipking analyzes the role of the abandoned woman's voice in poetry. He writes, "Almost every great male poet has written at least one poem in the voice of an abandoned woman. . . . Often these crossed-dressed poems have a crucial place, I shall argue, in the poet's development." He adds: "Again and again men have turned to abandoned women during a stage of poetic self-definition."[43] The history of operatic development in the Baroque offers a parallel example, where over and over again abandoned women provided a voice for composers struggling with the nexus at which music intersects with drama. It is Ariadne's lament that takes Monteverdi from the formal pageantry of *Orfeo* to the passionate expression of *Ritorno d'Ulisse* and *L'incoronazione di Poppea,* each opera buttressed respectively by the laments of Penelope and Octavia. Nicholas Lanier transferred the Italian achievement of passionate musical expression to England around 1630 in his *Hero and Leander,* in which Hero in her solo lament "expresseth passion, hope, fear, and despair, as strong as words and sounds can bear, and saving some pieces by Mr. H. Purcell, wee have nothing of this kind in English at all recommendable."[44] Purcell's own epiphany came with Dido's lament; his operatic masque *Dido and Aeneas* preceded all his great "dramatic operas," such as *King Arthur* and *The Fairy Queen.* For Handel, too, the adoption of a woman's voice during the early part of his Italian period represented a critical moment in the evolution of his musical style, teaching him how to plumb the depths of passion and extremes of emotion.

The voices of abandoned women do not simply offer a pathway to stylistic self-definition, however. As Lipking further demonstrates, poets often adopt the voice of an abandoned woman to express personal or public loss because no parallel tradition exists for an "abandoned man."[45] Ovid's Orpheus, perhaps the prototype for male loss, does not wail or curse, nor does he waver; instead, he conceives a plan and acts on it.[46] Further, his song for the gods of the Underworld is not an unconstructed lament but a carefully conceived artwork with clear purpose. Rather than trying to depict an abandoned man, then, male poets from the time of Ovid have typically put on the mask of a woman in order to lament. For example, Alexander Pope, Handel's English friend and colleague, suggests openly that he often used women's laments to disguise his own voice. In his clearest poetic imitation of Ovid's *Heroides, Eloisa to Abelard* (1717), Pope concludes the poetic epistle by having Eloisa herself invite the reader "to go back over the poem and interpret it as the confession of some personal trauma [of Pope's]."[47]

> And sure if fate some future Bard shall join
> In sad similitude of griefs to mine,
> Condemn'd whole years in absence to deplore,
> And image charms he must behold no more,
> Such if there be, who loves so long, so well;

Let him our sad, our tender story tell;
The well-sung woes will sooth my pensive ghost;
He best can paint 'em, who shall feel 'em most.

Pope even leaves a trail of biographical suggestion supporting his self-identifica-
tion with Eloisa's voice, as in a letter to his friend Martha Blount (1716): "The
Epistle of Eloise grows warm, and begins to have some Breathings of the Heart
in it, which may make posterity think I was in love."[48] Moreover, he openly acknowledges his "feminine side" in a letter of 1723 to Charles Mordaunt, third
Earl of Peterborow, in which he adopts the voice of an abandoned wife.

> [You] will own it a peculiar mark of Esteem and Gratitude, when I tell you I
> lose an hour of Mrs Howard's Conversation, to converse in this manner with
> You. She sits by my side, I look not on her, but on these lines; I give no atten-
> tion to her, but indulge the remembrance of you. These are my Merits as a
> Man, but as a Woman (for you know I am abhominably Epicœne) what mer-
> its have I not, that can remember & preserve my duty to my Husband after a
> Whole Fortnight's absence? I will now begin in the tender Strain, and ask you
> pathetically My dear Lord, is it my unhappy fate in particular, that I can no
> sooner learn to love, but I must be banish'd from what I love?[49]

Because music offers less obvious biographical information than words, it is
particularly difficult to assess when a composer might be using the voice of a
woman as a form of self-expression. In the case of Handel, the difficulty is com-
pounded by the survival of insufficient personal and biographical data to provide a key. However, the individual abandoned woman in music frequently
symbolizes a singular category of human loss or abandonment, perhaps most
obviously in sacred compositions where the soul abandoned by God or Christ is
conventionally portrayed with a woman's voice. Understanding the artist's use
of the abandoned woman as metaphor offers a way of approaching the artist's
own voice.

Handel's cantatas for abandoned women can be divided into three distinct
metaphorical categories on the basis of their texts. First, Armida and Agrippina
portray the irrationality associated with all women, which is not only dangerous
and fear-inspiring, but contagious to men who love women. Second, Lucrezia
represents a political metaphor, as when liberty, or the populace generally, is
(raped and) abandoned by those in power. Finally, the metaphor of a soul deserted by God may play a role in the depictions of Clori and Hero.[50] All three
types of abandoned women continue to appear in Handel's later works depicting not just women but, metaphorically, a more general sense of human loss.
Further, in rare instances, Handel moves beyond metaphor by having his male
characters speak directly in the voice of an abandoned woman.

Armida and Agrippina are the most obvious viragos in Handel's cantatas. Both reappear almost immediately in operas: Agrippina as the title character of Handel's opera for Venice (1709) and Armida in Handel's first opera for London, *Rinaldo* (1711)—though here she is tamed and converts to Christianity! Sorceresses with magical powers, such as Medea (*Teseo*), Melissa (*Amadigi*), and Alcina (*Alcina*), are among Handel's most interesting operatic characters, but strong, dangerous mortal women populate Handel's operas and oratorios as well, including Poppea (*Agrippina*) and Delilah (*Samson*). In *Hercules,* Dejanira causes the death of her husband Hercules, and her mad scene closely resembles an abandoned woman cantata in its flexible construction and vacillating affects; David Hurley has aptly analyzed this scene as a musical depiction of hysteria following eighteenth-century medical sources.[51] Handel's dramatizations of these abandoned women are not just structurally related, however; sometimes the women use the same musical voice. For example, Clori's exorbitant aria "Un pensier" is transferred to Poppea with the text "Per punir che m'ha ingannata saprò tessere un inganno" ("In order to punish the one who has deceived me I will know how to plot") as she plans revenge against Ottone.[52] Agrippina's first aria, "Orrida, oscura," calling on the heavens to erupt with thunder and lightning is transferred with new text ("Sibillando, ululando") to the sorceress Medea in *Teseo* as she calls forth spirits to torment her rival.

The depiction of magical and mortal viragos serves in part to illustrate the volatility of women and in part to warn men of the dangers of loving them. As repeatedly described in multiple cantata texts, women entrap and torture their prey, and men are urged to flee them. In *Dalla guerra amorosa* (before 1709), where "reason" calls the singer away from the "war of love," the stated danger of loving women is that men in love lose their rational sense (thereby becoming more like women). This idea that by loving women a man is subdued, weakened, and made effeminate (and thus irrational) continues to appear in Handel's later works. Samson provides the most obvious example. However, even Hercules's wife Dejanira, when she thinks he has "fallen" in love with another woman who is a "mere" captive, accuses him of effeminacy:

> O glorious pattern of heroic deed!
> The mighty warrior, whom not Juno's hate,
> Nor a long series of incessant labours
> Could e'er subdue, a captive maid has conquered!
> O shame to manhood! O disgrace of arms!

Further, in his opera *Orlando,* Handel musically depicts such "effeminate" love madness in a man by giving Orlando the voice of an abandoned woman. At the opening of *Orlando* (premiered in 1733), the magician and mentor Zoroaster shows the valorous knight Orlando the two paths he can follow: that of love or that of battle. He urges Orlando to purge from his heart all effeminate passions ("Purgalo ormai da effeminati sensi") and to follow glory. Nevertheless, Orlando chooses love and becomes a prisoner of his emotions. He strips himself of the outward signs of his masculinity and power by discarding his shield and sword, and, similarly, Handel strips him musically of his masculinity by having him sing like an abandoned woman in free forms that combine recitative and aria fragments. Orlando does not regain control of himself or of his music (by returning to *da capo* form) until Zoroaster restores his senses, at which time he vows to abandon love and follow valor. Whereas the instrumental cantatas depict the danger posed by irrational, abandoned women, the story of Orlando and Handel's setting of it depict the danger that by loving a woman too much, a man may himself become irrational and effeminate.

Lucrezia, in contrast, offers an example of a betrayed woman whose situation has political ramifications. Raped by Sextus Tarquinius, son of the Etruscan king of Rome, she commits suicide to expiate the dishonor that her loss of chastity, although not of her doing, has brought upon her family. Her husband and father avenge her honor and her life by overthrowing the Tarquins, thereby ending the tyranny of Etruscan rulers and establishing the Roman Republic. Lucrezia thus represents more than herself: she stands for all of the populace tyrannized and mistreated by the Tarquin kings, and, true to her role as a political metaphor for an oppressed people, Lucrezia, unlike Armida and Agrippina, never wavers in her condemnation of her betrayer. Although Lucrezia's story had a special resonance for Rome, given "her involuntary role in Rome's becoming a republic,"[53] the theme, as we have seen, was also popular in Bologna and northern republics such as Venice and the Netherlands.[54] *Lucrezia* is the only cantata of Handel's series on abandoned women that cannot be located by patron and place with assurance. It could emanate from Rome, as Handel's biographer Mainwaring states, except that Handel's autograph provides significant evidence that it predates his known arrival there, implying rather a provenance of Venice or Florence.[55] Although the Grand Duchy of Florence would not be an obvious place for such a "republic" cantata, it cannot be ruled out.[56] In 1690 Cardinal Pamphili had sent a musical setting of his own Lucrezia text to Cardinal Francesco Maria de' Medici, which suggests one possible scenario that places Handel's setting of a different Lucrezia in Florence as a carefully chosen part of his "letter of introduction" from the Medici to Pamphili, Handel's first Roman patron.

In Handel's later works, abandonment or endangerment as a result of political circumstance or intrigue is often depicted by women, such as Susanna and Esther. Like the viragos, they are musically associated with their cantata predecessors. For example, Susanna, under threat of death on false premises, sings "If guiltless blood be your intent," borrowed, as already shown (Examples P.5 and

P.6), from the cantata *Lungi n'andò Fileno,* a continuo cantata for an unnamed abandoned woman who says that she is "not permitted to hope except for the tyranny of a cruel death." In some cases, the borrowings indicate the permeable boundaries between categories of abandoned women. Although Agrippina may be a virago, in *Agrippina condotta a morire* she is also abandoned politically (and ordered killed) by her son Nero. Handel uses her music in *Esther* (transmitted through the *Brockes Passion*), where Haman, the chief minister of King Ahasuerus of Persia, has ordered the execution of "all the Jewish race." Esther, herself a member of the Israelite community, not only is personally threatened by the edict, but she risks death by approaching the king, her husband, without a summons to plead for her people. Entering the throne room under this double threat of death, she sings "Who calls my parting soul" as she sinks into a faint; the opening motive is derived from the beginning of Agrippina's *scena,* "Come, O Dio" (see Ex. 6.1).

As with the voice of women abandoned in love, men rarely take on this voice of political abandonment directly, but, there is at least one clear instance among Handel's works. In *Tamerlano,* the Turkish sultan, Bajazet, has been taken prisoner by Tamerlane, emperor of the Tartars. Finding no way to escape, Bajazet commits suicide, and in an extended *scena* at the end of the opera, the dying sultan alternately comforts his daughter and calls on the Furies to avenge him. His dying words echo those of Lucrezia, another victim whose death is politically charged.

Bajazet: Io sarò la maggior furia d'averno.	I will be the greatest fury in hell.
Lucrezia: Nell'inferno farò la mia vendetta.	I will wreak my vengeance in the Underworld.[57]

If there is any question that the setting of Bajazet's suicide derives from the musical topos of feminine instability, Handel helps to clarify the answer in his penultimate opera, *Imeneo,* by directly borrowing the accompanied recitative at the climax of Bajazet's suicide scene, "Si, figlia, io moro," for the feigned mad scene of the heroine Rosmene, "Ahi! che mancar mi sento."[58]

Finally, the cantatas about Clori (*Delirio amoroso*) and Hero (*Ero e Leandro*) seem to hint at the idea of the holy spirit or soul as an abandoned woman. That these are the only two cantatas about abandoned women that derive from the houses of cardinals (Clori was written by Pamphili and composed for him; Hero was composed for Ottoboni) may therefore be significant. Clori, distraught over the death of her beloved Tirsi, descends into hell to find him, but he does not welcome her there. She thereupon determines to transport them both to blessed Elysium (heaven), where they can live united. Hero, distraught over the death of her beloved Leander, tears out her hair and unites herself with him in death. In each case there is a possible religious metaphor. In *Delirio amoroso* the holy spirit or soul (Clori), separated from Christ, descends into hell (where they cannot live united) and then rises into heaven to be joined with Him. The image of the soul seeking Christ can be viewed as a reversal of the typical metaphor of Christ pursuing a reluctant soul, but it adheres to the common portrayal of the soul thinking (incorrectly in Christian theology) that it has been abandoned. Clori, whether an abandoned lover or a metaphor for an abandoned soul, is delusional; she thinks she is descending into hell, believes she is rejected, but longs to be united with her beloved/Christ in heaven. In *Ero e Leandro* the soul/woman (Hero) seeks to become the bride of Christ (with her hair as symbol of the earthly pleasures she is abandoning). In a religious reading, the suicide of Hero cannot, of course, be understood literally, but Hero's language is not wholly distinct from the text of the *Salve regina,* which Handel also set in 1707, in which the soul exclaims: "To thee do we cry, poor banished children of Eve, to thee do we send up our sighs, mourning and weeping in this vale of tears, . . . and after this our exile [life on earth] show unto us the blessed fruit of thy womb, Jesus [in life after death]." Graham Dixon suggests that this Catholic text could "hardly have been congenial to a convinced Protestant like Handel,"[59] but the equally potent metaphor of the abandoned soul in Lutheran imagery and the relation to secular texts of abandoned women doubtless would have rendered the language, at least, familiar.

Certainly the language of the lost soul and that of the abandoned lover are closely parallel. The first aria text in Handel's cantata *Figli del mesto cor* reads:

Son pur le lacrime	Tears are still
Il cibo misero	The wretched food
Ch'io prendo ognor.	That I always take.
Sempre tra gemiti	Always groaning,
Non spiro altr'aere	I breathe no other air
Che del dolor.	Than that of sorrow.

Psalm 42, the text that Handel chose to set both for his first Chapel Royal Anthem (1714) and his first Chandos Anthem (1716), begins in the Chandos version:

As pants the hart for cooling streams
So longs my soul for thee, O God.
Tears are my dayly food:
While thus they say, where is now thy God?[60]

Musical as well as textual parallels exist between the cantatas and the Chandos Anthems. In *The Lord is my light* (Chandos Anthem 10) the setting of

"They are brought down and fall'n" is modeled on Lucrezia's "Alla salma," and the musical setting of Armida's directions to the winds, "Venti, fermate," is used to set the text "It is the Lord that ruleth the sea." Specific and astonishing relationships occur between characters. Agrippina's "Come, O Dio,"

Come, O Dio! bramo la morte	How, O God, can I desire the death
a chi vita ebbe da me?	of one who received life from me?

was reworked in the *Brockes Passion* (1717?) to set a text of the Virgin Mary, "Soll mein Kind," before being borrowed for Esther's "Who calls my parting soul" in 1718.

Soll mein Kind, mein Leben, sterben,	Shall my child, my life, die,
und vergiesst mein Sohn sein Blut?	and does my son shed his blood?

Although both Agrippina and Mary are contemplating the death of their sons, their situations could not be more different. In one case the son chooses the death of his mother; in the other the son willingly accepts his own death. Nevertheless, Handel's borrowing emphasizes the common theme of a mother forcibly separated from her son by death.

The *Brockes Passion* also offers a prime example of a man taking on the voice of an abandoned soul. After Jesus is betrayed by Judas and taken away, the crowd flees for its life, but the apostle Peter remains alone and asks to be taken with Jesus (and not abandoned). His aria "Nehmt mich mit, verzagte Scharen" borrows its musical incipit from the aria of Clori in *Delirio amoroso*, "Lascia omai le brune vele," as she imagines sailing with her lover (Christ?) to Elysium. After Peter denies Jesus three times, his distress deepens. "Heul, du Fluch!" in which he berates himself (and declares that he should weep blood rather than tears of water) is based on the 1712 version of "Tears are my daily food" from *As Pants the Hart,* and "Schau ich fall in strenger Busse," which refers to the Prince of Night laughing at his fall, is based on Lucrezia's first aria, "Già superbo del mio affanno."

In sum, Handel's instrumental cantatas for women's voices hold a special, and somewhat complex, place in his compositional practice. First, their passionate expression reflects a long literary tradition depicting women in extreme situations, and their irregular structure is often an attribute of the texts themselves. However, the overall musical traits associated with women's voices also represent an early style both historically and within Handel's own composition; that is, as comparisons of Handel's and Marcello's settings of the Lucrezia text and Handel's own revisions of *E partirai, mia vita?* illustrate, the texts themselves do not govern absolutely the instability of the setting no matter how strongly they might suggest it. Finally, the voices of abandoned women do not disappear from Handel's music altogether but continue to resonate metaphorically in depictions of human loss, for Handel often returns to the voices of his early cantata women to portray political or spiritual suffering.

The question remains whether this extraordinary set of cantatas for abandoned women had any personal resonance for Handel. That is, if his male characters Orlando, Bajazet, and Peter speak with the voices of women, does Handel himself? It seems abundantly clear that Handel's Italian patrons did so—that, for example, Pamphili, in his poetic texts in female voice, and Ottoboni, through his collection of paintings of women, expressed personal emotion. Although it is easy to imagine that Handel, as a bachelor, German expatriate, and devout Lutheran in Catholic Italy, not only experienced but could have expressed a sense of emotional, political, or spiritual abandonment, it is not possible to make specific, biographical connections between his life and the voicing of such feelings. However, Handel's developing compositional voice can surely be heard in his cantatas for women, providing an example of the special connection advanced by Lipking between young poets' development of style and their use of abandoned women's voices wherein "the art of the exercise consists of knowing which rules to break."[61] Handel exercised this impassioned and unrestrained voice for the first time in Italy (his Hamburg opera *Almira* betrays barely a glimpse of it); but it was also in Italy, especially under the influence of leading members of the Arcadian Academy of Rome, that Handel had to learn to control this feminized voice with rational (masculine) principles of style and structure, a topic that will be taken up more fully in the following chapter. Like Orlando, he had to master the woman's voice within, or as the Aeneas-figure in Nahum Tate's *Brutus of Alba* cries out to the Queen (Dido) he is abandoning, "Hold, hold! by all that's good / Let me conjure you stifle that rash voice!" Handel's "Heroides" (his Italian cantatas for Lucrezia, Clori, Diana, Armida, Hero, and Agrippina) offered the young composer an opportunity to extend the boundaries of standard practice early in his career and provided a resonant resource for dramatic writing throughout his life. Handel found the breadth and depth of his own expressive voice by trying on the voices of abandoned women.

3

Pastoral Lovers

... shepherds of Arcady, you shall blazon my legend
Among your hills, for Arcady has no rival
In music ...
... and oh! To have been just one from among you,
Your keeper of sheep, or dresser of grapes empurpled.
For surely the shape that bewitched me, whether of Phyllis,
Amyntas, or any so ever, would now be lying
Beside me among the willows, and under the vine-loops.

Virgil, *Eclogues*

During the years Handel was in Italy, from late 1706 to early 1710, he composed more solo continuo cantatas than any other type of musical work. Fifty-two such cantatas can be definitely associated with the Italian years. Whereas his solo instrumental cantatas often depict specific mythological or historical characters, such as Armida, Agrippina, and Abdolonymus, the texts of the continuo cantatas typically lack this kind of dramatic specificity, offering instead a nameless and more conventional conceit, frequently based on classical and Renaissance models, of love pursued but rarely won. The only clear exceptions to this statement are the two continuo cantatas already discussed: *Hendel, non può mia musa,* in the voice of Pamphili comparing Handel to Orpheus, and *Lucrezia.*

Since the sex of the singing persona is so rarely identified in any of the continuo cantatas, as opposed to the solo instrumental cantatas, the best way of grouping the texts is by identification of the loved object. Of Handel's fifty Italian continuo cantatas with pastoral texts, thirty-two are directed to women: twenty-five address a faceless female beloved using a conventional, pastoral name (twelve to Clori, five to Nice, four to Fille [or Filli], and one each to Eurilla, Licori, Irene, and Dori), and another seven do so simply by the use of a feminine ending to identify the beloved (such as *pastorella, cara,* or *bella*). Ten cantatas are definitely addressed to men: four are directed to Fileno, two to Tirsi, and four to a nameless love. Among this group are the only four continuo cantatas that can be definitively assigned a woman's voice: two by name (Clori both times: *Partì, l'idolo mio* and *Sarei troppo felice*) and two by gender (the singer in *Se per fatal destino* refers to herself as *incauta* [imprudent woman]; in *Zeffiretto* she speaks of herself as *quella* [that female]). Finally, in eight cantatas, the loved one is unidentified by sex. *O lucenti, O sereni occhi* provides an example of such anonymity, addressing the eyes of the beloved as a symbol for the whole person.

All of these practices, including the use of conventional names such as Clori and Fileno, the substitution of gendered identifications for names, and the avoidance of gender altogether, are typical of pastoral texts and distancing. Whereas Handel's abandoned women cry out with individual voices that rise from the heart with wrenching and sometimes raw emotion, the shepherds and nymphs of the continuo cantatas sing more of the pains of love than of themselves; their voices are never individualized. The veil of elegant affectation makes it difficult to discover the personal and political situations that may be hidden in these cantatas. Nevertheless, it seems probable that behind the pastoral facade, gendered identifications, and gender avoidance are lurking the cultured elite of Rome, who took on pastoral names in the Arcadian Academy. Some pictorial evidence for this supposition can be found in a cantata manuscript now at Yale University that was compiled in 1693 for Andrea Adami, castrato, director of the pontifical chapel, and Ottoboni's favorite.[1] It seems likely that the eleven cantatas in this manuscript were copied for performance at the cardinal's *conversazione* or the Arcadian Academy, of which Adami, like Ottoboni, was a founding member.[2] One noteworthy aspect of the manuscript is the inclusion of a watercolor miniature by Pier Leone Ghezzi at the outset of each cantata, which may represent the earliest surviving work of this famous caricaturist. As Reinhard Strohm writes, these miniatures are remarkable for depicting entire theatrical scenes.

The "scenes" refer, of course, to the cantata text in each case—but those perpetually enamoured and love-sick shepherds are shown here in their noble living quarters and with the attitudes and costumes of the aristocratic patrons themselves. One is tempted to recognise Pietro Ottoboni in some of these versions of "Tirsi," "Aminta," etc. . . . It is a little surprising that Adami should have accepted these pictures. Perhaps he was disappointed, and that was the reason why [a subsequent volume of cantatas] is not illuminated although space was left. In any case, Ghezzi's work in *Misc. Ms. 166* does not conform to the rules of refinement and pastoral disguise to which the texts and the music are subjected. It is a glimpse behind that curtain of stylisation which the cantata genre was supposed to weave.[3]

Figure 3.1 Caricature illustrating Alessandro Scarlatti's cantata *Luci vaghe* (Rome, 1693) by Pier Leone Ghezzi (1674–1755). Gilmore Music Library (Misc. Ms. 166, fol. 63r), Yale University.

Ghezzi's bold lifting of the curtain will help point the way in my own attempt to penetrate the pastoral disguise of the cantatas, but Handel's conformity to the "rules of refinement" needs to be examined before it is possible to follow Ghezzi behind the veil of stylization in the typical continuo cantata.

The issue for Handel was how to write music appropriate to these elegant but conventional pastoral texts. To do so meant reining in the angular and chromatic outbursts that were characteristic of the abandoned women and finding a smoother and more controlled, if more ornamented, surface for men's voices. Handel's fifty-two continuo cantatas written in Italy thus serve to illustrate (1) his style shift from the passionate outpourings of female voices to the cultivated artifice of aristocratic shepherds; (2) the textual conventions, which, because of their plasticity, not only allowed multiple and hidden readings but encouraged them; and (3) the extent to which the distancing effected by pastoral voices masked a personal utterance.

Thirty-nine of the Italian continuo cantatas have been sufficiently identified to allow their placement within one of the following chronological groups (see Appendix 1 for the chronological underpinnings of these groups): pre-Rome 1706 (identified by its paper type as Moons 1706 group); Rome spring 1707 (comprising two chronological groups: Ruspoli 16 May 1707 and ?Spring 1707); Rome late summer/autumn 1707 (comprising ?Ottoboni 1707 and Ruspoli September/October 1707); Naples 1708; Ruspoli August/September 1708; and post-Rome 1709 (identified by its paper as Moons 1709 group). These cantatas are all based on the alternation of recitative (r) and aria (A), usually determined by standard distinctions in the text. Whereas recitative consists of lines of irregular length that sometimes rhyme in irregular patterns, arias generally follow regular metric patterns and rhyme schemes and contain lines of a consistent length. More specifically, recitative consists generally of a mixture of *settenari* (seven-syllable lines) and *undicisillabi* (eleven), whereas the lines of arias are usually more consistent with *ottonari* (eight-syllable lines), or, more rarely, *quinari* (five). The most common pattern for continuo cantatas is two rA pairs, where each aria text falls into two sections (AB) meant to be set in *da capo* form (ABA). However, individual texts differ in various important ways, including rhyme schemes, structure, length and placement of recitatives, and number and length of arias. Overall the cantatas illustrate a chronological movement in the texts toward a standard pattern of recitative-aria alternation, symmetrical structure in the aria texts achieved through rhyme and sections of equal length, and a more lyrical rhymed structure in recitative.

A chronological movement toward increased structure and regularity in the texts is reflected as well in the music. Only in 1706 and 1707 does Handel set *da capo* aria texts in non–*da capo* forms, and only the pre-Rome 1706 and Rome spring 1707 groups contain cantatas in which there is a blurred dividing line between recitative and aria, with the use of independent arioso (s) movements to heighten recitative essentially into aria. In *Lucrezia* (pre-Rome 1706), for example, the text of the arioso "Alla salma,"

. . . alla salma infedel porga la pena.   . . . do justice to my faithless body.

is not complete in itself, nor does it contain affective words like *martire* or *piange* that Handel later would set apart by word-painting. Rather, Handel chooses in these early examples, as in the early group of cantatas for women's voice to which *Lucrezia* belongs, to heighten the dramatic moment by loosening the formal patterning.

Provenance also plays a role in determining textual structure and Handel's response. Although we do not know the librettists of most of these cantatas, we do know that the movement toward textual regularity is one associated in particular with the Roman Arcadian Academy, whose primary goal was, as its founders described it, to rescue Italian poetry from the mannered artificiality and (feminine) excesses typical of seventeenth-century Italian verse. Twenty-eight cantatas by Handel can be placed in Rome during 1707 and 1708, all of which can confidently be associated with the Academy meetings or *conversazioni* of his Roman patrons.[4] If the classicizing literary goals of the first decade of the eighteenth century in Italy are clearest out of all his works in Handel's Roman cantata texts, it is because Rome was in the forefront of this movement.

The first two chronological groups of continuo cantatas, pre-Rome 1706 and Rome spring 1707, offer a striking set of contrasts that illustrate both the chronological trends within the overall group and the impact of Rome. (Tables 3.1 and 3.2 list the cantatas from each group and show their overall form and verse patterns.) Of the five 1706 cantatas, only one (*Fra tante pene*) follows the pattern rArA. Two consist of the shortened form ArA, and two have greatly expanded formal schemes with mixtures of recitative, arioso, and aria (*Lucrezia* and *Udite il mio consiglio*). By contrast, during the spring 1707 period, six of nine cantatas follow the pattern rArA, and the exceptions are less extended. *Del bel idolo mio* and *Ninfe e pastori* contain three rA pairs, and *Sei pur bella*, in the form ArsA, contains the only example of an arioso movement in this group, the final line of recitative text (*g*) being raised into the arioso "Vivi alla pace tua." The association of this trait with a discarded early style can be witnessed in the English revision (c. 1715) of *Sei pur bella*, where new text is substituted for the recitative and final aria, eliminating the arioso (see Appendix 2).[5]

The rhyme schemes are also quite different in the 1706 and early 1707 cantatas. In the 1706 group, *da capo* aria texts often have no rhyme within the internal sections, the most common pattern dividing a four-line stanza into a two-line A section and a two-line B section as follows: *ab | ab*. In the spring 1707 group, expanded patterns with rhyme within and across the sections become increasingly common. Whereas in 1706 only one of the ten *da capo* arias, "Non esce un guardo mai" in *Udite il mio consiglio*, follows the internally rhymed scheme (*aab | ccb*), in 1707 five out of twenty arias adhere to this specific pattern, and only six lack internal rhyme in at least one section. "Care luci" in *Aure soavi* is the only aria text in the group to adhere to the early abbreviated *ab | ab* pattern; the others, although lacking rhyme, are still extended, such as "Se non giunge quel momento" in *Filli adorata e cara* in the pattern *abc | abc*. It may not be a coincidence that "Care luci" is the only aria from this group not set by Handel as a *da capo*, as the lack of breadth in this verse pattern is not consistent with the increasingly expanding *da capo* form.[6] Later revisions underscore the shift to internal rhyme. In *Sei pur bella*, the original final aria, "Nascermi sento al core," follows the pattern *abc | abc*, but the replacement aria, "E certo allor," follows the increasingly common pattern *aab | ccb* (see Appendix 2).

Table 3.1   Pre-Rome 1706 (Moons 1706 group)

Chi rapì la pace?

A	*xa* | *a(bb)a*
r	*axa* | *xxbb*
A	*xxa* | *bba*

Fra tante pene

r	*xxaa* | *bb*
A	*aaxb* | *ccxddeeb*
r	*aaxxxbb*
A	*ab* | *ab*

Lucrezia (O numi eterni)

r	*xxxxaaxxbb*
A	*abc* | *abc*
r	*xxxxxxaa*
A	*ab* | *ab*
r	*xxaa* | *xxxxx*
s	*x*
r	*x*
s	*x*
r	*xxxxxxx*
a	*xxxxx* | *xxaaxbxb*

Sarai contenta un dì

A	*ab* | *ab*
r	*xxaxa*
A	*ab* | *ab*

Udite il mio consiglio

r	*axxxxbxbx(ax)xa* | *cxc*
s	*dd*
A	*xa* | *abba*
r	*xababcc* | *ddee*
A	*aab* | *ccb*
r	*xxxa*
s	*xa*

The following abbreviations are used in Tables 3.1 through 3.6: r = recitative; A = aria; s = arioso; | = sectional division in *da capo*, or sectional breaks in recitative; *x* = single unrhymed line; *( )* = single line with internal rhyme; F = refrain, shown in non-italic ( ) with rhyme preceding (*a*F) or (*x*F).

In the 1706 group, the recitatives rarely use rhyme throughout; often it is limited to a concluding rhymed couplet. In the Rome spring 1707 group, only one cantata, *Se per fatal destino,* follows this pattern, the others containing various and often complex rhyme schemes. Handel's setting of largely unrhymed recitative tends to be continuous, without the sectional cadences found in rhymed recitatives, and the musical style is generally more sustained and song-like, flowing easily into arioso sections typical of Handel's early works, such as *Lucrezia* and *Udite il mio consiglio.* Handel's setting of the rather short recitative from *Sarai contenta un dì* provides an example (Ex. 3.1).

Table 3.2 Rome spring 1707

Aure soavi (Ruspoli, 16 May)

r	*aabab | cc | dxxd*
A	*ab | ab*
r	*ababcc*
A	*aab | aab*

Del bel idolo mio (Ruspoli, May?)

r	xaaxbbc | xxc
A	*ab | accb*
r	*xxx*
A	*xa | bba*
r	*xxaa*
A	*abab | ccbb*

Filli adorata e cara (spring?)

r	*xaax | bxb | cdcd*
A	*abc | abc*
r	*axaxbxb*
A	*aab | ccb*

Nella stagion (Ruspoli, 16 May)

r	*axa | bb | cxc*
A	*abab | abab*
r	*abba | xcc*
A	*aab | ccb*

Ninfe e pastori (spring?)

r	*abab | xx | cc*
A	*ab | axb*
r	*axbbccddaa*
A	*aab | ccb*
r	*aabbcc*
A	*xa | xa*

Poiché giuraro amore (Ruspoli, 16 May)

r	*abccaadd | bexefxf*
A	*abbc | addc*
r	*aa | bb | cc | dd*
A	*abbc | addc*

Sei pur bella (Ruspoli, 16 May: version 1 in Appendix 2)

A	*a(ab) | c(cb)*
r	*xababcc | dedeffg*
s	*g*
A	*abc | abc*

Se per fatal destino (Ruspoli, 16 May)

r	*xxxxxxxxxxaa*
A	*xabc | xabc*
r	*xxxxxxxxxxxxxaa*
A	*xxa | bba*

Stelle, perfide stelle! (spring?)

r	*axxbb | xaxxcc*
A	*aab | ccb*
r	*axaxbbcc | xxdxd*
A	*aabc | aabc*

Ma con qual pena, O Dio!	(x)	But with what pain, O God!
Perché ingrata mi sei,	(x)	Because you are ungrateful to me,
M'offendi in guisa che me forzi al partir,	(a)	You offend me so that you force me to part,
E del partir io avrò la colpa	(x)	And for the parting I shall have the blame
E soffrirò il martire.	(a)	And suffer the torment.

The exclamation of the first line, despite the striking leap of a diminished seventh on *pena,* cadences neatly to B-flat minor. The second line sets off with a dominant seventh (4-2) of E-flat, but is wrenched away to C minor by the *b♮* (m. 3), cadencing (m. 4) on the third line ("you force me to part"). The fourth line, again outlining great distances in an angular vocal line encompassing leaps of a diminished seventh, octave, and a fifth while rising to the highest point on *colpa* (blame), cadences weakly to G minor. The last line ("and I suffer the torment") reaches a confirming final cadence in G minor through an extended arioso ending chromatically with a depiction of the word *martire.* Such arioso endings of recitative are completely lacking in the 1707 Ruspoli group.

Nella stagion offers an example from the 1707 group of Ruspoli cantatas. The opening recitative consists of eight lines of text:

Nella stagion che, di viole e rose	(a)	In the season when violets and roses
Il giardin si riveste,	(x)	Bedeck the garden anew,

Example 3.1 *Sarai contenta un dì,* recitative.

Per mitigar le fiamme sue amorose,	(*a*)	To assuage the flames of passion,
Amarilli vezzosa,	(*b*)	Pretty Amarilli,
Assisa in piaggia erbosa	(*b*)	Seated on a grassy bank
D'un mirto all'ombra,		In the shade of a myrtle tree,
con dogliosi accenti	(*c*)	with mournful voice,
Spiegò, mesta e piangente,	(*x*)	Unfolded, sad and weeping,
Al bel idolo suo questi lamenti:	(*c*)	These laments to her beloved idol:

The first three lines contain the first rhyme (*axa*), and despite the lack of a grammatical close, Handel reflects the closed rhyme with a cadence to C major, the first dominant-tonic cadence in the recitative (Ex. 3.2). The next two lines form a rhymed couplet (*bb*) and serve to introduce Amarilli, the main character of the cantata. Here Handel follows both the form and content of the text by introducing a new key (representing the introduction of Amarilli) through its seventh degree (G-sharp diminished seventh) and repeating this chord without resolution, just as the couplet repeats the rhyme. The final three lines of text are also closed (*cxc*), and Handel moves through a standard harmonic progression to a final cadence in A minor. While clearly taking into account the very structured rhyme scheme, Handel's harmonies are also able to preserve the grammat-

Example 3.2 *Nella stagion,* opening recitative.

ical continuity in a way that the rhymes cannot. The recitative begins in D minor, and the first cadence to C major is not strong but is comparable to the comma in the text. The chord used for the couplet represents the most sustained harmony in the recitative, but it is unstable and cries out for a resolution and, thus, continuity. This, of course, is given at the beginning of the *cxc* rhyme, and the full close in A minor coincides with the end of the sentence that makes up the recitative; it offers the first sense of musical, as well as grammatical, repose. In the music, then, Handel is able to satisfy and combine the conflicting demands of the rhyme scheme and the grammatical construction.

The first aria of *Nella stagion* consists of two quatrains rhymed *abab* in regular *ottonari* (eight-syllable lines, as opposed to the seven- and eleven-syllable lines typical of recitative).

Ride il fiore in seno al prato	(*a*)	The flowers smile in the meadow
A tornar la primavera	(*b*)	At the return of spring,
E con soffio delicato	(*a*)	And with gentle breath
Spira l'aura lusinghiera.	(*b*)	The caressing breeze blows.
Solo tu, crudele ingrato,	(*a*)	You alone, cruel and unkind,
Sdegni ognor la fé sincera	(*b*)	Do ever scorn the loyalty
Del mio petto innamorato	(*a*)	Within my loving breast,
Con sì barbara maniera.	(*b*)	In such a heartless fashion.

Here Handel is not concerned particularly with the rhyme scheme or grammatical construction, but, as is usual in arias, with the content of the text. The first quatrain tells of the happiness and beauty that occur in springtime, and he sets the lines without much textual repetition, depicting the pleasant scene, and perhaps specifically the smiling flowers, with rolling triplets (Ex. 3.3). In the second quatrain the text changes to a description of the beloved, who alone is cruel and disdainful. Handel makes the most of the textual contrast by eliminating the triplets and adding sharp dissonance to the vocal line—a diminished fifth, diminished third, augmented fourth, diminished fourth, and minor seventh follow one another in quick succession as a setting of the words, "Solo tu, crudele ingrato" (Ex. 3.4). Handel repeats the entire B section text in an altered setting, and then the A section returns to effect the *da capo*. The cantata is completed with another rA pair that shows many of the same stylistic traits.

The trajectory toward regular structures and more flowing melody and harmony illustrated by the two groups from 1706 and early 1707 is continued during Handel's next two years in Italy: each of the succeeding groups contributes to a tendency toward regularization, but each also contains unique stylistic traits.

Example 3.3 *Nella stagion,* first aria, beginning.

Example 3.4 *Nella stagion,* first aria, beginning of B section.

A second group of continuo cantatas for Rome can be grouped together around September 1707, five tentatively associated with Ottoboni's patronage and four identified with Ruspoli (Table 3.3). Four follow the rArA pattern, one adds an opening aria (ArArA), three add a closing recitative (rArAr), and one extends this by an additional rA pair (rArArAr). However, with one of these recitative-ending cantatas, *Qualor l'egre pupille* (rArAr), the decision to eliminate the final recitative was taken early: in the copy made for Ruspoli by his regular copyist, Angelini, the final recitative is crossed out and a written indication of the omission provided as well.[7] Whether this alteration was initiated by Handel or his patron is not clear.

Of twenty arias in this group, the pattern *aab | ccb* occurs most frequently and can be found in eight of the arias, one of which, "Altra speme or non alletta" in *Menzognere speranze,* is not set as a *da capo.* Only five arias lack internal rhyme in at least one of the sections. In a distinguishing feature of this group, the B section in six arias is longer than the A section, a textual pattern not consistent with the textual symmetry typical of the *da capo* or the musical emphasis on the A section. The use of rhyme in the recitatives is largely unchanged from the spring 1707 group.

A new stylistic trait is found in the first recitative of *Occhi miei,* where there is a textual refrain that is set also as a musical refrain (Ex. 3.5).

Table 3.3 Rome late summer/autumn 1707

Dimmi, O mio cor (Ottoboni?)

r	*xxaxaxxxxxxbxb*
A	*a(ab) | cc(dd)b*
r	*xxxxxaaxbxbcxc | cxdd*
A	*ab | aab*

E partirai, mia vita? (Ottoboni?)

r	*ababxcxxc*
A	*ab | ab*
r	*xxaab | bxcc*
A	*ab | ccab*

Menzognere speranze (Ruspoli, 22 September)

r	*xxaa(bb)cxc | dxeexxd*
A	*aab | ccab*
r	*axxaxaxbbcc*
A	*aabccb*

Ne' tuoi lumi (Ruspoli, 22 September)

A	*xa | bba*
r	*xxxaxx | abb*
A	*aab | ccb*
r	*xxxaaa | bab*
A	*(aa)b | (cc)b*

Occhi miei (Ottoboni?)

r	*(aF)xbbxx | xcca(aF)*
A	*abbc | addc*
r	*axab(bF)*
A	*abc | abc*

Qualor l'egre pupille (Ruspoli, 22 September)

r	*xxaa | xbb | cc | xdxd*
A	*aab | ccb*
r	*xaa | bb*
A	*ab | ba*
r	*aa | bb*

Sarei troppo felice (Pamphili; Ruspoli, 22 September)

r	*(xxaF)xbcc | bxb | xddee | xffa | (xxaF)*
A	*abc | abc*
r	*xxaaxxaab | (xxbF)*
A	*ab | ab*
r	*xxa | (xxaF)*

Venne voglia (Ottoboni?)

r	*aaxxb | xb | cc | ddee*
A	*aab | ccb*
r	*xxaa | bxb*
A	*xa | bba*
r	*aabbcc*

Vedendo Amor (Ottoboni?)

r	*ababxcc*
A	*aab | ccb*
r	*xxaabbccddee*
A	*aab | ccb*
r	*xaaxbbccdd*
A	*aab | ccb*
r	*axxa*

Example 3.5a *Occhi miei,* first recitative, opening.

Example 3.5b *Occhi miei,* first recitative, ending.

Example 3.5c *Occhi miei,* second recitative, ending.

(recitative 1)
Occhi miei, che faceste?   *My eyes, what have you done?*
Nel contemplar curiosi   By curiously contemplating
Quel vivo fuoco che dalle pupille   The lively fire that from her eyes
Vibra la vaga Fille,   The lovely Fille shoots,
. . . .
E libertade e vita al cuor toglieste.   You took both liberty and life from my heart.
Occhi miei, che faceste?   *My eyes, what have you done?*
(recitative 2)
Il misero innocente   The miserable one [the heart],
D'un delitto non suo   Innocent of a crime not its own,
La pena e il danno sente.   Suffers the pain and injury.
Del suo grave dolor voi siete rei.   For its grave sorrow you are guilty.
Che faceste, occhi miei?   *What have you done, my eyes?*

In this group, *Sarei troppo felice,* with a text by Pamphili, also contains refrains. The use of a refrain offers an alternative textual method of structuring recitatives other than rhyme; furthermore, setting the text refrains as musical refrains gives the recitatives a heightened quality akin to aria which is otherwise lacking, in the absence of arioso movements. Three other cantatas with such refrains, *Dalla guerra amorosa, Lungi da me, pensier tiranno!* and *Solitudini care,* cannot be specifically dated, but the first two appear in Ruspoli's accounts on 31 August

1709, placing them definitely in Italy and possibly at Ruspoli's. Handel's use of
refrains may be an aid to chronology, enabling us to assign all five cantatas to
Rome, during late summer 1707. The refrain structure is absent from his cantatas that can be dated later, and earlier use is rare. The single earlier instance occurs in the instrumental cantata *Tu fedel? tu costante?* which appears in Ruspoli's
account books on 16 May 1707, where the first recitative begins and ends with
the same line of text, and Handel takes the opportunity to use a musical refrain.
In *Aure soavi* (also from the Ruspoli 16 May group), the only continuo cantata
certainly from an earlier date that contains similar lines of text at the beginning
and end of its first recitative, Handel declines the opportunity to compose a
musical refrain (Ex. 3.6).

Aure soavi e liete,	*Soft and delightful breezes,*
Ombre notturne e chete,	*Hushed evening shadows,*
Voi dall'estivo ardore,	From summer heat you
Dolci ne difendete.	Give us sweet relief.
. . . . .	. . . . .
Di parlar a colei	I imagine speaking to her,
Che pur non m'ode,	Who does not hear me.
Aure soavi, ombre notturne io fingo.	*Soft breezes, evening shadows.*

    Arioso endings not associated with refrains occur only twice. One of these
appears in *Ne' tuoi lumi,* a cantata that is not in or altered to rArA form, providing a combination of traits that typifies an earlier style (Ex. 3.7). However, this
arioso section is a mere vestige of the arioso movements Handel created earlier

Example 3.6 *Aure soavi,* opening recitative.

Example 3.7 *Ne' tuoi lumi,* recitative cadence.

out of single lines of recitative in 1706 (*Lucrezia* and *Udite il mio consiglio*) and
early 1707 (*Sei pur bella*).

E fosco, in un instante,	And, in an instant,
M'appare il ciel d'amore,	The heaven of love appears dark to me,
Pria sì giocondo e luminoso al core.	Once so entertaining and bright to my heart.

The second recitative in *E partirai, mia vita?* also has an arioso ending (not a
separate arioso movement), but as in the case of *Sei pur bella,* a later English revision eliminated the passage (see Ex. 2.11).

In Naples between April and July 1708, Handel composed five solo continuo
cantatas as well as the large-scale serenata *Aci, Galatea e Polifemo* for three voices
and other trios. All of the cantatas identified with this period have the rArA pattern (Table 3.4). Seven of the ten arias have rhyme within both individual sections, and eight have sections of equal length. All arias are *da capo,* and no recitatives are treated as arioso. However, the elaborately rhymed recitatives often
include word repetition with surprising and elaborate word-painting, as, for example, in *Nell'africane selve:*

Nell'africane selve,	(*a*)	In the forests of Africa
Ove rei spaventi,	(*b*)	Where fearsome monsters,
O cada o sorga il giorno,	(*c*)	Whether at dawn or sunset,
S'odono sempre intorno—	(*c*)	Are heard all around—
Ululati di belve,	(*a*)	The howling of beasts,
Sibili di serpenti	(*b*)	The hissing of serpents
E d'augelli rapaci orride strida—	(*d*)	And the eerie screams of birds of prey—
Fiero leon s'annida,	(*d*)	The proud lion has his den,
Ed audace e maestoso,	(*x*)	And, bold and majestic,
Non soggiace al timor fra l'altre fiere;	(*e*)	Passes unafraid among the other animals;
Stampa nei boschi, altiere,	(*e*)	Proudly he prints
L'orme del passo errante,	(*f*)	His wandering footsteps in the forest,
Ma se mai, fra le piante,	(*f*)	But if ever through the branches
Un raggio lo ferisce	(*x*)	He is struck by a ray [of light]
D'insidiosa e lucida facella,	(*g*)	From an insidious bright torch,
L'audacia del leon non è più quella.	(*g*)	The lion's audacity then disappears.

Table 3.4   Naples 1708

Mentre il tutto è in furore

r	*axa* | *bbxxcddc*
A	*aab* | *ccb*
r	*xxaabcbc*
A	*xa* | *bba*

Nel dolce tempo

r	*xxaxbab* | *xccddx* | *eeaa*
A	*a(bb)c* | *a(dd)c*
r	*axxxbbxx* | *xxxxxaaaa* | *xxcc*
A	*aab* | *ccddb*

Nell'africane selve

r	*abccabddxeeffxgg*
A	*ab(bc)* | *addc*
r	*xaabxb* | *xccddee*
A	*xaab* | *xccb*

Quando sperasti

r	*abba* | *xcc*
A	*abc* | *abc*
r	*xaax* | *xxbxb* | *xccdd*
A	*aabc* | *ddbc*

Sento là che ristretto

r	*abbaccddxxe* | *exfggf*
A	*ab* | *ab*
r	*axxxbba* | *ccddee*
A	*abbc* | *dadc*

In the first eleven bars of this recitative, the word *cada* is set to a falling motive that tumbles nearly two octaves; *sorga* surges up a minor seventh, using sixteenth notes; *ululati di belve* is repeated with an impossibly high wail followed by a drop of a diminished twelfth; and *sibili* hisses (on the "si-" syllable) in a downward run of thirty-second notes over a tenth (Ex. 3.8).

The use of word repetition and extended word-painting in recitatives seems to be largely limited in Handel's works to the spring and summer of 1708, including *La resurrezione* (Rome, 1708) and *Aci, Galatea e Polifemo* (Naples, 1708). Although examples occur as well in *Apollo e Dafne* (1709), such recitative settings are not common in his earlier or in his later compositions. For example, in his 1706 setting of *Lucrezia* Handel ignores word-painting possibilities that are captured by Marcello, as in the phrase *voi con fochi tonanti* (with your thundering flames), as shown in Ex. 2.18; and in the London revision to the Neapolitan cantata *Sento là che ristretto,* Handel alters the second recitative to eliminate the word-painting on the word *naufragar* (shipwreck), the outburst on "think how my heart groans," and the final arioso ending that sets the words "I burn in the fire," with a resultant reduction of three bars (Ex. 3.9).

Son io Nice il ruscello,	Nice, I am the brook,
E di bellezza il mare	And the sea of beauty
È il tenero tuo seno	Is your soft breast
Ove, tra vivi scogli	Where, among living rocks,
Va del mio core a naufragar il pino.	The ship of my heart goes to be wrecked.
Or se fiero destino	Now if a cruel fate
Misero al par di quello,	As pitiful as that one there
Mi vieta il ribaciar	Forbids me from kissing once more
Di sì placido mar	The far shores
Le sponde estreme,	Of the very serene sea,
Pensa il cor quanto geme,	Imagine how much my heart groans,
E come in vario loco,	How in a different place,
Vittima troppo fida, ardo nel foco.	A too faithful victim, I burn in the fire.

This chronologically delimited practice of word-painting constitutes another way of giving the recitatives greater interest—albeit, unlike the refrains of late 1707, a completely musical one.

Handel returned to Rome in July 1708 and during that summer composed one final group of cantatas, associated particularly with the Arcadian Academy meetings which Ruspoli was hosting that summer. Seven cantatas can be linked to this period (Table 3.5); however, a number of these may be copies of earlier work (see Appendix 1). All end with an aria; six of the seven have the form rArA, the only exception being ArA. The textual patterns largely duplicate the earlier Ruspoli groups, with pervasive rhyme in both aria (within and across sections)

Example 3.8 *Nell'africane selve,* opening recitative, mm. 1–11.

Example 3.9a *Sento là che ristretto,* second recitative: original version.

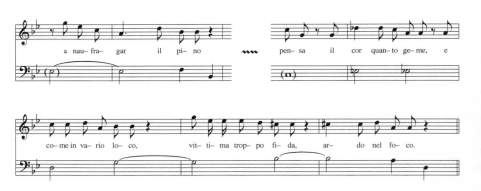

Example 3.9b *Sento là che ristretto,* second recitative: revised version.

and recitative (providing structural shape). The recitatives are generally simple, lacking refrains or word-painting. The recitatives of three cantatas include a few examples of arioso cadences on final, key words, a characteristic first seen in the 1706 *Sarai contenta un dì* (see Ex. 3.1), but now used more consistently in a way that seems to combine and control the more exuberant word-painting of the Neapolitan group and the extended ariosos on more neutral words (as in *Ne' tuoi lumi,* Ex. 3.7) characteristic of the earlier cantatas (Ex. 3.10).

The formal flexibility of the 1706 and early 1707 works is largely absent from the Ruspoli summer 1708 group, as are many of the melodic and harmonic freedoms. Whereas the earlier works contain arias in a variety of forms, all fourteen

Table 3.5 Ruspoli, August/September 1708

Clori, vezzosa Clori

r	*ababcxxc*
A	*aaxb	ccxb*
r	*xaabbxc	cddcee*
A	*aaxb	aaxb*

Ditemi, O piante

r	*xxaab	bxxcc*
A	*aab	xxxb*
r	*abxba	xcc	xxdd*
A	*aab	ccb*

Lungi da voi

r	*xxaaxbxxb	cxcddexexe*
A	*(aa)bc	(dd)bc*
r	*xaab	bxccdxd	xee*
A	*abbc	addc*

Lungi n'andò Fileno

r	*abxbaccd(ed)ee*
A	*aab	ccb*
r	*axb	bacc	dd*
A	*aab	ccb*

Manca pur quanto sai

r	*abab	cdc	dee*
A	*ab	accb*
r	*abba	xcc*
A	*aabc	b(bd)dc*

Se pari è la tua fé (first version in Appendix 2)

A	*abc	abc*
r	*xxxxxxxxx*
A	*xa	xa*

Stanco di più soffrire

r	*xaabcc	xbxddexe*
A	*ab	accb*
r	*axbbxcca	xdedexff*
A	*abcd	abcd*

of the arias from this set are in *da capo* form. Eleven of these use the increasingly standard five-part *da capo* pattern in the A section: ritornello–A1 [first setting of the A text modulating away from the tonic key]–ritornello–A2 [varied setting of the A text moving back to the tonic key]–ritornello; *da capo* arias from 1706 and 1707 are typically shorter and omit one or more of these five parts. Further, cantatas in the earlier groups often contain striking musical contrasts between the A and B sections of the *da capo* aria (see "Ride il fior" in *Nella stagion*, Exx. 3.3 and 3.4 above), but the Ruspoli summer 1708 cantatas increasingly use the same

Example 3.10a *Lungi n'andò Fileno,* first recitative: *pianto* (tears).

(i)

(ii)

Example 3.10b *Lungi n'andò Fileno,* second recitative: *martire* (torture) and *tempre* (destiny).

Example 3.10c *Lungi da voi,* second recitative: *lontananza* (separation).

Example 3.10d *Manca pur quanto sai,* first recitative: *doglia* (pain).

motivic material in the B section as in the A (Ex. 3.11). This "monothematic" style is particularly prevalent in and appropriate to the pastoral, which idealizes an idyllic continuity as opposed to strong contrast and disruption.

The final set of cantatas illustrates further the stylistic distinction between the Roman and non-Roman cantatas (Table 3.6). The four cantatas in this group can be linked to the 1706 pre-Rome group by the use of similar manuscript paper; however, strong chronological evidence is lacking that would per-

A

B

Example 3.11a *Manca pur quanto sai,* second aria.

A

B

Example 3.11b *Ditemi, O piante,* second aria.

A

B

Example 3.11c *Lungi n'andò Fileno,* first aria.

A

Se più   non   t'a—   mo,   non   ti   do—   ler,

B

Ma da   te   bra—   mo ca— ro pia— cer,

Example 3.11d *Stanco di più soffrire,* second aria.

Table 3.6   Post-Rome 1709 (Moons 1709 group)

Ah, che pur troppo è vero
r	aa | bbcxddc | xxxxee	
A	abc | abc	
r	xxaxa | xbbxcxc	
A	abab	
r	xxxaxabb	
A	aab | ccddb	

Clori, degli occhi miei
r	ababxccdd
A	abc | abc
r	aabccb
A	abcbde | axcbde

Non sospirar
A	xxa | bxba
r	xxxaxa
A	xa | bba

Un sospir
A	ab | ab
r	xaax | bxb
A	aab | ccb

mit a definitive dating.[8] Connected, at least tangentially, through paper analysis to Handel's opera *Agrippina* of 1709, the group has been provisionally placed later than the final Ruspoli group of 1708.

Like the 1706 pre-Rome group, these cantatas do not present a standard form. One follows the rArA pattern; one is extended (to three rA pairs); the other two follow a further reduced form of ArA, first seen in the pre-Rome group as something of an anomaly and then reappearing in one cantata from the final Roman group. It is this shortened form that dominates Handel's cantatas after he leaves Italy (see Chapter 5). Only two of the eight *da capo* arias (the second aria of *Ah, che pur troppo è vero* is not in this form) contain rhyme within both sections; three have unequal sections with the B text longer than A. The recitatives contain some scattered rhyme but are generally not organized into sections. None of the recitatives contain extended arioso sections, and there are no refrains or word-painting. One recitative from *Clori, degli occhi miei* has an arioso cadence on the word *piange* ("weeping"), as happens frequently in the Ruspoli summer 1708 group.

In *Ah, che pur troppo è vero,* the second of three arias, "Care mura," includes a written-out treble part for the cembalo. The only other continuo cantata in which this occurs is *Lucrezia* from the 1706 pre-Rome group, where in the closing ritornello to its extended arioso movement, based on a text fragment of a single line, the treble cembalo line wordlessly echoes the chromatic and diatonic descending lines of the voice (Ex. 3.12). In "Care mura" the treble instrumental

Example 3.12 *Lucrezia*, passage with treble part for continuo.

line also appears in a heightened musical setting, but here the text, as is typical of the later period, is a complete statement that could potentially be set as a *da capo* (*ab | ab*). Handel chooses instead to use a through-composed setting. In this cantata a lover sings of being separated from his beloved. The walls he addresses (of the city, a cloister, a cemetery, a family villa?) are "dear" either because they once contained Clori (before her departure) or because they now cloister her even as they separate her from him. In the second aria the lover sings directly to the "dear walls":

Care mura! in voi d'intorno	Dear walls! Since around you
Già ch'in van raggiro il piede,	Now I wander in vain,
Se accoglieste Clori un giorno,	If once you received Clori,
Accogliete or la mia fede.	Receive now my faith.

The bass consists of a sixteenth-note pattern that divides into two melodic lines: a rising scale repeatedly moving from the third to the sixth scale degree, supported by a repeated cadential pattern that never "arrives" but is deflected to the sixth degree and an unchanging alternating-note figure. Against this bass that paints the image of the trembling lover (alternating note) and the repeated unsuccessful attempts to reach the beloved (scale to sixth degree), the treble line traverses wide, disjunct intervals in angular and almost aimless motion. Hardly melodic, this line seems something like a directionless walking bass transplanted into the treble register.[9] As such, it contributes to the depiction of the lover who "wanders in vain"; for him there is no resolution. In contrast, or in addition, it might also represent the teardrops falling in "rivers" that the lover describes in the recitative preceding the aria. The combined effect of this relentless treble line against the repeated failure of arrival in the bass creates a portrayal of despair that is as exceptional as it is convincing (Ex. 3.13).

The two non-Roman groups of cantatas may originate from the same place and perhaps from the same patron. The texts, which are closely related in style and structure, do not follow the precepts of the Arcadian Academy, being both more asymmetrical and more dramatic than the conventional pastoral. The unusual cembalo writing in a single cantata from each group also brings to mind that the fortepiano was developed in Florence by Bartolomeo Cristofori during these years. It is tempting to think that these special cembalo parts were written for a Cristofori instrument.

The six chronological groups of cantatas depict a stylistic trajectory over a period of three years toward greater surface control and formal regularity, a style shift that is typical of the period and parallels a similar trajectory in the cantatas of Scarlatti and Mancini (see Chapter 2). This musical trend is consistent not only with the changing structure of the texts but with a shift in content from di-

Example 3.13 *Ah, che pur troppo è vero,* "Care mura," opening *(continued overleaf).*

rect personal utterance of (feminine) expression to the (masculine) filtering of emotion through the artifice of pastoral texts based on classical and Renaissance models that was especially typical of the Arcadian Academy. In a parallel trend, Francis Haskell pointedly describes how visual artists succumbed to the "classical ambience of Rome" under the influence of Cardinal Ottoboni's patronage and produced work that was "gentle, sweet and academic."

Such was indeed the effect of Ottoboni's circle on most of the painters who worked for him. Sebastiano Conca . . . gradually lost the vigorous brio of his

Example 3.13 (continued)

early years when he came to Rome in about 1706 and was taken up by the
Cardinal and his friends. Gaulli [see Figure 2.1], another favourite, also became flaccidly academic as the years went by. . . . In so far as one can point to
any specific influence of Pietro Ottoboni on the arts it must be sought in a
rather bland sweetness, restrained by the rules of academic classicism from
verging too far in the direction of the rococo, and tending towards a certain
cool anonymity. It was a style . . . easily appreciated by princes and general
public alike. It lacked the vigour of the true Baroque, the intricate fantasy of
French rococo, with which it was contemporary, and the severity of later eighteenth-century painting.[10]

In cantatas, the change has been less heralded, but I suggest that during Handel's Italian years, and in his compositions for Rome in particular, we can watch
a related shift taking place as the young composer responded musically to Arcadian reform texts and the tastes of his patrons.

Following Arcadian precepts, the texts reverberate with echoes of classical
and Renaissance poetry. A reflection of the passionate love poetry of Catullus
can be found, for example, in the final aria of *Quando sperasti*. Where Catullus

famously writes (poem 5: "Vivamus, mea Lesbia"), "Give me a thousand kisses, then a hundred, then another thousand, then a second hundred, then still another thousand, then a hundred," Handel's anonymous text reads, "I wish to give you thousands and thousands of sweet kisses, O dear Fille, so that they serve as chains, to keep you always with me, and I want to give you hundreds and hundreds of such caresses in a moment" (the *mille* and *centum* of the Latin little altered in the *mille* and *cento* of the Italian). The influence of Italian chivalric love poetry is even stronger, and the borrowing of images from Petrarch is particularly common. For example, compare Handel's *Chi rapì la pace?* (see Appendix 2) with Petrarch's description of the beloved's eyes as darts that wound like Cupid's arrows:

Si tosto come aven che l'arco scocchi,	As soon as he has released the string,
buon sagittario di lontan discerne	a good archer discerns from afar
qual colpo è da sprezzare et qual d'averne	which shot is futile and which
fede ch'al destinato segno tocchi;	he can believe will strike the intended target;
similemente il colpo de' vostri occhi,	thus you, Lady, felt the shot from your eyes
Donna, sentiste a le mie parti interne	pass straight into my inward parts,
dritto passare, onde conven ch'eterne	wherefore my heart must overflow
lagrime per la piaga il cor trabocchi.	through the wound with eternal tears.[11]

Similarly, the image of a lover's thoughts or sighs flying to the beloved in Handel's *Fra pensieri* finds direct precedent in Petrarch:

	[If a mountain pass were opened,]
I miei sospiri più benigno calle	my sighs would have a kinder path
avrian per gire ove lor spene è viva;	to go toward where their hope still lives;
or vanno sparsi, et pur ciascuno arriva	now they go scattered, but still each one
là dov'io il mando, ché sol un non falle;	arrives where I send him, for not one fails;
et son di là sì dolcemente accolti,	and over there they are so sweetly welcomed,
com'io m'accorgo, che nessun mai torna,	as I see, that none of them ever comes back,
con tal diletto in quelle parti stanno.	with such delight they stay in those parts.[12]

Although certainly influenced by passionate classical poetry and mediated through Petrarchan imagery of unrequited love, the texts and, equally important, the context of Handel's cantatas found their primary antecedents in classical pastoral poetry, where shepherds (supposedly) extemporized verses individually or in competition. Like the *Idylls* of Theocritus and the *Eclogues* of Virgil in particular, the cantata texts contain portrayals of same-sex love.[13]

Stories of famous same-sex couples recur throughout classical literature. Ovid, in the *Metamorphoses,* relates the stories of Jupiter and Ganymede ("The King of Heaven once was fired with love / Of Ganymede") and of Apollo and Hyacinth ("Hyacinth was [Apollo's] favourite"),[14] and in Theocritus's *Idyll* XII,

directed to a beloved boy, Ganymede is used as the measure to judge the sincerity of his kisses. The story of Hylas and Hercules can be found in Theocritus's
Idyll XIII: "The bronze-hearted son of Amphitryon, too, / who withstood the
savage lion, loved a boy, / the graceful Hylas with the flowing hair."[15] Legendary
and historical heroes offered similar models. In his *History* Thucydides tells the
story of the "love affair" of Aristogiton and Harmodius, Athenian heroes im-
mortalized for assassinating the tyrant Hipparchus, beginning: "Harmodius was
then in the flower of youthful beauty, and Aristogiton, a citizen in the middle
rank of life, was his lover and possessed him."[16] Theocritus in *Idyll* XXIX refers
to the love of Achilles for Patroclus, whose death Achilles avenged during the
Trojan War: "when you wear / the beard of manhood on your cheeks, we'll be /
Achilles and his friend to one another."[17] In the *Aeneid,* Virgil describes (or in-
vents) the story of Nisus and Euryalus, both Trojan warriors; after young
Euryalus was killed, Nisus single-handedly attacked his slayers and died on
Euryalus's bosom: "One gate was held by Nisus, the most aggressive of fighters
. . . / Euryalus was beside him, his friend . . . / That lad with the bloom of
youth on his unshaven cheeks / These two were one in love."[18]

It was, however, in the fictive realm of pastoral poetry, apart from mythological, legendary, or historical references, that same-sex love reached its lyrical
heights. Virgil's *Eclogue* II tells of the passion of Corydon for Alexis ("Corydon
the shepherd burned for fair Alexis, / His master's darling"),[19] and the final *Eclogue,* most of which Virgil puts in the voice of his friend, the poet Cornelius
Gallus, offers the paean to Arcady (partially quoted in the epigraph to this
chapter) that makes equal the love of men and the love of women:

> Yet, shepherds of Arcady, you shall blazon my legend
> Among your hills, for Arcady has no rival
> In music. And oh! How softly my bones would nestle
> If flutes of yours in the future voiced my sorrows
> In love, and oh! To have been just one from among you,
> Your keeper of sheep, or dresser of grapes empurpled.
> For surely the shape that bewitched me, whether of Phyllis,
> Amyntas, or any so ever, would now be lying
> Beside me among the willows, and under the vine-loops,
> Phyllis to gather me garlands, Amyntas to finger
> The delicate reed-stops. And what if Amyntas be swarthy?
> Violets are dark, and dark are blueberries also.[20]

In the early modern period, because of religious and social proscriptions, ex-
pressions of same-sex love were more veiled than in the classical period, but poetic traditions offered an acceptable outlet. On the one hand, same-sex desire, as
an integral element of the classical heritage, could be openly imitated; on the

other, contemporary distancing technique in both rhetoric and music permitted an ambiguity that allowed for a same-sex interpretation. In his edition of the poetry of Michelangelo, James Saslow demonstrates how traditional love poems "could be translated almost without alteration, except for the pronouns, into the service of describing and justifying homosexual love as it was constructed by Michelangelo and his culture." Given Michelangelo's documented homosexual desire, it is not surprising that such gender shifts occur even in his own poetry. Saslow points to two poems ultimately addressed to one of Michelangelo's male loves "that make use of earlier drafts originally addressed to a woman, simply altering the addressee from *donna* to *signore* without changing the sentiment or images." Another poem, originally addressed to a woman, was altered in a later draft probably intended for another of Michelangelo's loves, but "as prepared by Michelangelo for publication, reverts to female pronouns and references, suppressing the intermediate male stage and making the poem more comprehensible and acceptable to a public audience in traditional terms, both social and literary."[21]

With Handel's cantatas, such specific textual evidence is lacking, but gender flexibility can be read in their deliberate ambiguity. Saslow writes that Michelangelo "softened or obscured intended references" with the "avoidance of any term or pronoun that would indicate gender." Rather than describing the specific beloved, "these poems describe instead only the beloved's attributes."[22] In the texts of Handel's cantatas, such gender avoidance is evident in those cantatas where the love object is rhetorically represented, as for example in *Lungi da voi* by "the languid eyes" (*languidi lumi* and *languide pupille*), so that the sex of the loved one is left (or, perhaps, can be left) unidentified.

Even when the beloved's sex is specified, gender ambiguity remains an important element of contemporary Baroque performance practice. For example, in Handel's cantata *Lungi da me, pensier tiranno!* (copied for Ruspoli in 1709), the singer addresses a male lover as "handsome Tirsi" and "beloved Tirsi, my adored god!" and in *Lungi n'andò Fileno* (copied for Ruspoli in 1708), the singer cries out to a male love, "Fileno, the better part of my life, Soul of my soul, Heart of my heart!" In neither case is the sex of the singer identified, and, given the literary and social context, one cannot simply assume that the "voice" is a woman's. Even if, as is likely, these cantatas were sung in Ruspoli's household by the female soprano Margarita Durastante, who at this time was his only regularly paid soloist, the sex of the "voice" is not thereby determined, for the sex of the singing voice was frequently masked by a tradition that freely exchanged male and female performers on treble parts. Thus the role of the abandoned woman in Pamphili's *Delirio amoroso* (1707) was written for the castrato Pasqualino,[23] while in the cantata *Oh, come chiare* (1708), the role of Ruspoli himself depicted in his Arcadian guise of the shepherd Olinto was played by Durastante.[24] Eighteenth-century performing practice encouraged gender play.

A glimpse of the Virgilian interchangeability of gender (either/or, Phyllis or
Amyntas) can be found in the Handel sources. In *Lungi da me, pensier tiranno!,*
directed to the male beloved Tirsi, the last aria, "Tirsi adorato," contains a
gendered reference to the beloved as *caro* (a male beloved). In most of the English sources *caro* is transmuted into *cara,* a female beloved.[25] Although this is
likely a case of scribal unfamiliarity with Italian, it does illustrate how easily
genders can shift in these cantatas. Often a name is the only gendered identification, and a differently gendered name of equal syllable count can easily be
substituted without any disruption to the rhyming pattern or metrical scheme;
in most of these cantatas, Clori and Tirsi or Irene and Fileno are poetically interchangeable. The following excerpts demonstrate how simple it would be to
shift genders in Handel's cantata *Aure soavi.*

Onde fra voi solingo,	Wherefore alone among you,
Di parlar a colei [*colui*]	I imagine speaking to her [*him*],
Che pur non m'ode,	Who does not hear me,
Aure soavi, ombre notturne io fingo.	Soft breezes, evening shadows.
Pietà, Clori [*Tirsi*], pietà	Pity, Clori [*Tirsi*], pity,
Se quel che pietà sia	If that which is pity
Dentro al tuo cor si sa.	Is known inside your heart.
Un'aura flebile,	A gentle breeze
Un'ombra mobile	A passing shadow,
Sperar me fa	Makes me hope
Che Clori [*Tirsi*] amabile,	That lovely Clori [*Tirsi*]
Nell'alma nobile	In [*her/his*] noble soul
Senta pietà.	Feels pity.

Handel's own view of the either/or nature of these texts can perhaps be found
in his later use of the music. For example, the cantata *Mi palpita il cor,* first
composed early in his London years as an accompanied cantata with flute, is addressed to Clori. Some years later (c. 1722) Handel took the opening arioso-style
recitative and attached it to a revision of the continuo cantata *Dimmi, O mio
cor,* which is addressed to Fileno.

Mi palpita il cor	My heart flutters,
Né intendo perchè.	But I know not why.
Agitata è l'alma mia,	My soul is agitated,
Né so cos'è.	But I know not what it is.

This expression of desire is completely ungendered; it could be sung by a man
or woman to a man or woman, as Handel realized. Even cantatas that include
a gendered referent were treated by Handel with flexibility. The aria "Fra

pensieri" provides a particularly rich example. It started life as the first aria of the cantata *Fra pensieri,* with melismatic groups of four sixteenths on alternate downbeats depicting the (male) singer's thoughts as they waft toward Clori. The aria next appears, in slightly altered form, in three strikingly different situations. In *Rodrigo* (autumn 1707) it provides the final aria in which a leading male character, having won back his kingdom, sings of being reunited with his beloved, using a text that could just as easily come from a cantata: "I am yours, fair eyes, my soul shall live for you."[26] Here the sixteenth-note groups seem to depict a barely contained flood of emotion. In *Il pastor fido* (London, 1712), a female character uses the same music to voice similar sentiments (although in this case the character is neither honest nor successful): "You, O stars, have fulfilled the fine hope of my love at last."[27] In the instrumental cantata *Echeggiate, festeggiate* (London, 1710), honoring the Hapsburg archduke Charles as King of Spain, the aria is given to the goddess Juno, and the sixteenth notes take on a triumphant tone approaching the sound of a trumpet call: "With the valour of a strong arm you gave liberty to the world."[28] Much later, after additional operatic appearances and further altered, the aria finds its way into the mouth of Juno once again in *Semele* (London, 1744); by changing the sixteenth-note turn into an alternating-note figure, Handel aptly depicts Juno's jeering triumph over her rival Semele: "Above measure is the pleasure that my revenge supplies" (Ex. 3.14).[29]

The plasticity of "Fra pensieri" in both affect and voice offers a striking con-

Example 3.14a *Fra pensieri,* "Fra pensieri."

Example 3.14b *Echeggiate, festeggiate,* "Col valor."

Example 3.14c *Semele,* "Above measure" (voice and bass only).

trast to the specificity of the voices of abandoned women, which are clearly female. Handel reuses his female-gendered cantata music with care. He transfers it from woman to woman, only letting men speak with a female voice in the most extreme situations, as shown in Chapter 2. Handel's more artificially distanced continuo cantatas, by contrast, can be understood equally in male or female voice directed to a male or female beloved. This flexibility of interpretation presents a clever way of disguising the possible representation of living persons and of same-sex love.

The pastorals of Theocritus and Virgil include, in addition to mythological stories and imaginary shepherds, references to friends and contemporaries of the authors and to contemporary political issues. For example, Theocritus addresses his *Idylls* to specific friends with whom he says he has shared same-sex love (see Chapter 4); he speaks directly in his own voice in "Lines to a Boy" (*Idyll* XXIX and XXX): "When you will, my day is like to the immortals', / and when you are unwilling, much in darkness."[30] Virgil's *Eclogues* are set in the aftermath of the assassination of Julius Caesar and the defeat two years later of Brutus and Cassius at Philippi by Antony and Octavian; in *Eclogue* I, for example, Meliboeus laments the confiscation of his lands for returning soldiers. The poetry of Catullus is also full of personal references. His beloved Lesbia very probably represents a real-life figure; his boy-lover Juventius, although a more generic representation, is no less real.[31] Similarly, Petrarch writes of contemporary issues. He addresses the head of the Colonna family of his day as *Gloriosa Columna* (glorious column) and insisted that his beloved Laura, although thought by some contemporaries to be an imaginary figure, represented a real person.[32]

However, the precise identification of friends and lovers in the works of Theocritus, Virgil, Catullus, and Petrarch is less important than the tradition that held the poetry to be thinly veiled autobiography. For example, Aelius Donatus (fl. 350) in his *Life of Virgil* "reports that the poet was rustic in appearance, shy and hesitant in manner and bisexual" and specifically connects the story of Corydon's homosexual love for Alexis in *Eclogue* II with Virgil's purported love for the slave Alexander, who belonged to his patron Pollio.[33] Although the details of this interpretation have been largely discounted today (while the idea that Virgil was writing from a more general experience of a disappointed homosexual love retains currency), the interpretation from Donatus represented the dominant tradition and would have been known to any classically educated person from the Renaissance through the eighteenth century.[34] It is partly this contemporary belief that the classical pastorals presented real stories behind an Arcadian facade that suggests the possibility, perhaps greater than previously thought, that Handel's cantata texts similarly represent contemporary persons and political affairs.

Of course, *Hendel, non può mia musa* (1707) is in the voice of Pamphili and about Handel. Another obviously biographical cantata, the instrumental *Oh, come chiare* (August 1708), contains three characters: Olinto pastore, Tebro fiume, and Gloria. Referring to the War of Spanish Succession, the text tells how Ruspoli (identified by his Arcadian name) will rouse Rome (represented by the Tiber River) to its old glory (which the figure of Glory confirms). All three singing figures are led by an *astro clemente* (goodly star), referring to Pope Clement XI much as Petrarch refers to Colonna.[35] Biographical references in cantatas that come between *Hendel, non può mia musa* and *Oh, come chiare* similarly refer to events and persons related to Handel's Italian circle.

After he oversaw the production of *Rodrigo* in Florence late in 1707, Handel may have gone on to Venice for the opera season or he may have returned to Hamburg for the January 1708 performances of *Florindo* and *Daphne*. In any case, he was back in Rome by early spring. The Ruspoli documents include a bill for copying an unnamed cantata by Handel on 26 February 1708; Handel specifically signed his cantata *Lungi dal mio bel nume* with place and date—Rome, 3 March 1708; and during the same month *Il trionfo del tempo* was revived by Pamphili, although "perhaps not with Handel's participation."[36] On 8 and 10 April 1708 Handel's largest Roman work, *La resurrezione,* was produced under the patronage of Ruspoli. Around the end of April, Handel traveled on to Naples. The Ruspoli account books refer both to the return of the bed "hired for *Monsù* Endel" and a payment to a provisioner for the food consumed by Handel and his companion.[37]

Handel's "companion" is a mystery. Mattheson speaks of Handel leaving Hamburg (in 1709) and traveling to Italy "with von Binitz,"[38] but there is no way of knowing whether or not the "companion" in the Ruspoli accounts of 1708 is the same person. In any event, Ruspoli apparently hosted the two in some luxury. Kirkendale writes that "we cannot help but marvel at the payment of 38.75 *scudi* for the food consumed by Handel and his companion. Measured against the monthly salary of 20 *scudi* for the primadonna, 15 for the first nobleman of the *famiglia alta,* 10 for the later *maestro di cappella* Caldara . . ., down to 10 every year for the bass violinist–this sum, devoured in two months, conjures up mountains of fruit, pheasants, nectar and ambrosia, making the marble tables bend."[39] The Ruspoli documents provide the only evidence that Handel at this time was traveling with a companion. There are no documents indicating whether Handel thereafter journeyed to Naples on his own or in company.

Mainwaring describes this trip:

From Rome he removed to NAPLES, where, as at most other places, he had a palazzo at command, and was provided with table, coach, and all other accommodations. While he was at this capital, he made ACIS and GALATEA,

the words Italian, and the Music different from ours [the English *Acis and
Galatea* of 1718]. It was composed at the request of DONNA LAURA . . .
[who] lived, acted, and conversed with a state truly regal. . . .

   While he was at Naples he received invitations from most of the principal
persons who lived within reach of that capital; and lucky was he esteemed
who could engage him soonest, and detain him longest.[40]

Mainwaring's account is largely confirmed in other evidence. Handel dated his
autograph of the serenata *Aci, Galatea e Polifemo* "Napoli li 16 di Giugnio. 1708.
d'Alvito," and the trio *Se tu non lasci amore* is signed "G. F. Hendel/ li 12 di
luglio/ 1708/ Napoli."[41] The serenata was performed "within reach" of Naples as
part of the celebrations surrounding the wedding of Tolomeo Saverio Gallio,
Duke of Alvito, and Beatrice Tocco on 19 July 1708,[42] and we can now identify
Mainwaring's "Donna Laura" as the bride's aunt, Aurora Sanseverino, who also
instigated revivals of the serenata for wedding celebrations in Piedimonte (1711)
and Naples (1713).[43]

   The serenata and cantatas associated with Naples seem to have strong ties to
contemporary events and persons, beginning with *Aci, Galatea e Polifemo,* specifically tied to the Duke of Alvito's wedding. Although not previously considered so, the continuo cantatas also appear to be related to the wedding couple,
perhaps even more intimately than the serenata. Reinhard Strohm first identified the cantata *Nel dolce tempo* with Naples because of its reference to the
Volturno River that flows nearby.[44] More recent research has identified the geographic location even more closely with Piedimonte d'Alife, the primary residence of Aurora Sanseverino. In *Nel dolce tempo,* a shepherd relates how he saw
and fell in love with a shepherdess. He tells her how her beauty has inflamed his
heart. She responds bashfully that his "gentle manner and pleasing face" have
also awakened a sweet flame in her heart, but continues that "honesty is greater
than love." The shepherd responds: "Your charming appearance pleases me,
lovely one, but still more the rare virtue of your soul. The more I love you because you are honest, the more you are dear to me." In the concluding aria the
shepherd asks the nymph to listen to the birds who sing not only of her beauty
but of her "honest and faithful love" (see Ex. P.1). This is one of only four continuo cantatas by Handel to include two specific voices (though the shepherd
tells the whole story himself, quoting the responses of the shepherdess), and it
seems very likely that the shepherd and shepherdess couple depicted here are of
the aristocratic type represented by Ghezzi and meant to represent the bride and
groom.

   Both *Nell'africane selve* and *Sento là che ristretto* are addressed to a woman
named Nice, a familiar but relatively rare female pastoral name; within Handel's
cantatas it appears only five times as compared to Clori's twelve. If this name

was chosen specifically to represent the bride, Beatrice, it would place both cantatas figuratively in the voice of the bridegroom. In *Nell'africane selve,* the singer
describes himself vividly as a lion who has been captured by the beauty of Nice's
eyes. He declares his love and faith and asks only for love in return. In *Sento là
che ristretto,* the singer longs to be united with Nice's soft breast and worries that
a "cruel fate" will keep him from kissing his beloved. Continuing the analogy to
the bride and groom, this "fate" may refer to the fact that the wedding was taking place within the context of the War of Spanish Succession. *Mentre il tutto è
in furore* seems to refer specifically to this war, describing how brave Fileno remains "thinking of soft love" while "the raucous sound of the timpani and
trumpet fills the night and day with uproar." The singer (representing Beatrice?)
paraphrases Julius Caesar, urging Fileno to "Go, yes, see and conquer, and then
return to me" so that "I will be able to say that I am loved by one who on the
battlefield seemed like thunder and lightning."[45] Finally, in *Quando sperasti* the
lover sings, imitating the love poetry of Catullus, that he would like to give his
beloved Fille hundreds and thousands of kisses.

These five Neapolitan continuo cantatas thus form an interesting set in terms
of contemporary reference. *Nel dolce tempo* identifies its provenance in its text;
Mentre il tutto è in furore identifies the context of the War of Spanish Succession. All can be associated, some with more confidence than others, with the
wedding of Beatrice Tocco and the Duke of Alvito. In two cantatas Beatrice
seems to be represented by the rhyming Nice; in one Alvito is possibly portrayed by the metrically equivalent Fileno. The use of substitute names is typical
not only of Catullus, who substituted the name Lesbia for the metrically equivalent Clodia, but also, of course, for the members of the Arcadian Academy,
who took on pastoral names. Three of the cantatas in this group echo specific
classical or Renaissance authors: *Nel dolce tempo* probably takes its incipit from
a poem by Petrarch that describes his own love as more intense than a long sequence of loves described in Ovid's *Metamorphoses; Quando sperasti* seems to
echo one of Catullus's most ardent love poems; and *Mentre il tutto è in furore*
quotes Caesar's famous "Veni, vidi, vici."

Because Handel's time in Rome was not similarly centered on a single event
and stretched over a much longer period involving a wider circle of people, it is
more difficult to decipher personal and political situations that may be represented. There is, in addition to *Hendel, non può mia musa,* at least one Roman
cantata by Handel that clearly is biographical. In *Stelle, perfide stelle!* the singer
laments leaving Rome: "I forsake you, flowered and beautiful banks of the
Tiber, dear walls, I leave you." Handel heads this cantata "Partenza di G. B.
Cantata" at the top left of the autograph and "di G. F. Handel" on the right. A
similar heading appears, also in Handel's hand, in his autograph of *Rodrigo,*
composed in Rome, 1707. Both paper evidence and the reuse of a discarded

manuscript page with this cantata heading in the *Rodrigo* autograph indicate that the cantata, too, was composed in Rome, 1707.[46] Like most of the Ruspoli 1707 cantatas, it follows the pattern rArA. The recitatives, although not pervasively rhymed, include rhymed couplets which act as important points of demarcation both grammatically and musically. Both the arias are in *da capo* form and include rhyme within and across sections. For many years the left-hand heading, "Partenza di G. B.," was understood to provide the title ("Departure") and (by analogy to the phrase "di G. F. Handel" on the right) the initials of the librettist (by G. B.).[47] More likely the entire left-hand heading is a title referring to the "Departure *of* G. B.," as is now generally assumed. In an English manuscript source from about 1730, G. B. is identified as Giovanni Bononcini.[48] Bernd Baselt has suggested that the initials might rather refer to (Georg) von Binitz.[49] Of course, G. B. need not be a musician or anyone related to Handel at all. Nevertheless, the heading clearly indicates a specific biographical background to this cantata.

Stelle, perfide stelle! is one of the nine cantatas by Handel that avoid any sexual referent. It opens in recitative with a wrenching cry to the "treacherous stars" and "evil fate" that have "predestined" this leave-taking. Handel sets the tone immediately by having the voice enter a major seventh above the bass on *stelle,* sustained on repeated quarter notes over half a measure. The voice carries the "root" of the diminished seventh harmony in F-sharp minor suspended against the tonic note in the bass, providing not only a searing dissonance but a sense of having started not just *in medias res* but at the end, the moment of parting. The harmony moves in the second measure to the tonic of F-sharp minor, then to the subdominant in first inversion and, finally, at the beginning of the third measure, to the dominant (C-sharp major), ending the direct address. Thereafter the harmony shifts out of F-sharp minor by moving not to the tonic but to an A major chord, beginning a progression that will end with a full cadence to C-sharp minor at the end of the first couplet. The second part of the recitative recapitulates this harmonic pattern, moving to F-sharp minor, again sustaining a diminished seventh chord over its note of resolution (here A-sharp diminished over B), which chord becomes IV of the final tonic. The singer declares the sentiment that Handel depicts with his harmony: "I forsake the flowered banks of the Tiber, I leave the dear walls, I desert the beloved stones, but even if my feet take me far away, my abiding faith remains with you." That is, the major seventh created by suspending a diminished seventh of the subdominant against the subdominant itself may seem distant from the tonic, but in fact remains, however dissonant (or distant), closely tied to it (Ex. 3.15).

The first aria, "Se vedrà," depicts the lover's tears and sighs manifesting themselves in Rome despite his absence. Handel here as elsewhere depicts distance by creating a bass line that divides into two parts: one that remains constant and one that moves against it. His use of dotted rhythms in a slow tempo, as is often

Example 3.15 *Stelle, perfide stelle!*, first recitative.

the case, indicates pain. Compare in Ex. 3.16 the pattern here with that in *Non sospirar* (another cantata with no gendered referent that depicts distance). In "Care mura" from *Ah, che pur troppo è vero,* discussed earlier (Ex. 3.13), Handel uses the same kind of pattern without the dotted rhythms, but the close similarity to the opening of "Se vedrà" allows for the possibility of a direct connection. Perhaps the phrase "care mura" reminded him of the similar phrase in *Stelle, perfide stelle.*

The tears that flow like waves are ultimately depicted in a striking melisma using staccato articulation and ever faster-flowing tears (Ex. 3.17). It is certainly difficult, but Chrysander exaggerates in calling it "rather unsingable."[50] Such unusual melismas, which do not grow out of the motivic fabric, are typical of arias in Handel's early cantatas, especially those dealing with distance. Compare the melisma in the first aria of *Lungi da voi* (Ex. 3.18) on the word *lontananza* (distance).

Example 3.16a Bass pattern in *Stelle, perfide stelle!*

Example 3.16b Bass pattern in *Non sospirar.*

Example 3.17 *Stelle, perfide stelle!*, "Se vedrà," melisma on *pianto*.

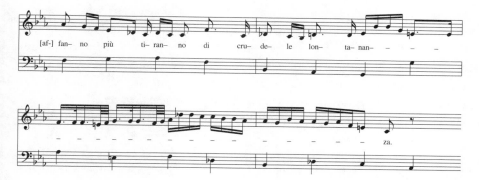

Example 3.18 *Lungi da voi*, "Un affanno più tiranno," melisma on *lontananza*.

The second recitative in *Stelle, perfide stelle!* contains three semantic sections, each concluding with a rhymed couplet. First, the singer does not know where the path will lead, but tears will leave a trail for the beloved; then the singer worries that on returning to Rome, the beloved will no longer be there or interested; and, finally, the singer embraces silence, knowing that no declaration of love can be made. Handel provides only two cadences, after the second and third sections, using the same compositional process and same harmonic goal (E minor) in both parts. Rather than offering a sustained harmonic progression in any one key, he simply provides a series of chords, harmonically coherent of course, preceded by their dominants. Lacking the piercing dissonance of the first recitative, this setting depicts a harmonic pathway that could go in any number of directions. The sequence of temporary tonics (representing the stones on the path that are bathed by tears) comprises A major (m. 3), F-sharp minor (6), E minor (9–11), A minor (13), D major (15), G major (17), E minor (19).

The final aria in 12/8 *allegro* suddenly offers a possibility of happiness. The turning figure of the accompaniment strikes a giddy note; today one would say it sounds like a carousel. Handel's setting, however, adheres to the conditional tense and resists affirmation. The text of the A section reads:

Quando ritornerò,	When I return,
Se in voi ritroverò	If I find in you
L'amato mio tesor,	My loving treasure,
Sarò felice.	I will be happy.

In the first full statement of this text Handel moves harmonically, as one would expect, to the dominant. However, rather than allowing this cadence to stand, he repeats the last line, modulating to the relative minor. This unexpected shift into minor for the repetition of the text *sarò felice* undercuts any sense of expectation, leaving instead a wistful sense of what might have been. Handel repeats this undermining of hope with each iteration of the full text. The second full statement cadences to G major with both voice and bass moving to the tonic, but Handel repeats the word *felice,* moving instead to the third of the scale. Although the melodic line moves downward, this inconclusive "echo" adds a hesitation or question mark to the preceding tonic close. On the final iteration of text, Handel moves again toward G major on the phrase *sarò felice,* but this leads instead to a deceptive cadence that delays and weakens the arrival of the final cadence. When Handel used the music of this aria later as the basis for the final duet in *Giulio Cesare* (1724) between Caesar and Cleopatra, he rewrote the bass, omitting the turning motives, and deleted the sections that undermined musically the sense of hope expressed in the text of the cantata.

The text of the second section of the aria recapitulates and strengthens the sentiment first voiced in the second recitative that this love cannot be spoken: "But to reveal my love, my heart is not allowed." The whole text of this section reads:

Sperando soffrirò,	I will suffer with hope,
Tacendo l'amerò,	I will love [her/him] in silence,
Ma di scoprir l'ardor	But to reveal my love
Mio cor non lice.	My heart is not allowed.

Here the issue of a gendered referent becomes critical. In the first part of the aria, the beloved is referred to as *l'amato mio tesor* (my loving treasure), the masculine gender of *tesor* providing no indication of the sex of the beloved. Indeed, in three of Handel's cantata texts "mio tesor(o)" specifically refers to a female beloved: in *Lungi dal mio bel nume* to Clori, in *Nella stagion* to Amarilli, and in

Nice, che fa? to Nice. In a fourth, *Da sete ardente afflitto,* the sex of the beloved, as here, is not identified. The most critical moment for the sexual identification of the beloved in *Stelle, perfide stelle!* occurs in the second section with the phrase *tacendo l'amerò.* The "l" refers specifically to the beloved and must take the correct gender; however, the pronoun (*la* or *lo*) automatically elides with "amerò" so that the necessity is bypassed. In the one other instance of a similar construction in Handel's cantatas, from *Sarei troppo felice* by Cardinal Pamphili, the singer is identified as Clori and her lover as Fileno, so that "l'amo" means "I love him."

Stelle, perfide stelle! offers no incontrovertible evidence for any specifically gendered reading. The voice could be that of a man or a woman, and the beloved could be, in either case, male or female. However, its context makes a homosexual reading of the cantata not only possible but probable. The singing persona of *Stelle, perfide stelle!* has been assumed, rightly I believe, to be a man's. Instrumental and continuo cantatas in women's voices are clearly identified, and I see no reason to make an exception for this work, especially given the heading provided by Handel: "Partenza di G. B"—as the use of initials would have been more usual in reference to a man. The sex of the beloved also seems to be male. The careful obfuscation of the sex within the text points to this conclusion, especially because the masking of homosexual desire by the elimination of any sexed referent, as we have seen, was simple and common. The care that has been taken here to avoid disclosure is striking. Moreover, the text itself speaks of a desire that cannot be expressed, a love that the heart is not allowed to reveal.

Although many of the cantatas depict heterosexual love, a number of others tell of same-sex desire, even though the distinction is not always obvious. Among Handel's cantatas, those where the beloved is not identified by sex offer a clear instance of possible same-sex interpretation; these include, in addition to *Stelle, perfide stelle!, Chi rapì la pace?, E partirai, mia vita?, Lungi da voi, Non sospirar, O lucenti, O sereni occhi, Qualor l'egre pupille,* and *Da sete ardente afflitto.* The cantatas addressed to Fileno or Tirsi when the singing voice is not identified as female also fall into this category: *Dimmi, O mio cor* and *Lungi n'andò,* addressed to Fileno, and *Lungi da me, pensier tiranno!* and *Manca pur quanto sai,* addressed to Tirsi. Even cantatas that identify themselves as heterosexual can be considered as part of this group. Not only were the cantata texts and settings flexible enough to allow gender transfer, which change Handel himself effected in the arioso movement "Mi palpita il cor" and in a number of later borrowings, but heterosexuality could be used as a thin facade, as Saslow has shown in the works of Michelangelo. *Sarei troppo felice* by Cardinal Pamphili provides a likely cantata example. The singer, who complains of Fileno's unfaithfulness, begins: "I would be very happy if I were able to give laws to my thoughts. What avails beauty and judgment, love, faith, constancy, cleverness or wisdom, in my grave danger?" At the beginning of the second recitative, the singer suddenly names herself in the third person while continuing in the first person: "Clori, scorned Clori, I remember the offense but do not know how to drive the offender from my heart." The awkwardness only highlights the weakness of this identification. The text offers only one other gendered association with the singer, the feminine form *altera* ("proud one"), but both it and the name Clori occur at the end of unrhymed lines, where "altero" and any two-syllable name would fit just as easily.

The cantata texts possibly associated with same-sex desire, as well as many others, repeat a number of common topics: concealing one's love or pain with silence, trying to control one's thoughts, and hoping to overcome a distance that is surely more metaphorical than geographic. As Saslow points out with reference to Michelangelo, the conflict of same-sex desire with the teachings of the church created a moral and religious obstacle to the fulfillment or even expression of those desires. It is difficult to imagine that the early eighteenth-century Roman circle of cardinals, princes, and artists did not encounter similar conflict between their desires and their beliefs, and the continuo cantatas offered a place where such desires could be expressed. The heritage of the classical pastoral lent legitimacy to the experience of same-sex desire. The tradition of chivalric love offered the trope of lifelong desire and unconsummated love. The practice of Italian poetry permitted the sex of the beloved to be concealed, and the performance of cantatas allowed the sex of the lover who sings to be obscured. The poetry itself described a separation of lovers that could not be bridged regardless of proximity, and this virtual distance was further emphasized by a poetic and musical style that favored artifice rather than direct passion. However, the cantata texts, as indicated by some specific references (to Handel, Ruspoli, the Volturno and Tiber Rivers) and depicted in Ghezzi's watercolors, were not merely conventional lyrics without contemporary allusion. Like the pastoral names assumed by the members of the Arcadian Academy, the mask of poetic, pastoral, and chivalric convention allowed the cultural elite to speak of their illicit loves and desires (whether homosexual or heterosexual). Handel's Italian style shift, especially in the cantatas he wrote for Rome, shows him moving from the unrestrained expression of highly charged emotion modeled on the voices of women to an intimate idiom tightly controlled by artifice that permitted the manly expression of innermost feelings through concealment.

4

Cantata Couples and Love Triangles

Therefore, we have to read the myth more or less as we would read an orchestral score, not stave after stave, but understanding that we should apprehend the whole page and understand that something which was written on the first stave at the top of the page acquires meaning only if one considers that it is part and parcel of what is written below on the second stave, the third stave and so on.

Claude Lévi-Strauss, *Myth and Meaning*

In addition to solo continuo and instrumental cantatas, Handel composed a small group of cantatas for more than one voice. These can be divided by their texts into three overlapping categories: pastoral, mythological, and political. Three cantatas follow the pastoral tradition. In *Arresta il passo* (also titled *Aminta e Fillide*) the shepherd Aminta pursues the shepherdess Fillide and wins her; in *Amarilli vezzosa* (also titled *Il duello amoroso,* "the love duel") Daliso pursues Amarilli without success; in *Cor fedele* Tirsi and Fileno both pursue Clori without success. Two larger works tell mythological stories that replicate the typical pastoral plot. In *Aci, Galatea e Polifemo* the monster Polyphemus woos Galatea, but she and her lover Acis remain faithful to each other even after Acis's death; in *Apollo e Dafne,* the god chases Daphne, who eludes his grasp through transformation. Finally, two cantatas, in addition to their pastoral or mythological overtones, depict political situations. The trio *Oh, come chiare* represents Ruspoli as Rome's defender during the War of Spanish Succession; the five-voiced *Echeggiate, festeggiate* celebrates a later moment in the same war: the anticipated (but never achieved) accession of King Charles III of Spain. All seven works, ranging in length from the five arias of *Amarilli vezzosa* to the eighteen arias, duets, and trios of *Aci, Galatea e Polifemo* (which because of its size and dramatic content is called a serenata rather than a cantata), include instrumental accompaniment, sometimes of great richness and variety. In addition, there are a few continuo cantatas that include multiple voices. *Nella stagion* narrates the story of Amarilli and a "handsome boy," giving one aria to each; in *Nel dolce tempo* a shepherd narrates how he fell in love and how the shepherdess responded; and in *Sans y penser,* Handel's only French cantata, Silvie and Tirsis fall in love "without thinking about it," but fail to connect with each other. Because *Sans y penser* apparently calls for two singers, unlike *Nel dolce tempo* and *Nella stagion,* which are narrated stories, it will be included in this discussion of multi-voice cantatas and added to the pastoral group.

Just as the solo instrumental cantatas predominantly date from 1707 with only one or none from a later date in Rome, so too the multi-voice cantatas can be grouped into chronological and geographic patterns. Only two of them can be dated definitively to 1707: *Cor fedele* and *Sans y penser. Arresta il passo* may also have been composed in this year and then revised in 1708. *Amarilli vezzosa, Aci, Galatea e Polifemo,* and *Oh, come chiare* were all composed in 1708. Further, a revised version of *Arresta il passo* can be connected to a performance at the Arcadian Academy of 1708 through the Ruspoli documents (14 July 1708), and *Cor fedele* may have been revised for performance in Naples in 1708, given the use of Neapolitan paper for part of the revision; at any rate, this revision occurred either in Naples or shortly thereafter.[1] The initial version of *Apollo e Dafne* was probably composed in northern Italy in 1709 and later revised or finished in Hanover. Thus, six of the seven multi-voice instrumental cantatas (excluding only *Echeggiate, festeggiate,* London, 1710), can be associated in composition or revision to 1708–1709.

The geographic and chronological distribution of the multi-voice cantatas is shown in Table 4.1. The pastoral cantatas, *Arresta il passo, Sans y penser, Cor fedele,* and *Amarilli vezzosa,* are all Roman, while the two mythological cantatas, *Aci, Galatea e Polifemo* and *Apollo e Dafne,* are not. The distinction holds as well for the political cantatas: *Oh, come chiare* for Rome adopts a pastoral voice, placing Ruspoli in his pastoral persona in the role of a shepherd, while *Echeggiate, festeggiate* for London makes use of a mythological metaphor. My discussion will focus on the six pastoral and mythological cantatas (five instrumental and one continuo), referring to the two political works only as part of the pastoral and mythological groups.

Table 4.1 Handel's multi-voice cantatas

Date	Roman	Non-Roman
1707	[*Arresta il passo* ?] *Sans y penser* (continuo: September) *Cor fedele* (October)	
1708		*Aci, Galatea e Polifemo* (Naples: July) [*Cor fedele* ?] (revised Naples: July?)
	Arresta il passo (July) *Amarilli vezzosa* (August) *Oh, come chiare* (August)	
1709		*Apollo e Dafne* (Venice?)
1710		*Echeggiate, festeggiate* (London)

Not surprisingly, the Roman pastoral cantatas partake of the academic tradition already witnessed in the continuo cantatas. There is little in the way of characterization, and it is sometimes difficult to tell the characters apart. Further, the structure of these multi-voice pastorals remains very regular; there are no ariosos, no accompanied recitatives, no unusual aria forms. They illustrate well what Francis Haskell deemed typical of this Roman artistic period—"a rather bland sweetness . . . tending toward a certain cool anonymity."[2] Nowhere is this more obvious than in *Amarilli vezzosa*. The shepherd Daliso, tired of pursuing the shepherdess Amarilli, declares he will have her by force. She responds that taking pleasure by force will come to nothing. She urges Daliso to use his sword to pierce her heart, but he recoils from this deed and relinquishes his fight. Amarilli laughs at him and says he could have had her if only he had persevered. They conclude with a duet: he singing that he wants his heart back; she that he lacks the torch to kindle passion. Daliso (mezzo-soprano) and Amarilli (soprano) each have two arias; three of these are in triple or compound meter, and three are in major keys. All are *da capo,* and all are accompanied by unison violins. The major distinction between the parts is that Daliso has the one minor-key aria, full of sighs and silences, and Amarilli has the one aria in duple meter, which depicts a raging storm with a concertato solo violin (Ex. 4.1).

Although it could be argued that these arias show Daliso to be the weaker character, it is also true that it would not significantly alter the cantata if Amarilli sang a minor-key aria about sighs and Daliso used the metaphor of the sailor lost at sea. Handel underlines this seeming musical interchangeability in the final duet, in which the two singers each sing through the same minuet separately with different words, after which their voices join in counterpoint (Ex. 4.2). The duet suggests that Daliso and Amarilli are not actually at odds and that their roles of pursuit and resistance have been mutually chosen and are mutually dependent. This impression is perhaps reinforced by Handel's later use of this music as a love duet between husband and wife in *Poro* (1731).[3]

The non-Roman cantatas are distinguished from the Roman pastoral cantatas not just by their mythological topics, but, as with the non-Roman continuo cantatas discussed in Chapter 3, by their verve, musical characterization, and inventiveness. One measure of this is vocal range, which provides a significant distinction between the pastoral idiom and the more dramatic mythological stories. The Roman cantatas, again following the pattern of the continuo cantatas, are all for treble voices, while the bass roles of Polyphemus and Apollo bring compositional and timbral variety to the mythological stories.

Both mythological and pastoral multi-voice cantatas generally depict an action, as in *Amarilli vezzosa,* whose ending is not happy, nor even particularly satisfying, for the affected parties. In the mythological stories, for example,

Example 4.1a *Amarilli vezzosa,* "È vanità d'un cor" (Daliso).

Example 4.1b *Amarilli vezzosa,* "Quel nocchiero che mira le sponde" (Amarilli).

Example 4.2 *Amarilli vezzosa,* "Sì, sì, lasciami, ingrata / Su, su, restati in pace" (voice and bass only).

Daphne eludes her pursuer but loses her life; Acis dies and is turned into a stream. As E. J. Kenney writes more generally of Ovid's *Metamorphoses:*

> Ovid depicts a universe in which human beings, and more often than not the gods who are supposed to be in charge, are at the mercy of blind or arbitrary or cruel, and always irresistible, forces. . . . In this dangerous and uncertain world the happy ending is the exception.[4]

In its dramatic form the pastoral always incorporated a happy ending, as in Guarini's *Il pastor fido* and Tasso's *Aminta,* but pastoral cantatas, like Ovidian myths, eschew this convention. Unhappy endings, although most obvious in the largest, "operatic" cantatas, can be found in the smaller multi-voice and solo works as well. Indeed, as a genre, the Baroque cantata differs strikingly from contemporary opera specifically in its avoidance of the *lieto fine.* The difference, then, between the multi-voice cantatas and the solo cantatas lies not in the outcome (typically an unhappy ending), but rather in whether or not the action that leads to the outcome is depicted.

The solo voices of abandoned women and pastoral shepherds represent the stasis of perpetual unhappiness—the women in a constant state of grieving or revenge, the shepherds in a constant state of desire. Both states are described as unchanged by death. Agrippina sees herself after death as both vengeful ("a dark shade, a wandering ghost, a fury of cruelty") and grieving ("I will be a lonely sorrowful shade"),[5] and Lucrezia vows that she will wreak vengeance from the Underworld on her ravisher. The pastoral shepherds are equally clear, if not even more precise, about the continuation of their emotional state after death. In *Filli adorata e cara,* the shepherd vows:

Ma se volesse mai mia cruda sorte,	But if my cruel fate ever wished,
Che pria di riveder tue luci amate,	That before seeing your loving eyes,
Il rio dolore mi chiamasse a morte,	An evil sadness would call me to death,
Sappi, O Filli, mio Nume,	Know, O Filli, my goddess,
Che estinto ancor t'adorerà costante	That even dead my loving spirit,
La fredda salma mia,	My cold corpse,
Lo spirto amante.	Would adore you constantly.

The abandoned women and the pastoral shepherds are not frozen still (like the victims of the sorceress Alcina who are turned into stone), nor is their pain iterative (like that of Prometheus, who was condemned to have a vulture feed daily on his liver, which immediately would grow back). Rather, like Tantalus, whose Underworld punishment was always to be just out of reach of food and water, the voices of the solo cantatas are locked into an eternal gerundive state of mourning or desiring with no hope of amelioration. As expressed in the cantata *Poiché giuraro:*

Io senza speme di cangiar mai tempre	I, without hope of ever changing the nature
Nel mio dolor sarò l'istesso sempre,	Of my sadness, will be always the same,
Sol nel mesto mio core.	Alone in the sadness of my heart.
Col tempo il duol diverrà maggiore.	With time the sadness will only become greater.

By contrast, the duet and trio cantatas deal directly with change. Needless to say, the mythological cantatas based on Ovid's *Metamorphoses* are intrinsically about transformation (metamorphosis), but change is also integral to the pastoral cantatas. In *Cor fedele,* for example, Clori's inconstancy forces Tirsi and Fileno to change their attitude toward love: "let our hearts be slaves of caprice, and not of love." In *Arresta il passo,* Fillide is transformed, unusually, by love's awakening. Moreover, the element of change in these works transcends content. Myths, including the pastoral "myth" or story of pursuit, not only tell of transformation, but are themselves transformed in telling and retelling, and their telling transforms the listener.

As has been widely demonstrated, relationships between myths, both within and between cultures, demonstrate "astounding similarity."[6] Joseph Campbell has described what he calls the overriding "monomyth": "The standard path of the mythological adventure of the hero is a magnification of the formula represented in the rites of passage: *separation—initiation—return:* which might be named the nuclear unit of the monomyth."[7] More recently, Wendy Doniger has replaced Campbell's "static" formulation with the theoretical construct of "micromyth" as the most stripped-down, basic version of a story that is open to "wildly different variants," and the "macromyth" as a "composite of the details of many variants."[8] Another way of describing these variations on mythic themes has been to speak of the "multiformity" of myth, where the variations on a single theme are "multiforms" of one another.[9] Using this terminology, Handel's duet and trio cantatas each represent a "multiform" of the story of (failed) pursuit. However, as Doniger points out, groupings of myths depend on point of view, a trait that she, using a musical analogy, refers to as "multi-vocality."[10] Thus, the male characters Apollo, Polyphemus, and Aminta may all be singing variations on the same song of desire, but the same cannot be said for the women, Daphne, Galatea, and Amarilli, all of whom experience "wildly different" outcomes. However, just as Apollo's pursuit is replicated in many myths, so, too, Daphne's transformation into a vegetative state is a multiform. Choosing only from Apollo's amours, it is possible to pick a bouquet of such cases. Daphne, who spurns the god, is transformed into a laurel; Clytie,

who is scorned by the god, is transformed into a heliotrope; Clymene, who returns his love, is turned into a "shrub of frankincense"; and Hyacinth, one of his
male lovers, is turned into a flower named for him after being accidentally
killed.

Myths repeat the same story because the story is meaningful. The same is
true of fairy tales. "Little Red Riding Hood" and "Hansel and Gretel" are, at
one level, multiforms of the same story, which is retold because its message continues to resonate: children who stray into the dark wood and speak with
strangers (the wolf, the witch) can end up in deep trouble. The "pursuit" myth,
somewhat less pedagogic in function, maintains a still stronger psychic hold on
humanity in general and lies at the basis of all of Handel's multi-voice cantatas.
Usually at some point, Handel paints the pursuit musically. *Arresta il passo* introduces this chase motive in the second, *furioso,* section of the overture, which
depicts Aminta chasing Fillide; it is abruptly cut short by Aminta calling out for
Fillide to stop ("Arresta il passo"), as shown in Ex. 4.3. In *Apollo e Dafne,* the
"chase scene" comes at the end. Daphne, represented by the solo violin in sixteenth notes, flees from Apollo, represented by the solo bassoon in eighth notes;
just as his steps begin to match hers (by moving into sixteenths), she is transformed before his eyes, and the musical fabric of the aria disintegrates into accompanied and then simple recitative as Apollo stands amazed (Ex. 4.4). A
chase is probably also depicted in the overture to *Amarilli vezzosa,* where the
imitation and chains of suspensions in the two violins seem to paint Daliso's
pursuit of Amarilli. Again, the pursuit is interrupted, here by a surprising deceptive cadence(*), which initiates a transition into a minuet. By having this
minuet foreshadow the final duet of Daliso and Amarilli (see Ex. 4.2), Handel
seems to offer in his opening "sonata" a glimpse of the cantata's dramatic arch:
from chase to enforced formality (Ex. 4.5, p. 138).[11]

The main crux for interpreters and listeners in understanding the pursuit
myth and distinguishing one type from another is the identity of the object of
desire; as a shepherd asks Acis in John Gay's libretto to Handel's later, English
version of the Acis and Galatea myth (discussed in Chapter 6): "Shepherd, what
art thou pursuing?" Just as the metaphor of the abandoned woman can be understood asexually to represent personal loss, a lost soul, or political abandonment, so too can the pursued shepherdess be understood to represent various
personal, professional, religious, and political goals. Therefore, the nymph in
stories of pursuit should not be seen simply as a sexual trope, but as also representing a (sometimes thwarted) goal. Petrarch, for example, makes it very clear
that his pursuit is not only for the woman he desires but also for the fame he desires as an artist, and he does so by his choice of name: with the alteration of a
single letter his beloved Laura is transformed into *lauro,* the laurel wreath that
denotes the greatest glory for a poet. Like Apollo, Petrarch failed to catch the

Example 4.3 *Arresta il passo,* overture, ending.

nymph, but he accepted the laurel wreath as substitution (transformation/subli-mation): he was crowned poet laureate on Easter Sunday, 1341, in Rome.[12]

Multiformity, as well as the relation of the pursuit theme to both myth and pastoral, plays a critical role in the transmission of the stories Handel sets to music. This can be seen with particular clarity in the classical depictions of Polyphemus's pursuit of Galatea, by tracing the fable backwards from Ovid's *Metamorphoses* to Virgil's *Eclogues* to Theocritus's *Idylls*. It is only in Ovid that the story becomes a love triangle with the addition of the character of Acis, whose transformation is necessary to the inclusion of the story among the *Metamorphoses*. In Theocritus the tale is more directly one of failed pursuit in which Polyphemus's love cannot bridge the differences between himself and Galatea. The Cyclops and the nymph are "unmatched" not just because he is a giant

Example 4.4 *Apollo e Dafne,* "Mie piante correte," ending.

monster and she is "fairy flesh" (*Idyll* VI, l. 15), but more because she is a sea nymph and he, although the son of Neptune and the sea nymph Thoösa, is earthbound (*Idyll* XI).[13] Polyphemus pleads: "Leave the green sea gulping against the dry shore. You'll do better o' nights with me, in my cave. . . . O[h], won't you come out, Galatea, and coming out forget . . . to go back home! You'd learn to like to shepherd sheep with me" (*Idyll* XI, ll. 42–43, 60–62). It is this image of unmatched love, rather than the specific characters, that Virgil later in-

Example 4.4 *(continued)*

corporated into his *Eclogue* II, a same-sex pastoral based directly on Theocritus's *Idyll* XI and sung by the shepherd Corydon to the fair youth Alexis. However, Corydon is depicted as unequal not directly to Alexis, even though that may be the case, but to his rival in love, "his master" whose "darling" is Alexis. From here the addition of Acis by Ovid is a small step. Re-instituting the specific characters of Galatea and Polyphemus, Ovid has the nymph not simply reject the suit of the Cyclops but prefer someone else both better matched and more desirable. Acis, son of the river nymph Symaethis and King Faunus of Latium, had parents strikingly parallel to those of Polyphemus, but in contrast to the Cyclops, Acis was "beautiful" (*Metamorphoses* XIII).

Example 4.5 *Amarilli vezzosa,* Sonata, end of *allegro* to beginning of *menuetto.*

All three multiforms of this story depict the wooing in strikingly similar terms. Polyphemus (or Corydon) emphasizes the bounty of his fields and flocks and argues that, having seen himself in the water, he is not ugly. In Theocritus, Polyphemus states:

> I'd have you know, I graze a thousand sheep, and draw
> the best milk for myself to drink. I am never without
> cheeses, summer or fall: even in midwinter
> my cheese nets are laden. (*Idyll* XI, ll. 33–36)

> Certainly I'm not ugly, as they call me;
> for lately I looked in the sea—there was a calm—
> and I thought my cheeks and my one eye showed up handsome,
> and my teeth shone back, whiter than Parian marble. (*Idyll* VI, ll. 36–39)

Virgil has Corydon sing (*Eclogue* II):[14]

> You scorn me, never asking who I am—
> How rich in flocks, or flowing with snowy milk.
> A thousand lambs of mine roam Sicily's hills;
> Summer or winter, I'm never out of milk. (ll. 19–22)

> Nor am I ugly: once by the shore I saw
> Myself in the wind-calmed sea. I would not fear to
> Compete for you with Daphnis: mirrors don't lie. (ll. 25–27)

In Ovid, Polyphemus's bragging is more detailed and effusive (*Metamorphoses* XIII):[15]

> All this fine flock is mine, and many more
> Roam in the dales or shelter in the woods
> Or in my caves are folded; should you chance
> To ask how many, that I could not tell:
> A *poor* man counts his flocks. Nor need you trust
> My praises; here before your eyes you see
> Their legs can scarce support the bulging udders.
> And I have younger stock, lambs in warm folds,
> And kids of equal age in other folds,
> And snowy milk always, some kept to drink
> And some the rennet curdles into cheese.
> . . . [S]purn not my gifts, but come!
> For sure I know—I have just seen—myself
> Reflected in a pool, and what I saw
> Was truly pleasing. See how large I am!
> No bigger body Jove himself can boast
> Up in the sky—you always talk of Jove
> Or someone reigning there. My ample hair
> O'erhangs my grave stern face and like a grove
> Darkens my shoulders; and you must not think
> Me ugly, that my body is so thick
> With prickly bristles.

Moreover, in all three versions, Galatea (or Alexis) is offered an animal gift: "I'm rearing eleven fawns, all with white collars, for you, and four bear cubs" (*Idyll* XI, ll. 39–40); "Also, a pair of wild kids which I found deep in a valley, their skins still spotted white; they suck my she-goat dry; and they're for you" (*Eclogue* II, ll. 40–42); "I found one day among the mountain peaks, for you to play with, twins so much alike you scarce could tell, cubs of a shaggy bear. I found them and I said 'She shall have these; I'll keep them for my mistress for her own'" (*Metamorphoses* XIII).

Even while enumerating instances of similarity, the differences among the versions become clear. Theocritus and Ovid, telling the story of Galatea and Polyphemus, emphasize the awkwardness and humor of the Cyclops's suit. In both versions his lack of appropriateness is so grotesque that it is funny, including his puffed-up pride in huge numbers of flocks with their bulging udders, his description of himself as handsome, and his courtship gifts to the water nymph of bear cubs. Virgil, by contrast, emphasizes the poignancy of the ill-fated, "country" lover: though he "has not forgotten the comic effect of Polyphemus'[s] vain and resentful threats, he makes us take Corydon seriously."[16] Closely following his model in Theocritus, Virgil's change in scale to a human relationship means that nothing Corydon says of himself is out of place. His beloved Alexis may think him poor in comparison to his master Iollas, but he is rich in flocks; he has realized that, even if he is not as elegant as someone from the upper classes, he is not bad-looking; and he has found a pair of beautiful young kids (not bears) to give to his beloved. Virgil's version shows us that what is humorous about the Cyclops is his lack of physical, aesthetic, and rhetorical proportion; however, it also encourages by analogy our sympathetic consideration of the monster's plight.

The pastoral versions by Theocritus and Virgil, although they differ in their choice of character and in their use of comedy, are closely similar in other ways. Foremost among these is the importance of same-sex love. *Idyll* VI of Theocritus presents a meeting of two herdsmen, the young Daphnis and the younger Damoetas, who engage in a singing match. This gentle competition, a love trial of worthiness, was "desired" and initiated by the older Daphnis, who begins in the voice of a shepherd warning Polyphemus that Galatea is taunting him. Damoetas's response in the voice of the Cyclops wins Daphnis's approval and love. The poem concludes with only slightly veiled sexual play. The shepherds exchange pipes and play sweetly together, while the herd itself dances to their music. The last line reads: "Neither was victor; both unvanquished proved." In Virgil's *Eclogue* II the homosexual content is transferred from the frame to the central story. It begins with the lines: "Corydon the shepherd burned for fair Alexis, his master's darling, and he hadn't a hope" (ll. 1–2). The main body of the poem, Corydon's personal lament, exists within the wider context of pastoral loves. Alexis's refusals make Phyllis's "moody rages or haughty whims" or even Menalcas's tanned body (as opposed to Alexis's "gleaming white" body) seem preferable. Corydon, who cannot win Alexis away from his master Iollas, thinks he could nevertheless compete with Daphnis in beauty and with Damoetas in music, thus naming the shepherds in the poetic model by Theocritus. However, he threatens to give the love gift he has for Alexis to the nymph Thestylis. In both pastoral poems, same-sex love represents a natural half of the passionate world. In Theocritus, the homosexual lovers use a heterosexual relationship as the basis of their love trial; in Virgil, Corydon compares his passion for Alexis to other possible love objects, male and female.

Theocritus and Virgil also may be compared in the extent to which these poems represent the poet's own voice. In the opening verses of *Idyll* VI, Theocritus directly addresses Aratus—"It happened one day, Aratus"—whose homosexual love he describes graphically in *Idyll* VII. *Idyll* XI is addressed to Nicias, a doctor, with whom Theocritus probably had been friendly since student days, so that their "common interest in love affairs is particularly understandable."[17] In contrast to the personal address of Theocritus, Virgil distances himself by providing a narrative opening frame—"Corydon the shepherd burned for fair Alexis"—and trusting the poem and its ending to Corydon's voice. Yet he identifies his own voice beneath the shepherd's mask in *Eclogue* VI, where he presents himself openly in the person of the shepherd Tityrus and quotes from Corydon's lament.[18] "In this case we can say quite literally that the shepherd has come to speak for the poet and the poet to express himself in the shepherd's words."[19]

What is most remarkable about the more intimately personal attributes of Theocritus's poetry is the power invested in pastoral song. In *Idyll* VI, the song competition represents a method of evaluating the worthiness of a lover, and the levels on which this occurs are overlaid one upon the other. Polyphemus sings in his own voice but fails as a lover because his song, not just his person, is monstrous and grotesque. At the second level, Damoetas uses the voice of Polyphemus to advance his personal desires and succeeds as a lover because he wittily responds to Daphnis's challenge; "by his graceful responsiveness, [he] has proved himself Daphnis' peer."[20] At the third level, Theocritus uses the voices of Damoetas and Polyphemus in his song to Aratus. Theocritus later describes Aratus's love as "prosaic and a cause hardly worth wearing oneself out over,"[21] but we cannot tell from this statement whether his song succeeded or failed.

In *Idyll* XI, addressed to the doctor Nicias, Theocritus claims that only art can cure love.

> Love's a complaint, Nicias, against which no drug known
> to Nature is effective: not an ointment, not a powder—
> save for the Muses: through their art can men with this disease

be eased, and sweet relief they find—but few can find it.
And this I ween you know full well, being a physician,
and held in love exceeding by the selfsame Nine. (ll. 1–6)

Theocritus then provides Polyphemus's song as an example of such a catharsis. At the climax of the lament, the monster cries out to himself, "Cyclops, Cyclops! Where is this mad flight taking you?" (l. 69), and decides to look for love elsewhere. Theocritus concludes:

In this way did Polyphemus shepherd his love with song;
and he found a readier cure than if he had paid hard cash. (ll. 77–78)

Virgil's *Eclogue* is not as explicit, but Corydon, like Polyphemus, is able to rouse himself: "Ah, Corydon, what madness seizes you? . . . You'll find another lad, if this one's cold" (ll. 69 and 73). The powerful model in Theocritus leads to the conclusion that Corydon's transformation is not simply a change from lamenting but a change that occurred on account of the lament itself.

In Ovid's version, the distancing of the poet has taken another step, for the *Metamorphoses* places the song of Polyphemus in the tear-choked voice of Galatea. Yet Ovid's *Metamorphoses* makes clear not only that the art of poetry determines the success of a suit, as in a love competition, but also that it provides a catharsis for love through sublimation. This can be demonstrated by comparing Ovid's version of the story of Polyphemus and Galatea with that of Apollo and Daphne. The *Metamorphoses* begins with the story of the creation of the world, the flood, the generation of all forms of life from the earth, the growth of human population from Deucalion and Pyrrha (the only survivors of the flood), the birth of the serpent Python, and its destruction by Apollo. The story of Apollo and Daphne follows immediately, as the first transformation linked to love. In contrast, the story of Polyphemus and Galatea occurs near the end of the sequence of transformations, as an interruption in the history of Rome from the wanderings of Aeneas to the apotheosis of Julius Caesar that ends the *Metamorphoses*. Ovid's trajectory over the course of his epic leads downward hierarchically from gods to heroes to men, and by placing Apollo and Polyphemus near opposite ends he sets off these two lovers in particular relation to each other.

Both suitors are poet-singers. Apollo says to Daphne: "I shape the harmony of song and strings." Polyphemus prepares his song by taking his pipe "made of a hundred reeds; his pastoral whistles rang among the cliffs and over the waves." Both pursue water nymphs: Daphne's father is the river-god Peneus, and Galatea's father the sea-god Nereus. Both think the nymphs flee from them because they do not realize who their suitors are. Apollo cries out, "Yet ask who loves you. No rough forester am I, no unkempt shepherd guarding here his flocks and herds. You do not know—you fly, you madcap girl, because you do not know." Polyphemus wonders at Galatea's flight "swifter than the winds," and adds, "Though, if you knew, you would repent your flight, condemn your coyness, strive to hold me fast." Both offer their father as proof of their worthiness: Apollo asserts, "I am the son of Jupiter," and Polyphemus says, "Moreover in your sea my father [Neptune] reigns; him I give you—my father, yours to be." Both, of course, lose the nymph, but whereas Apollo gains the laurel in Daphne's stead (the sublimation of sexual desire through art as described and depicted by Theocritus), Polyphemus is left with nothing. His song lacks elegance and proportion, as is evident from its very opening when he uses a litany of thirteen comparisons to depict Galatea's beauty ("Fair Galatea, whiter than snow, taller than alders, flowerier than the meads, . . .") followed by thirteen comparisons to draw her obstinacy ("Yet, Galatea, fiercer than wild bulls, harder than ancient oak, falser than waves," and so on). As E. J. Kenney writes, "Ovid's Cyclops is made to expand these hints [from Theocritus and Virgil] into a prodigious apostrophe to the nymph of nineteen verses, incorporating what must surely be the longest sequence of comparative ablatives in Latin literature. . . . This was certainly an in-joke."[22] As in Theocritus, Ovid's Polyphemus fails as a lover because he fails as a poet, but more severe than Theocritus, who permits the Cyclops catharsis through poetry, Ovid disallows him even that relief, emphasizing the incompetence of his song by placing the story in Galatea's voice.

These "multiforms" of the myth of pursuit by Theocritus, Virgil, and Ovid—the various versions of the Galatea and Polyphemus story, the pastoral love complaint of Corydon, and the story of Apollo and Daphne—illustrate a number of points critical to the context of Handel's multi-voice cantatas. As in Theocritus's poem, the shepherd's voice often provides a mask for the poet, something made manifest by the adoption of pastoral identities in the Arcadian Academy. As in Virgil's transference of the pursuit from Polyphemus to Corydon, the stories of gods and goddesses represent parables of human histories. The pursuit itself, as in Theocritus and Virgil, is equally and equivocally heterosexual or homosexual. As in all precedents, the success of the poem determines the success of the outcome. However, the goal need not be requited love, but rather catharsis for unrequited love or poetic achievement.

The multiformity of the classical sources is evident in Handel's cantata librettos. For example, the text of *Aci, Galatea e Polifemo* recalls explicitly the story of Apollo and Daphne when Galatea in her second aria compares herself to the laurel:

Benché tuoni e l'etra avampi	Though the heavens may resound and burn
pur di folgori e di lampi	with thunder and lightning
non paventa il sacro alloro.	the sacred laurel tree shows no fear.
Come quello anch'io pur sono	I am like that laurel,
ché non cedo e m'abbandono	for I neither yield nor resign myself
a timor di rio martoro.	to fear of harsh torment.[23]

That is, like Daphne, Galatea will successfully resist her unwanted suitor. Further, Galatea's plea to her father, Nereus, to transform Acis so that she may be united with him for eternity faintly echoes Daphne's plea to her father, Peneus, to transform her in order to protect her from her suitor.

E tu, mio genitore,	And may you, my father,
quell'infelice salma,	change that unhappy body,
trofeo di cruda morte,	the victim of cruel death,
deh, fa che si converta in fresco rio;	into a cool stream;
ché quando al mar che freme	when he reaches the foaming sea
con tenero d'amor dolce desio,	filled with sweet and tender desire of love
fia che giunga in tributo	let him pay his tribute,
poiché per mio dolore	so that where to my sorrow
sopra le nude arene estinto giacque	he once lay dead on the bare sands,
lo goderò, lo stringerò fra l'acque.	I shall enjoy him and embrace him in the waters.

However, the transformation of Acis into a stream, occurring as it does in a composition celebrating a wedding, is less a tragedy than a metaphor for the eternal union of Acis's desire and Galatea's welcoming arms. It fulfills an unspoken prophecy in the cantata itself: in Acis's first recitative, he describes himself as a stream rushing to kiss the shore of the sea.

Vanti, O cara, il ruscello	The stream, my dearest, utters
di fremer gorgogliando	gurglings of rage
rotto fra sterpi e sassi	as it breaks over stumps and rocks,
finché poi mormorando	until it comes, murmuring,
con gl'argentei suoi passi	with silvery steps
arrivi a ribaciar del mar l'arene;	to kiss the sea's shore;
ché sol da te, mio bene,	when alone, my love,
quando lontan son io,	and far from you,
misero al par di quello	I am as wretched as that stream
provo nel fido sen duolo più rio.	but feel a greater grief in my faithful heart.

The depiction of a stream rushing to unite itself with the sea as a metaphor for passionate pursuit and union is also the basis of one of the Neapolitan continuo cantatas—possibly in the "voice" of the Duke of Alvito as bridegroom—*Sento là che ristretto*.

Son io Nice il ruscello,	Nice, I am the brook,
E di bellezza il mare	And the sea of beauty
È il tenero tuo seno	Is your soft breast
Ove, tra vivi scogli	Where, among living rocks,
Va del mio core a naufragar il pino.	The ship of my heart goes to be wrecked.

Specific word comparisons leave little doubt that the continuo cantata is related to the Acis transformation as a "multiform," and the repetition of specific words and phrases (highlighted in italics below) suggests the same author.[24] The following example compares the beginning of Acis's recitative with the opening of the continuo cantata (the English translation of the *Aci* text is given above, that of *Sento là che ristretto* in Appendix 2):

Aci, Galatea e Polifemo	*Sento là che ristretto*
Vanti, O cara, il ruscello	Sento là che ristretto
di fremer gorgogliando	nell'angusto confin *di sterpi e sassi*
rotto *fra sterpi e sassi*	*degli argentei suoi passi*
finché poi *mormorando*	limpido ruscelletto
con l'argentei suoi passi	la già perduta libertà sospira. . . .
arrivi a *ribaciar del mar l'arene.*	ascolto *alfin* che geme. . . .
	con lento *mormorio,*
	belle *arene del mare*
	non vi posso *baciare.* . . .

The men of these cantatas are always the pursuers; women, the pursued. However, the gender distinctions previously noted between passionate women's voices and masked male anonymity are little in evidence. Here there are no abandoned women, but rather feminized, but little characterized, objects of desire, just as the male voices in the solo cantatas and most of the multi-voice cantatas are also generalized and anonymous. A certain amount of musical sharing among these and other female pastoral characters betrays a relative lack of specificity, as shown in Ex. 4.6. Clori's metaphor aria about the nightingales, "Va col canto," uses an accompaniment of triplets in 3/8 meter in two-part violin and recorder *(flauti dolci)* doublings (mostly in thirds) with harmonic and motivic support from the violas and bass.[25] Handel adapts this for Galatea's aria

Example 4.6a *Cor fedele,* "Va col canto."

Example 4.6b *Aci, Galatea e Polifemo,* "S'agita in mezzo all'onde."

"S'agita in mezzo all'onde," a metaphor aria that describes the waves of the sea.
He then transforms the accompaniment for his English version of the Galatea
and Polyphemus myth in Galatea's bird song, "Hush, ye pretty warbling choir."
In other examples, Clori's "Amo Tirsi" becomes the English Galatea's "As when
the dove" (Ex. 4.7, p. 148), and the Italian Galatea's "Se m'ami, O caro" is transferred with its text (but with a reduction of orchestral forces) into the voice of
the shepherdess Dorinda in Handel's pastoral opera *Il pastor fido* (London,
1712), as shown in Ex. 4.8 (pp. 149–150).

The examples of shared textual images (laurel), metaphors (the stream that
runs to the sea), and musical depictions (of the pursued nymph) illustrate some
of the multiformity of Handel's cantatas of pursuit. The very repetition suggests
not only the importance of the story, but also the likelihood of multiple and
metaphoric meanings. As the discussion of each cantata will show, these meanings vary. Some chases are explicitly sexual, some metaphoric; sometimes the

Example 4.6c *Acis and Galatea,* "Hush, ye pretty warbling choir."

pursued nymph is a sexual object of desire, sometimes the object of desire must be viewed asexually; sometimes the nymph represents a lost soul. Particularly striking are the occasions when the pursuit leads to a substitution for the original desire. The single repeated theme of these multi-voice cantatas, as with Theocritus's Polyphemus, is the catharsis of desire through sublimation or transformation.

Only in *Cor fedele* is the female object of desire, Clori, presented in such a way as to distinguish her from the general pastoral surroundings and transmit at least a hint of the danger associated with such female types as the voracious virago (like Agrippina) or the killer virgin (like Diana). Clori's four arias generally use expanded forms with large accompanimental forces. "Va col canto" (mentioned above) has recorders and violins; "Conosco che me piaci" uses violins and oboes in unison; "Barbaro, tu non credi" includes a violin solo, violin and oboe doubling in two parts, viola, and bass; and "Amo Tirsi" uses oboes and violins in various combinations.[26] Clori's arias, all in major keys, progress from F (one flat) to G (one sharp) to keys with ever more sharps (first A, then E), keys that would later feature in Handel's characterization of other seductresses, such as Cleopatra.[27]

Example 4.7a *Cor fedele,* "Amo Tirsi."

Example 4.7b *Acis and Galatea,* "As when the dove."

Clori's recitatives are set musically with dissonance and harmonic deception. As she tries to persuade Tirsi of her fidelity, she repeatedly says *credimi* ("believe me"), but this is always set with a striking dissonance, and with each iteration she moves further into the sharp keys (from B minor through C-sharp minor to F-sharp minor, cadencing in C-sharp minor), as shown in Ex. 4.9 (p. 151).

Tirsi, mio caro Tirsi, ah! se non vuoi	Tirsi, my dear Tirsi, ah! if you do not wish
da ferr'omicidial verdermi estinta	to see me slain by a deadly blade,
credimi, e sappi, che tu solo puoi	*believe me,* and be assured that you alone
di quest'anima mia regger l'impero;	can hold sway over this soul of mine,
credimi ch'il pensiero	*believe me,* that my thoughts
non vanta fuor di te pensier più degno;	boast none more worthy than of you;
e se a me più non credi,	and if you no longer believe me
perché sdegno tu celi,	because you harbour anger,
credilo a miei sospiri,	*believe it* from my sighs,

Example 4.8a *Aci, Galatea e Polifemo,* "Se m'ami, O caro."

alle lacrime, O Dio!	from the tears, O God!
che spargo a torto,	which I am unjustly shedding,
e ti diran fedeli	and they will tell you faithfully
che Tirsi è la mia pace e il mio conforto.	that Tirsi is my consolation and my comfort.[28]

In Clori's final recitative, as she tries to convince Tirsi that her declaration of love for Fileno, which he has overheard, was only a game for her, the dissonance is combined with harmonic deception. Beginning over a C-sharp pedal, the vo-

Example 4.8b *Il pastor fido,* "Se m'ami, O caro."

cal line leaps an augmented fifth on the word *ahi,* creating a major seventh with
the bass. On the word *amorose* (amorous) the harmony moves to an E-major
sixth chord, possibly implying a cadence to A, but this is deflected by downward chromatic motion in the bass from *g♯* to *g♮*. A progression of sixth chords
leads to a D-major chord on the name Fileno, suggesting a cadence to the key of
G, but this expectation is thwarted by a shift to a G-sharp diminished triad that
leads instead to an A-major chord on *scherzo gentil* ("an innocent joke"), finally
shifting into C-sharp minor for the cadence.

T'inganni, ahi! sì, t'inganni;	You are mistaken, alas, yes, you are mistaken;
quelle note amorose,	those amorous sounds
che poco anzi ascoltasti	which a little while ago you heard
scoglier dal labbro mio	fall from my lips
col pastorel Fileno	with the shepherd Fileno
furo sembianze ascose	were the deceptions
d'uno scherzo gentil che uscì dal seno.	of an innocent joke devised by my heart.

The harmony not only paints superficially the "deception" Clori claims to have
engaged in, but suggests the deeper deception that this entire speech is false (or

rather that she is equally false to Tirsi as to Fileno), as is clarified in the second half of the recitative. Beginning with a G-sharp pedal, Handel repeats the harmonic progression leading this time to a G-sharp minor cadence as Clori (deceptively) assures Tirsi that she is faithful to him alone.

The music that Handel composes for Tirsi and Fileno is strikingly different from Clori's. Fileno's four arias are all in flat keys (D minor, F major, C minor, F major), and the accompaniments are minimal. "Sai perchè l'onda del fiume" is accompanied only by continuo but includes an instrumental closing ritornello

Example 4.9 *Cor fedele,* "Tirsi, mio caro Tirsi," recitative for Clori.

(there is no opening ritornello). "Son come quel nocchiero" uses the wonderful combination of first and second recorder *(flauto)* and first and second viola; nevertheless, the vocal sections are largely accompanied only by continuo. Fileno's third aria, "Povera fedeltà," is a miniature continuo aria (the A section is only nine measures long). "Come la rondinella" stands out from Fileno's other arias by its inclusion of a concertato part for solo archlute, but this accompaniment largely functions as an elaborately realized continuo aria. Fileno's recitatives are all harmonically straightforward, if not simple.

Tirsi's four arias vacillate between major and minor, sharps and flats (G major, G minor, D major, B minor). Overall, these are the smallest arias, and, like Fileno's, they generally use reduced accompaniments. "Cor fedele" is a continuo aria; "Povero Tirsi" is largely *senza bassi;* "Tra le fere," although composed with six instrumental parts (Oboe 1 and 2, Violin 1 and 2, Viola, Bass), uses these forces principally in the ritornellos, leaving the voice either accompanied by continuo alone or *senza bassi;* finally, "Un sospiretto" is a continuo aria with a closing ritornello for strings. The use of *senza bassi* accompaniments distinguishes Tirsi's arias from Fileno's and depicts him as "unsupported." Tirsi's arias are also marked by silences in the vocal line. In "Cor fedele," he sings, "A beautiful woman considers her thoughts to be ignoble if she accepts into her heart the affections of just one lover," and Handel depicts the lover *(vago)* broken in two and suspended over a dominant pedal (on *B*) that doesn't resolve until the next phrase begins three measures later (Ex. 4.10). In "Quell'erbetta," Tirsi

Example 4.10 *Cor fedele,* "Cor fedele," setting of *vago.*

Example 4.11 *Cor fedele*, "Quell'erbetta," use of silence.

describes the "young grass" and the "golden vine" and asks: What does it say? What does it think? What does it do? What does it want? Handel follows these questions with rests in the vocal part and leaves their dominant harmonies unresolved. Just before the final cadence of each complete setting of the A text, the silence cuts through the entire musical fabric (Ex. 4.11).

The cantata *Cor fedele* thus depicts a musically attractive and well-endowed nymph who through discord and deception causes pain and unresolved tension for two musically honest, simple, and unprotected shepherds. The continuo cantatas repeatedly warn against this situation. In *Udite il mio consiglio* (1706), the shepherd Fileno begins:

Udite il mio consiglio,	Listen to my advice,
Inesperti d'amor pastori, udite;	You shepherds inexperienced in love, listen;
Se inconstraste giammai	If you ever encounter
Qui dove suole	Here where she is used to

guidar l'errante greggia	guiding the wandering flock
Dal colle al piano, o dalla selva al fonte,	From hills to valley, or from wood to spring,
Picciola pastorella,	A little shepherdess,
Di membra agili e pronte,	With quick and agile limbs,
D'atti languidi e schivi,	Gestures languid and bashful,
Che ha nero ciglio in bianco volto,	Who has black eyes in a white face,
E fregia della guancia	And, decorating a pale cheek,
Il pallor labbro vermiglio,	Red lips,
Fuggite, ah! sì fuggite,	Flee, ah! yes, flee,
Que' suoi furtivi sguardi,	Those furtive glances of hers,
E quelle sue semplicità mentite.	And her misleading simplicity.
Innocente rassembra, e pur niun'altra	She appears innocent, and yet no one else
È al par di lei cruda fallace e scaltra.	Is as cruel as she is false and cunning.

In *Menzognere speranze* (Rome, 1707), the nameless, deceived shepherd has given up love:

Alle lusinghe, non credea quest'alma.	In her enticements, my soul does not believe.
Spezzerò d'ogni amante	I shall shatter every lover's
I simulati affetti,	False sentiments,
E se talun costante	And if I see wounded
Vedrò piagato, lacrimar d'amore,	Such a constant one, crying of love,
Sarà suo maggior vanto	It will be his greatest glory
Ch'io non rida al suo pianto,	If I mock not his tears,
O pur sua maggior sorte,	Or his greatest fortune
Trovar in me pietà della sua morte.	To find in me pity for his death.

Venne voglia and *Vedendo Amor,* a pair of cantatas (Rome, 1707), describe an elaborate scene in which Cupid sets up as a birdcatcher, making his nets out of "chestnut brown, blond, and black hair" and using as his decoys "eyes, cheeks, lips and breasts." The singer falls into the trap once and manages to escape, but he is recaptured:

Rise Eurilla, rise Amore,	Eurilla laughed, Love laughed
Che di già mio vincitore	That already my conqueror
Mi teniva in servitù.	Held me in servitude.
Ed io misero non spero,	And I, miserable, do not hope,
Or ch'io son lor prigioniero	Now that I am their prisoner,
Di goder pace mai più.	To enjoy peace ever again.

In *Dalla guerra amorosa* (Italian, before 1709), the listener is again warned to fly from love:

Non v'alletti un occhio nero,	Do not be charmed by any dark eye[s]
Con suoi sguardi lusinghiero	Alluring with their glances
Che da voi chieda pietà.	That may beg pity from you.
Che per far le sue vendette,	For in order to take revenge,
E con arco e con saette,	With both bow and arrow,
Ivi amor nascoso sta.	Love stands hidden there.
. . . . .	. . . . .
Fuggite, sì fuggite!	Fly, yes fly!
A chi servo d'amor vive in catena,	To one who, a servant of love, lives in chains,
È dubbioso il gioir,	Joy is doubtful,
Certa la pena.	Pain certain.

Cor fedele acts out the static situations narrated in such continuo cantatas. Tirsi and Fileno are charmed, but deceived and hurt, by the lovely Clori. Their recourse is to turn to each other and to declare that they will no longer take love seriously. Fileno says:

Tirsi, amico e compagno,	Tirsi, friend and companion,
già che tanto si avanza	since so much in evidence is
l'incostante desio	the inconstant desire
di sesso imbelle,	of the fair sex,
scacciam da noi gelosa cura,	let us drive jealous care from us,
e il core sia servo del capriccio	and let our hearts be slaves of caprice,
e non d'amore.	and not of love.

The overall layout of the work emphasizes this conclusion. Tirsi begins the cantata with two arias. There follow three distinct scenes: one between Clori and Fileno, to which Tirsi listens, consisting of four arias leading to a duet; the next between Clori and Tirsi, containing a duet and three arias; and the last between Tirsi and Fileno, consisting of three arias leading to a duet. That is, in a composition of fifteen arias and duets, Clori leaves the scene after the eleventh number and is thereafter absent from about the last third of the work. Hinting at the myth of Orpheus, who reacts to his loss of Eurydice by turning to the love of boys, Tirsi and Fileno respond to their loss of Clori with male friendship.

In *Between Men*, Eve Kosofsky Sedgwick has argued that the classic love triangle, as in *Cor fedele*, illustrates the importance of male friendship (male bonding) in heterosexual relationships; she demonstrates how two men pursuing or pursued by the same woman frequently act out their desire for each other in terms of approval, admiration, or love.[29] Even more specifically, George Haggerty's discussion of the superiority of male love in Nathaniel Lee's play *The Rival Queens* (London, 1677) resonates with the pastoral characters of Clori, Tirsi, and Fileno: "women's love," he writes, is presented as more violent and less powerful than the relations among men. The women in this play are given to spectacle, and their scenes, which become the model for tragic conflict, tend toward the histrionic. . . . Masculine desire becomes an alternative center of value here. . . . Sexual desire between men and women is seen as dishonest, scheming, and debilitating. But the love that Alexander and Hephestion share is powerful, public, and intimidating.[30]

The male rejection of heterosexual love with a potentially dangerous and histrionic woman, and its replacement with an idealized same-sex love, lies at the heart of Handel's *Cor fedele.* Anthony Hicks writes: "When the men discover the game [Clori] is playing, they decide to renew their friendship and make the best of the situation, delivering some disparaging comments on women in general . . . their remarks may have had some topical or domestic significance now lost to us."[31] The likelihood of a specific, personal meaning is supported in part by a later change to the ending of the cantata. The use of Neapolitan paper for this revision has led Hans Joachim Marx to conclude that the alteration, which softens the ending and brings Clori back for a final trio, was written for that city.[32] Certainly the original, misogynistic ending would not have been appropriate for the wedding festivities with which Handel was engaged in Naples, but regardless of its provenance, the alteration, like that Handel made to *Il trionfo del tempo,* discussed in Chapter 1, suggests the existence of a homosexual (and possibly specific) subtext that could be recognized and considered inappropriate in a changed context.[33]

Cor fedele is not, of course, openly homosexual, and the male friendship achieved at the end is ambiguous in its implications. On the one hand, most radically, one can interpret the conclusion as a simple substitution of same-sex for opposite-sex sexuality. On the other hand, conservatively, one can view it as a victory for male friendship, superior because it is free from the taint of carnal desire. Because same-sex passion hides easily behind the facade of friendship, such ambiguity is often deliberate, and questions of interpretation surround depictions of male friendship from the most secular to the spiritual. In *Cor fedele* the newfound friendship of Tirsi and Fileno replaces either man's serious pursuit of Clori and, whether interpreted sexually or not, depicts a sublimation of heterosexual love.

Playing a critical role in all of Handel's multi-voice cantatas, the act of sublimation ranges from the ridiculous to the sublime. At the far comic end of the spectrum, the cantata *Sans y penser,* possibly written for Cardinal Ottoboni in 1707 (two years before he succeeded Cardinal Francesco Maria de' Medici as Protector of France), depicts the ill-fated love of Silvie and Tirsis. The shepherdess Silvie describes the situation: she has made Tirsis fall in love with her without thinking about it *(sans y penser),* but he has also claimed her heart.

Figure 4.1 Portrait of Cardinal Pietro Ottoboni (Rome, c. 1700–1705) by Francesco Trevisani (1656–1746). The Bowes Museum, Barnard Castle (Durham, England).

Tirsis decries the infidelity of women and of Silvie in particular. Silvie declares that pleasures are fleeting and concludes, "Let us seek to enjoy its pleasures; let us love." However, in the recitative immediately following she falls into mourning over Tirsis's departure. Tirsis apparently has decided that a brief fling is not what he wants. He ends the cantata with an air in which he chooses drink as a better companion than a faithless shepherdess:

Non, non je ne puis plus souffrir	No, no, I can no longer bear
Les infidélités	The faithlessness
D'une ingrate bergère	Of an ungrateful shepherdess.
Ma bouteille sera	Now this bottle will
Désormais mon plaisir.	Henceforth be my pleasure.
Si quelquefois elle devient légère	And if perchance it gets light,
J'en suis quitte pour la remplir.	All I need to do is refill it.

Handel's setting of this cantata illustrates his extraordinary sensitivity to national styles. A true French cantata, rather than an "Italian" cantata with a French text, it captures the flow not just of French song but of the heightened speech-song of French recitative that is so different from Italian declamation. Handel seems to enjoy in particular painting the situation/sublimation in Tirsis's final air. The air begins with the first line set to a definitive full cadence to E minor; the next two lines lead to a cadence on the dominant. After this is repeated, the expectation is that the second section, following the typical binary dance pattern, will proceed to balance the first melodically and harmonically, moving back to the tonic. Handel accomplishes this with a difference. Whereas the first section is set as a four-square statement in common time, with the bass moving in rhythmic partnership with the voice, the second begins with seeming imitation for one measure, but then passes through a transitional measure of 2/4 and slides neatly into triple time for the remainder of the air. Both the interruption of duple with triple meter at the words *ma bouteille* and the use of an imitative lag between bass and voice paint an already tipsy Tirsis celebrating his decision (Ex. 4.12).

At the other end of the spectrum from Tirsis's secular and self-indulgent choice between women and wine is the stark life-choice between sensuality and spirituality. Visual representations of this decision based on the mythological choice of Hercules were among the most popular visual images of the eighteenth century.[34] Cardinal Pamphili's text for Handel's *Il trionfo del tempo* offers an allegorical representation of this dilemma: as in a traditional love triangle, Beauty is wooed by Pleasure on the one hand and, on the other, by Time assisted by Truth. Pleasure's allures are significant, seemingly including Handel as an image of same-sex desire and music (see Chapter 1), and Beauty (Pamphili himself?) is torn:

Io vorrei due cori in seno	I would like to have two hearts in my breast
Un per darlo al pentimento;	So as to give one to repentance;
Al piacer l'altro darei.	The other I would give to pleasure.

However, she/he ultimately renounces pleasure and chooses spirituality.

Pure del Cielo intelligenze eterne,	Pure and eternal spirits of heaven,
Che vera scuola a ben amare aprite,	Who disclose the true path of loving well,
Udite, angeli, udite il pianto mio.	Listen, you angels, hear my weeping.
E se la Verità dal Sole eterno	And if Truth from the eternal sun
Tragge luce immortale, e a me lo scopre,	Draws down immortal light, and reveals that to me,
Fate che al gran desio rispondan l'opre.	Grant that my good works may balance my great devotion.[35]

   The depiction of sensuality and spirituality as suitors for the soul returns us to the metaphor of the soul as a woman. Just as the image of an abandoned woman can represent a soul that feels abandoned by God, so too the pursued

Example 4.12 *Sans y penser,* "Non, non je ne puis plus souffrir," transition into triple meter.

nymph or shepherdess can represent a soul pursued by the voice of God. At issue is whether the soul, like Beauty in *Il trionfo del tempo,* will answer the call, and whether the soul will be faithful. One of Handel's multi-voice cantatas appears to depict just this theme. *Arresta il passo* stands out as the only pastoral cantata that ends with the shepherd winning the nymph, and Ursula Kirkendale has suggested a religious motive linking it to the Arcadian Academy. In a striking conjunction of classical, contemporary, and religious pastoral images, the reed pipes of the god Pan served as a symbol for the "shepherds" of the Academy; the late Queen Christina was named their *basilissa,* or empress; and the infant Jesus was chosen as their protector, for simple shepherds of Bethlehem had been the first to be told of the savior's birth.[36] Thus, Kirkendale posits that the *Dio bambin* of the text, while superficially depicting Cupid, the god of Love, metaphorically represents the infant Jesus. At the moment of her "conversion," Fillide sings of the *Dio bambin* piercing her breast:

Sento ch'il Dio bambin	I feel that the boy-god
col strale suo divin	with his divine arrow
m'ha il sen piagato.	has pierced my breast;
E già questo mio cor	And already this heart of mine
più non ricusa amor	no longer rejects love,
ed è cangiato.	and is changed.[37]

Unlike the abandoned women and the pursuing shepherds who will never change, Fillide is transformed by divine fire.

The multiformity of myth means not only that many myths tell the same story, but also that individual myths contain multiple meanings. Although *Arresta il passo* can be read as a religious allegory of the soul pursued and won by God, other interpretations also present themselves. For example, Aminta's final aria before Fillide's acceptance of his suit depicts his longing with the now familiar metaphor of the river running to the sea as an image of eternal union. That Handel was perfectly clear about the sexual meaning of this metaphor and considered it in his setting is suggested by his transfer of this remarkable aria into *Rinaldo,* placing it in the voices of Sirens who lure Rinaldo to join them in the sea (Ex. 4.13, pp. 161–162).[38]

However, going one step further, the music of "Se vago rio" is also redolent of Spanish dance with its heavily accented groups of three beats (here organized into 12/8 meter), its E-mode harmony with pervasive use of the lowered leading tone, the repeated tonic and quick turn at the cadences, and the full pizzicato string accompaniment following exactly the movement of the voice in imitation of a guitar strumming.[39] *Arresta il passo* may have been written at the same time as Handel's Spanish cantata, *No se emenderá jamás,* and the Spanish flavor here

Example 4.13a *Arresta il passo,* "Se vago rio."

implies the possibility of a political interpretation of the pursuit story: just as Aminta successfully woos Fillide, Spain was successfully pursuing Rome, or Ruspoli specifically, as an ally in the War of Spanish Succession. *Arresta il passo,* therefore, can be interpreted as a political allegory, as a straightforward and unusually successful love story, or as a religious allegory. Given the recognized flexibility of the pursuit myth, there is no reason to assume that only one interpretation is valid. For the Roman Arcadians, probably all three of these meanings were immediately audible, and it is likely that the multiple levels of meaning are what made these pastoral stories so appealing to eighteenth-century audiences. *Arresta il passo* depicts a pursuit that is at once sexual, religious, and political.

Like *Arresta il passo,* the myth of Apollo and Daphne can be read in multiple ways. Campbell's interpretation, based on this theory of "monomyth," describes Daphne as the "hero" who, frozen by the "power of the fixating parent," refuses the "call to adventure."[40] The religious reading is similar, casting Daphne as the soul who refuses the god's call; as a result she is rendered spiritually dead, leaving the god to weep over her in the final aria, "Cara pianta." Both interpretations, however, derive from a focus on Daphne. The story is at least as important from the point of view of Apollo, who is forced to accept a sublimated object of desire—the laurel wreath of poetry or military victory rather than the consummation of sexual love. A dominant image in Petrarch's poems, where the transformation of love into poetry—Laura into *lauro*—is a core topic, the experience of Apollo would certainly have continued to be heard as a significant part of the Apollo and Daphne story by the literary community of Italy. Apollo's acceptance of a sublimated love object may also have held special importance for Handel, who had already set a different version of the story in Hamburg.

The libretto of Handel's Hamburg version of the Apollo and Daphne story, by Heinrich Hinsch, is bursting with additional incident and characters and is

Example 4.13b *Rinaldo,* "Il vostro maggio."

quite different from the Ovidian version that provides the basis of Handel's Italian cantata. Once set to music, the opera was so long that it had to be split into two: *Der beglückte Florindo* (Fortunate Florindo) and *Die verwandelte Daphne* (Transformed Daphne). As in Ovid's *Metamorphoses,* Apollo has just rid the countryside of a dangerous dragon called Python, and he boasts that his arrows are stronger than Cupid's. Cupid wounds Apollo with love's arrow just as Daphne is about to crown him with flowers for his heroism. So far the story, although more detailed, follows Ovid's narration. The opera differs from Ovid in that Daphne has pledged her love to Florindo; thus—parallel to Galatea's rejection of Polyphemus—she rebuffs Apollo's suit because she loves another. Nevertheless, Cupid, worried that she will yield, wounds her with one of Vulcan's lead arrows, causing her to spurn all love. As a result, she interrupts her wedding ceremony and renounces love. This leads to multiple complications: Florindo and Apollo continue to pursue Daphne; the deceitful shepherdess Lycoris says she has seen Daphne embracing a satyr; the shepherd Damon, deceived by Lycoris, says that Daphne has made advances to him; and Apollo says Daphne has made advances to him as well. Daphne prays to her father to prove her innocence, and in the middle of her aria she is turned into a laurel tree. Apollo acknowledges Cupid's power and accepts the laurel as his special tree. Florindo accepts the loss of Daphne and embraces another nymph, Alfirena, in her stead. Daphne, a victim of Cupid's pride, is guiltless, but loses all: her love and her human life.

The score for *Florindo* and *Daphne* does not survive. The libretto itself lacks the power and concision of the later Italian cantata, but it is interesting to see from the text that even in this version, Daphne's transformation interrupts the flow of an aria. Among the musical fragments associated with the opera, one seems to be the model for the second-movement minuet of the instrumental sonata that opens *Amarilli vezzosa* and also forms the basis of its concluding duet.[41] It seems likely that Handel would also have recalled his earlier setting when faced with the Italian version and perhaps borrowed from it. Would that it were possible to compare the musical settings of the transformation scenes in the two works. In the cantata, Daphne's metamorphosis is musically remarkable (see Ex. 4.4 above). Following it, Apollo's aria, which concludes the cantata, represents his own transformation, from the *piante* (steps) of the preceding chase ("Mie piante correte") depicting him as pursuer, to the *pianti* (tears) of a forsaken lover, to the poet who accepts the laurel (*pianta* [plant]) as a sublimation for love. Even though *pianta* initially precedes *pianti* in the text, just as Daphne's transformation precedes Apollo's tears, Handel eliminates the phrase *co' miei pianti* ("with my tears") on the repetition of the A section text and reverses the opening two words (from *cara pianta* to *pianta cara*), making it clear that the laurel crown will survive the tears and that the verbal progression from *piante* to *pianti* to *pianta* symbolizes the artist's journey of creation and transformation from pursuit through pain to poetry.

Cara pianta, co' miei pianti	Beloved plant, with my tears
il tuo verde irrigherò.	I will water your leaves;
De' tuoi rami trionfanti	With your triumphal branches,
sommi eroi coronerò.	I will crown the greatest heroes.
Se non posso averti in seno,	If I cannot have you on my breast,
Dafne, almeno	Daphne, at least
sovra il crin ti porterò.[42]	I will wear you on my brow.[42]

This measured lament projects a sense of nobility and restraint. Having failed in his pursuit of Daphne, Apollo remains in control of his art and must do so in order to wear the laurel. Not for him the out-of-control abandonment of women's voices: he acknowledges and embraces the sublimation of sensual pleasure in art (Ex. 4.14).

Example 4.14 *Apollo e Dafne,* "Cara pianta."

Apollo's restraint and control, his artistic if not sexual success, can be compared to the depiction of Polyphemus. Of course, from the point of view of Acis and Galatea, and probably that of the entire wedding party in Naples, this story is about undying love and fidelity, in which Polyphemus represents an implacable obstacle. However, from Polyphemus's point of view, the story is one of failed pursuit. When Galatea declares her steadfast refusal of the Cyclops in the *Aci* libretto by comparing herself to a laurel, the connection to Apollo's similarly failed suit is made manifest. As in *Idyll* XI by Theocritus, Polyphemus fails in his suit because he and Galatea are mismatched and because he fails as a singer. However, his artistic excesses, which as in Ovid demonstrate his monstrosity, prevent either catharsis (as in *Idyll* XI) or sublimation (as in the Apollo myth). The arias that depict Polyphemus's anguish ("Sibilar l'angui d'Aletto") or rage ("Precipitoso nel mar"), although tumultuous and frightening, are accurate portraits of the giant's size and strength. It is in his love pangs that Handel's Polyphemus so clearly reveals his lack of artistic finesse. He sings of his plight by comparing himself to a confused moth, a common operatic metaphor.[43]

Fra l'ombre e gl'orrori	Amid shadows and gloom,
farfalla confusa	when the torch is put out,
già spenta la face	the bewildered moth
non sa mai goder.	can never find joy.
Così fra timori	Thus amid its fears
quest'alma delusa	My deluded spirit
non trova mai pace	finds no peace
né spera piacer.	nor hopes for pleasure.

Handel's setting of this text translates the excesses of Ovid's Polyphemus into music. He depicts Polyphemus's gigantism in outsized arpeggios and leaps. First the moth descends into the horrid shadows in descending arpeggios covering an octave and a fifth. Then it flutters upward in sixteenth notes but falls precipitously over as much as two octaves. The accompaniment adds to the picture: the slow eighth-note pulsing motion of the muted violins (with recorder doubling the first violin at the octave) apparently depicts the wing motion of the moth, while orchestral trills, extending even into the lowest bass register, illustrate its futile fluttering. In its bass sonorities, prodigious range, and orchestral accompaniment, the aria portrays a moth of terrifying and prehistoric proportions (Ex. 4.15). As in Ovid's depiction, one has to admire the virtuosity (here of the performer as well as the composer) while recognizing the joke. In effect, both Ovid and Handel take on the role played by Damoetas in Theocritus's *Idyll* VI, who proves his worth by wittily conjuring up the love-sick giant.

Unlike Theocritus's Cyclops, however, Handel's Polyphemus forfeits his art

Example 4.15 *Aci, Galatea e Polifemo,* "Fra l'ombre e gl'orrori."

Example 4.15 *(continued)*

as well as his love; in the last dramatic scene of the cantata, Polyphemus fails to raise his song into aria form, and he loses own voice, singing the words of Acis in accompanied recitative (the beginning of which is given in Ex. 4.16 and in the following text).

Stupido! ma che veggio?
Aci, disciolto in fiume,
siegue l'amato bene, e mormorando
così si va lagnando:
Vissi fedel, mia vita,
e morto ancor t'adoro;
e de' miei chiari argenti
col mormorio sonoro
non lascio di spiegare i miei tormenti.

Fool that I am! but what do I see?
Acis, dissolved into a river,
follows his beloved, and in his murmuring
laments thus:
Faithfully I lived, O my life,
and in death I still adore you;
and in the murmuring sound
of my bright silvery waters
I shall not fail to make known my
          torments.

Example 4.16 *Aci, Galatea e Polifemo,* "Stupido! ma che veggio?"

Polyphemus begins, like the Cyclops in Theocritus, by calling himself to attention ("Cyclops, Cyclops! Where is this mad flight taking you?"), but rather than
finding relief and identity in his work, he is left voiceless. This point is made
particularly clear in the libretto, not only by the use of recitative text but by
having Polyphemus's echo of Acis's watery voice itself echo Acis's first words in

the cantata, where he compares himself to a stream that murmurs in silvery steps. Handel emphasizes the point musically by setting Polyphemus's words in simple recitative, only heightening Acis's words with *accompagnato*.

The story of pursuit can be told and interpreted in many ways, and Handel's pastoral and mythological multi-voice cantatas offer multiple versions that suggest multiple readings. Furthermore, the multi-vocality of these myths demands that, even within a single reading, we hear the multiple voices. Listening to Handel's setting of *Apollo e Dafne* or *Aci, Galatea e Polifemo* is, as Wendy Doniger writes of all myth, somewhat similar to listening to the quartet from *Rigoletto*, "when each character speaks from his or her heart, each voice contributing to a single tapestry of song."[44] One must listen to the voice (story) of Apollo as well as the voice of Daphne, to the voice of Polyphemus as well as the voices of Acis and Galatea.

For Handel and his patrons, one important element of these pastoral and mythological stories must have been their depiction of the sublimation of sensual pleasure. Related to the choice of Hercules, Handel's setting of Pamphili's *Il trionfo del tempo* depicts the "love triangle" of sensual pleasure, spiritual truth, and the soul. In *Il trionfo del tempo* the soul (Beauty) rejects Pleasure for Truth only with difficulty. *Arresta il passo*, viewed as a religious allegory, portrays the difficulty with which Aminta (God or his representative) woos and wins the faithful love of Fillide (the soul). As frequently depicted in eighteenth-century painting illustrating moral choice, the sublimation of sensuality in spirituality represented the desirable but more difficult path.

It was perhaps easier for men simply to give up women as inconstant and deceitful. Even to flirt with them was dangerous, in part because it led to a loss of freedom and control. Orpheus, despite his extraordinary artistic powers, loses control of himself (and looks back) because of a woman. Nero (in Handel's *Agrippina*) happily gives up Poppea for the throne, so as not to lose political power. In Handel's opera of 1732, Orlando goes mad because of the love of a woman; when he is returned to his senses he gives the woman to his rival, saying of himself: "He quell'd inchantments, and in combat conquer'd, and often laid the fiercest monsters low; now he's victorious o'er himself, and Love."[45] Among Handel's multi-voice cantatas, Tirsis in *Sans y penser* (comically) prefers the bottle (and the resultant lack of control it brings) to an unfaithful woman. More seriously, in the original ending of *Cor fedele* Tirsi and Fileno choose male friendship over Clori's inconstancy. Although this could mean a retreat from sensual pleasure (as perhaps occurs with Orlando), it could also represent the path taken by Orpheus, and more scandalously by Nero, to same-sex relationships. Orpheus says (in the words of Poliziano), "Let the love of woman bind me no longer . . ., the married man I urge to seek divorce, and all to flee the company of women," and turns to pederasty. In one of its possible readings for some portion of his audience, Handel's *Cor fedele* depicts the sublimation of the love of woman in same-sex love between men.

Most important for the artist among the images of sublimation in these cantatas is the replacement of love (or love of women) with art. In Theocritus's *Idyll* XI, as we have seen, Polyphemus cures himself with art: "In this way did Polyphemus shepherd his love with song / and he found a readier cure than if he had paid hard cash." The myth of Apollo and Daphne makes sublimation a central part of Apollo's story: he accepts the laurel rather than the nymph. The myth of Polyphemus, in Ovid's and Handel's versions, can be read as a variant of Apollo's. Like Apollo, Polyphemus desires a water nymph, but, unlike Apollo, his art is not adequate for catharsis or sublimation; by the end of the cantata his voice is silenced. As with the love of women, the issue is one of control. By the time of the composition of *Aci, Galatea e Polifemo* Handel's style in the continuo cantata had moved from an emotionally charged (female) voice to a (masculine) voice tightly controlled by artifice. Polyphemus loses his quest because his voice, like a woman's voice, lacks this control. In *Aci, Galatea e Polifemo* and *Apollo e Dafne,* two multi-voice cantatas that represent the culmination of his Italian visit, Handel clearly affirms, in Polyphemus's loss of voice, the importance of artistic control and illustrates, in Apollo's lament, the ideal possibility of sublimating sexuality in artistic excellence.

5

Silence and Secrecy

A Break, or Pause in Poetry is sometimes more significant than any Thing, that might have been said; so in Music, a Rest in its proper Place has often a wonderful Effect, and from the Beauty of its Surprize, makes the Suspension of Harmony itself agreeable.

Hildebrand Jacob, *Of the Sister Arts; An Essay* (1734)

There is no binary division to be made between what one says and what one does not say; we must try to determine the different ways of not saying such things, how those who can and those who cannot speak of them are distributed, which type of discourse is authorized, or which form of discretion is required in either case. There is not one but many silences, and they are an integral part of the strategies that underlie and permeate discourse.

Michel Foucault, *The History of Sexuality* (1978)

After Handel left Italy, he continued to live and work within the patronage system. In June 1710 he accepted a position as *maestro di cappella* at the court of Hanover, but with advance permission to "be absent for a twelve-month or more, if he chose it; and to go whithersoever he pleased."[1] By the end of 1710 he had arrived in London, where he performed for Queen Anne and composed his first opera for the English stage. In Hanover again by mid-1711, Handel was back in London by the autumn of 1712. During his first sojourn in London, Handel seems to have attended and played at musicales arranged in private homes. Some of these were hosted by well-to-do merchants, such as Mr. Thomas Britton, the "Small-Coal Man," famous for presenting what were long thought to be the first public music concerts in London.[2] Others were held in the homes of the aristocracy, much like the weekly *conversazioni* at Rome in the houses of Ottoboni, Pamphili, and Ruspoli. Sir John Hawkins tells us that "at that time there were weekly concerts at the houses of the duke of Rutland, the earls of Burlington and Essex, lord Percival, father of the late earl of Egmont, and others of the nobility."[3] Handel most likely met Lord Burlington through this network of private concerts, and in 1712 he was invited to reside at Burlington House. Hawkins paints a vivid picture of this arrangement:

Handel received a pressing invitation from the earl of Burlington, whose love
of music was equal to his skill in architecture and his passion for other liberal
studies, to make his house in Piccadilly the place of his abode. Into this hospi-
table mansion was Handel received, and left at liberty to follow the dictates of
his genius and invention, assisting frequently at evening concerts, in which his
own music made the most considerable part. The course of his studies during
three years residence at Burlington-house, was very regular and uniform: his
mornings were employed in study, and at dinner he sat down with men of the
first eminence for genius and abilities of any in the kingdom. Here he frequently met Pope, Gay, Dr. Arbuthnot, and others of that class.[4]

This lively arrangement must have been suspended for a year beginning in May
1714 when Burlington left for the Continent, but may have resumed after April
1715 on his return: Handel's opera *Amadigi* (1715) is dedicated to Burlington and
described as composed in his "Family."

By 4 August 1717, Handel's presence is documented in Cannons outside London at the villa of James Brydges, then Earl of Carnarvon and in 1719 created
Duke of Chandos (by which title I will refer to him here). By 1719, Handel was
primarily engaged in the establishment of the Royal Academy of Music for the
production of Italian opera in London, for which purpose he traveled to the
Continent to hire singers. From this year Handel's principal activity became
that of public opera composer, and in July 1723 a move into his own house in
Brook Street finally ended the period of private cantata composition that had
begun on his arrival in Italy and was coterminous with his residence at aristocratic houses.

The cantatas that Handel composed in England between 1710 and 1722 cannot all be dated with pinpoint accuracy, although the evidence provided by
their paper clearly proves their English origin.[5] As a set, this group is more dif-
fuse than any from Italy: the compositions cover a much broader period of
time, and many cannot be assigned to a specific patron. Nevertheless, their distinguishing attributes are familiar. As in Italy, the solo cantatas can be divided
on the basis of their accompaniment: either continuo or instrumental. The
London continuo group is further divided between newly composed works and
revisions that probably were made for pedagogical use. Although some of the
revisions probably were composed after 1723, when Handel became music tutor
to the royal princesses, they are included here because of their proximity to the
main compositional group and for the information they provide on Handel's
stylistic development. All of these new and revised solo cantatas are set to Italian
texts. In addition Handel composed two large-scale, multi-voice works with
English texts at Cannons in 1718: *Esther* and *Acis and Galatea*. As private music
in the sphere of oratorio and serenata, these can be directly compared with
Handel's Italian-texted *Il trionfo del tempo* (Rome, 1707) and *Aci, Galatea e*

Table 5.1   Handel's London solo cantatas

New Works	
CONTINUO	INSTRUMENTAL
Bella ma ritrosetta	*Splenda l'alba*
Deh! lasciate	*Mi palpita il cor* (HWV 132c with flute)
Dolc'è pur d'amor l'affanno	*Crudel tiranno Amor*
Ho fuggito	
L'aure grate	
Siete rose	
Son gelsomino	

Revised Cantatas	
Dolc'è pur d'amor l'affanno (HWV 109b)	*Mi palpita il cor* (HWV 132b with oboe)
E partirai, mia vita? (HWV 111b)	
Lungi dal mio bel nume (HWV 127c)	
Mi palpita il cor (HWV 132a; revision of *Dimmi,*	
O mio cor [HWV 106])	
Ninfe e pastori (HWV 139c)	
Sei pur bella (HWV 160c)	
Sento là che ristretto (HWV 161c)	
Se pari è la tua fé (HWV 158c)	
Son gelsomino (HWV 164a)	

Polifemo (Naples, 1708) and will form the basis of the next chapter. The solo cantatas, both continuo and instrumental, will be the focus of this chapter. The English set of Italian-language solo cantatas is shown in Table 5.1.

Despite being spread over a much longer time span than any set of continuo cantatas identified in Italy, the London set is equally, if not more, consistent in its stylistic features. A comparison with the Italian cantatas is generally illustrative.[6] Of the three London instrumental cantatas, none depicts a named singer (as was typical of the early Italian instrumental cantatas, such as *Armida* and *Abdolonymus*) and all adhere to a reduced formal scheme typical of Handel's later works. *Crudel tiranno Amor* (1722) is the longest, with three arias (ArArA). *Mi palpita il cor* follows the more typical rArA pattern, with the inclusion in the first recitative of an arioso that Handel must have liked particularly: not only did he use it repeatedly in variant revisions of this cantata, but he also appended it to the opening of his revision of the continuo cantata *Dimmi, O mio cor.* *Splenda l'alba* is based on a further reduced scheme of ArA. Remarkably, all seven of the continuo cantatas also fall into the pattern ArA. Moreover, the bit of recitative remaining is reduced in its musical function to a harmonic transition between the arias, which often are in strikingly distant keys. This change is evidenced in the scores by the lack of key signature in the recitatives of all but what is perhaps the first of the cantatas, *Bella ma ritrosetta*. The regular use of recitative key signatures in Handel's cantatas composed in Italy typifies the seventeenth-century conception of the cantata, where ariosos and arias bloom out of the recitative frame; in the London cantatas, by contrast, the arias take over the structural role and are joined by connective, recitative tissue. The rather sharp distinction between the cantatas written in Italy and in England can be illustrated more specifically with a comparison of two continuo cantatas: *Figli del mesto cor* (Rome, 1707?) and *Ho fuggito* (London, c. 1718).

Figli del mesto cor begins and ends in recitative in the pattern rArAr. It opens and closes in D minor and is in flat keys throughout, the first recitative and aria carrying a signature of one flat, the second recitative and aria two flats, and the final recitative one flat. The recitatives provide the cantata's harmonic structure, in which the arias represent expanded moments. Each aria flows unceasingly. "Son pur le lacrime," for example, has no rests whatsoever, the lack of any break making the rhythm feel particularly relentless. Handel enhances this effect through his use of melismas on the final syllable of words, creating a sense of wordless wailing as he connects the phrases. Disjunct motion also creates striking effects in the vocal line of both the recitative and aria, while dissonance and chromaticism pervade the harmony. All these traits assist in providing a general feeling appropriate to the text (Ex. 5.1).

Son pur le lacrime	Tears are still
Il cibo misero	The wretched food
Ch'io prendo ognor.	That I always take.
Sempre tra gemiti	Always groaning,
Non spiro altr'aere	I breathe no other air
Che del dolor.	Than that of sorrow.

Ho fuggito, by contrast, follows the formal scheme of ArA. There is no recitative framework to provide a harmonic structure, and the cantata, as is typical of the English works, begins and ends in different keys: the first aria is in A minor, the second in D major. The medial recitative carries no key signature and functions primarily to move the harmony from the key of the first aria to that of the second. The shift in function for recitatives from underlying the harmonic fabric to bridging a harmonic disjunction parallels a concurrent change in Handel's compositional process. Whereas in works written in Italy Handel seems to have composed his scores from beginning to end (*Rodrigo* provides a clear example), he began in London to compose the arias first and fill in the recitatives only afterwards. In the new paradigm, a harmonic link, put in place only after the aria was fully composed, between the cadence of the recitative and the cadence of the B section of the following aria became the one essential relationship between an aria and the preceding recitative.[7] As is typical of Handel's mature works, the recitative cadence in *Ho fuggito* (F-sharp minor) previews the cadential key of the B section of the following aria.

Example 5.1 *Figli del mesto cor,* "Son pur le lacrime."

"Ho fuggito," the first aria of the cantata, describes a process of breaking free of the bonds of love but then voluntarily returning to captivity. The A section reads:

Ho fuggito Amor anch'io,	I too have fled from Love,
Ho spezzato i lacci suoi:	I have broken its bonds:
Ma che poi?	But what then?
Son tornato in servitù.	I have returned into bondage.

Handel's setting of this text is both less atmospheric and more sophisticated than his treatment of *Figli del mesto cor;* it represents not a continuous outpouring of emotion but a struggle to remain in control. The angular opening melody is embodied in a finely chiseled rhythmic pattern that, alternating between dotted quarter and dotted eighth groups, never repeats from measure to measure. The punchy rhythm and irregular melody perfectly depict the singer's "breaking the bonds" of love. Following the question, "But what then?" Handel provides a silent pause in the music, after which the "return to bondage" is portrayed with a simple scale running down to the tonic. On the repetition of this question and answer, Handel expands the "return" by a deflection into a deceptive cadence. However, the apparent resistance or hesitation is quickly overcome on the second try, making the sense of servitude all the more final (Ex. 5.2).

The use of a pause after a question is not unusual; Handel does much the same in Tirsi's aria "Quell'erbetta" from *Cor fedele* (see Ex. 4.11), although the pause there, in all but one instance, is in the voice alone. What is striking about "Ho fuggito" is that the silences not only grow in length but begin to infect other sections of the text. First, Handel introduces a complete silence not just after the question, but also after the statement about breaking the bonds of love. This pause previews the "What then?" question by indicating a lack of achievement or arrival or, perhaps, the emptiness that causes the question to be asked. Then, in the final section of the aria, Handel once again provides a deceptive cadence on the phrase "I have returned into bondage," but this time, rather than immediately quashing the hesitation with a full cadence, Handel further

Example 5.2 *Ho fuggito,* "Ho fuggito," mm. 5–17.

Example 5.3 *Ho fuggito,* "Ho fuggito," mm. 19–35.

extends the struggle. As the singer begins to repeat the text, he stops after the first two words *(son tornato),* and the entire musical fabric is broken for two full quarter-note rests before the singer can start again and speak the whole phrase ending with the words *in servitù* ("I have returned"—[break]—"into bond-age"). The final vocal cadence with its falling fifth and rising sixth seems to be dragged out of the singer (Ex. 5.3). Thus in "Ho fuggito," as in other of the English cantatas, Handel's use of silence moves far beyond the kind of text painting that would include a rest after a question. Here the silence represents a deep-seated difficulty with expression and a momentary inability to continue.

The increased use of silence in Handel's work in England coincides with an in-creased use and appreciation of gaps and silences in literature and drama; this was a period of heightened political and social tensions that also emphasized the value of silence and secrecy. Handel cannot have been unaware of the tensions and factions swirling around him. During his years in Italy, he maneuvered, ap-parently successfully, around both sides of the War of Spanish Succession. Upon leaving Italy he was forced into ever more delicate situations not only concern-ing that war, but also in regard to both the Hanoverian Succession in England

and the Jacobite threat to that succession. He must have learned early the value of personal silence (not to be confused with humility), both as one who benefited from the patronage system and as a composer dependent on his public. In the face of Handel's careful preservation of his music manuscripts, the lack of surviving letters, notebooks, or other personal documents implies a decision on his part not to keep such material. His silence leaves many gaps in our knowledge of his final months in Italy and subsequent travel.

Handel's biographical trail begins to fade immediately after the performance in Rome on 9 September 1708 of the dramatic cantata *Oh, come chiare*. Despite such specific markers as the performances of *Agrippina* in Venice from late December 1709 to late January 1710 and the clear documentation of his appointment in Hanover on 16 June 1710, his tracks remain indistinct even after his arrival in England late in the same year. The questions begin with Handel's last year in Italy. If he traveled to Florence for the autumn 1708 opera season, as he had the previous year, he would have heard G. A. Perti's *Ginevra*. Handel's use of this libretto as the basis of his opera *Ariodante* (1734) strengthens the likelihood of his presence in Florence, as it fits into a pattern of adaptations of librettos from performances Handel himself probably had attended.[8] Because copying bills for some of Handel's cantatas appear in the Ruspoli accounts on 28 February and 31 August 1709, it has been suggested that after the opera seasons in Florence and Venice Handel again spent time in Rome.[9] However, of the twenty-four works listed during that year, at least seventeen can be dated earlier, most with absolute certainty; thus Handel's presence in Rome during 1709 has to be considered very doubtful, especially so in Ruspoli's household after the appointment in March 1709 of Antonio Caldara as Ruspoli's *maestro di cappella*. Moreover, it would have been an interesting year in which to spend more time in Florence, given the marriage of the former cardinal Francesco Maria de' Medici and the related visit of one of Handel's Roman patrons, Cardinal Ottoboni. Furthermore, the set of continuo cantatas on northern Italian paper associated with 1708/1709 places Handel most likely in Florence or Venice. On 9 November 1709, Prince Ferdinand de' Medici wrote a letter recommending Handel to Duke Karl Philipp von Neuberg at Innsbruck.[10] Assuming that Handel was in Florence at least at this point, the letter probably signals Handel's final departure from that city.[11] Handel was undoubtedly in Venice for the performance of his opera *Agrippina* at the Teatro San Giovanni Grisostomo, the second opera performed during the Venetian season and the first of carnival season in 1709/1710.[12] It premiered on 26 December, and Mainwaring writes that it played for "twenty-seven nights successively."[13] After this, in early 1710, Handel quitted Italy.

Although it is easy in hindsight to attribute direction to what were possibly unpremeditated wanderings, Handel does seem to have moved with decision from Venice to Hanover. On 9 March 1710, Karl Philipp wrote back to Ferdinand that Handel had not needed his assistance. By early June, Handel was in Hanover, and he was appointed Kappellmeister, or *maestro di cappella,* on 16 June 1710.[14] The Electress Sophie (mother of the Elector Georg Ludwig, later George I of England) writes in a letter dated 4 June 1710 of "the music of a Saxon who surpasses everyone who has ever been heard in harpsichord-playing and composition," adding that "he was much admired in Italy." Ten days later, she confirms Handel's appointment in Hanover: "There is not much to say from here except that the elector has taken on a Master of the Chapel named Handel, who plays marvellously on the harpsichord."[15] The question remains what drew Handel to Hanover.

The Electress offers some tantalizing personal information about Handel: "He is quite a handsome man, and gossip says that he has been in love with Victoria." This Victoria can likely be identified as the singer Vittoria Tarquini, called la Bombace ("the bombshell"), who is romantically linked with Handel by Mainwaring:

> VITTORIA, who was much admired both as an Actress, and a Singer, bore a principal part in this Opera [*Rodrigo*]. She was a fine woman, and had for some time been much in the good graces of his Serene Highness [Prince Ferdinand]. But, from the natural restlesness [*sic*] of certain hearts, so little sensible was she of her exalted situation [as mistress of Ferdinand], that she conceived a design of transferring her affections to another person. HANDEL's youth and comeliness, joined with his fame and abilities in Music, had made impressions on her heart. Tho' she had the art to conceal them for the present, she had not perhaps the power, certainly not the intention, to efface them.[16]

Mainwaring associates Vittoria not only with *Rodrigo,* but also with *Agrippina* and, possibly, with the cantata *Apollo e Dafne*:

> This Opera [*Agrippina*] drew over all the best singers from the other houses. Among the foremost of these was the famous VITTORIA, who a little before HANDEL's removal to Venice had obtained permission of the grand Duke to sing in one of the houses there. At [the opera] AGRIPPINA her inclinations gave new lustre to her talents. HANDEL seemed almost as great and majestic as APOLLO, and it was far from the lady's intention to be so cruel and obstinate as DAPHNE.[17]

The mention here of Apollo and Daphne might offer evidence of the Italian origins of *Apollo e Dafne,* except that the cast lists of *Rodrigo* and *Agrippina* do not

Figure 5.1 Portrait miniature of Handel (c. 1710) by Christoph Platzer (photograph of lost original). Händel-Haus, Halle.

corroborate the participation of Vittoria in these performances, making Main-waring's whole account doubtful.

Vittoria is listed in 1707 among the singers in the service of Ferdinand,[18] and she had a leading role in the September production of *Dionisio re di Portogallo* (music by Perti; libretto by Antonio Salvi),[19] an opera Handel most likely heard (as he was in Florence for the performance of his *Rodrigo* later that autumn) and whose libretto was later adapted for him in London under the title *Sosarme*.[20] In addition to being Ferdinand's mistress, Vittoria was the wife of the composer

Jean-Baptiste Farinel (b. 1655), whom she had married in 1689.[21] Electress Sophie's particular interest in the rumored relationship arises from the fact that Farinel was a violinist and composer in the service of the Elector.

Whether or not a personal reason played a role in attracting Handel to Hanover (and if he did indeed have an affair with Vittoria, the city in which her husband was employed might not have been an obvious first choice), he would surely have been drawn at least in part by musical motives. Hawkins quotes Handel as saying:

> When I first arrived in Hanover I was a young man, under twenty [he was twenty-five]; I was acquainted with the merits of Steffani [a copy of this composer's chamber duets owned by Handel is dated Rome, 1706],[22] and he had heard of me. I understood somewhat of music, and . . . could play pretty well on the organ [this, of course, is ingenuous understatement]; he received me with great kindness, and took an early opportunity to introduce me to the princess Sophia [the Dowager Electress Sophie] and the elector's son [Georg August, later George II of Great Britain, a man of Handel's age], giving them to understand, that I was what he was pleased to call a virtuoso in music; he obliged me with instructions for my conduct and behavior during my residence at Hanover; and being called from the city to attend to matters of public concern, he left me in possession of that favour and patronage which himself had enjoyed for a series of years.[23]

Although it is possible to confirm Steffani's presence in Hanover at this time,[24] his tenure as *maestro di cappella* ran only from 1688 to 1696, after which his service to the Elector was in the field of diplomacy.[25] Furthermore, at the death of the previous Elector and the accession of Georg Ludwig in 1698, the Court Opera in Hanover had been suspended. Handel's appointment to the position of *maestro di cappella* may indicate an attempt to revive opera in Hanover, but it is also possible that it represents a diplomatic maneuver of some sort. As Vitali suggests, Prince Ferdinand's letter to Karl Philipp at Innsbruck, which speaks of Handel's "honest sentiments, civility of manners, and full command of several languages, and a talent more than mediocre in music," implies that the composer was being recommended to that court for "diplomatic activities in the manner of Agostino Steffani."[26] Not only the diplomatic service Steffani had already provided to the Hanover court, but also the fact that the Elector, on becoming George I, appointed the composer Farinel as the Hanoverian resident, raises the possibility that Handel was similarly engaged to fill such a position.

Most likely, Handel made his decision to go to Hanover in Venice. He probably met Prince Ernst August II, younger brother to the Hanoverian Elector Georg Ludwig, in that city during the 1707–1708 season,[27] and during the

1709–1710 season he met the Baron Johann Adolf Freiherr von Kielmansegge, the Elector's deputy master of the horse. As Mainwaring writes,

> At Hanover there was also a Nobleman who had taken great notice of HAN-DEL in Italy. . . . This person was Baron KILMANSECK. He introduced him at court, and so well recommended him to his Electoral Highness, that he immediately offered him a pension of 1500 Crowns per annum as an inducement to stay. Tho' such an offer from a Prince of his character was not to be neglected, HANDEL loved liberty too well to accept it hastily, and without reserve. He told the Baron how much he owed to his kind and effectual recommendation, as well as to his Highness's goodness and generosity. But he also expressed his apprehensions that the favour intended him would hardly be consistent either with the promise he had actually made to visit the court of the Elector Palatine, or with the resolution he had long taken to pass over into England, for the sake of seeing that of LONDON. Upon this objection, the Baron consulted his Highness's pleasure, and HANDEL was then acquainted, that neither his promise nor his resolution should be superseded by his acceptance of the pension proposed. He had leave to be absent for a twelve-month or more, if he chose it; and to go whithersoever he pleased. On these easy conditions he thankfully accepted it.[28]

Thus Kielmansegge's offer of a position could explain Handel's choice of Hanover as a destination, his quick departure from the court at Innsbruck to which he had an introduction from Prince Ferdinand, and the speed of his employment after his arrival.[29]

The Elector Palatine at Düsseldorf, Johann Wilhelm, was married to Anna de' Medici, sister to Gian Gastone and Ferdinand. Handel's sense of obligation to visit this court undoubtedly derived from Prince Ferdinand himself, to whom the Elector Palatine wrote on 13 September 1710 that "the virtuoso Handel" had been with them for some weeks, sharing with them "all his singular talents for which he enjoys a just place in your kind estimation."[30] There were, however, also relations between Düsseldorf and the court at Hanover. Not only was the Dowager Electress Sophie related to the Palatinate family, but Steffani had served this court from 1703 to 1709, primarily in areas of diplomacy.[31] For political reasons, then, the court of Hanover would not have minded the idea of Handel visiting Düsseldorf. It also would not have balked at his spending some time in London.

With the impending Hanoverian succession to the throne of England, there was a good deal of interest in Hanover about Queen Anne's health and other events in London. The Queen had refused requests from the Hanoverian court to send a member of the family to London, but a Hanoverian Resident,

Christoph Friedrich Kreyenberg, did take up a position in London from September 1710, and a number of Hanoverian diplomats served as special envoys.[32] Given the proven diplomatic service of Steffani (and the historical use of musicians in diplomatic business), the placement of a composer employed by the Hanoverian court in London might have seemed advantageous. The arrangement gave Handel the means to accomplish his stated goal of traveling to England and provided the Hanoverian court with another presence in the English capital city. Kielmansegge, who continued to play a role in Handel's career after the Elector was crowned King of England, may have recognized this mutually advantageous possibility when, and if, he first approached Handel.

Thus, despite his formal employment there, Handel spent little time in Hanover. He was appointed in June 1710 and by September had already visited and left Düsseldorf. Mainwaring writes that "the Elector Palatine was much pleased with the punctual performance of his promise, but as much disappointed to find that he was engaged elsewhere."[33] Handel must have arrived in London shortly thereafter in the autumn of 1710. He returned to Hanover again by traveling through Düsseldorf; letters from the Elector Palatine dated 17 June 1711 to the Hanoverian Elector and the Dowager Electress express apologies for detaining Handel. Handel may have attended the baptism of his niece at Halle in November 1711, and less than a year later, in October 1712, he was back in London for good.[34]

When Handel first arrived in London, probably late in 1710, the Hanoverian court undoubtedly provided entrée, for Handel was quickly welcomed at court. On 6 February 1711, an Italian "dialogue" was performed in honor of the Queen's birthday "set to excellent Musick by the famous Mr. *Hendel,* a Retainer to the Court of *Hanover,* in the Quality of Director of his Electoral Highness's Chapple."[35] Handel also had other English contacts. Among them was Charles Montagu, Fourth Earl of Manchester, British ambassador in Venice, who brought the castrato Nicolini (Nicolò Grimaldi) to London for the 1708–1709 season.[36] Handel would probably also have retained letters of introduction from the English Resident in Hamburg, John Wych.[37] Through these and other contacts, Handel had access to a wide spectrum of London society.

February 1711 brought Handel not only a performance at court but also a great public triumph in the production of his first London opera, *Rinaldo.* When he returned to Hanover shortly thereafter, it was with royal encouragement to find his way as soon as possible to London again. According to Mainwaring, he had promised to do so:

> When he took leave of the Queen at her court, and expressed his sense of the favours conferred on him, her Majesty was pleased to add to them by large presents, and to intimate her desire of seeing him again. Not a little flattered

with such marks of approbation from so illustrious a personage, he promised to return, the moment he could obtain permission from the Prince, in whose service he was retained.[38]

That Handel planned for this return is clear from his contacts with friends and musicians not of the aristocracy. He wrote in French to his German compatriot, the composer Andreas Roner, in London:

Please convey my best compliments to Mr. Hughes. I shall take the liberty of writing to him at the earliest opportunity. If however he wishes to honour me with his commands and add thereto one of his charming poems in English, that will afford me the greatest possible pleasure. Since I left you I have made some progress in that language.[39]

Handel's cantata *Venus and Adonis* with a text by John Hughes may therefore be the first English text set by Handel. No autograph exists of this work; perhaps Handel received the text and composed it in Hanover as part of his study of English. Hughes's poetry also found its way later into the text of *Acis and Galatea,* which Handel set in 1718. Handel must have met Roner and Hughes during his first trip to London, probably through Britton's concerts; Hawkins identifies Hughes as a regular there.[40] In the autumn of 1712, when "he obtained leave of the Elector to make a second visit to England,"[41] Handel initially "accepted an invitation from one Mr. Andrews of Barn-Elms, in Surrey, but who also had a town residence, to apartments in his house."[42] Shortly thereafter, he moved to Burlington House.

Lord Burlington, although at least superficially a member and supporter of the Whig party loyal to the Hanoverian Succession, may actually have been, as has been argued by Jane Clark, a leader of the Jacobite party that was working through both political and military channels to restore the Stuarts to the throne of England.[43] Burlington's musical patronage has not yet been fully assessed in light of this theory, but any Jacobite leanings would surely have affected the work he supported.[44] Roger Turner has shown that Burlington's clerics were Jacobite,[45] and the villa at Chiswick of Burlington's own design has been reinterpreted as a Jacobite shrine.[46]

Hawkins writes that during Handel's "three years residence at Burlington-house . . . he composed three operas, namely, *Amadis, Theseus,* and *Pastor Fido.*"[47] In both *Il pastor fido* (1712) and *Teseo* (1713) Handel is identified, as in the earlier *Rinaldo* (1711), as "Maestro di Capella [*sic*] di S. A. E. d'Hanover." *Teseo* is dedicated to Burlington. Handel's next opera, *Silla,* dated 2 June 1713 in the dedication, was perhaps performed privately at the Queen's Theatre in honor of the French ambassador, Louis-Marie D'Aumont Rochbaron, to whom it is dedicated; Burlington is one possible patron for such a performance.[48] Given the French dedicatee (the French harbored the Stuarts and were openly viewed as supporting a Stuart succession)[49] and in light of Burlington's possible Jacobite connections, the text of *Silla* becomes a particularly interesting object of study.

Duncan Chisholm has already tied the libretto to Tory and Jacobite political views, arguing that Silla might represent a "Tory caricature" of the ambitious Duke of Marlborough as "the monstrous Silla of Handel's opera."[50] It might also have represented, more subversively, a negative characterization of the Elector himself. It was well known that George had divorced his wife, Sophia Dorothea, in 1694 and placed her under house arrest in Ahlden (where she died thirty-two years later). English anti-Hanoverian propaganda after 1714 used this situation continually to discredit and undermine George I, with exaggerated rumors about his sexual appetite and many affairs.[51] Sir John Percival, later first Earl of Egmont, wrote on 26 January 1715 about the Tories who "have used very vile arts to alienate the minds of the people from the king," saying that "it would dirty my pen to write the load of lesser scandall invented by the Kings Enemies to serve their purpose among the vulgar."[52] Among the gossip he is willing to communicate is "That [the King] keeps two Turks for abominable uses," referring to accusations of homosexuality.[53] However exaggerated the various sexual rumors might have been, they were afforded substance, perhaps undeserved, by known facts. George had repudiated his wife; he did have a number of mistresses; and he also kept as personal attendants two Turks, Mehemet and Mustafa, who were so much a part of the royal household that they were depicted in the murals of Kensington Palace.[54] Moreover, the accusations largely parallel the dramatic circumstances in *Silla*.

In the libretto of Handel's opera, Silla enters Rome (by analogy, London) by armed force, and not content with the title he has (Elector) declares himself "Perpetual Dictator" (King). "He divorced many wives without cause" and led a "dissolute and lascivious life."[55] The libretto graphically depicts Silla's "indecent assaults" on other women,[56] and the mute character of Scabro, "*Favorito di Silla*," is probably meant to represent, like Anicetus in *Nero*, a homosexual attendant (the name itself implying licentious and indecent [scabrous] behavior), even though Scabro refuses to carry out Silla's evil plans and assists his enemies. Plutarch reports that despite his many marriages, Silla "yielded without resistance to any temptation of voluptuousness, from which even in his old age he could not refrain," and lists a number of Silla's male and female lovers, specifically mentioning the "archmime" Sorex (which may be the source for the mute Scabro in Handel's opera), but identifying his favorite as Metrobius, a female impersonator.[57] The opera concludes with Silla voluntarily relinquishing the throne, reconciling with his wife, and going off to the countryside

(Ahlden?), an action which the Jacobites fervently hoped George would imitate. As Jane Clark writes of a later period, "Possibly . . . Lord Burlington hoped to persuade the usurper to invite the exiled [Stuarts] to return and go back to his own lawful lands in Germany."[58]

The possibility that *Silla* was in any way a propaganda tool for the Jacobites makes it "seem extraordinary," as Chisholm writes, "that Handel should, as a servant of the House of Hanover, be involved with this particular opera."[59] It is, however, the last opera in which Handel is identified as *maestro di cappella* of the Hanoverian court. *Amadigi* (1715), Handel's next opera and the last one composed before the opening of the Royal Academy in 1720, is, like *Teseo,* dedicated to Burlington. The dedication, by the impresario John Jacob Heidegger, reads in part:

> *My LORD,* My Duty and Gratitude oblige me to give this Publick Testimony, of that Generous Concern Your Lordship has always shown for the promoting of Theatrical Musick, but this Opera more immediately claims Your Protection, as it is compos'd in Your own Family.[60]

Handel is identified neither by name nor position, and letters published by Donald Burrows indicate that for political reasons Handel had been dismissed from his Hanoverian position.[61] Although the letters do not mention *Silla,* and the decision to dismiss Handel most probably preceded the performance on 2 June, any news of the opera that reached Hanover could not have pleased the Elector, who was fighting against France in the War of Spanish Succession.

England's unilateral negotiations with France, beginning in 1711, broke a ten-year military alliance with Imperial and Dutch forces. The withdrawal of British troops from the conflict in 1712 left the allied armies at a great disadvantage, and the Hanoverian Elector conveyed his displeasure to Queen Anne. Nevertheless, Handel, commissioned by the Queen, composed a Te Deum and Jubilate to celebrate the peace treaty of Utrecht. This news was communicated to the Elector in a letter dated 13 January 1713, stating that the Queen wished that Handel "remain here for a while" to complete the commission and the performance. Although the correspondent writes that "I didn't doubt that Your Highness would be pleased that one of your servants would have the honor of serving Her Majesty in some way,"[62] the Elector must have responded angrily at having one of "his servants" associated with the peace he had so strongly opposed. Handel was quickly dismissed.

The terms of the dismissal are given in a letter from the Hanoverian resident Kreyenberg dated June 1713: "A few days ago I wrote to you on the subject of Mr Handel, that since His Highness was determined to dismiss him, Mr Handel submitted to that wish, and desired nothing save that the affair be con-

ducted with a good grace and he be given a little time here so that he could enter the queen's service."[63] As the letter continues, however, it is clear that the
dismissal was not conducted as delicately as might have been desired, especially
as "Mr Handel could have been extremely useful." Kreyenberg goes on to say
that the Queen's physician (Dr. John Arbuthnot), who "enjoys the queen's confidence, is [Handel's] great patron and friend, and has the composer constantly
at his house." Apparently, Handel had been able to give Kreyenberg information about the Queen's health, and, because of the planned succession, the Elector would have found such news of significant interest. Kreyenberg concludes
by saying, "I arranged things so that Mr Handel could write to M. Kielmansegg
to extricate himself gracefully, and I let slip a few words to inform him that,
when some day His Highness comes here, he might re-enter his service."[64]

Both Mainwaring and Hawkins attribute the reconciliation of Handel and
the Elector after his arrival in London to Kielmansegge, who, they say, arranged
a water party at which Handel's music would be played. Handel's *Water Music*
was possibly premiered at such an occasion on 17 July 1717,[65] but by then the
King had heard Handel's music on many occasions, initially on his very first at-
tendance at Sunday service in the Chapel Royal (September 1714).[66] The dismissal of Handel seems in retrospect a necessary political act rather than an attack on Handel. Another letter from Kreyenberg dated July 1713 clarifies this:

> I am pleased that you have written to me about Mr Handel. I had not ex-
> pected that he would remain in His Highness's service, nor was I considering
> that but merely the manner of his dismissal; I have done it in such a way that
> he is quite content, giving him to understand that he is by no means in dis-
> grace with His Highness, and dropping a few words to the effect that he will
> be quite all right when the elector comes here. He will continue to tell me all
> he knows.[67]

Kreyenberg's letters seem to confirm that Handel was serving the Hanover
court in the role of political informant. They not only make Handel's position
quite clear but unequivocally identify the physician Arbuthnot as a source of
Handel's information. One wonders if Arbuthnot, no stranger to politics, was
alert to this arrangement. Author of the famous John Bull pamphlets of 1712
that satirized the bitter divisions in England over the conduct of the War of
Spanish Succession, Arbuthnot definitely supported Queen Anne's peace negotiations and not the position of Hanover.[68] It does not seem likely that he would
willingly have passed information on to the Hanoverian court. It may be that
Handel was a political innocent, and the commissions to compose the Utrecht
Te Deum and *Silla* were deliberate, political acts (by the supporters of Queen
Anne, on the one hand, and by Jacobite supporters, on the other) in which

Handel was used as a pawn against his employer, the Hanoverian Elector, but this seems unlikely. Rather, Handel appears to have been a savvy political opportunist who successfully achieved both a position in Anne's court and continuing cordial relations with Anne's successor.

Political maneuvering demanded dissembling and concealment. As Sir Robert Walpole wrote at the time of the Jacobites:

> No man of common prudence will profess himself openly a Jacobite; by so doing he not only may injure his private fortune, but he must render himself less able to do any effectual service to the cause he has embraced; therefore there are but few such men in the kingdom. Your right Jacobite, Sir, disguises his true sentiments. . . . These are the men we have most reason to be afraid of: they are, I am afraid, more numerous than most gentlemen imagine.[69]

Lord Burlington, who was assigned the name Mr. Buck in coded Jacobite correspondence, provides an example of a man who lived one political life in public and another in private. Politics, however, was not the only reason for silence. The concealment of same-sex acts followed the same path, and one could easily substitute "sodomite" for "Jacobite" in Walpole's statement, the similarities between the two identities magnified by the legal and biblical view that equated homosexuality with the overthrow of the state. Same-sex desires were rarely proclaimed, and Burlington, in addition to an apparent double life in politics, may also have been someone who concealed private desires behind a public facade.

Burlington married in 1720, and the union produced three daughters. In the same year as his marriage, however, he brought the Italophile English architect William Kent back from Rome to become part of his household. Of this relationship, one scholar writes, "All his life Kent lived with Burlington: his place in the Burlington household was a very special one, and there is no reason not to presume a close homosexual relationship,"[70] while another responds that it represented "genuine affection, uninhibited by class distinction and uncomplicated by any suggestion of homosexuality."[71] Of course, if there had been an erotic relationship, one would not expect it to be documented,[72] but such an arrangement would not have been unusual. The situation of a married man having a long-term same-sex relationship with an unmarried man of lower status had many models, classical and modern, ranging from the emperor Nero to the Medici princes. Further, the artistic coterie that surrounded Burlington, especially between 1710 and 1720, consisted of a number of artists who have been associated with homosexuality or homoeroticism, including the authors Alexander Pope (1688–1744) and John Gay (1685–1732), both of whom later contributed to texts which Handel set.

When Handel first joined this circle, around 1713, Burlington was not yet

twenty. Pope was twenty-five; Handel and Gay were twenty-eight. Both Pope
and Gay paint a picture of life at Burlington's two residences, Burlington House
in London and Chiswick House outside the city, as a new Arcady that encom-
passed all the muses, along with abundant natural and intellectual pleasures. In
his *Trivia* (1716), Gay writes of London:

> Yet *Burlington's* fair Palace still remains;
> Beauty within, without Proportion reigns.
> Beneath his Eye declining Art revives,
> The Wall with animated Picture lives;
> There *Hendel* strikes the Strings, the melting Strain
> Transports the Soul, and thrills through ev'ry Vein.[73]

Pope writes of Chiswick House in 1716, "I am to pass three or four days in high
luxury, with some company, at my Lord Burlington's. We are to walk, ride, ram-
ble, dine, drink, & lye together. His gardens are delightfull, his music ravish-
ing."[74] And again in the same year, "His Gardens flourish, his Structures rise, his
Pictures arrive" accompanied by the activity of "*Italian* Chymists, Fiddlers,
Bricklayers and Opera-makers."[75] Gay writes in his *Epistle to the Right Honour-
able the Earl of Burlington* (1716):

> While you, my Lord, bid stately Piles ascend,
> Or in your *Chiswick* Bow'rs enjoy your Friend;
> Where *Pope* unloads the Bough within his reach,
> Of purple Grape, blue Plumb, and blushing Peach;
> I journey far.——[76]

Implicit in every description of this verdant and artistic hothouse atmosphere is
its luxurious and indolent sensuality, but, of course, no specifics are given.
"However," as one biographer of Gay has stated, "recent scholarship, examining
the prevailing atmosphere of the Burlington House milieu, has discerned a distinct homo-erotic undertone within this cultural coterie, raising a suggestion
which is worth exploring further."[77]

For artists who experienced the emotion of same-sex love, silence increasingly
became the only form of expressing it. In the seventeenth century such attraction could be more openly represented in poetry and drama, as, for example, by
Lord Rochester, but the increased prohibitions, arrests, punishments, and executions in the early eighteenth century meant that even as the "molly" subculture was thriving, the necessity of concealment was growing.[78] This would have
been true especially of the public artist. The poet Thomas Gray (1716–1771)
provides a good example. As Raymond Bentman writes,

In the period between Hervey and Beckford, many men suspected of sodomitical desire were forced to flee to the continent. Gray did not have the resources of the aristocrats who fled from England; or the power of Hervey, who
could live in defiance of public opinion; or the wealth of Beckford, who could
live in luxurious isolation. He had little choice but extreme discretion or silence to deal with his desires.[79]

Silence also covered all public discussion of sexual acts between men, which
were commonly identified as an unnamable vice, as in *The Third part of the Institutes of the Laws of England* (1644), where sodomy is described as that "detestable and abominable sin, amongst Christians not to be named."[80] Even in so explicit a document as *Plain Reasons for the Growth of Sodomy in England* (c. 1730),
the name is covered in silence: "It is the Action of a *Man* to beget a *Child,* but it
is the Act of a *Beast,* nay worse to ———— I scorn to stain my Paper with the
Mention."[81] This manner of leaving a gap in the narrative was standard even in
published trial documents, sometimes to the point of ludicrousness: "The Prisoner said ———— and ————, and Jack said ————, and the Prisoner said —
————, by which I concluded that they were committing Sodomy together."[82]
Gaps in narrative structure, as must have been clear to the Grub Street writers,
offered imaginative possibilities more potent and salacious than any factual description.

The power of silence openly expressed in blanks and gaps became equally important in more elevated literature and drama in England during the first half of
the eighteenth century. The classical model for such expressed silence comes
from the treatise attributed to Longinus, *On the Sublime,* which was translated
and repeatedly published during this period in England.[83] Longinus, as an example of sublimity, cites the passage in the *Odyssey* where the living Ulysses
greets Ajax in the Underworld and asks pardon for causing Ajax's death:

> Well, I have written elsewhere to this effect: 'Sublimity is the echo of a noble
> mind.' Thus, even without being spoken, a simple idea will sometimes of its
> own accord excite admiration by reason of the greatness of mind that is ex-
> pressed; for example, the silence of Ajax . . . is grand, more sublime than any
> words.[84]

Clearly paraphrasing Longinus, Hildebrand Jacob writes in *Of the Sister Arts*
(1734): "A Break, or Pause in Poetry is sometimes more significant than any
Thing, that might have been said."[85]

Silence in the eighteenth-century English novel grew to encompass not only
verbal description, as Homer describes the silence of Ajax, but also elaborate vi-

sual depictions on the page itself. For example, Samuel Richardson's epistolary novel *Clarissa* (1747), which presents the supposed writings of Clarissa herself, uses disordered fragments arranged helter-skelter around the page to offer a visual image, more powerful than description, of her disorientation following her rape. In *Tristram Shandy* (1759), Laurence Sterne takes expressed silence further, by using dashes, asterisks, and typography, as well as blank, marbled, or completely black pages.[86] For example, when he introduces the widow Wadman, Sterne declines to describe her, leaving that rather to the imagination of the reader and providing a page and a half of blank space on which to write (vol. 6, chap. 38). More often, Sterne uses either asterisks or dashes to indicate ellipses, some of which represent single words or names, but others of which go on for lines. In volume 9, chapters 18 and 19 are completely blank, and chapter 20 begins with ellipses, only turning to words to describe and then "translate" a further silence:

```
_____        *       *       *       *       *       *       *       *
*       *       *       *       *       *       *       *       *       *
*       *       *       *       *       *
        *       *       *       *       *       *       *       *       *
*       *       *       *       *       *       *       *       *       *
*       *       *       *       *       *       _____
```

—You shall see the very place, Madam; said my uncle Toby.

Mrs. Wadman blushed—looked towards the door—turned pale—blushed slightly again—recovered her natural colour—blushed worse than ever; which, for the sake of the unlearned reader, I translate thus—

Although often, like Grub Street authors, leading the reader to lewd imaginings that could not be printed, Sterne also used expressed silence to comic and ironic effect and commented on the more dramatic and expressive effect of silent interruptions in contemporary theatrical representations, especially in the work of the actor David Garrick (1717–1779). He parodies the reaction of self-important audience members who hear only the grammatical effects of Garrick's use of silence (all punctuation and dashes are in the original):

—And how did Garrick speak the soliloquy last night?—Oh, against all rule, my Lord,—most ungrammatically! betwixt the substantive and the adjective, which should agree together in *number, case,* and *gender,* he made a breach thus,—stopping, as if the point wanted settling;—and betwixt the nominative case, which your lordship knows should govern the verb, he suspended his voice in the epilogue a dozen times, three seconds and three fifths by a stopwatch, my Lord, each time.—Admirable grammarian!—But in suspending his voice—was the sense suspended likewise? Did no expression of attitude or countenance fill up the chasm?—Was the eye silent? Did you narrowly look?—I looked only at the stop-watch, my Lord.—Excellent observer![87]

Sterne's burlesque presumably is based on discussions and critiques that he heard at dinner parties and coffee houses, for Garrick's published correspondence shows that his use of silence prompted just such reactions.[88] In response to his playing of Hamlet in 1742–1743, one writer begins: "I take the liberty to send you a few remarks upon your manner of playing, which, excellent as it is, may receive, perhaps some improvement from what I am now going to mention. . . . Your chief mistake is a want of attention to the proper stops and pauses: which, however inconsiderable it may seem, is a gross neglect, and would hardly be excused in a reader of ordinary judgment."[89] He concludes a long list of alleged errors with a rule that will prevent future errors: "Never disjoin the verb from the accusative case, or from the concluding members of the sentence which it governs."[90] Another writer offers exactly such an example of an "injudicious" pause in the line, "I think it was to See—My Mother's Wedding," to which Garrick responds tellingly by distinguishing between a "stop" and a "suspension."

I certainly never *stop* there, (that is close the *sense*) but I as certainly *suspend* my voice, by which your ear must know that the sense is suspended too; for Hamlet's grief causes the break, and with a sigh he finishes the Sentence—"my mother's Wedding." I really could not from my feelings act it otherwise.[91]

Garrick's description proves as appropriate to the silences in Handel's English cantatas as it is of his own acting. Handel's notated pauses also "suspend" the voice, just as they suspend the harmony and, sometimes, the meter. They also create similar grammatical breaks, as between the verb and its dependent clause in *Ho fuggito* ("I returned—[long pause]—into bondage"). Handel's English cantatas specifically notate the kinds of pauses that Garrick would later insert as a matter of performing practice to increase the tension and emotional impact of his characterizations. Notably, Hildebrand Jacob's treatise of 1734, seven years before Garrick's London debut, considers the expressive role of silence in music equally with that in literature: "In Music, a Rest in its proper Place has often a wonderful Effect, and from the Beauty of its Surprize, makes the Suspension of Harmony itself agreeable."

The most comprehensive discussion of music and silence today appears in a study by Anna Danielewicz-Betz, *Silence and Pauses in Discourse and Music.*[92]

She pointedly remarks on the lack of musicological investigation into this topic, as opposed to the substantive work in linguistics and literary theory ("Generally speaking, musicological studies have paid little attention to rests in music"),[93] and she surveys the rather small field of theoretical publications, including Riemann's *Pausenlehre* (1903) and Cage's *Silence* (1961). The categorization she proposes distinguishes between silence that is external to the musical composition, including boundary silence that frames a performance of music and the silent breaks between movements, and internal silences or pauses; and she further divides both kinds of silence into two categories which she names "acoustical" (represented by an extremely low level of intensity, such as background noise or a *pianissimo*) and "perceptual" ("where no sound signals are perceived by the listener").[94]

More limited typologies of silence, excluding both acoustical silence (including music composed to represent silence) and boundary silence beyond the border of the composition or movement, were offered at a symposium entitled *Musique et silence* in 1994 at the University of Tours. In a discussion of late Baroque instrumental music, Raphaelle Legrand distinguished between functional pauses that result from specific styles (such as the French overture), ornaments (for example, *coupé*), articulations (*staccato, style brisé*), and respirations, and various expressive silences identified by such seventeenth-century rhetorical terms as *aposiopesis* (silence throughout all voices), *abruptio* (pre-cadential silence), and *tmesis* (expressive sigh).[95] Eric Gaudibert presented a more general categorization that comprised five types of silence: dramatic (the goal of a crescendo or decrescendo), questioning (a hesitation), plaintive (emotional, interruptive), integral (detached articulation, such as *staccato,* notated or implied), and articulative (phrase articulation).[96] Although these typologies are useful (and related), none is text-dependent or based on vocal music. Handel's cantatas thus suggest a different categorization.

In the following analyses of Handel's London cantatas, I use the word "silence" exclusively to mean an internal pause or gap notated by rests in every part simultaneously. Boundary silence and pauses that result from detached articulation or performance style (integral or functional silence) are not considered. Although Handel later became a master at depicting silence by musical sound (a form of acoustical silence), as, for example, in the choruses "He sent a thick darkness" from *Israel in Egypt* and "Let no rash intruder" from *Solomon,* he did not pursue this in the cantatas, even those whose texts are about silence—at least in part, I assume, because of the miniature scale of the performing forces. I would categorize the silences in Handel's cantatas as madrigalistic (pauses that depict such words as "die" or "sigh" or that follow a question), grammatical (pauses that function as musical punctuation to articulate musical phrases, including the silence that often precedes the final cadence), and disruptive (the silences that interrupt the musical flow without regard either to a specific word or to grammar).

Silence enters Handel's cantatas through the texts. In contrast to the passionate outbursts of women, the male voice of the pastoral lovers who "suffer with hope and love in silence" *(Stelle, perfide stelle)* parallels Thomas Gray's silence in the face of "a hopeless love." In *Se per fatal destino* (1707), the lover asks, "If, through fatal destiny . . . fate wishes I be silent and loving . . . then should I speak? No, I want to be silent in suffering my death." And in the final words of *Stelle, perfide stelle* (Rome, 1707) the lover declares: "I will love in silence, for to reveal my love . . . is not allowed." Repeatedly described in the Italian cantata texts, silence slowly enters the sound structure of the cantatas as well. Although madrigalistic and grammatical silences appear throughout Handel's cantata repertory, disruptive silence that cuts through the score and temporarily halts the flow of speech and music is a particular feature of his English set. With the understanding that the three categories overlap, each can be discussed in turn.[97]

The madrigalistic use of silence pertains to a form of word-painting (named for its distinctive use in Italian and English madrigals of the sixteenth and early seventeenth centuries) in which the rest depicts (or imitates) an act of respiration (breathing, sighing) or a break in activity (as a command to stop, or depictions of death or dying). Handel's use of rests to interrupt the settings of individual words provides a small lexicon of such effects: *so-spirando* (sigh) in *Armida abbandonata; tre-mo-li* (quivering) in *O lucenti; inciam-pa* (stumbles) in *Nell'africane selve;* and *pe-na* (pain) in *O numi eterni.* As in the later use of disruptive silence, the unusual or unexpected word break is often the most interesting. In *Cor fedele,* for example, the title aria expands the typical repertory by breaking the word *va-go* (lover), thus describing Tirsi himself as a "broken" lover (see Ex. 4.10).

Rests occurring immediately before or after a word follow a similar pattern. Handel repeatedly uses a rest following phrases dealing with death, as in *Arresta il passo,* where rests consistently follow the word *morir* (to die). In "Per voi languisco" in *O lucenti,* Handel sets off the phrase "for you I languish and die" with rests; in "Tormentosa, crudele" in *Partì, l'idolo mio,* quarter-note rests highlight the phrase "you ought rather to have deprived me of life"; the only rests throughout the system in "Basterebbe a tor di vita" in *Poiché giuraro amore* paint the phrase "it would suffice to take from life a thousand hearts." Handel seems also to have a preference for depicting the word *solo* (alone, meaning "only" or "set apart") with rests, as in "Ah, crudele" in *Armida abbandonata* ("that you alone [rest], you alone, alone [rest]"); "Ride fiore" (see Ex. 3.4) in *Nella stagion* ("you alone [rest], you alone [rest]"); and "Con linfe dorate" in *Echeggiate, festeggiate* ("the King of Iberia is Charles alone [rest] Charles alone").

In a related example from *Lungi da me, pensier tiranno!* the text of the second aria begins:

Fuggi da questo sen,   Fly from this breast,
O barbaro pensier,   O barbarous thought,
Lasciami in pace!   Leave me in peace!

Handel sets the entire text in a rush of sixteenth notes (depicting *fuggi*), but then repeats the phrase *in pace* with half and quarter notes set off by rests, so that the singer is left "alone" (lonely) without the "barbarous thoughts." The ornamentation in the Bodleian Library copy at Oxford, shown in Ex. 5.4, implies a suspension of metered time in addition to the isolating rests.[98] Rests also depict coming to a halt, as in "Per te lasciai" in *Delirio amoroso,* where twice the command *ferma* (stop) is followed by five beats of silence (Ex. 5.5). This aria also uses silence to depict the phrase "tu vuoi partir" (you want to leave). At first the silence simply follows the word *partir,* leaving the singer alone. It then breaks the phrase itself in two (Ex. 5.6).

An important subgroup of madrigalistic silence is Handel's frequent use of rests following a question. Although one could argue that silence following a question mark should fall into the category of grammatical pauses, discussed below, I have placed it here, first, because the silence is descriptive of the response to a rhetorical or unanswered question and not simply an articulation, and, second, because there are many close ties to other forms of word-painting.

Example 5.4 *Lungi da me, pensier tiranno!,* "Fuggi da questo sen."

Example 5.5a *Delirio amoroso,* "Per te lasciai," setting of *ferma,* mm. 71–78.

Example 5.5b *Delirio amoroso,* "Per te lasciai," setting of *ferma,* mm. 80–91.

Example 5.6 *Delirio amoroso,* "Per te lasciai," setting of *partir.*

The simple use of rhetorical silence can be seen in "Superbetti occhi amorosi" in *Ne' tuoi lumi,* where the only rests follow the first completion of the question in the text (Ex. 5.7):

Superbetti occhi amorosi,	Proud, loving eyes,
Sì crudeli, sì vezzosi,	So cruel, so charming,
Perché siete, O Dio, con me?	Why are you, O God! with me?

Handel suspends the silence on a dominant harmony, as is typical of his practice, only thereafter arriving, with a repetition of the phrase "O Dio, con me," at a grammatical close. In "Quell'erbetta" from *Cor fedele,* the questions are similarly suspended, but without resolution (see Ex. 4.11). Rhetorical questions often cross the boundary into descriptive silence, as when they concern death—"Do you want to kill me?" being the most common. Thus in the duet "Fermati—No, crudel!" in *Cor fedele* the silences in the opening section of the duet refer to the word *fermati* (stop), while those in the second section follow the question "vuoi che m'uccida?" (do you want to kill me?). Sometimes other-

Example 5.7 *Ne' tuoi lumi,* "Superbetti occhi amorosi."

wise inexplicable silence can be attributed to Handel's understanding of the text
as a question. In "Per te lasciai" in *Delirio amoroso* (Ex. 5.6 above), the silence
following "tu vuoi partir" (you want to leave) can be explained madrigalistically
as leaving the singer "alone." However, the phrase also implies a heart-wrench-
ing question that remains hanging in the air despite the lack of a question mark
in the sources: "Now that love brings me to see you again, you want to leave
me?" Similarly, the break of almost two measures in the duet "Senza occhi"
from *Cor fedele* seems to derive from an interpretation of the text as a question.
In the modern edition the text and its translation appear as follows:[99]

E se non è il pastore	And if the shepherd
semplice e tutto amore,	is not simple and all love,
nol prende per suo vago,	she will not take him as her lover,
perché lo vuol così.	because that is how she wants him to be.

However, the musical setting at one point indicates a different meaning when it
divides the last line between the two singers—Fileno: "Perché?" Tirsi: "lo vuol
così" (Why? She wants it so).[100] The long silence following the last jointly sung
"perché" may thus be understood as a typical, if longer than normal, compositional response to a question suspended on a dominant harmony (Ex. 5.8).

The general category of grammatical pauses stands in opposition to interrogative silence: first, because the rests tend to be very short, and second, because
the silences are usually associated with a form of harmonic closure (half or full

Example 5.8 *Cor fedele,* "Senza occhi."

cadence). Some of the early cantatas contain no rests at all (for example, "Son pur le lacrime," as shown in Ex. 5.1); in others, Handel only uses rests to articulate the vocal part from the ritornellos, as in "Non esce un guardo mai" in *Udite il mio consiglio,* where the rests come at the beginning and end of each vocal section (Ex. 5.9, p. 201). Handel's general stylistic development tends toward an ever-greater use of articulating rests, even if these are not silences throughout the system. For example, when he revised his Italian setting of "Sei pur bella," from the cantata of the same name, in London, he strengthened the harmony and improved the bass line, but the primary change in the vocal line is the addition of articulating rests (Ex. 5.10, p. 202).[101] "Tergi il ciglio lagrimoso" from *Nella stagion* (Rome, 1707) provides an early example of the use of rests throughout the system to set off the beginning of lines, articulate the verse structure and punctuation, and demarcate word repetition (Ex. 5.11, p. 203).

Tergi il ciglio lagrimoso,	Dry those tears,
Acciò torni più vezzoso	So that the loveliness of your face
Del tuo volto il bel seren.	Returns more beautiful.

The pre-cadential pause fits into the category of grammatical silence by its preparation for and articulation of the final cadence and by its typical lack of the descriptive purpose of madrigalistic silence. This hiatus, sometimes momentary, sometimes longer, provides an extended upbeat that implies the intake of air and the pulling together of forces necessary to reach a finality; like the interrogative silence, it is usually suspended on a dominant. The effect can be monumental, and Handel uses it this way in many of his later oratorio choruses, perhaps most famously in the "Hallelujah" in *Messiah.* In the cantatas, the pre-cadential pause is often more like a fleeting breath to punctuate the final closure. "Chi rapi la pace," in the cantata of the same name (1706), contains a sixteenth-note pause before the final cadence of both sections of the aria: in the first case the cadence preceding the rest is a weak tonic cadence to a first inversion triad; in the second case the rest follows a sustained dominant after a deceptive cadence (Ex. 5.12, p. 204).

Of course, pre-cadential silence can have an affective meaning overlaid on its otherwise functional purpose. The expansion of the pre-cadential pause for affective purpose is, not surprisingly, most common among the English-period works. For example, the silence after the words "Carlo solo" in "Con linfe dorate" from *Echeggiate, festeggiate* not only emphasizes *solo,* as described above, but also functions as an emphatic pre-cadential pause (Ex. 5.13, p. 204).[102] Despite a secondary descriptive or grammatical purpose, however, the truly disruptive silence of the English cantatas can usually be distinguished from its functional relative.

Example 5.9 *Udite il mio consiglio,* "Non esce un guardo mai."

Example 5.10a *Sei pur bella,* "Sei pur bella," Italian version.

Example 5.10b *Sei pur bella,* "Sei pur bella," London version.

Example 5.11 *Nella stagion,* "Tergi il ciglio lagrimoso."

Example 5.12a *Chi rapì la pace?*, "Chi rapì la pace?," A section.

Example 5.12b *Chi rapì la pace?*, "Chi rapì la pace?," B section.

Example 5.13 *Echeggiate, festeggiate*, "Con linfe dorate."

The disruptive break at the end of the first section of "Ho fuggito" (Ex. 5.3 above), for example, is clearly related to a pre-cadential silence. The independent importance of this expressive silence, however, can easily be illustrated by editing out the disruption and leaving only a grammatical pre-cadential pause (Ex. 5.14). Handel's "addition" of a failed cadential attempt broken off in mid-phrase decisively overrides any grammatical purpose.

The climax of "Ho tanti affanni in petto" in *Mi palpita il cor* (London, c. 1711) is a long silence after an indefinite pause on the dominant harmony. This graphically portrays the text of the aria and its final line: "I cannot say." Although descriptive and pre-cadential, the rest moves far beyond decorative word-painting, identifying "silence" as the core of the aria. The very use of notated rests following a fermata is meaningful for being musically unneces-sary,[103] and it is of further significance that Handel reserves silence for this moment, providing otherwise in the course of the entire aria only an eighth-note (grammatical) pause before the start of the second section. Like the other silences of the same period, this climactic break, which suspends time and meter, moves beyond word-painting to depict in dramatic terms the condition of the singer (Ex. 5.15).

Ho tanti affanni in petto,	I have so many sorrows in my breast
che quel sia il più tiranno,	that that which is the more oppressive
io dir, io dir nol so.	I cannot, I cannot say.[104]

The importance of silence to the English set of cantatas can also be seen in revisions. The addition of grammatical pauses to the first revision of the aria "Sei pur bella" has been discussed above. In the second, also English, revision, Handel takes the opportunity to rewrite the aria completely, putting grammati-

Example 5.14 *Ho fuggito*, "Ho fuggito," rewritten cadence.

Example 5.15 *Mi palpita il cor,* "Ho tanti affanni in petto."

cal pauses in the vocal line alone, but including significant pre-cadential silences in both sections of the aria. Similarly, the aria "Mi piagò amor" from *Dimmi, O mio cor* as revised for *Mi palpita il cor* (HWV 132a, a revised version of the earlier cantata) highlights an increased use of rests, including a shifting of pauses in the bass part from the fourth to the first beat, the addition of grammatical pauses in the vocal line, and a silence throughout the score following the word *fatale* ("fatal"), as shown in Ex. 5.16.

In addition to disruptive pauses, Handel's English cantatas also offer some of the earliest examples of settings in which the vocal line is composed in short, broken and, often, repeated sections at a very slow (usually *Largo*) tempo. This fragmented style was to become an essential part of Handel's toolbox, as in the aria "He was despised" in *Messiah*. Fragmentation always depicts extreme emotion. In "He was despised," the singer (perhaps once again the Christian soul) describes the rejection of Christ in emotionally impeded speech. The use of rests depicts this difficulty of expression: "He was despised [rest], despised and rejected [rest], rejected of men [vocal rest], a man of sorrows [vocal rest], a

Example 5.16a *Dimmi, o mio cor,* "Mi piagò amor."

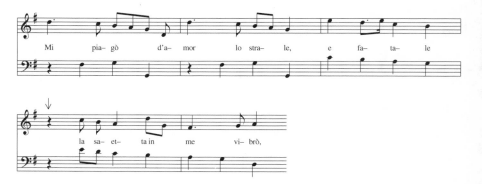

Example 5.16b *Mi palpita il cor,* "Mi piagò amor."

Example 5.17 *La solitudine,* "L'aure grate."

man of sorrows and acquainted [vocal rest] with grief [vocal rest], a man of sorrows, and acquainted with grief." Handel's setting has so impressed itself on most listeners of *Messiah* that it is difficult to imagine the biblical text without this slow, halting, and repetitive delivery. An early example of this fragmented style in Handel's cantatas is Apollo's lament in *Apollo e Dafne* (1709/1710): "Beloved plant [rest], with my tears [rest], I will water your leaves [rest]; with your branches [rest] triumphant [rest], the greatest heroes [rest], the greatest heroes I will crown."

In "L'aure grate" (*La solitudine,* 1718) the text depicts the pleasures of nature, which are no less real for the bittersweet fact that they are said to replace the pleasures (and pains) of love. The first section of text is set in seven small units, each of which (with the exception of the final phrase) is made up of only four to seven notes (Ex. 5.17). The breathless "Siete rose" from the cantata of the same name is similar (see Ex. P.3), even though most of the rests are in the vocal line only. Like most of Handel's fragmented arias, both "L'aure grate" and "Siete rose" are marked *Largo.*

Although their origins may sometimes be found in descriptive word-painting or grammatical pauses, disruptive and fragmenting silences represent a separate category because, despite being notated, they are tied more to performance than to the text. That is, these silences transform the disembodied cantata voice into a theatrical presence struggling with expression. The silences tear the fabric of sound; they suspend time; they disrupt grammar. Sometimes they place the comprehension of the affect ahead of the comprehension of the text. In all these ways, the silences of Handel's English cantatas preview the growing use of silence in literary texts—where notated blanks and dashes leave gaping holes—and more particularly the naturalistic stage acting represented especially by Garrick.

"Deh! lasciate" offers a final example. The aria proceeds without any rests through the system until the word *ingrata* in the B section, after which the music stops completely for three quarter-note rests (Ex. 5.18).

Deh! lasciate e vita e volo	Ah! leave both life and flight
All'amabile usignuolo,	To the sweet nightingale,
Cacciatori, per pietà.	O hunters, for pity's sake.
Col suo flebile lamento,	With his plaintive song
Ei ridice il mio tormento	He tells of my torment over and over
All'ingrata che lo fa.	To the ungrateful one who causes it.

This silence is noteworthy because there is no immediate textual reason for it. *Ingrata* ("ungrateful one" [female]) does not conjure up a rest on the basis of word-painting as does "sigh" or "stop," and its position in the middle of a line marks no point of articulation in terms of either punctuation or rhyme scheme. Moreover, this remarkably long break of three quarter notes differs from the typically shorter rests that serve to paint words or articulate phrasing. Especially because there is no silence in the cantata before this moment, the total suspension of the music for such a long break at the first mention of the "ungrateful one" presents a particularly theatrical pause; it moves beyond painting the text to depict the singer as a *dramatis persona* who is emotionally unable to continue. Although the introduction of dramatic silence that is neither madrigalistic nor structural is often attributed to later composers, the continuo cantatas that Handel wrote in England demonstrate his significant use of this musical resource.

The growing use of silence in Handel's London cantatas between 1710 and 1722 derives in part from the persistent imagery in earlier texts of noble male silence as opposed to female volubility. In Handel's settings from the Italian period, the voice of the singer is disguised and could represent equally, or concur-

Example 5.18 *Deh! lasciate*, "Deh! lasciate" (London, c. 1720).

rently, the author, the patron, an auditor, or the composer, among other possibilities. In contrast, the expressed silences of the London cantatas, which exceed
a descriptive or grammatical "reason" and go beyond the text, more dramati-
cally capture the voice of a specific persona or individual actor in performance.
That is, by moving beyond described silence to expressed silence, Handel's London settings "perform" the texts, much as Garrick later performed written texts,
adding silences and breaks where none is indicated. These expressed silences
seem to speak particularly in Handel's own voice. In his young career, he had already dealt with the love of a woman who was the mistress of his patron and
then had obtained a position in the city where her husband worked; in securing
patronage he had successfully played both sides of the War of Spanish Succession more than once; and in England, as in Italy, he worked in clearly homoerotic circles. The necessity of silence in both illicit love and diplomacy must
have been clear to him. Not surprisingly, this life lesson found its way into his
music. In cantatas that tell of love's pleasures and pain, Handel increasingly expresses emotion through silence. As Garrick would declare two decades later in
response to a critic of his pauses and interruptions, "I really could not from my
feelings act it otherwise."

Culmination of the Private

Since my Last I have been at Canons [*sic*] with E. of Carnarvon who Lives [as] an Prince
. . . . He has a Chorus of his own, the Musick is made for himself and sung by his own
servants, besides which there is a Little opera now a makeing for his diversion whereof
the Musick will not be made publick. The words are to be furnished by M^rs [Messrs]
Pope & Gay, the musick to be composed by Hendell. It is as good as finished, and I am
promised some of the Songs by Dr. Arbuthnot who is one of the club of composers.

Letter to Hugh Campbell from Sir David Dalrymple (27 May 1718)

Hawkins writes that "after three years residence at Burlington-house . . . Handel received a pressing invitation from the duke of Chandois [*sic*] to undertake the direction of the chapel at his superb mansion, Cannons," and he wonders what might have induced Handel "to enter into engagements that rendered him somewhat less than master of himself and his time."[1] Although Hawkins errs in assuming Handel ever took on a salaried position at Cannons, it is clear that Handel was often at Cannons and composed a significant body of music for James Brydges, then Earl of Carnarvon, later Duke of Chandos (to whom I will refer by his ultimate title of Chandos).[2] Handel and John Arbuthnot are noted as being together at the Cannons estate in a diary entry dated 4 August 1717.[3] Then on 25 August, Chandos writes to Arbuthnot: "Mr. Hendle has made me two new Anthems very noble ones & Most think they far exceed the two first. . . . You had as good take Cannons in on your way to London."[4] On 27 May 1718 Sir David Dalrymple writes in a letter that "there is a Little opera now a makeing" at Cannons, "the musick to be composed by Hendell."[5] Handel and Arbuthnot are recorded as dining at Cannons in April 1718 in the company of the composer John Christopher Pepusch, whose presence at Cannons is first documented on 15 December 1717 and who by the middle of 1719 had become Chandos's salaried music director.[6] With Chandos, as in the case of Ruspoli, the salaried appointment of a composer was made only after the conclusion of Handel's less formalized residency. During a seemingly narrow window of less than two years, Handel composed for Cannons, among a number of smaller works, the ten so-called Chandos Anthems, a Te Deum and a reduced version of the Utrecht Jubilate, and the "little opera" *Acis and Galatea,* as well as his first dramatic work based on an Old Testament story, *Esther*, called "Oratorium" in the Cannons inventory.[7]

In many ways *Acis and Galatea* and *Esther* are twins. Not only were both probably composed for performance at Cannons in 1718, but both are likely the result of an artistic collaboration by the same authors and Handel, and both use the same combination of five voices, where the leading characters (Galatea-Acis-Polyphemus and Esther-Ahasuerus-Haman) are soprano, tenor, and bass, to which two smaller tenor roles are added (in *Esther*, Mordecai and Habdonah; in *Acis*, Damon and Corydon). The close connection between these works in terms of their chronological and creative origins suggests that one Cannons drama should not be considered entirely apart from the other. In fact, *Esther* and *Acis and Galatea* can be seen as a double culmination of Handel's period of private patronage that had begun with his arrival in Italy in 1706.

The libretto of *Esther* has been variously attributed to Alexander Pope and to Dr. Arbuthnot. Sir John Percival names Pope in his diary after hearing the private revival at the Crown and Anchor Tavern in 1732; in advertisements for the public performance later that year, not authorized by Handel, Pope is also named as author. Arbuthnot is named in three early Dublin librettos and in the posthumous edition of his works (1751). Although general consensus now leans toward Pope, and the modern Twickenham edition of Pope's works accepts his authorship, it is likely that more than one hand was involved. Pope, Arbuthnot, and John Gay, all part of the Burlington circle, often worked collaboratively and did so especially in this period. They co-authored the play *Three Hours Before Marriage* in 1717, and Dalrymple (see the epigraph at the beginning of this chapter) names Pope, Arbuthnot, and Gay as collaborating with Handel in 1718 on "a little opera," probably *Acis and Galatea*.[8]

Acis and Galatea offers an entirely new version of the Ovidian story that Handel had set in Naples as *Aci, Galatea e Polifemo*, discussed in Chapter 4. Brian Trowell has argued that like *Aci*, the English *Acis* began life as a trio for the main characters.[9] He sees "discontinuities" in the libretto and music of the version that has come down to us, but his most convincing argument has to do with the part-writing of the ensembles, which he shows either to have been conceived originally for three voices or borrowed from ensembles for three voices. For example, "Galatea, dry thy Tears" is based on the trio, "Lieto il Tebro," that ends *Agrippina*, and "Mourn all ye Muses" derives from the Trio of Believers, "O Donnerwort! O schrecklich Schreien," from the *Brockes Passion*. The apparent expansion of *Acis* from three voices to five during composition parallels the expansion of the Chandos Anthems from three to five voices as the Cannons Concert (the assembled group of employed musicians) grew in size.[10] *Esther*, by contrast, was larger at the outset (did not grow from a three-voice vocal texture), requires a larger orchestra, and contains a "second set" of five soloists (four unnamed Israelites and a Persian officer) that nearly duplicates the vocal ranges of the main roles.[11] Further, the ensembles in *Acis* can be and probably were sung by the soloists, but the ensembles in *Esther* were probably designed as true choruses with multiple voices on a part; at one point in the score, for example, the bass choral part splits into two lines. The larger forces of the oratorio imply that it followed *Acis,* if only by a matter of months. Whereas the use of shared subject matter and possible three-voice origin connects *Acis and Galatea* to the Neapolitan serenata and the Italian cantata tradition despite its language, ensembles, and expanded size, the score of *Esther,* because of its even greater number of ensembles, still larger forces, and biblical source, is, by comparison, quite removed from that tradition. Nevertheless, just as *Il trionfo del tempo* is closely tied to Handel's Italian cantatas on account of Pamphili's authorship and Roman context, *Esther* is tied to *Acis* by common creative background and provenance.

The literary heritage of both *Acis and Galatea* and *Esther* can be traced from an ancient source through a late seventeenth-century adaptation of high quality to a minor dramatic work published shortly before the Cannons compositions. That is, the libretto of *Acis* derives from Ovid through John Dryden's 1693 translation, and is closely tied to a 1716 masque based on the story of Apollo and Daphne. *Esther,* a more straightforward adaptation, derives from the Old Testament story through Racine's play *Esther* of 1689 and the English translation of Racine by Thomas Brereton, *Esther, or Faith Triumphant* (1715). The story of *Esther* tells of the deliverance of the Jewish community in Persia from a sentence of death. As presented in the libretto, Haman, the evil minister of King Ahasuerus, threatens to annihilate the Jews in Persia. In the biblical story this edict has a more complicated history, as Haman there persuades the king himself to condemn the Jews, which the king does without knowing either the identity of the population or that his wife, Esther, is Jewish; further, as a command of the king, the edict becomes non-revocable. Although the king has decreed death to all who enter his presence other than by his command, Esther, urged by her cousin and guardian Mordecai, who earlier had saved Ahasuerus's life, enters the throne room, is welcomed by the king, and invites the king and Haman to dinner. At the dinner, she reveals her Jewish identity to her husband and pleads for her nation. Ahasuerus thereupon acknowledges the loyalty of the Jewish population, rescinds the edict, honors Mordecai for having earlier saved his life, and punishes his minister Haman with death.

As both Winton Dean and Ruth Smith have noted, the Cannons authors in framing Handel's libretto seem to have worked directly from Brereton, sometimes borrowing quite closely. In the following example the connection is obvious, although the speaker is changed and the decasyllabic (heroic) couplets of the Brereton text are altered to shorter lines more suited to musical setting as an aria.[12]

BRERETON, ACT I	ESTHER, SCENE I
Mordecai:	*Haman:*
Both root and branch they seek to spoil our race!	Pluck root and branch from out the land;
	Shall I the God of Israel fear?
A gen'ral massacre is here declar'd . . .	Let Jewish blood dye ev'ry hand,
Nor age nor sex shall scape th'invet'rate steel.	Nor age nor sex I spare.

The story of *Acis and Galatea,* like Handel's *Aci, Galatea e Polifemo* of 1708, follows Ovid's version, but the English libretto has a more immediate model in John Dryden's translation. This had recently been republished, in 1716, as part of a collaborative translation of the *Metamorphoses* to which Pope and Gay contributed.[13] Although Pope had also translated the Acis and Galatea story, perhaps as early as 1702, his version did not appear in print until 1749 (when it was titled "Polyphemus and Acis").[14] The reliance of the Cannons libretto on Dryden's translation is underscored by its complete lack of relation to Pope's.

Polyphemus's two recitatives, "I rage, I melt, I burn" and "Whither fairest," both owe some of their wording directly to Dryden, as do parts of the climax: Acis's "Help Galatea" and Galatea's "Must I my Acis still bemoan" and "Heart the seat of soft delight." Some couplets are borrowed essentially intact, such as Acis's final words:

DRYDEN'S OVID (LL. 206–207):	*ACIS AND GALATEA*
Help, Galatea! Help, my parent gods,	Help, Galatea, help ye parent gods,
And take me, dying, to your deep abodes!	And take me dying to your deep abodes.

Pope's translation differs strongly (ll. 141–143):

Acis too run, and help, oh help! He said,
A wretch undone: O parents help, and deign
T'admit your offspring in your watry reign.

The collaborators sometimes altered Dryden's words to adjust for the change from narrative description to direct address or to enliven the dramatic characterization, as in these lines for Polyphemus:

DRYDEN (LL. 58–59):	*ACIS AND GALATEA*
A hundred reeds, of a prodigious growth,	Bring me a hundred reeds of decent growth,
Scarce made a pipe proportioned to his mouth.	To make a pipe for my capacious mouth.

Pope's translation of the same passage is unrelated (ll. 45–46):

His whistle (which a hundred reeds compose)
With all his strength the giant-lover blows.

In some cases the alteration of Dryden is greater, especially when (as in the borrowings from Brereton's *Esther*) the decasyllabic lines are abandoned for a simpler and shorter rhythmic pattern. Still, the indebtedness is clear, as in these lines for Polyphemus (where, once again, there are no echoes in Pope's translation):

DRYDEN (LL. 103–111; 116–117):	ACIS AND GALATEA
My palace in the living rock is made	Thee, Polyphemus, great as Jove,
By nature's hand; a spacious pleasing shade,	Calls to empire and to love,
Which neither heat can pierce, nor cold invade.	To his *palace in the rock,*
My garden filled with fruits you may behold,	To his dairy, to his flock,
And *grapes* in clusters, imitating gold;	*To the grape of purple hue,*
Some blushing bunches *of a purple hue;*	To the plumb of glossy blue,
And these, and those, are all reserved for you.	*Wildings* which *expecting stand,*
Red strawberries in shades *expecting stand,*	*Proud to be gather'd by thy hand.*
Proud to be gathered by so white a hand.	
Nor chestnuts shall be wanting to your food,	
Nor garden-fruits, nor *wildings* of the wood.	

Dryden's unquestionable influence on the Cannons version did not extend to an earlier English musical setting of this story. One of a series of entertainments inserted in a revival in 1701 of *The Mad Lover* by John Fletcher (1579–1625), the masque of *Acis and Galatea,* written by Peter Motteux and set to music by John Eccles, takes a comic approach.[15] Acis was played by the singing actress Anne Bracegirdle, who specialized in "breeches parts," opposite Elizabeth Bowman as Galatea. Not only does the restoration of Acis provide a happy ending in this version (Neptune decrees "Live, *Acis,* live, and quit the shore. / A watry God; and mortal now no more"), but the Acis story frames a comic subplot about a rustic bride and bridegroom named Roger and Joan. When the bridal party enters, Acis woos all the girls and (like Don Giovanni) gets into an altercation with the bridegroom. This portion of the masque (without reference to the Acis and Galatea story) was frequently revived on its own with the title *The Country Wedding.* The only verbal echoes between the two masques are some common rhymes, such as the swain(s)/plain(s) of the two opening numbers:

MOTTEUX, OPENING ARIA FOR ACIS	*ACIS AND GALATEA*, OPENING CHORUS
Come, ye Nymphs, and ev'ry Swain, *Galatea* leaves the Main, To revive us on the Plain.	Oh, the pleasure of the plains! Happy nymphs and happy swains.

Dreary as Motteux's *Acis and Galatea* can be (Dean writes that "the construction of the plot is lamentable, and its classical charm is degraded to a coarse and vulgar farce"), it nevertheless partakes of a tradition of sung masques to which the Cannons *Acis and Galatea* belongs. The leading creative contributors to this musical-theatrical form were the librettists John Hughes and Colley Cibber and the composers John Christopher Pepusch and John Ernst Galliard. Handel had known Hughes from his earliest days in London and had received from Hughes the first English words he set to music, the cantata *Venus and Adonis*. Pepusch was the "other" Cannons composer. Some of the immediate precedents for the Cannons *Acis* include *Calypso and Telemachus* (1712), an opera by Hughes and Galliard; *Venus and Adonis* (1715), a masque by Cibber and Pepusch; *Myrtillo* (1715), a "pastoral interlude" by Cibber and Pepusch; and *Apollo and Daphne* (1716), a masque by Hughes and Pepusch. Hughes is one of the known contributors to the libretto of the Cannons *Acis,* and, as Dean writes, "there can be little doubt that Hughes' *Apollo and Daphne* . . . was the actual model for Gay's *Acis and Galatea*."[16]

Given the parallelism between Apollo's love of Daphne and Polyphemus's love of Galatea as multiforms of the same story of pursuit (see Chapter 4), it is not surprising to find that the writing team behind the Cannons *Acis and Galatea* turned to Hughes's *Apollo and Daphne*. Dean lays out a number of examples showing the correspondences: Daphne's first air, "How happy are we," finds echoes in the opening chorus (see above) and in the love duet, "Happy we"; Apollo's first air, "Fair blooming creature," is turned into Damon's aria, "Would you gain the tender creature"; and Daphne's second aria dismissing Apollo's suit, "Cease to sooth[e] thy fruitless Pain," is adapted for Polyphemus as he determines to give up the lover's role:[17]

HUGHES, APOLLO AND DAPHNE	ACIS AND GALATEA
Cease to sooth[e] thy fruitless Pain; Why for Frowns wilt thou be suing? Cease to languish and complain. 'Tis to seek thy own Undoing Still to love, and love in vain.	Cease to beauty to be suing, Ever whining[,] love disdaining. Let the brave their aims pursuing, Still be conqu'ring not complaining.

Hughes's close relation to Handel and to Pepusch suggests that he might have been an active rather than passive partner in the artistic collaboration that created *Acis and Galatea*.[18] Other partners in the collaboration also incorporated earlier work. Handel, for example, turned to his early pastoral trio *Cor fedele*, adapting Galatea's first two arias from two arias for Clori. The bird song of "Va col canto" is used in "Hush, ye pretty warbling choir," and Clori's final aria, "Amo Tirsi," for "As when the dove" (see Ex. 4.7).[19] Although "Va col canto" was also adapted in the Neapolitan serenata for Galatea's song about the waves of the sea, "S'agita in mezzo l'onde," it would seem, not just from the closer similarity of the accompanimental patterns but also from Handel's use of another of Clori's arias, that he went back directly to *Cor fedele* and not to his earlier setting of the Acis story (see Ex. 4.6). This should not be surprising. As discussed in Chapter 4, Handel seems to have viewed the nymphs of his cantata pastorals as somewhat interchangeable.

Verbal echoes of Pope's poems are found in both *Esther* (from *The Rape of the Lock*) and *Acis and Galatea* (from "On a fan"). Moreover, the climactic trio of *Acis*, "The flocks shall leave the mountains," borrows from Pope's poem "Autumn" from his *Pastorals* (ll. 40–46).[20] Leaving aside the changes of meter, which are to be expected of verse transformed into a singing text, the transfer of the conceit is clear, including both the depiction of love's vows as more durable than nature's course (*Pastorals*, ll. 1–3; *Acis*, ll. 1–4) and the iterative statements, posed in the negative, that describe the pleasures and sustenance given by love (*Pastorals*, ll. 4–7; *Acis*, ll. 5–8); the last lines borrow words and phrases exactly but out of order.

POPE, "AUTUMN" FROM *PASTORALS*	ACIS AND GALATEA
The Birds shall cease to tune their Ev'ning Song,	The flocks shall leave the mountains
The Winds to breathe, the waving Woods to move,	The woods the turtle dove,
And Streams to murmur, e'er I cease to love.	The nymphs forsake the fountains,
	Ere I forsake my love!
Not bubbling Fountains to the thirsty Swain,	*Not show'rs to larks so pleasing,*
Not balmy Sleep to Lab'rers faint with Pain,	*Nor sunshine to the bee,*
Not Show'rs to Larks, or Sunshine to the Bee,	*Not sleep to toil so easing,*
Are half so charming as thy Sight to me.	*As these dear smiles to me.*

Most striking of all, both *Acis and Galatea* and *Esther* appear to borrow a vivid description of Neptune from Pope's translation of the *Iliad*. In *Acis and Galatea* this is logically transformed into a description of Polyphemus, Neptune's son. The same words describe the coming of Jehovah in *Esther*, where their use was probably cued by a similar line in Brereton's *Esther*. Yet the verbal parallels make the dual borrowing from the same source clear. The Twickenham edition of Pope's poems goes so far as to suggest that this double borrowing "may seem to indicate" Pope's active hand in both librettos.[21]

POPE, *ILIAD*

Fierce as he past, the lofty *Mountains nod,*
The forests shake! Earth trembled as he trod
And felt the footsteps of th'immortal God.
From Realm to Realm three *ample Strides*
   he took,
And, at the fourth, the distant Aegae shook.

ACIS AND GALATEA

Behold the monster, Polypheme,
See what *ample strides* he takes,
The *mountain nods, the forest shakes.*
The waves run frighten'd to the shore.

ESTHER

He comes to end our woes,
And pour his vengeance on our foes.
Earth trembles, lofty mountains nod.
Jacob, arise to meet thy God!

BRERETON, *ESTHER*

At his least nod *earth trembles,* roars the deep.

Handel's musical settings of these lines, although necessarily similar in affect, resist comparison, largely because in neither does "the (lofty) mountains nod" become a dominant musical motive. Nevertheless, the shared textual borrowing further illustrates the twin origins of *Acis* and *Esther.*

Both *Acis and Galatea* and *Esther* are, on their surfaces, straightforward stories: the one a tragic tale of doomed love, the other a triumphant story of evil overcome. Even so, both are open to multiple interpretations. With the Neapolitan serenata, for example, we have seen that the meaning can change as the focus shifts from one character to another; that is, the story is different depending on whether it is seen through the eyes of Acis, Galatea, or Polyphemus. In addition, both stories can support layers of meanings or hidden subtexts. This is particularly clear with *Esther.*

The Esther story, whose central message is the deliverance of a people, was often read in England as an allegory of British political and religious identity. As Ruth Smith documents in her detailed study of Handel's oratorio texts,[22] the Book of Esther was the most popular scriptural source for sermons in Thanksgiving Day services (5 November) celebrating English deliverance from the Gunpowder Plot of 1605, when a group of English Roman Catholics had planned to blow up Parliament. This political association was strengthened with the landing of the Protestant William of Orange at Torbay on 5 November 1688 (the culmination of the "Glorious" Revolution to overthrow the Catholic James II), "affording a parallel with the Jews' deliverance from religious tyranny." Moreover, Brereton's 1715 translation of Racine's play, on which Handel's libretto is based, was dedicated to Archbishop William Dawes, who was particularly known for a sermon delivered on 5 November 1696 that had referred to the Esther story.[23] However, Esther's connection to the common allegorical equation between the biblical Israelites and English Anglicans as the chosen people can only be made in the most general terms. A specific allegory, in which the characters of the biblical drama represent particular contemporaries, and which also takes into account the different nationalities and religions of Ahasuerus and Esther, the king's gullibility, and Haman's extraordinary evildoing, would be next to impossible to construct. For example, the accession of William and Mary was viewed as a parallel in terms of deliverance, but a specific reading of William and Mary into the roles of king and queen would not only reverse their nationalities (Mary was the daughter of James II and William was foreign) and describe the queen's religion (which in Mary's case was the national religion) as a persecuted minority, but would paint William (in the role of Ahasuerus) as thoughtless and cruel. In 1732, when Handel's *Esther* was publicly produced for the first time, the situation was no more conducive to specific interpretation, unless, as in one possible reading offered by Smith, all the characters are personifications: "the king is the state, Esther is the Church, enlisting the state's defence of true Protestant religion, and Haman is Catholicism."[24]

In contrast to the complexity of interpretive parallels between Esther's people and the English Protestant majority, the opposite interpretation, in which the Jewish minority represents loyal English Catholics within the larger Protestant (in *Esther*, Persian) majority, offers a simple and straightforward political allegory. As Smith states, "contemporaries referred to James II as Ahasuerus and [his wife] Mary of Modena as Esther, interceding with her husband for the international Catholic cause as represented by the British minority."[25] Indeed, James II and his wife, Mary of Modena, had been present at one of the first performances of Racine's play on 5 February 1689, only months after the king had fled to France. Earlier, the Esther story had been a frequent subject in English Catholic plays of the sixteenth and seventeenth centuries, and later, in 1731, Edmund Gibson, Bishop of London, "investigated a disturbing report of a sermon preached at St George's, Hanover Square (Handel's parish church), which was said to have promulgated opposition views and was on a text from the Book of Esther." In 1732, it was Gibson who forbade a staged performance of Handel's *Esther*, thereby initiating the subsequent history of English oratorios as unstaged dramatic works. One reason for his decision could have been that he took issue with the text itself. That is, despite alterations to the 1732 *Esther* in order to emphasize its connections with the Hanoverian party, in part by the addition of two of Handel's Coronation Anthems, Gibson "would surely have

Figure 6.1 Portrait of Alexander Pope (London, c. 1714) by Charles Jervas (c. 1675–1739). Bodleian Library, University of Oxford (Poole Portrait 243).

been aware of the possibility of reading Jacobite propaganda in *Esther,* whose libretto was publicly said to be by a Tory Papist [Alexander Pope]."[26]

Linked by their literary and political views, Pope, Gay, and Arbuthnot, together with Jonathan Swift and Thomas Parnell, had instituted a club in 1714 to combat pedantry and pretense in scholarly and literary writings. Pope had suggested establishing a satirical monthly periodical late in 1713, at a time when Pope and Gay were both actively involved in the Burlington circle. Instead, primarily during 1714, these authors, calling themselves the Scriblerus Club, penned the *Memoirs of Martin Scriblerus* (which was not published until 1741 in the works of Pope). Arbuthnot and Pope played the major roles in the writing of these *Memoirs* during the club year of 1714 (when Burlington was away from London) and again during the period 1716 to 1718 when Pope, Gay, and Arbuthnot revived the Scriblerus project.[27] Given Handel's association with these authors during the specific years of their Scriblerus activity, it seems likely that he must at times have been a witness, if not a participant, in discussions concerning this work. Among the list of already written but unpublished works mentioned in the *Memoirs* is "The Case of Queen *Esther,* with the whole Process of her *Purification.*"[28] Unfortunately, no trace of a treatise (if that is what it was) on Esther's purification survives. Its topic, according to Kerby-Miller, "would have been almost impossible to handle . . . without offending some," and he speculates that it might have been destroyed because it was sacrilegious.[29] Nevertheless, the very mention of Esther in the *Memoirs of Martin Scriblerus* would seem to bear significant relation to the libretto of Handel's *Esther,* also written by the Scriblerian authors.[30] Kerby-Miller suggests that "the idea of such a treatise [on Esther] no doubt came to Pope or Arbuthnot while they were preparing the libretto for Handel's oratorio *Esther.*" However, the reverse chronology seems equally plausible—that earlier Scriblerian work on Esther had brought the literary sources used in Handel's libretto to hand.

In regard to "why Pope and his friends might have taken an interest in Racine's play," Smith writes: "For Pope, a Catholic and a Jacobite sympathiser" and for "the libretto's other putative author, their mutual friend Arbuthnot, whose brother fought on the Jacobite side in the 1715 Rebellion," this story offers an easy allegory for Catholics and Jacobite sympathizers in early Georgian England. Such an allegory would also have appealed to Handel's patrons. In the previous chapter I discussed Burlington's political leanings and drew a relation between his possible Jacobite position and Handel's opera *Silla* of 1713. Chandos, too, sympathized with Jacobite beliefs and was in correspondence with the exiled Lord Bolingbroke in France, who served the son of James II as the rightful heir to the English throne. Bolingbroke may himself have passed on word about the allegorical possibilities of the Esther story. Not only was he a close friend of Pope, but his mistress at the time of the Cannons *Esther* had performed in Racine's play before James II.[31] Smith concludes that the Esther story

> has obvious potential, in the years immediately after the 1715 Rebellion, as an allegorised plea for justice for loyal Catholics indiscriminately victimised by punitive taxation as well as continued exclusion from public office. For Pope, and for any Catholic, this interpretation would have had the additional satisfaction of an allegorical takeover: the text used each year by Protestants to

congratulate themselves publicly on victories over 'evil' Catholic forces was now used to represent Catholics in the role of the chosen people saved from misfortune.[32]

As Smith so clearly illustrates, the potential allegorical meanings of the Esther story are multiple. From the Protestant point of view alone there are many ways of reading the story; for example, Esther can be interpreted as Queen Caroline, as the personification of Britannia, the "guardian of constitutional liberties," or as the Anglican Church, "enlisting the state's defence of true Protestant religion."[33] From the Catholic point of view, Esther was often associated specifically with Mary of Modena, James II's Catholic queen. As a Jacobite text, Esther more generally represented "an unexceptional plea for tolerance of minority views."[34] Moreover, viewing the story of Esther in this way as a general entreaty for tolerance opens up the interpretive possibilities to ever-widening circles. For example, one could substitute any number of religious minorities (including the Jewish minority itself) for the Catholic reading, and national difference could also be substituted for religious difference. For Handel's Esther, however, the Jacobite reading proposed by Smith seems to fit best with the specific group of artists and patrons associated with the work.[35]

An indication that Handel may have recognized a political allegory in Esther occurs in his choice of setting for Esther's words, "Who calls my parting soul," as she faints in the presence of her husband, King Ahasuerus, who has decreed death to all who approach him uncalled. The music can be traced back to Agrippina's only tender Adagio, "Come, O Dio," as she awaits her death on the order of her son. Both works use the topos of a forsaken woman in terms of political abandonment. As mentioned in Chapter 2, Agrippina's aria found its way into Esther through an intermediate setting in the Brockes Passion as the solo beginning of a duet, "Soll mein Kind," where Mary senses her son's imminent death: "Shall my child, my life, die, and does my son shed his blood?" Here again the melodic theme expresses a woman's experience of death and abandonment; although Mary's situation is the result of very different, but still political, circumstances, she, like Agrippina, is contemplating the death of a son and separation from him (Ex. 6.1).

In contrast to the probable religious and political allegories of Esther, the possible allegorical meanings of Acis and Galatea relate more to the primary literary aims of the Scriblerus Club: to expose pedantry and pretense through satire (as in the Memoirs) and (similar to the aims of the Arcadian Academy) to maintain and improve literary standards through a close association with the classical tradition. Thus it is no surprise that, in contrast to Motteux's Acis and Galatea of 1701 or even the Neapolitan serenata, the Cannons Acis closely follows Ovid's story. The role of Polyphemus in each of these versions offers a particularly

Example 6.1a *Esther*, "Who calls my parting soul" (voice and bass only).

Example 6.1b *Brockes Passion*, "Soll mein Kind" (voice and bass only).

Example 6.1c *Agrippina condotta a morire*, "Come, O Dio" (voice and bass only).

interesting comparison. Motteux drastically reduces the monster's part: after a brief confrontation with the lovers, Polyphemus exits in order to ask for Galatea's hand in marriage from her father, leaving the stage open for the extended scene between Acis and the rustic couple Joan and Roger. His longest set of lines comes at his exit:

> Now, Dear, this is well. I find you are wise,
> My Person you prize, and that Boy you despise.
> I'll hie me to *Nereus,* and call him ashore:
> We'll marry and then———I need say no more.

The Neapolitan serenata more closely follows Ovid by emphasizing the monster's grotesque gigantism, which is made most apparent in the aria "Fra l'ombre," in which the outsize Cyclops operatically compares himself to a fluttering moth (see Chapter 4). The Cannons authors, by contrast, repeatedly turn to Dryden's translation of Ovid for Polyphemus's language, and they follow Ovid's characterization closely. For example, in his first aria, "O Ruddier than the cherry," the use of comparatives and the progression from positive to negative attributes follow Ovid closely, even though the Cannons text has no exact borrowings from Dryden's (or Ovid's) poetic language.

DRYDEN (LL. 67–82):

Oh lovely *Galatea,* whiter far
Than falling snows, and rising lillies are;
More flowry than the meads, as crystal
   bright,
Erect as alders, and of equal height:
More wanton than a kid, more sleek thy skin
Than Orient shells, that on the shore are seen.
Than apples fairer, when the boughs they lade,
Pleasing as winter suns or summer shade:
More grateful to the sight, than goodly planes;
And softer to the touch, than down of swans;
Of curds new turn'd: and sweeter to the taste
Than swelling grapes, that to the vintage haste:
More clear than ice, or running streams, that stray
Through garden plots, but ah more swift than they.
Yet, *Galatea,* harder to be broke,
Than bullocks, unreclaim'd to bear the yoke,
And far more stubborn, than the knotted oak:
[etc.].

ACIS AND GALATEA

O ruddier than the cherry,
O sweeter than the berry,
O nymph more bright than moonshine
   night,
Like kidlings blithe and merry.
Ripe as the melting cluster,
No lily has such lustre;
Yet hard to tame as raging flame,
And fierce as storms that bluster.

The change in poetic language from Dryden/Ovid to the Cannons text paints a particularly clear picture of Polyphemus as an uncouth artist who will not be able either to win Galatea or to find solace (like Apollo) through his art. It also points to a contemporary literary controversy concerning the pastoral, which was near and dear to the Scriblerians, and which had arisen following the publication in close succession of sets of pastoral poems by Ambrose Philips (1708) and Pope (1709).[36]

Whereas Pope in his *Pastorals* maintained the classical tradition of Theocritus's *Idylls* and Virgil's *Eclogues,* writing in an elevated style of Thyrsis and Daphnis in the Golden Age of Arcadia, Philips took the stand that the true pastoral should reflect simple English rusticity both in the names of its characters (Hobbinol and Colin Clout) and in its language. Gay supported Pope with parodies of "realistic pastorals" in *The Shepherd's Week* (1714), where "Thou wilt not find my Shepherdesses idly piping on oaten Reeds, but milking the Kine, tying up the Sheaves, or if the Hogs are astray driving them to their Styes,"[37] and then even more pointedly in *Trivia* (1716), where he sets his pastorals in the City of London. Pope himself attacked Philips directly in *The Guardian* (no. 40, 27

April 1713); posing as a neutral third party supporting Philips, he compared passages in their pastorals:[38]

> But the better to discover the Merits of our two Contemporary Pastoral Writers, I shall endeavour to draw a Parallel of them, by setting several of their particular Thoughts in the same light, whereby it will be obvious how much *Philips* hath the Advantage. With what Simplicity he introduces two Shepherds singing alternately.

Hobb[-inol] *Come,* Rosalind, *O come, for without thee*
            What Pleasure can the Country have for me:
            Come, Rosalind, *O come; my brinded Kine,*
            My snowy Sheep, my Farm, and all is thine.
Lanq[uet]   *Come,* Rosalind, *O come; here shady Bowers*
            Here are cool Fountains, and here springing Flow'rs.
            Come, Rosalind; *Here ever let us stay,*
            And sweetly wast, our live-long Time away.

The other Pastoral Writer [Pope himself], in expressing the same Thought, deviates into downright Poetry.

Streph[on] *In Spring the Fields, in Autumn Hills I love,*
            At Morn the Plains, at Noon the shady Grove,
            But Delia *always; forc'd from* Delia's *Sight,*
            Nor Plains at Morn, nor Groves at Noon delight.
Daph[ne]   Sylvia's *like Autumn ripe, yet mild as* May,
            More bright than Noon, yet fresh as early Day;
            Ev'n Spring displeases, when she shines not here.
            But blest with her, 'tis Spring throughout the Year.[39]

Pope's choice of parallel passages by Philips and himself strikingly replicates the difference between Ovid's voice and that of Polyphemus in the Cannons *Acis*. It seems likely that Pope and Gay, in their contributions to the pastoral masque of *Acis and Galatea,* took the opportunity to satirize Philips, in the character of Polyphemus, as a monster who destroys the true pastoral idyll of the classical tradition, personified by Acis.[40] This reading seems particularly likely when one considers that Acis's death comes at the moment when he is actually singing words from Pope's *Pastorals* in the trio "The flocks shall leave the mountains."

Handel's setting of "O Ruddier than the cherry" replicates in music the long and obsessive sequence of comparatives which Ovid puts into Polyphemus's mouth and which one commentator has called "certainly an in-joke" (Ex. 6.2).[41] Handel borrows the basic motive for this aria from a bass motive in an aria in Reinhard Keiser's *Janus* that has a very different affect (Ex. 6.3). Agrippina, the leading woman (no relation to the Agrippina of Handel's opera and cantata), has been treacherously thrown in prison and told that her lover has ordered it so that he can marry someone else. She is allowed to see her lover once again on condition that she does not speak to him ("When I see you once more, my lips must be still, and my sighs must express what is in my speaking heart").[42]

Although Handel probably felt competitive with Keiser,[43] he, unlike Pope in relation to Philips, was heavily indebted to the older composer.[44] Despite this (or perhaps because of it), he might have enjoyed parodying Keiser in a country where the beauties of Keiser's composition were not known.[45] Interestingly, there is a possible musical endorsement to such an interpretation. Just

Example 6.2 *Acis and Galatea,* "O Ruddier than the cherry" (voice and bass only).

Example 6.3 Keiser, *Janus,* "Wann ich dich noch einst erblicke."

as the use of Pope's pastoral at the moment of Acis's death at the hands of the inept and destructive monster, Polyphemus-Philips, helps to cue the literary reading, Handel's possible association of Keiser with the destructive power of Polypheumus derives some support from his use of Keiser's Italian duet *Caro autor,* specifically at the point in "Wretched lovers" where the chorus introduces "the monster Polypheme." Handel deploys all three of Keiser's contrapuntal motives (Ex. 6.4, pp. 227–228). Perhaps the long chain of borrowing through his own works of the birdsong accompaniment in "Hush, ye pretty warbling choir" had allowed Handel to forget that that aria too found its origin in Keiser.[46] His colleagues would not have known this detail, but it seems likely that for Handel, as for his collaborators, the characterization of Polyphemus as an artist lacking artistry here took on a more personal aspect than in either Ovid's version or Handel's earlier setting of the myth.

In Handel's Neapolitan version, as in Theocritus's *Idylls,* the story focuses on Polyphemus—his inappropriate love and the possibility of curing lovesickness with art. Although that serenata was written for a wedding, for which the message was undoubtedly that true love survives even death, the young couple are never portrayed as happy, and Polyphemus dominates the score just as he dominates them. Furthermore, as in Ovid, Handel's Italian Polyphemus can be compared unfavorably with his Apollo. While the sun god's unrequited love for Daphne is transformed into a love for artistic achievement (as represented by his final elegiac aria), the monster's inability to control his passionate outbursts of love and rage contradicts the male ideal of restrained eloquence and leaves

Example 6.4a Keiser, *Caro autor,* "Da gl'amori flagellata" (voices and bass only).

him, like a wrathful woman, abandoned, alone and, ultimately, voiceless. In contrast to his Italian setting's emphasis on Polyphemus, Handel's English version of this story is primarily about Galatea, whose voice is the first and last to be heard individually in the work. Polyphemus appears only in the center of the work and is not heard from again after Acis's death, having fulfilled his function as the necessary catalyst to bring about the tragic denouement. In the most significant alteration from Handel's Neapolitan setting, this Galatea does not call on her father, Nereus, to transform Acis, but does so herself. She turns her loss into a creative act.

The emphasis on Galatea in the English version supports a possible literary allegory. In this reading, Galatea represents the Cannons circle or perhaps Pope explicitly, and she is shown to prefer the classical tradition (Acis) to the coarse and inelegant style of the rustic pastoral (Polyphemus).[47] The parody of Philips may have added humor to the Cannons version, but its ending is tragic. Polyphemus does not just lose Galatea or his artistic voice, as he does in the Neapolitan serenata; rather, he destroys the classical literary tradition, represented by Acis, leaving only Pope and the Scriblerians (Galatea and her friends) to mourn and honor its memory ("Be thou immortal, tho' thou art not mine"). This ending differs strikingly from the Neapolitan version where Galatea and Acis are eternally united, like the stream and the ocean, and Polyphemus is left alone to interpret Acis's continuing song of love.

Example 6.4b *Acis and Galatea,* "Wretched lovers" (voices and bass only).

As we have seen, both *Acis and Galatea* and *Esther* contain multiple possible meanings. In *Esther* these include two diametrically opposed political-religious allegories (each with its own variants), one celebrating the deliverance of the majority Protestants from Catholic domination and the other depicting tolerance for minority Catholics. In *Acis and Galatea* the meanings range from a story of true love that survives death to an allegory on the death of classical liter-ature at the hands of artistic charlatans.

Such multiplicity permits and encourages the consideration of further ave-nues of interpretation. In the twentieth century, for example, the Esther story has been interpreted as a closet drama related to homosexuality. As Eve Kosofsky Sedgwick points out in her book *The Epistemology of the Closet*, Mar-cel Proust implies such an interpretation of Racine's *Esther* by what she calls "in-sistent suggestions" in the "Sodom and Gomorrah" books of *A la recherche du temps perdu* (1921).[48] Sedgwick, however, does not cite any of the many passages in Proust that refer to or quote from Racine's *Esther*. One of these, as an exam-ple, comes as M. de Charlus reveals to M. de Vaugoubert, at a party, which staff members of an unnamed embassy are inclined to homosexuality:

> Certain names mentioned by M. de Charlus, indignant if he himself was cited for his peculiarities, but always delighted to give away those of other people, caused M. de Vaugoubert an exquisite surprise. Not that, after all these years [of self-denial], he dreamed of profiting by any windfall. But these rapid reve-lations, similar to those which in Racine's tragedies inform Athalie and Abner that Joas is of the House of David, that Esther, enthroned in the purple, comes of Yiddish stock, changing the aspect of the X—— Legation, or of one or another department of the Ministry of Foreign Affairs, rendered those palaces as mysterious, in retrospect, as the Temple of Jerusalem [*Athalie*] or the Throne-room at Susa [*Esther*]. At the sight of the youthful staff of this Embassy advancing in a body to shake hands with M. de Charlus, M. de Vaugoubert assumed the astonished air of Elise [Esther's attendant in Racine's *Esther*] exclaiming, in *Esther*: "Great heavens! What a swarm of innocent beau-ties issuing from all sides presents itself to my gaze! How charming a modesty is depicted on their faces!" Then, athirst for more definite information, he cast at M. de Charlus a smiling glance fatuously interrogative and concupiscent. "Why, of course they are," said M. de Charlus with the knowing air of a learned man speaking to an ignoramus. From that instant M. de Vaugoubert (greatly to the annoyance of M. de Charlus) could not tear his eyes from these young secretaries whom the X—— Ambassador to France, an old stager, had not chosen blindfold. M. de Vaugoubert remained silent, I could only watch his eyes. But, being accustomed from my childhood to apply, even to what is voiceless, the language of the classics, I made M. de Vaugoubert's eyes repeat the lines in which Esther explains to Elise that Mardochée [Mordecai], in his zeal for his religion, has made it a rule that only those maidens who profess it shall be employed about the queen's person. "And now his love for our nation has peopled this palace with daughters of Sion, young and tender flowers

wafted by fate, transplanted like myself beneath a foreign sky. In a place set apart from profane eyes, he" (the worthy Ambassador) "devotes his skill and labour to shaping them."[49]

Building on the cumulative effect of such passages, Sedgwick lays out a homosexual allegory for Racine's *Esther*, in which Esther represents the closeted homosexual and Ahasuerus the personification of the laws or dictum that would send all who practice same-sex sexual relations to their death.[50] Although an intimate of Ahasuerus, Esther realizes that "the king is to this day unaware who I am" (Racine, Act I, l. 90), but her deception "is made necessary by the powerful ideology that makes Assuérus categorize her people as unclean . . . and an abomination against nature." Esther's guardian, Mordecai, representative of her conscience and, more broadly, the collective homosexual conscience, tells her: "Go, venture to declare to the king who you are" (Racine, Act I, l. 190). Esther agrees, saying in the Bible (Esther 4:16), "And if I perish, I perish." In Racine's ending, Ahasuerus does not see the revelation as affecting his love for Esther nor as damaging to himself; rather, he immediately recognizes his error, countermands his order to kill all of "Esther's people," and punishes the advisor who proposed and supported the massacre.

Whereas the use of the Esther story as a political and religious allegory can be documented in contemporary sermons and biblical commentary, as Ruth Smith has done, I know of no contemporary written record that associates the Esther story with homosexuality in the eighteenth century. Still, the allegorical connections are sufficiently interesting to warrant further discussion. Sodomy was punishable by death, and men who committed this act were increasingly considered an identifiable minority. In 1707–1709 and again in 1726–1727, suspected homosexuals were rounded up in London in significant numbers and sentenced to the pillory, to hang, or both in succession (if they survived the pillory).[51] For those directly affected by the laws against sodomy, Ahasuerus's thoughtless condemnation of a minority community would have resonated with the frequent calls for the rooting out and death of all who engaged in homosexual acts. There is no written record of which I am aware from the first half of the eighteenth century that expresses antipathy to or outrage against such extreme punishments. The earliest such statement appears to occur in the private, unpublished papers of the English jurist Jeremy Bentham (1748–1842), whose utilitarian theory that the object of law is to achieve the "greatest happiness of the greatest number" was published in *An Introduction to the Principles of Morals and Legislation* (1789). At his death, he left hundreds of pages in manuscript (dating from throughout his life) on sodomy law reform based on this theory. Sounding a little like Esther, he wrote:

A hundred times have I shuddered at the view of the perils I was exposing my-self to in encountering the opinions that are in possession of men's minds on [this] subject. As often have I resolved to turn aside from a road so full of prec-ipices. I have trembled at the thoughts of the indignation that must be raised against the Apologist of a crime that has been looked upon by many, and those excellent men, as one among the blackest under Heaven. But the dye is now cast, & having thus far adhered with that undeviating fidelity [to] the principles of general utility I at first adopted, I will not at last abandon them for considerations of personal danger. I will not have to reproach myself with the thought that those principles which my judgment has approved, my fears have compelled me to abandon.[52]

On 11 April 1780, following another horrible death of a convicted sodomite in the pillory (and the permanent injury of another), Edmund Burke, in what was perhaps the first public statement on this issue to the House of Commons, pro-posed a bill that would have abolished this form of punishment.[53]

It can hardly be doubted that these ideas, written and spoken in the second half of the eighteenth century, were current earlier, even if those thinking them did not have Bentham's courage to write them down, even privately, or Burke's courage to speak them publicly. For example, Bentham's statements about ho-mosexual sodomy that "the extreme horror and indignation with which this Vice is regarded by the generality of people in this country will occur obviously enough as a reason for continuing the punishment for it" but "to destroy a man there should certainly be some better reason than mere dislike to his Taste, let that dislike be ever so strong"[54] expand on the simpler words of William Brown, a married man convicted of sodomy in 1726, who was fined, and sentenced to the pillory and twelve months in prison. He was quoted in court as having said at the time of his arrest: "I did it because I thought I knew him, and I think there is no crime in making what use I please of my own body."[55]

The only way for a man not so accused (and not therefore *in extremis*) to speak would be through allegory, and the Esther story offers a particularly good way to express the idea of tolerance—not just of religious dissenters, but also, by analogy, of those whose sexual practices needed to remain hidden on fear of death and disgrace. Could the authors of *Esther* have considered such a private reading of this story? It is not, of course, possible to answer this question di-rectly. The consideration of a homosexual reading needs to take into account the likely homoeroticism of the artistic circle and the strong prohibitions that existed against urging tolerance for same-sex acts. However, if such a reading was intended by the authors, it is clear that the traditional political allegories in-vested in this story would have provided ample cover.

Perhaps the best evidence for considering a homosexual interpretation of Handel's *Esther* is the stronger homosexual reading of *Acis and Galatea,* written by the same group of artists in relation to the same patron in the same year. The key to such a reading is the use of Pope's "Autumn" as a model for the climactic trio, "The flocks shall leave the mountains" (see the extracts earlier in this chapter). Although this borrowing is frequently cited, what has not generally been noted is that Pope's poem, as written in 1704, published in 1709, and republished in 1717, describes Hylas's same-sex passion for the shepherd Thyrsis.[56] In 1736, when Pope published his collected works, he hid the same-sex element of "Autumn" by changing the name of Thyrsis to Delia, thus creating a heterosexual facade which continues to this day. At the time of the composition of *Acis,* however, this change had not yet taken place, and the only version of the poem that would have been known to the collaborative group of writers at Cannons was the homosexual one. Although two modern commentators have questioned the significance of the textual parallel between Pope's poem and the trio in *Acis* (but not on account of the same-sex content of the poem, which they appear not to have known),[57] the importance of Pope's poem as a model for *Acis* can be documented not just by comparing the two texts but by tracing the lineage of Pope's pastoral.

"Autumn," as Pope states, is based on Virgil's eighth *Eclogue* in content and structure: both tell a double story of unrequited love using a double refrain. In Virgil's poem both stories are narrations: first Damon sings of Maenalus's love for Nysa (based on Theocritus, *Idyll* III), and then Alphesiboeus sings of an unnamed woman's love for Daphnis (based on Theocritus, *Idyll* II). In Pope's poem, Hylas and Aegon sing of their own loves, and the borrowing into *Acis* derives from Hylas's song only. Although the double form of "Autumn" is based on Virgil's eighth *Eclogue*, Hylas's same-sex love is modeled directly on Virgil's second *Eclogue,* which tells of Corydon's love for Alexis.[58] This eclogue, as we have seen in Chapter 4, is based on *Idyll* XI of Theocritus, in which Polyphemus sings of his unrequited love for Galatea, and the related *Idyll* VI, in which Daphnis and Damoetas cement their same-sex love through a singing competition on the subject of Galatea and Polyphemus. The literary trajectory is thus from Theocritus's *Idylls* which tell of the love of Polyphemus for Galatea in the context of same-sex love (not just of the imaginary Daphnis and Damoetas, but also of Theocritus and Aratus, to whom *Idyll* VI is addresssed), to the *Eclogues* of Virgil in which Theocritus's *Idyll* XI becomes the textual model for a poem about the same-sex desire of Corydon for Alexis (where Virgil was thought to be speaking in the voice of Corydon), to Pope's "Autumn," a pastoral that models itself on Virgil's *Eclogues* and tells of the same-sex love of Hylas for Thyrsis, to the libretto of Handel's *Acis and Galatea* which returns to Theocritus's original story, making the circle complete.

Pope's poem and Handel's libretto can be further connected to a depiction of same-sex love through the use of specific names that may serve as codes. Hylas, the lover in Pope's poem, was the homosexual love of Hercules, and Thyrsis, a common name in pastorals, repeats the name used in Handel's continuo cantatas containing male love objects (Tirsi) and also the name of one of the two men, Tirsi and Fileno, who choose male friendship over the love of Clori in *Cor fedele*, a work that, to judge from the evidence of his borrowings from it, was apparently on Handel's mind during his composition of *Acis*, perhaps in part because of the use of Pope's poem. Further, in the very lines of "Autumn" reused in *Acis*, Pope borrows from the seventeenth-century Scottish poet William Drummond of Hawthornden, whose works had recently been published in London (1711). Drummond frequently writes of the loves of Damon and Alexis, the names referring to himself (Damon) and his friend Sir William Alexander (Alexis); this practice, as in Pope's poetry, seems to refer back to Virgil's Corydon and Alexis.[59] In the Cannons *Acis*, the two shepherds added to the cast of the three principals are Damon and Corydon, both names used in classical poetry to represent same-sex lovers. Moreover, in the direct sources of Pope's poem, Corydon and Damon are both linked (Corydon by Virgil and Damon by Drummond) homoerotically if not homosexually with a shepherd named Alexis, the name that Pope gives himself throughout the *Pastorals*.

The textual borrowing from Pope's *Pastorals* into the *Acis* trio and the broader use of coded names suggests the possibility that the Cannons authors used the traditional story of Acis and Galatea, as frequently happens in published works with homoerotic origins, as a disguise for a story about a same-sex couple. Reading *Acis* as a heterosexual masking of a homosexual story would lend a completely new significance to Acis's death, when, at the end of the trio, he is crushed with a stone hurled by the monster Polyphemus. He is killed for no other reason than that he loves Galatea, who cries out after the deed:

> Must I my Acis still bemoan,
> Inglorious crush'd beneath that stone!
> Must the lovely charming youth
> Die for his constancy and truth?

Through the multiformity of myth, this death of the "lovely charming youth" by stoning resembles the death of Orpheus, who is attacked with stones and dismembered and whose head and lyre later float down the Hebrus river murmuring in mournful harmony; in *Acis*, by comparison, Galatea transforms the dead youth into a bubbling fountain that "murmurs still his faithful love." Seen within a homosexual context, Acis's death also resonates (as did Orpheus's) with the horrific Georgian stonings of homosexuals in the pillory.

In a homosexual reading of *Acis and Galatea,* Polyphemus could represent the "monstrous" law condemning men convicted of same-sex acts to death, parallel to Sedgwick's reading of Haman in *Esther.* Alternatively, he could represent a male homosexual in a position of power who, with "monstrous" hypocrisy, carries out these executions. Indeed, there is a classical precedent for this reading in Euripides' *Cyclops,* a play loosely based on the story of Polyphemus and Ulysses from the *Odyssey,* where Polyphemus in drunken enthusiasm declares his preference for boys.[60]

> This is pleasure unalloyed. I think I see the heaven and the earth swimming around together, I see Zeus's throne and the whole revered company of the gods. Shall I not kiss them? The Graces are trying to seduce me. No more! With this Ganymede here I shall go off to bed with greater glory than with the Graces. And somehow I take more pleasure in boys than in women.[61]

If, however, Acis's death is a reference to the death of Orpheus, and, by parallel association, to the deaths in the London pillories of men convicted of homosexual acts, then the sex of Acis's attacker must be considered. Not only did Orpheus die at the hands of vengeful women, but throughout the eighteenth century the assailants of convicted sodomites in London consisted largely of women who were encouraged thus to revenge the supposed insult inflicted on them by men who loved other men. In 1785, this practice was condemned in print in the complete works of Voltaire: "The law of England, which exposes guilty men to all the insults of the mob, and above all the women who torment them, sometimes to death, is at the same time cruel, indecent, and ridiculous."[62]

The most striking evidence for reading Polyphemus as a vengeful woman lies in the music. Polyphemus's opening recitative, "I rage, I rage, I rage, I melt, I burn," and his following aria, "O Ruddier than the cherry," are both modeled on arias sung by betrayed women in extreme situations. The opening of the recitative clearly evokes the opening of Marcella's mad song by John Eccles in Thomas D'Urfey's *The Comical History of Don Quixote,* where, crazed from unrequited love, she sings "I burn, I burn, I burn, I burn" (Ex. 6.5). Premiered by Mrs. Bracegirdle in the role of Marcella, this song was widely known and repeatedly published; Henry Purcell even commemorated it in a song written the next year entitled "Upon Mrs Bracegirdle Singing (I Burn &c) in ye play of Don Quixote." Eccles's "I burn, I burn, I burn, I burn" continued to be popular in the early eighteenth century, and from 21 December 1715, it was used in Gay's play *What d'Ye Call It* as an afterpiece. Therefore, Marcella's song would undoubtedly have been known to the authors of the Cannons *Acis,* and its association with a woman who not only specialized in breeches parts but sang the role of Acis in the Motteux-Eccles version of the Acis and Galatea story is probably

Example 6.5a Handel, *Acis and Galatea*, "I rage."

Example 6.5b Eccles, The Comical History of Don Quixote, "I burn."

not insignificant. One can imagine that a musical parody might have been suggested to Handel by one of his collaborators.[63]

The following aria for Polyphemus, "O Ruddier than the cherry," similarly incorporates motives from an aria for a woman in an extreme situation, in this case Agrippina from Keiser's *Janus* (see Exx. 6.2 and 6.3). Agrippina's aria might have been used by Handel as part of a private meaning shared by the authors of *Acis,* in which the monster Polyphemus was understood to represent a woman in male attire. Women who cross-dressed had been described in England in just such terms as women who,

> from the top to the toe, are so disguised, that though they be in sexe Women, yet in attire they appeare to be men, and are like *Androgini,* who counterfayting the shape of either kind, are in deede neither, so while they are in condition women, and would seeme in apparell men, they are neither men nor women, but plaine Monsters.[64]

Just as Pope later hid the homosexual origin of his poem "Autumn" by masking the sex of one member of the couple, so too does the possible sexual reversal of both Galatea and Polyphemus hide what may have been a secret homosexual allegory in *Acis and Galatea.* This meaning would have been accessible only to those who were aware of the clues, but not to the general audience. In this allegory, the male beloved in a same-sex relationship is "disguised" as the woman Galatea, and the vengeful (Thracian or English) woman is "disguised" as the monster Polyphemus. The common use of gender reversal in Baroque opera and drama would have facilitated this reading. Travesty, for example, was a common plot element. Women characters frequently disguised themselves as men. Less frequently (Gay's *Achilles* and Handel's *Deidamia* provide examples) men disguised themselves as women. Even more to the point, contemporary performance practice permitted, and perhaps even encouraged, transgendered performance. The frequent use of castrati made such exchange relatively simple, as many male and female roles were composed in the same vocal range. In Handel's *Aci, Galatea e Polifemo* the part of Acis was written for a soprano castrato with a higher part than that of the mezzo-soprano Galatea; in Eccles's masque Acis was a breeches role sung by Mrs. Bracegirdle.[65]

An allegorical interpretation of Polyphemus as a monstrous woman also relates to the operatic tradition of setting roles for witches and sorceresses in the natural male (bass or tenor) voice. English models for this practice occur in settings of *Macbeth* by both John Eccles and Richard Leveridge (about 1696 and 1702, respectively), where the role of Hecate was written for bass, and in Purcell's *Dido and Aeneas,* where at least in 1700 the role of the Sorceress seems to have been played by a bass.[66] Handel himself followed this tradition when he wrote the role of the Witch of Endor in *Saul* (1738) for a male tenor. Thus the idea of a bass singing the role of a woman was not foreign, and the choice of modeling Polyphemus's opening musical line on the familiar mad song of a crazed woman may be the specific musical clue for this reading, just as Pope's poem is the primary textual clue for the homosexual interpretation of Acis and Galatea.

Viewed as part of a same-sex allegory, Galatea and Acis represent a same-sex couple based on Pope's Hylas and Thyrsis but disguised as a heterosexual couple, just as Hylas and Thyrsis are later disguised by Pope as Hylas and Delia. Polyphemus, as the cause of the tragedy, could represent the English law making sodomy a capital crime, or he could be a man with same-sex desires himself, as in Euripides, and thus would kill Acis either out of jealousy or as a hypocritical defender of the legal code. More provocatively, Polyphemus might represent a woman disguised as a man, as in the travesty tradition, and more specifically, a dangerous woman depicted by a low male voice, following the English musical convention of bass witches and sorceresses. Whereas the Neapolitan Polyphemus loses his suit because his song lacks the manly attributes of control and reason, the Cannons Polyphemus may actually be a portrait of an abandoned and vengeful woman. If so, then Acis could specifically represent a convicted London sodomite stoned in the pillory, or, as a mythological multiform, Acis could symbolize Orpheus, stoned by the Thracian women.

It is also possible that the same-sex allegory was not invested in the specific characters of *Acis and Galatea* but rather in the use of the story as a private artistic collaboration. In such a reading none of the characters undergoes sexual transformation, but rather the very act of collaborating is erotically charged. The classical antecedent for this reading occurs in *Idyll* VI of Theocritus, where two male lovers, the cowherds Damoetas, whose "beard was already halfway grown," and Daphnis, "on [whose] cheek was the golden flower of manhood," engage in an erotic singing match on the subject of Galatea and Polyphemus, which concludes with this sexual imagery:

> When he had done, Damoetas kissed Daphnis
> and gave him a pipe, and a fine flute Daphnis gave.
> Damoetas fluted and herdsman Daphnis piped,
> and the heifers began to prance on the soft sward.
> Neither was victor; both unvanquished proved.[67]

By their use of musical and textual borrowings, the Cannons circle of artists may have recreated a similar singing of the story of Acis and Galatea in which their various contributions combined to create a privately understood homosexual meaning.

Acis and Galatea and *Esther* represent the artistic culmination of the period of private patronage in Handel's life, both works offering ample evidence of the depth and richness of Handel's musical expression. Both also provide culminating examples of important attributes in Handel's cantatas.

Galatea and Esther are further examples of "abandoned women," through whose voices at least three of their creators, Handel, Pope, and Gay, sought emotional expression—Handel in his Italian cantatas for women and Pope in his heroic epistle *Eloisa to Abelard* (1717), as well as, more pointedly, in a private letter to the third Earl of Peterborow (1723) in which he takes on the voice of an abandoned wife (see Chapter 2). In Gay's *Epistle to Burlington* (1716; published in 1720), he writes of the pleasure of borrowing women's clothing while his own is being washed.

> If women's gear such pleasing dreams incite,
> Lend us your smocks, ye damsels, ev'ry night!

Taken metaphorically—although there is no reason not to understand him literally as well—Gay describes the pleasure of trying on women's voices. In the two multi-voice works from Cannons, both the hesitantly brave Esther and the steadfast Galatea seem to speak allegorically for their authors in various guises—political, religious, and sexual, as well as, in the literary reading of *Acis and Galatea* where Galatea may represent Pope (and the other Scriblerians), professional.

In contrast to the artistic freedom possible in female impersonation, the male voice continued to represent the ideal of controlled emotion. In Italy, this ideal was supported by the Arcadian Academy in opposition to seventeenth-century poetic effusions. The texts of Handel's continuo cantatas largely derive from this movement toward a rhetoric distanced by artifice, and Handel's settings all move in this direction (see Chapter 3). Polyphemus offers a prime example of the poet-singer who cannot control his emotional expression. In Handel's Neapolitan setting, despite Acis's death, the danger posed by this lack of discipline is personal: Polyphemus loses his own artistic voice. In the Cannons setting, by contrast, the danger is expressed outward so that artistic ineptitude is viewed as hazardous not just to the artist but to the entire literary canon.

In Handel's Italian cantatas, intertextuality between the texts of the continuo cantatas and the poems of Petrarch (Chapter 3) and the multiformity of myth (Chapter 4) offer clues to multiple meanings and interpretations. In the Cannons works, the extraordinary network of intertextual relations between classical sources, contemporary translations, and the previous artistic work of a number of the authors similarly expands the possible avenues of interpretation, especially in *Acis and Galatea.* Musically, the intertextuality of Handel's borrowings, both from himself and others, also provides a rich background to a more complete and complex reading of the scores.

The role of silence in the Cannons works is largely metaphoric. Aside from typical grammatical pauses and the few madrigalistic silences, as in "Mourn all ye Muses" in *Acis and Galatea* where the chorus sings "the gentle Acis [rest] is no more [longer rest]," there is little expressed silence of the kind discussed in Chapter 5. In a reversal of the outcome of the Neapolitan serenata, where Polyphemus loses his own voice only to echo Acis's "murmurings," in the Cannons version it is Acis, possibly representing either the classical literary tradition or a same-sex lover (like Orpheus), who is silenced.

The possible use of the Acis story as a mythological multiform of the Orpheus story brings us back to Handel's cantata, "Hendel, non può mia musa," set to Pamphili's text (Chapter 1), and unites the themes of artistic excellence and same-sex love. Orpheus is killed by raging women; and Polyphemus, who kills Acis, is associated—in Ovid by contrast to the masculine ideal of Apollo—with the uncontrolled and unrestrained female voice. Because the emotionally impassioned voices of women represent a danger to life, love, and art, man must learn to control this voice not only in women but also in himself. According to legend, the Thracian women were unable to kill Orpheus until they drowned out his voice with their shouts, for as long as his voice could be heard their weapons would not harm him. In the Cannons *Acis and Galatea,* Acis's classical voice, while singing words of Pope, is overcome and silenced by Polyphemus's simple-minded patter, paralleling the Scriblerian fear that literary mediocrity would overcome true literary merit. The equation of artistic excellence with the ideal male voice sets up a same-sex motive as both text and subtext. Orpheus is killed by the Thracian women because of his preference for men and boys, and classical artistry (represented by Acis) is killed because of its allegiance to masculine artifice.

While an eighteenth-century same-sex reading of Handel's *Esther* is possible, but only tentatively, a same-sex reading of Handel's *Acis and Galatea* is not only possible but strongly probable. It is supported by the intertextuality of the literary borrowings, especially the chain that links Pope's same-sex pastoral to the *Idylls* of Theocritus, which tell the same story in a same-sex context. Moreover, by its inherent contrast of classical (masculine) and uncontrolled (feminine) voices, by its role as a mythological multiform, not just to previous tellings of the same myth but to those of Apollo and Daphne and of Orpheus, and by its metaphor of enforced silence, a same-sex reading of *Acis and Galatea* grows out of and is the ultimate product of the private, homoerotic context of the entire cantata repertory.

Epilogue: "True Representation"

Allegories and riddles, trifling as they are, afford the mind amusement: and with what delight does it follow the well-connected thread of a play, or novel, which ever increases as the plot thickens, and ends most pleas'd, when that is most distinctly unravell'd?

William Hogarth, *The Analysis of Beauty*

After Handel moved out of the realm of private patronage and into a house of his own in 1723, he ceased to be involved in the composition of cantatas, and his attention turned decisively to large-scale works for public performance. The body of private music he wrote between 1706 and 1723 ranges from continuo cantatas with two arias and a connecting recitative to such large-scale works as *Il trionfo del tempo* and *Acis and Galatea*. One shared aspect of this private repertory, whether for the Florentine court, the Roman Arcadian Academy, or the Burlington circle in London, is its relation to and growth out of a privileged male culture that embraced same-sex love. Although Handel's cantatas definitively place him in that context, they do not and cannot offer defining evidence about his desires or actions.

Documentation of same-sex desire, of course, would be unlikely during this period, and more so for a public artist such as Handel. As the cases of the dramatists Isaac Bickerstaff and Samuel Foote later in the century would show, an accusation of sodomy was sufficient to ruin a career. Even the aristocratic class, traditionally less affected by an accusation or acknowledgment of same-sex desire than were artists, merchants, or laborers, was slowly retreating behind a wall of silence. Although at the end of the seventeenth century Lord Rochester could banter publicly in his writings about his same-sex loves, Lord Hervey in the eighteenth not only avoided any public commentary about himself but when accused in 1731 of being a "pathick" (the passive partner in a sodomitical relationship) fought a duel to protect his honor before retreating into silence. When Lord Bateman separated from his wife in 1738 on account of his "male seraglio," he seems to have been spared legal action partly because he maintained a facade of silence. His wife's grandmother, the Duchess of Marlborough, wrote of him at this time: "They say Lord Bateman has consented to do great things in this separation, which, if true, shows he is very much frighted."[1]

As the dates of the incidents concerning Lord Hervey and Lord Bateman indicate, by the 1730s there had been a change in England from a society that by and large tolerated same-sex desire among the aristocracy, ignored it among the lower classes, and represented it on the stage, to one that restricted even the mention of same-sex love. It is not surprising, therefore, that the decade of the 1730s offers particularly interesting artistic evidence about same-sex love in terms of coded depictions and veiled allusions. For example, it was in 1735 that Pope altered his poem "Autumn" for republication by changing the same-sex relationship to a heterosexual one. In his revisions of the 1730s, Handel too erased same-sex allusions from the private music of his cantata period. In order to understand these artistic changes, it is necessary first to understand the social changes that define the decade historically. The altered afterlife of Pope's and Handel's earlier creative work during this decade can then be assessed in light of a social climate that lent a new, and largely negative, reading to assigned (sexual) identities.

During the first two decades of the eighteenth century, the frequently cited image of the rake or libertine with a prostitute on one arm and a pathic on the other gave way before the simultaneous development of the network of molly houses and the Societies for the Reformation of Manners. The molly houses, although many who frequented them had wives and children at home, represent a landmark in the development of a separate identity for men who engaged in same-sex acts. At the same time, the political instability of the late seventeenth and early eighteenth centuries, including the fear of external attack and internal revolution, of popery and absolutism, led to a rise of zealous reformers who called for a moral renewal to protect England from the fate of Sodom and Gomorrah. The identification of certain establishments as molly houses made them particularly vulnerable to attack, the more so because the customers were typically members of the merchant and lower classes and the reforming societies "dared not attack the aristocracy, at least not directly."[2] The Society for the Reformation of Manners was founded in 1690; by 1699 there were nine societies, and by 1701 there were twenty in London alone.

The Societies quickly began their work of rounding up sodomites for prosecution, and by 1698 a few individuals had been targeted for entrapment; 1699 saw the first successful group arrest, as mentioned in a pamphlet of that year recounting the trial and execution of the Earl of Castlehaven in 1631 for sodomy and other sexual crimes:

Another Abomination that shocks our Natures, and puts our modesty to the Blush, to see it so commonly perpetrated, is the *Devilish and Unnatural Sin of Buggery.* . . . This Sin being now Translated from the *Sadomitical* [sic] Original, or from the *Turkish* and *Italian* Copies into *English;* not only in the Infamous Example of that Monster Ri—by, and other Notorious *Sodomites;* but

. . . also that there is at this time several taken up at *Windsor,* and others of
the same Gang now Committed to *Newgate,* who were ingag'd in a more
than Beast-like Confederacy among themselves, for exercising this *Unnatural
offence.*[3]

In 1707 a larger raid netted (according to differing contemporary reports) between forty and one hundred arrests. At least three of these men committed suicide.[4] In his book *The History of the London Club[s]* (1709), Edward Ward writes
in his chapter "Of the Mollies Club":

> Thus, without detection, they continued their odious society for some years,
> till their sodomitical practices were happily discovered by the cunning man-
> agement of some of the underagents to the Reforming Society.[5]

Handel arrived in London in 1710, following the 1707 raid and its aftermath,
and for many years there were no significant arrests for sodomitical activity. At
their fifteenth annual meeting in 1710, the Societies for the Reformation of
Manners claimed that by their efforts "our streets have been very much cleansed
from the lewd night-walkers and most detestable sodomites."[6] The period of
calm following the 1707 raid permitted the molly houses to return to a more
public operation and gave relative comfort to those who frequented them. This
situation changed definitively in 1726 with the Societies' "best organised and
most comprehensive" raid.[7]

After months of preparation and infiltration, in February 1726 Mother Clap's
molly house was surrounded and forty men taken in arrest. Within months,
about twenty other houses were raided as well. Although many of those arrested
were released for want of evidence, in fifteen cases of sodomy brought to trial
between 1726 and 1730 four men were hanged; eight were fined and sentenced
to prison and the pillory (from which one died); and three were acquitted.
These numbers can be compared to twelve heterosexual rape cases from the
same period, where one was hanged, one punished, and ten acquitted.[8] One
reason for the difference stemmed from the virtue invested in procreation—that
is, the growth of the population was considered a wholly good result regardless
of the means. As stated in *Plain Reasons for the Growth of Sodomy in England,*
published about 1730:

> An old *Proverb* says, *There is no Harm done where a good Child's got.* Faults of
> this Nature must be confess'd to proceed from a Richness in *Constitution,* and
> therefore are more excuseable than *base* and *unmanly Practices.*[9]

Another reason, not entirely unrelated to the first, lay in the identification of
sodomy as an activity considered dangerous to the health of the state; in partic-

ular, the association of homosexual sodomy in England with Italy, Catholicism, and Popery made it more than a private act. Religious reformers worried that sodomy would cause God's wrath to fall upon the city and country as in the biblical Sodom and Gomorrah, while others associated it with the downfall of the state through treason.

The raids, trials, and public punishments or executions between 1726 and 1730 led to a rash of pamphleteering on the evils of sodomy, with titles such as *Plain Reasons for the Growth of Sodomy in England* and *A Hell upon Earth, or, The Town in an Uproar . . . Occasion'd by the Late Horrible Scenes . . . of Sodomy, and other Shocking Improprieties,* both published around 1730. Then in 1730 and 1731 the Netherlands initiated a far more horrific purge in which hundreds of men were arrested for sodomy and at least sixty were publicly executed by ghastly means, such as strangling and burning, drowning in a barrel, or strangling and drowning tied to a 100-pound weight.[10] These executions were widely publicized in London.

Not surprisingly, the public attitude toward same-sex love and desire changed with these events. Whereas in earlier decades aristocrats could own their same-sex desires and the lower classes could, despite the isolated raids of 1699 and 1707, engage in same-sex activities with relative impunity (as indicated by the fast and steady rise of molly houses after 1707), after 1730 such talk was silenced and such actions hidden. Public behavior also changed: men were encouraged to desist from fancy (effeminate) dress and from publicly greeting other men with a kiss, there being no custom "more hateful, predominant, and pernicious."[11] Concurrently, public accusations increased as the sodomite label became the most damning insult one could hurl at an enemy. These years were so decisive that they formed a boundary recognized by history. In 1813, Robert Holloway wrote in *The Phoenix of Sodom, or the Vere Street Coterie*:

> Many years previous to the reign of George I the sin was permitted without any exemplary punishment:—but about the twelfth year of that reign [i.e., about 1726] a number of those wretches were apprehended, and convicted of the most abominable practices, some of whom were put to death; which gave check to the evil for some time.[12]

In 1738, with the initial blast of reformers' zeal expended and public concern over paid informers rising, the Societies for the Reformation of Manners disbanded, giving themselves the credit in their final report for "instigating the prosecution of numbers of sodomites and sodomitical houses."[13]

My discussion of Handel's Italian Orpheus cantata in Chapter 1 showed that public (and semi-public) references to homosexuality frequently occurred through the use of classical names understood as coded epithets; that context is a critical factor in reading such codes; and that implicit homoerotic references can often be confirmed by their deliberate alteration or elimination in later revisions of works. These conclusions have resonated throughout this book, and they become especially relevant for the 1730s in London. The four years of aggressive prosecution of alleged homosexuals immediately preceding 1730 gave special meaning both to the thinly veiled accusations and the defensive maneuvers of this period. A series of events relating to Alexander Pope illustrates the interconnectedness of such actions.

Pope was frequently attacked in the press, and one allegation that recurs is his sexual impotence with women. In an example from 1727 this is spelled out in a statement that takes off from the idea of social inequality between a suitor (identified as the character of Gulliver) and a socially superior lady:

> And besides, the inequality of our Stature rightly consider'd, ought to be for us as full a Security from Slander, as that between Mr. *P—pe,* and those *great* Ladies who do nothing without him; admit him to their Closets, their Bedsides, consult him in the choice of their Servants, their Garments, and make no scruple of putting them on or off before him: Every body knows they are Women of strict Virtue, and he a harmless Creature, who has neither the Will, nor Power of doing any farther Mischief than with his Pen.[14]

In 1730, Aaron Hill (the author of Handel's first opera for London, *Rinaldo,* and in 1732 of a letter to Handel urging the composer to set English texts) published a similar attack on Pope entitled *The Progress of Wit: A Caveat.*[15] He calls Pope "the Ladies Play-thing," and amplifies this characterization by identifying Pope as "Alexis" throughout the poem, only identifying him by name toward the end.[16]

As we have seen, one of the best-known classical images of same-sex love is that of Corydon for Alexis in Virgil's Second *Eclogue.* Pope echoes this story in his Pastoral "Autumn," where Hylas sings of his same-sex love for Thyrsis. In defense of his classically based *Pastorals* (first published in 1709), and in opposition to the party supporting rustic (realistic) pastoral, Pope's anonymous essay in *The Guardian* in 1713 purported to support that party against himself while obviously proving his own poetic superiority. The essay begins facetiously by showing how, according to the "Rule of Pastoral" used by his opponent Ambrose Philips, all but two of the *Eclogues* of Virgil must be disallowed to the pastoral genre, and it lists the reasons for eliminating each, including that "*Corydon's* Criminal Passion for *Alexis* throws out the Second."[17] Pope's open acknowledgment of the same-sex desire of Corydon for Alexis makes his decision to refer to himself throughout the *Pastorals* as Alexis potentially meaningful. And in the context of the 1730s, Hill's use of the epithet "Alexis" in his attack on Pope becomes potentially damning.

Indeed, Hill's use of the name "Alexis" in his attack on Pope gives special significance to two changes Pope made in the publication of his collected works in 1735. In *An Epistle from Mr. Pope to Dr. Arbuthnot,* originally published in January 1735 with a publication date of 1734, Pope censures with satire a number of writers in addition to Ambrose Philips. In the 1734 publication of this poetic epistle he attacks Lord Hervey under the name of Paris, but in the 1735 collected works he changes the name to Sporus, the eunuch who became Nero's "wife." Pope himself explains the change in a note saying that the name Paris allowed a "contemptible Character" to be considered "a Noble and Beautiful Person," so "the Author changed it to this of *Sporus,* as a Name which has never yet been so mis-applied." The change creates a specifically sexual meaning, making explicit the innuendo in accusations published in 1730–1731 by William Pulteney, M.P., from which Pope borrows directly, that Hervey was a hermaphrodite and a pathic.[18] One reason for making this accusation may have been to take an offensive posture in response to Hill's criticism—in other words, to raise himself above moral suspicion by attacking more vigorously just that vice for which he was impugned, the label of Sporus being far stronger, more specific, and more scurrilous than that of Alexis. Simultaneously, Pope also took a defensive posture by changing the names in his pastoral poem "Autumn," eliminating the same-sex love between Hylas and Thyrsis.

The context of the 1730s gives resonance to the names Alexis and Sporus and special importance to the sexual alteration of the beloved in Pope's "Autumn" from Thyrsis to Delia. Also in this decade, Handel erased homoerotic implications from his earlier, private works. As suggested in Chapter 1, Handel may have destroyed his autograph or reserve copy of the Orpheus cantata at this time. He certainly altered *Il trionfo del tempo,* also based on a text by Cardinal Pamphili. For its first public performance in 1737 Handel deftly removed the reference to himself in Pleasure's kingdom by rewriting the heavenly music heard by Beauty for violin rather than keyboard. Similarly, Handel's revisions of *Acis and Galatea* for its first public performances eliminated most of the references that could have led to a homoerotic reading.

After the premiere of *Acis and Galatea* in 1718 at Cannons, Handel seems to have paid little attention to the score for years. However, the music circulated. Some of the songs, without attribution to Handel, were published in 1722; then in 1727 excerpts were performed in Bristol. In 1731 a performance, apparently of the complete Cannons version, was given in London as a benefit for the singer Philip Rochetti. Then in 1732 Thomas Arne mounted a full-scale professional performance, possibly staged. His major changes were to divide the work into three acts, to have the five-voice ensembles sung by full chorus, and to conflate the roles of Damon and Corydon into one character named Damon but sung by a woman. Handel probably did not countenance any of these performances, but Arne's he could not overlook. He quickly advertised his own *Acis and Galatea* for June of that year.[19]

If Handel meant to overwhelm his competition with the 1732 *Acis,* he certainly did so in sheer size. He combined the Neapolitan *Aci* and the Cannons *Acis,* interleaving them from beginning to end. Most of the English *Acis* was translated into Italian, but some was not, making the production bilingual. To this structure he added still more arias from other pastoral works: the instrumental cantatas *Cor fedele* and *Arresta il passo,* and the opera *Il pastor fido.* He divided this much-enlarged production into three acts: the first depicting the happiness of Acis, Galatea, and the pastoral community, taken largely from the Cannons *Acis* with additions from the other pastorals; the second introducing Polyphemus and the central conflict, combining the two versions; and the third depicting the crisis and denouement, taken largely from the Neapolitan *Aci.* Each act begins and ends with choruses, and these were borrowed, where necessary, from the *Birthday Ode* and *Brockes Passion.*[20]

Discussions of Handel's 1732 *Acis* are usually dominated by the size of the revised work, but the elimination of the cues to a homoerotic reading is at least as striking. Two of the most important are deleted: the Italian translation of "The flocks shall leave the mountains" eliminates the obvious reference to Pope's "Autumn," and all allusion to the rising triadic repetitions ("I burn, I burn") of Marcella's Mad Song is omitted, with only Polyphemus's opening run preserved in a later recitative, as shown in Ex. E.1 (compare Ex. 6.5). Furthermore, the names of both Corydon and Damon are eliminated for no obvious reason; their music is retained, and additional music for friends and confidants added. The landscape is thus clearly altered by the use of common pastoral names—Clori, Filli, Sylvio, Dorindo and Eurilla—with no obvious homoerotic overtones. Although any one of these changes might be considered inconsequential in other circumstances, the combined force of the 1730s context, the importance of code names, and the fact of the alterations themselves, as in the examples in Pope's work, gives them weight. Handel never performed the Cannons version complete on the public stage. Only after the public was familiar with the enlarged work did Handel revert to an all-English version, in 1739, but, among other differences, he never restored the names Damon and Corydon.[21]

A comparison of alterations made by Pope and Handel to their works in the 1730s raises the question of whether Handel, like Pope, might have been motivated by a specific allusion to his sexuality, or if the context of the period alone was sufficient to suggest these changes. Although I know of no public reference to Handel's sexuality that definitely predates the alterations he made to *Acis* and *Il trionfo del tempo* in the 1730s, there is evidence that Handel was publicly associated with homoeroticism. As discussed in the Prologue, the eighteenth century viewed same-sex love through three separate filters: legal, classical, and ex-

Example E.1 *Acis and Galatea* (1732), Polyphemus's recitative.

otic. By the end of the century, one writer combined all three into a single descriptive sentence defining homosexuality as "the passion contrary to nature [legal] which the Thracian dames avenged by the massacre of Orpheus [classical], who had rendered himself odious by gratifying it, the inconceivable appetite which dishonoured the Greeks and Persians of antiquity [which] constitute[s] the delight, or, to use a juster term, the infamy of the Egyptians [exotic]."[22] Although the cantata repertory privileged the classical view almost to the exclusion of the others, and depicts Handel only through the classical lens as Orpheus, Handel in England was depicted in all three categories.

The most vicious image of Handel appears in a caricature by Joseph Goupy (Fig. E.1). The original chalk drawing on canvas, which remained in Goupy's hands until after Handel's death, is now in the Fitzwilliam Museum.[23] Its date is uncertain. A print of this drawing, probably by Goupy, appeared around 1749

Figure E.1 Caricature of Handel (London, c. 1740?) by Joseph Goupy (1686–1770). Fitzwilliam Museum, Cambridge.

(Fig. E.2), and two anonymous prints closely related to it appeared later, one in 1754 (Fig. E.3) and the other probably later but in the same general period. In the following discussion I will refer to these four known states of the image as follows: Goupy drawing, Goupy print, 1754 print, and "final" print. The thrust of the image in all its versions has generally been understood to reflect Handel's gluttonous appetite. The only known motive for this drawing was published in 1822 by Laetitia-Matilda Hawkins as an anecdote told her by her father John

Hawkins, the music historian. According to this story, around the time in 1733 when he was facing intense opposition to increased prices for admission to his oratorio *Deborah*, Handel invited Goupy to supper, warning him that it would have to be "plain and frugal." Goupy, one of Handel's best friends, accepted on that basis. After dinner, Handel excused himself, but was gone so long that Goupy rose from his chair and caught sight of Handel in an adjoining room eating just such a meal as he had told his friend he could not afford. The supposed upshot of this event was the portrait of Handel, the termination of their friendship, and the loss of a legacy for Goupy in Handel's will.[24] If the drawing is actually the result of such an event around 1733, however, Handel either did not know of it or ignored it, as he and Goupy remained close friends for a number of years. Apparently the two bachelors had a reputation for kicking up their heels, for in 1740, when Handel journeyed to the baths at Aix-la-Chapelle for health reasons, his decision to travel with Goupy led the Earl of Radnor to write to his friend James Harris, "Mr. Handel set out for Germany Thursday last in company with Goupee, therefore there is little hopes of his *Amendment*."[25] It may be that Goupy's drawing dates from after 1743, in which year the two men were still friendly, but perhaps Handel only learned of the drawing or only took offense when Goupy made his print.

Certainly *one* of the thrusts of Goupy's caricature is Handel's enormous appetite and his bulk. He is depicted as a grossly fat hog or boar seated on a keg at an organ. A ham and a fowl hang from the side of the organ, and oyster shells are scattered around the floor. In the late anonymous prints, this aspect of the caricature is further emphasized by the elimination of other details and the addition of still more food, wine bottles, and a long grocery list hanging out of Handel's pocket. The 1754 print, entitled "The Charming Brute," further points up this meaning with the following verses:

> The Figure's odd—yet who wou'd think?
> Within this Tunn' of Meat & Drink
> There dwells the Soul of soft Desires,
> And all that HARMONY inspires:
> Can Contrast such as this be found?
> Upon the Globe's extensive Round.
> There can—yon Hogshead is his Seat.
> His sole Devotion is—to EAT.

The eliminated details of Goupy's drawing and print certainly matter, however. As the painter and critic Jonathan Richardson had written in 1719, "painting is another sort of writing."[26] Emblems offered a code, published in collec-

Figure E.2 "The true Representation and Character &c" (c. 1741?), engraving by Joseph Goupy (?). Copyright © The British Museum, London.

Figure E.3 "The Charming Brute" (1754?), anonymous engraving. Copyright © The British Museum, London.

tions such as Cesar Ripa's *Iconologia* (London, 1709), whereby artists could depict a point of view that viewers could interpret. Jenny Uglow writes in her study of Hogarth:

> Nearly all contemporary satire used emblems, partly because they were safe, not obviously personal, slanderous or treasonable. The habit of "deciphering" was deeply engrained.[27]

Emblematic images provided "the learned with arcane wisdom while providing the ignorant with enjoyment."[28] Caricature, the exaggeration of features for comic effect and/or attack, also played a key role, becoming especially important in England in the 1730s following the English publication of the relatively genial and gentle caricatures of Ghezzi, some of whose images were discussed in Chapter 3 (see Figure 3.1). However, caricature also offered a method of public punishment "when the culprit had put himself beyond . . . reach."[29] For example, "unbelievably gross" satires and caricatures of George II appeared by 1737.[30] As Uglow writes, satirical images "were *weapons* as well as portrayals."[31] Goupy's image of Handel is more than a satire about his weight and appetite; it is an attack on his person. Goupy's drawing and its copies, as Donald Burrows has written, "may have gained credibility from some streak of gluttony in Handel's personality, but the purpose behind the caricature has yet to be explained convincingly; it is likely that some wider social or political intention dictated the nature of the images."[32]

Richard Wallace has demonstrated that Goupy's work is modeled in part on a print by Jusepe Ribera entitled "Drunken Silenus."[33] Silenus, a mentor to and follower of Bacchus, is always represented as a grossly fat old man, always drunk and usually riding a donkey. (In reference to Silenus, satyrs, the disciples of Bacchus, were often called Sileni.) In its first three states the caricature of Handel contains a creature leaning out from behind the organ holding up a mirror, emblematic of vanity, to Handel. In the two versions by Goupy, an identification of the creature is not absolutely clear. Edward Rimbault (1876) identifies it in the drawing as "Aesop," the ancient, and possibly fictitious, author of animal fables; Wallace (1983) identifies it from the print as a monkey.[34] In the 1754 print, by contrast, the creature holding the mirror is certainly a satyr, probably borrowed, as Wallace suggests, from the Ribera print. In the final version of the print this figure holding the mirror is eliminated. The association of the satyr figure in the 1754 print with Silenus points to a meaning in all versions that encompasses both sexuality and bestiality. That is, the image portrays Handel as an animal, just as "Aesop's Fables" used animals to depict human frailties such as avarice. Moreover, the satyr itself was a creature half man, half animal. The monkey symbolizes man's baser self (lust in particular and vice in general), and the combined figure of a mirror held by a monkey specifically represents lust in addition to vanity.[35]

Goupy's drawing also makes striking reference to loud music by surrounding Handel with drums, horn, trumpet, and bassoon, considered by Jacob Simon (1985) as a depiction of Handel's "fondness for loud orchestral effects."[36] Rimbault colorfully describes the scene as it appears in Goupy's print: "In the midst of the chamber, which is in great disorder, are kettle-drums, a hunting horn, a side drum, and an enormous trumpet; and through the open window are visible a donkey's head, braying, and a park of artillery which is fired, without cannoniers, by the blazing music of the organist."[37] The addition of "smoking cannons," unique to the Goupy print, is generally considered a reference to the use of cannons at (but not in) the performance of Handel's Fireworks Music of 1749 and is used to date this particular version. Although the reference is likely, it should also be mentioned that at least as early as 1742 Pope had used the term "cannon" (in reference to kettle drums) in the *Dunciad* to describe the rousing quality of Handel's music; he writes concerning Handel's "removal" to Ireland in 1741–1742 where *Messiah* was premiered:

> Mr. *Handel* had introduced a great number of Hands, and more variety of Instruments into the Orchestra, and employed even Drums and Cannon to make a fuller Chorus; which prov'd so much too manly for the fine Gentlemen of his age, that he was obliged to remove his Music into *Ireland*.[38]

Both the number and the prominence of the musical instruments are reduced in the anonymous copies of the drawing, which also include a musical score on the floor behind Handel, identified only in the final print as *Messiah*.

The musical instruments (and cannons), which certainly refer to the famed "noisiness" of Handel's music, contribute to the identification of Handel as the subject of the caricature, but this was not their only meaning. The trumpet, for example, is specifically emblematic of the sin of pride; Ripa's *Iconologia* identifies the trumpet with boastfulness, or the opposite of beneficence.[39] This meaning links the image of the trumpet with the mirror, reinforcing the depiction of vanity and pride. Ripa also associates music generally with flattery and with the danger of being charmed,[40] giving perhaps a different twist to the title of the 1754 print, "The Charming Brute." More specifically, Ripa's emblem for scandal contains a figure with a lute in the left hand and an oboe and a music book at the feet.[41] Granted the substitution of the organ as a further identifying feature of Handel, Goupy's image is close enough to Ripa's that this meaning too can be layered with the others. Finally, the relation of the image to Silenus offers a reading of the loud drums and pipes as part of the worship of Bacchus, as described by Ovid:

> Bacchants and Satyrs are your followers,
> And that old drunkard [Silenus] whose stout staff supports
> His tottering steps, who sits so insecure
> Upon his sagging ass. Wherever your
> Course leads you, young men's shouts and women's cries
> Echo afar with noise of tambourines
> And clashing bronze and long-bored pipes of box.[42]

Goupy's original drawing contains a riderless but saddled horse (which seems much too small within the perspective of the drawing) behind the figure with the mirror. Typically an emblem of death, the riderless horse may signify the death of friendship through pride and greed. Rimbault suggests that the wall and entrance gate behind the horse resemble the gate to Burlington House;[43] indeed, Henry Angelo in his *Reminiscences* states that Lady Burlington collaborated with Goupy on the original satire.[44] If so, the horse may indicate the end of patronage. In the Goupy print, the gateway is transformed into a more elaborate and fanciful architecture, and a braying donkey, drawn directly from Ribera's "Drunken Silenus," replaces the horse.[45] The donkey clearly refers to the ass on which Silenus rides. In addition, the ass is emblematic of sloth or idleness.[46] Ripa also associates asses' ears with arrogance and luxury.[47] Neither the horse nor the donkey appears in either of the later prints.

In both Goupy versions, a scroll (trampled) beneath Handel's feet reads "Pension Benefit Nobility Friendship." The scroll seems to have a double-edged meaning, referring both to Handel's lack of these qualities (as in the dinner with Goupy) and lack of gratitude to others for offering him these gifts. Simon suggests the latter only, writing that this emblem is "less easy to interpret but may be a reference to patronage and friendship disdained."[48] In light of the other depictions of vanity, arrogance, luxury, and idleness in this drawing, such an interpretation supports the emblematic reading of the horse in the first version as the death of patronage and friendship. In the later anonymous versions, the scroll is changed to read "I am myself alone."

In sum, Goupy's two versions of this image are far more damning than a simple representation of gluttony; only in the later anonymous copies is the caricature largely reduced to that single attribute. In his "true Representation and Character &c" of Handel, as his print is titled, Goupy specifically depicts Handel as lustful, proud, gluttonous, slothful, and contemptuous of "pension, benefit, nobility, and friendship." This combination of character traits had a specific meaning in seventeenth- and eighteenth-century England when homosexuality was viewed as an outgrowth of the general sin of debauchery. Edward Coke in *The Third Part of the Institutes of the Laws of England* (1644) states that the basis of homosexuality is "pride, excess of diet, idleness, and contempt of the poor."[49]

This legal description derives directly from its biblical source, Ezekiel 16:49: "Behold, this was the guilt of your sister Sodom: she and her daughters had pride, surfeit of food and prosperous ease, but did not aid the poor and needy."[50]

A homosexual reading of Goupy's caricature presents Handel as having unbridled appetites. His gluttony is shown by his characterization as a hugely obese hog, by the excess of food strewn about him—the beer and wine kegs and, later, bottles—and by a parallel to Silenus. His sexual appetite is suggested by the monkey (later the satyr) and the combination of loud drums and pipes associated with Bacchic orgies, and, following Ripa's emblematic codes, a scandal is hinted at by the placement of wind instruments and, later, a music-book on the floor (and, indeed, the very surfeit of musical noise depicts yet another kind of unrestrained appetite). The specific type of lust is described with emblems representing a combination of traits specifically thought to coincide with same-sex desire: vanity (mirror, monkey holding a mirror, trumpet), gluttony, idleness (boar or pig, donkey) and luxury (asses' ears, abundance of wine, food, and music), and lack of generosity and gratitude (the scroll under Handel's feet, the riderless horse, the possible reference to Burlington). This reading is affirmed by the owl on Handel's head in the Goupy drawings. Rimbault rather hopefully suggests that the owl alludes to Handel's "habits of retirement."[51] More correctly, the owl is associated with deceit (Simon) and with "darkness, bad augury and evil" (Wallace).[52] Like all birds of prey, it also indicates avarice (and thus appetite once again).[53] The bird's negative connotation is further emphasized by what Wallace gently describes as "misbehaving" (defecating) on Handel's head. Finally, in a meaning not openly published in contemporary lists of emblems, but probably available at least to Burlington and Goupy through Italian contacts, the owl designated a homosexual and, specifically, a pathic, as documented by Michael Rocke in his research on Florence.[54] The owl, like most of the emblems that would connect this image with homosexuality, was eliminated in the later anonymous prints.

A homosexual reading also clarifies the meaning of the verses attached to the Goupy print:

> Strange Monsters have Adorn'd the Stage,
> Not Afric's Coast produces more.
> And yet no Land nor Clime nor Age,
> Have equal'd this Harmonious Boar.

In contrast to the verses on the 1754 print, these lines not only do not emphasize gluttony, they do not directly mention it. Rather they refer to "strange monsters" on the stage, alluding certainly to the castrati of Italian operas, making the connection to Africa's shores, a locale the English frequently associated with eunuchs and the origin of sodomy. In sum, Goupy's images of Handel, especially the later print, depict Handel as a homosexual by emblematic association with the legal and biblical definitions of the period. In the later, anonymous copies of this satire, the homosexual imagery is largely omitted, recalling the alterations made by Pope and Handel in their own work.

An accusation of homosexuality is not the same thing as a confirmation, and the same culture of antagonism to same-sex desire that led to the elimination of homosexual references in artistic works also created a healthy climate for false accusations and blackmail. During this period, robbers and highwaymen were known to keep their victims from calling out for help by threatening to accuse them of sodomy, and a few such were hanged for making false accusations.[55] The homosexual epithets "Alexis" and "Sporus" in the published quarrels between Hill and Pope and between Pulteney and Hervey may similarly be the result of seeking the most defamatory personal slur possible, but they may also be factual (as in the case of Hervey they most certainly were). The same is true of the Goupy print. It contains a number of insults, one of which seems to be an accusation of homosexuality. This could be a reading that Goupy hoped his viewers would find and he could deny intending; but, like the other embedded insults, it could represent a truth.

Whereas the use of biblical and legal imagery was always damning, the appeal to classical authority for same-sex desire could be neutral as well as negative. Pope directly attacked Hervey with the name Sporus, while names such as Alexis and Corydon offered a more gentle and ambiguous allusion. If the use of such names was questioned as a personal reference to same-sex desire, it was possible for an author to plead classical literary precedent. The name of Orpheus in particular was ambiguous: on the surface it could simply refer to musical or poetic superiority, but it could also carry a subtext of homosexuality. Throughout his life Handel was often referred to as Orpheus. Although the intended balance between the two meanings of the name cannot always be determined, it is clear that a homosexual reading does not generally take priority. That is, the homosexual reading suggested by Pamphili's cantata text, *Hendel, non può mia musa,* derives from its special context and cannot be generally applied.

In terms of a sexual reading, the most interesting parallels between Handel and Orpheus are those that specifically refer to the end of the legend rather than those that permit an association with Orpheus winning Eurydice back from Hell through his musical abilities. Between about 1739 and 1746 a situation arose that made the end of the story an obvious choice for allegory. Following the turmoil of 1733 to 1737 when Handel was forced to compete with a second company in London, the Opera of the Nobility, another opera company was formed in 1739 under the direction of Lord Middlesex. Although Middlesex's company was supported by many of Handel's former friends and patrons, as well as some of those who had supported the Opera of the Nobility, Handel refused to participate. No doubt in retaliation, a group of women subscribers to Middlesex's opera refused to attend Handel's oratorios, setting up conflicting parties and events. Mrs. Delany writes in 1744 that "all the opera people are enraged at Handel," and singles out the "fine ladies, petit maîtres, and ignoramus's."[56] In 1744 Handel's librettist Jennens writes of "ladies" opposed to Handel,[57] and Mainwaring in his biography of 1760 states that in 1743 Handel fell "under the heavy displeasure of a certain fashionable lady."[58]

The one woman specifically associated with the opera party's opposition to Handel is Lady Margaret Cecil Brown. Although she was certainly not Handel's only adversary—nor indeed is it likely that his opposition could have consisted only of a small group of ladies[59]—the image of the male musician overwhelmed by feminine ranting fed the stereotype of the destructive power of the female voice, whether internal (in terms of conquering the female voice within, which Polyphemus fails to do) or external. Orpheus's death offered a clear analogy. The earliest example seems to be a poem written in 1739, entitled "Advice to Mr. *Handel:* Which may serve as an Epilogue to *Israel in Egypt.*"

> In vain thou hop'st to charm with Sounds divine
> The Fiend, who stops her Ears to Sounds like Thine;
> Deaf to the Charmer's Voice, tho' 'ere [*sic*] so wise:
> The more thy Art to sooth her Malice tries,
> The more her Javelin of Detraction flies,
> But flies in vain; her Javelin let her throw,
> Superior Merit still eludes the Blow.[60]

Although Orpheus is not mentioned by name, the relationship to the following lines of Ovid about the Thracian women illustrates the parallel.

> "Look!" shouted one of them, tossing her hair
> That floated in the breeze, "Look, there he is,
> The man who scorns us!" and she threw her lance
> Full in Apollo's minstrel's face, but, tipped
> With leaves, it left a bruise but drew no blood.[61]

This connection is confirmed in a poem of 1745 that not only mentions Orpheus and the Thracian women, but also emphasizes the relation to Ovid's telling of the story in ample footnotes. Further, its final line ("And vanquish ev'ry Fiend of *Thrace*") echoes the designation of the enemy in the earlier poem as

"The Fiend." Entitled "To Mr. Handel," the poem was published in the *Daily Advertiser* (21 January 1745) and includes the following lines:

> While you, Great Master of the Lyre;
> Our Breasts with various Passions fire;
> The Youth to Martial Glory move,
> Now melt to Pity, now to Love;
>
> . . . . .
>
> How hard thy Fate! that here alone,
> Where we can call thy Notes our own;
> Ingratitude shou'd be thy Lot,
> And all thy Harmony forgot!
> Thou'dst feel, alas! the like Disgrace
> Thy Father *Orpheus* felt in *Thrace.*
> There, as dear *Ovid* does rehearse,
> (And who shall question *Ovid's* Verse?)
> The Bard's enchanting Harp and Voice
> Made all the Savage Herd rejoice,
> Grow tame, forget their Lust and Prey,
> And dance obsequious to his Lay.
> The *Thracian* Women 'tis wellknown,
> Despis'd all Music, but their own;
> But chiefly ONE, of envious Kind,
> With Skin of Tyger *capuchin'd,*
> Was more implacable than all,
> And strait resolv'd poor *Orpheus* Fall.[62]

As David Hunter has shown, Lady Brown is specifically identified here by the adjective "capuchin'd," referring to a popular style of a dress with a hood that was modeled on the *brown* tunics worn by the Franciscan order of Capuchins.[63] She is even more clearly identified in a poem published the following year (April 1746) entitled "Orpheus and Hecate." Here Orpheus descends to Hell and succeeds in winning Eurydice, only to find his return path opposed by "*Brown* Hecate."[64] In a footnote to this poem, Hecate is described, according to the "Atients," as having three heads, "that of a Horse, a Bitch, and a Savage; the second is suppos'd to be the Head used on this occasion."

These poems primarily attack Handel's enemies, specifically the women who opposed him, by referring to the Orpheus legend. They are not, like Goupy's print, an attack on Handel. Nevertheless, the repeated references to Orpheus's death as told by Ovid would have raised the issue of sexuality to anyone who knew the story. Henry Fielding's *Eurydice,* a farce that played in February 1737, makes it clear that the story was familiar. In the opening scene, where the Author and Critick discuss the play, the Critick fears "some part of the Audience may not be acquainted with it"; to which the Author responds, "No, No; any Man may know as much of the Story as my self, only by looking at the End of *Littleton's* Dictionary, whence I took it. Besides Sir, the Story is vulgarly known. . . . Dear Sir, every School-Boy knows it." Fielding depicts Pluto "conquered" by Orpheus, and Charon consoles the bard for his loss of the termagant Eurydice, stating: "I believe the Devil [Pluto] would be very glad to go with you, if he could leave his Wife behind him." Orpheus then sings in "recitative":

> Ungrateful, barbarous Woman!
> Infernal *Stygian* Monster!
> Henceforth Mankind
> I'll teach to hate the Sex.

In such lines, Fielding's play depicts Orpheus's misogyny and alludes to his preference for same-sex love, offering also "some innuendo on the sexual preferences of the castrati."[65] The repeated use of the death of Orpheus as a metaphor for Handel's situation in the 1740s similarly contains sexual innuendo.[66]

During the same period as the Orpheus poems, this metaphor of Orpheus's death also appears as a refrain in the letters from the circle of the renowned philosopher James Harris, who arranged Milton's *L'allegro* and *Il penseroso* for Handel's setting of that text.[67] In January 1744, for example, the Oxford classical scholar and tutor John Upton (1717–1760) sent Thomas Harris (brother to James, friend of Handel, and a London lawyer) the following lines, attributing them to Pope:

> An Epigram by Mr Pope
> On Handel's &c. &c.
> "Orpheus of old drew only stones and stocks:
> Our Orpheus draws the *wise* as well as blocks."[68]

As a riddle, these lines are not immediately transparent. "Stocks" could refer to the main stems of plant life, making the first line mean simply that Orpheus attracted trees and stones. "Blocks" might then refer not just to the stupid (blockheads) in contrast to the "wise," but could mean dull and lifeless, setting up a contrast between those who are intellectually alive (wise) and those who are like the stones and stocks (blocks). Somewhat differently, "stones" and "stocks" could refer to the objects thrown by the Thracian women, stones and lances/javelins, which could lead to an interpretion of the epigram as saying that Orpheus of old drew the wrath of women but ours attracts wise (masculine) ears as well as insensitive ones (with a gendered reading strongly implied). "Stones" and "stocks" could also refer to contemporary punishments for sodomy, stoning and the pillory, meaning that while the old Orpheus was killed for his same-sex desire, the new Orpheus attracts wise men as well as female opposition.

In the Harris correspondence, the Orpheus story continued to be closely connected with Handel for years. On 14 February 1745 Thomas Harris writes to his brother about the competitive entertainments set up by Handel's female enemies: "I had thought the Thracians would have filled it [the opera *L'incostanza delusa*] in opposition to Orpheus, but find they reserve themselves for their puppet-shew."[69] Upton continually compares Handel to Orpheus. In 1750 he writes, "Here I keep Lent, and this doleful season I expect consolation from the Lute of our Orpheus. You know what animals he drew. And shall not an equal Orpheus have equal power? Consider what an animal I subscribe myself in musick, & yet I think I am paid for loss of time & money. But you that have *ears to hear*—how you can stay away I know not."[70] And in 1752: "I am constant attendant on Mr Handle [*sic*], just as the Brutes were on Orpheus; to hear, admire, and stare."[71]

The Orpheus myth thus runs as a thread through Handel's life, its same-sex implications always available, but rarely obvious. In Pamphili's Orpheus cantata text of 1707, a same-sex reading can be plausibly argued, based on the social context and the individuals connected to it. With the epigram attributed to Pope, similar circumstances apply. Pope and Handel collaborated during Handel's first decade in London in an environment of private patronage that was imbued with homoeroticism. Pope's *Pastorals* play with classical images of same-sex desire, and his contribution to *Acis and Galatea* provides a key to a homosexual reading of that text potentially connected to the Orpheus myth. In the 1730s Pope and Handel both revised artistic work from earlier years, eliminating same-sex references. Whether or not the poems published between 1739 and 1745 associating Handel's situation with the end of the Orpheus story contain a specific homosexual subtext, they openly suggest that men were more attracted to Handel's music and better able to understand it. Any educated Englishman who had read the classics would have understood this same-sex attraction in terms of Ovid's version of the story. Indeed, the poem "To Handel" in 1745 specifically asks "And who shall question Ovid's Verse?" "Pope's" epigram surely picks up the double meaning of these references.

The image of same-sex desire as foreign seems to have begun as a way of distancing homosexuality from England. To a certain extent, any non-English origin was acceptable, and the root of same-sex desire was variously traced to France, Italy, and Egypt, among other locales. Italy and Greece were frequently linked because of their classical authority, but the alleged relation of same-sex desire to Catholicism and political upheaval equally paired France and Italy as the "original theatre" of this "crime."[72] However, the association of same-sex love with Turkey and Persia increased throughout the eighteenth century as the English became ever more fascinated with the Middle East. On the one hand, romantic literature, travel books, and the increase of trade to that area as a result of the East India Company made Eastern culture and artifacts fashionable. On the other hand, Eastern religions and societies were, unlike Europe, mysterious and remote, and the association of same-sex love with the East gave it a heightened sense of personal danger and allure. Without a direct connection to England's political and religious enemies in Europe (such as had been posited by the Societies for the Reformation of Manners), the practice of homosexuality could be seen as romantically foreign and distant. By the end of the century, this "romantic" view had largely superseded the "classical" one. During Handel's life, however, exoticism was in its nascence.

The exotic origin of same-sex desire was typically located in Turkey or Persia. In the preface to the pamphlet of 1699 concerning the trial and condemnation of the Earl of Castlehaven, homosexuality is described as "translated from . . . *Turkish* and *Italian* copies into *English*."[73] In 1715 Sir John Percival wrote that the opposition had spread rumors "that [George I] keeps two Turks for abominable uses."[74] At the end of the century Charles Sonnini described same-sex passion as "the inconceivable appetite which dishonoured the Greeks and Persians of antiquity."[75]

Readers of travel books and history had many additional opportunities to make the association between Persia and same-sex love. For example, Thomas Herbert's *A Discription* [sic] *of the Persian Monarchy* (1634) had been repeatedly reprinted into the eighteenth century.[76] Herbert describes many royal banquets at which "Ganymede boys in vests of cloth of gold, rich bespangled turbans and embroidered sandals, curled hair dangling about their shoulders, with rolling eyes and vermilion cheeks, carried in their hands flagons of best metal; and went up and down, proffering the delight of Bacchus to such as were disposed to taste it."[77] He also tells of a usurping prince who escaped from his enemies, whereupon they "cut in pieces an accursed catamite who was his bed-fellow."[78] A manuscript catalogue of the library of James Harris's son, the first Earl of Malmesbury, provides valuable information on the extensive holdings of James Harris in the area of Persian history.[79] His books about Turkey and Persia include *Customs of the East Indies* (London, 1705), Fryke's *Two Voyages into the East Indies* (London, 1700), *Turks, History of* (London, 1683), Knolles's *History of the Turks* (London, 1610), Sandy's *Travels thro' Turkey, Egypt etc* (London, 1621), and Tavernier's *Voyages through Turkey into Persia & the East Indies* [trans.] by Phillips (London, 1678).

Mrs. Delany's comment of 1738 in a letter to her sister that "my Lord [Bateman] you must know has some times been famous for a male seraglio" illus-

trates how the exotic (Persian or Turkish) representation of homosexuality provided words and images that allowed the subject to be discussed in polite
company. In the same year, James Harris's correspondence discusses the premiere of Handel's *Xerxes,* King of Persia, the subject of which seems to have suggested various bantering allusions. On 22 April 1738, Harris writes to his friend
Upton:

> You mention nothing of our Timotheus the Great Handel. What success has
> Xerxes? Is he followed by Millions now as he was formerly, or was the Spirit of
> Fear and Servitude then able to work greater Wonders than the love of Art &
> Genius is now? At present I Heartily wish him good Success tho a Persian & a
> Monarch.

Then on 4 May the Fourth Earl of Shaftesbury writes to Harris:

> The concern you show about poor Xerxes's welfare is really commendable; 'tis
> to be hoped you are coming to think a little more favourably of great Mon-
> archs. . . . But to be serious, Xerxes is beyond all doubt a fine composition.[80]

These texts suggest a number of riddles. First, it appears that the name "Xerxes"
is applied at different times both to the opera and to Handel. When first used
by Shaftesbury it may refer to Handel and to the opera as well; later, however, it
clearly means the opera. Harris's letter is harder to interpret. He first calls Handel "Timotheus," the great Greek musician who roused Alexander the Great
with his music. The reference is certainly to Dryden's *Alexander's Feast,* which
Handel had set the previous year, in which "Timotheus to his breathing flute /
and sounding lyre, / Could swell the soul to rage, or kindle soft desire." The
scene of the Ode is the Persian city of Persepolis "at the royal feast, for Persia
won / By Philip's warlike son" (Alexander's defeat of Darius, King of Persia).
Harris then asks about Xerxes, appearing to move on to the opera, but his next
question, "Is he followed . . .?" maintains the personification. Possibly Harris is
using here the historical Xerxes as a symbol of the opera, asking whether "he"
(the character of Xerxes) is still followed by millions or whether "the Spirit of
Fear and Servitude" (instilled by the historical Xerxes) was more effective than
the "Art & Genius" (of Handel as represented in the opera), concluding that he
wishes "him" (the operatic character and opera) well "tho a Persian & a Monarch." However, Harris may also be incorporating Handel in his commentary
on the operatic character, just as he equates the composer with the character of
Timotheus. If so, the most interesting statement occurs in the final line: "At
present I Heartily wish him good Success tho a Persian & a Monarch." Although the sentence continues to play on the texts of Handel's recent composi-

tions (either *Xerxes* or *Alexander's Feast* could have elicited the phrase "Persian and a Monarch"), the construction of the sentence also makes clear that this description is negative. The growing eighteenth-century association of Persia with same-sex love, in addition to Harris's extensive library holdings on the culture of ancient and modern Persia, points to the possibility that the subtext of this statement is homosexuality.

The history of ancient Persia, predating that of ancient Rome, repeatedly tells of eunuchs and same-sex love in the royal courts. Xenophon's *Cyropaedia*, reportedly one of Harris's favorite books,[81] explains that Cyrus the Great preferred eunuchs as personal bodyguards because their allegiance was not divided by the love of a wife or ambitions for their children; thus Cyrus "selected eunuchs for every post of personal service to him, from the door-keepers up."[82] This tradition was continued and expanded by his successors, whose sexual use of the eunuchs becomes ever clearer. As a modern author has written, "The harem of Darius III of Persia included both concubines and eunuchs, as did that of Artaxerxes. After Alexander the Great defeated Darius he began to copy Persian ways, adding to his harem a number of eunuchs whom he took as sexual partners."[83] Given what is known of their education and reading, Harris, Upton, and Shaftesbury would all have known that any of the Persian monarchs, native or conquering, implied in this exchange—Xerxes, Darius III, and Alexander—would have kept boys and eunuchs for their enjoyment.

All three of the sexually implicit images of Handel—legal, classical, and exotic—take strength from a factual basis and some interconnection. Goupy's drawing presents Handel as enjoying a surfeit of food and composing with a surfeit of sound, incontestable attributes of the composer. That Handel also was at times vain and arrogant can be read from anecdotes about his temper and stubbornness. The Orpheus poems and references depict a period in which Handel was opposed by a group of society women who apparently were angry at Handel for refusing (their desire for him) to compose an opera for the Middlesex company, and the scroll that Handel tramples in the Goupy drawing may, depending on its date, refer specifically to Handel's rejection in 1743 of this request, in which Goupy was used as an emissary.[84] The comparison of Handel to Persian monarchs draws on the obvious fact that Handel, like those monarchs, employed eunuchs (castrati). The sexual allusions in these images cannot, of course, be similarly proven, but whether true or false, accusation or slur, they are based on codes easily deciphered in the eighteenth century. The combination of traits portrayed in Goupy's drawing, and particularly its emphasis on unconstrained appetite, combine to form the contemporary legal definition of a sodomite. The Thracian women, who successfully silenced Orpheus, attacked him because he refused them and preferred same-sex love. The sexual image of the Persian monarch did not refer solely to the employment status of eunuchs, but to the monarchs' sexual desire for eunuchs and boys (as well as women); and, with this reading in mind, it is possible that the turbaned and bearded "Aesop figure" in the Goupy drawing represented a Persian or exotic, who, like either the satyr or Aesop, depicts unbridled sexuality holding up a mirror to Handel.

Harris's library provides all the keys necessary to unlock coded messages in any of the three eighteenth-century images of homosexuality. His collection of materials on Persia offers the essential background for an understanding of the exotic image. For a sodomitical reading of Goupy's caricature, one would only need to know the Bible. Harris, who had studied law at Lincoln's Inn,[85] also owned Coke's *Institutes* in which the biblical description is translated into legal code. Further, Harris would surely have followed the 1739 legal proceedings against Robert Thistlethwayte, Warden of Wadham College, for an attempted sodomitical attack on a commoner student. Not only was there significant publicity concerning this case,[86] but it would have held special importance for Harris, who had been a gentleman commoner at Wadham ten years before. In addition, Harris's deep background in the classics would have allowed him to understand the sexual reference in such classical code names as Ganymede and Alexis, to realize the potential double meaning in the name Orpheus, and to comprehend the sexual inferences in the literary chain leading from Theocritus to Handel's *Acis and Galatea*. His library contained three copies of Theocritus's *Idylls,* two copies of Ovid's *Metamorphoses* in Latin and one in the Sandys translation (London, 1740), and multiple copies of Virgil's complete works.

In a review of 1990, Donald Burrows wrote about the complexity of writing a biography of Handel:

> The biographer is faced with a number of difficult choices: whether to take Mary Granville's [Mrs. Delany] or Goupy's view of Handel's personality . . ., and Canaletto's or Hogarth's of 18th-century society? When music begins to intrude into the biography the difficulties are even greater.[87]

I believe the answer to the question of which choice to make can only be "all of the above." Handel did not live only in Canaletto's or Hogarth's London, and his close friends included both Goupy and Mrs. Delany. To confine our view to a single perspective limits our sense of the man and his time, and to separate the music from the context that created it restricts our ability to comprehend it fully.

Same-sex love and desire played a critical role in eighteenth-century Italy and England. Through personal, legal, literary, and historical (not to mention trade) routes it permeated all levels of society, and it would be surprising if Handel's music had been unaffected. Despite periodic prosecutions and horrific executions, artists publicly and individuals privately found ways to include same-sex love in their plays, novels, letters, and conversation. The nonchalance of Mrs. Delany in writing to her sister of Lord Bateman's male seraglio gives the lie to those who think everyone adhered to the views of the Societies of the Reformation of Manners, and her explanation of same-sex allusions in Garrick's *Miss in her Teens* illustrates that this aspect of the play was grasped at the time. Handel's cantatas offer the listener many avenues of exploration toward a better understanding of their cultural context and intrinsic beauty. Their association with same-sex desire in the eighteenth century does not exclude other meanings, as I hope to have shown, but rather adds an essential element to their full appreciation.

Cantata Chronology

This appendix provides in semi-tabular form a chronological survey of the cantatas based on documentary evidence, of which a significant portion derives from paper studies of the autographs. Although the details of Handel's autographs and the data collected from various archival sources are largely incontrovertible, the chronological reading of this factual information depends on interpretation. The chronology presented here derives from my previous work, modified where necessary in the light of more recent scholarship; as much as possible, references are provided parenthetically, using the shortened citations listed in the Bibliographic Abbreviations. Longer explanatory notes are given at the end of the Appendix. I have tried to present clearly those situations where the chronological interpretations of this data conflict and to indicate the reasons for my conclusions. Interested readers should thus be able to consider for themselves the problems inherent in a chronological analysis of the cantatas. The reader who does not want to pursue this investigative track should be assured that significant differences of opinion are limited in scope. It is, of course, valuable to compare the chronological analysis presented here with the musical analyses presented earlier in the book, especially in Chapters 2 and 3.

Categories of evidence

By conflating and interpreting information from different sources, it is possible to identify groups of cantatas organized by geographical location, patron, and date. My groupings appear below in chronological order, with evidence provided for each in terms of the following four categories.

1. *watermarks:* On the premise that Handel acquired his music paper in batches and worked through a single lot before requesting or purchasing more, it is possible to group and often to date his scores on the basis of the paper itself as indicated by the paper maker's watermark. Thus, at the most obvious level, typical Roman paper with a *fleur de lis* ("Fleur") watermark can be distinguished

from paper of Venetian manufacture with three crescent moons ("Moons"). I take the names of these papers and their subclassifications from Burrows/Ronish, *Catalogue,* where watermarks are named by identification of the main image (Fleur, Moons), subgroups within categories are identified by numbers in increments of 10 (Fleur 10, Moons 10), and further distinctions are made on the basis of initials in the countermark (Moons SS10). In previous publications, including my own, different names have been used; for example, "Moons" has been referred to as Three Moons, Triple Crescent, Three Crescents, and so forth.

2. *page layout:* Further distinctions can be made by examining the layout of the page. Handel's paper probably was acquired blank and then ruled with musical staves (most likely by a professional scribe). The implement used for this purpose (a rastrum) may be familiar from the use of an oversize version for drawing chalk staves on school blackboards. Because rastra varied both in the width and number of staves they could draw at one time, one batch of ruled paper can often be distinguished from another of the same paper type ruled differently. The detailed measurements given here come exclusively from Burrows/Ronish.

3. *documentary evidence:* An important source of evidence derives from the account books of Handel's patrons. In these, we often find the dated payment records for copies made of music performed in the patron's house. Further chronological information is provided by contemporary diaries and letters. Finally, manuscript copies and collections of the cantatas and archival documents concerning these copies offer significant evidence about the performance and transmission of the cantatas.

4. *compositional aspects:* Pertinent chronological information for specific cantatas can frequently be gleaned from various aspects of the sources. For example, Handel appears to have composed the cantata *Ah! crudel* on a discarded folio. The title of a different cantata, "Qual ti riveggio," provided in a scribal hand, is crossed out, and Handel has added "A Crudel." This may indicate that *Ah! crudel,* although it first appears in the Ruspoli accounts on 10 October 1711, was written at the same time as *Qual ti riveggio (Ero e Leandro),* placing it around September 1707. In addition to data collected from such unique circumstances, voice range and musical style also provide tentative chronological evidence, and Watanabe uses handwriting analysis to group individual cantatas, as cited below.

Listing of compositional groups of Handel's chamber vocal works:

- continuo cantatas are listed first and set off by a row of asterisks; instrumental cantatas next; then other works (such as *Il trionfo del tempo* and

Acis and Galatea) in general order of size for Italian periods and in chronological order for London periods.
- alternate titles are provided in parentheses (titles in italics and first lines in
  quotation marks).
- identifying chronological information in parentheses follows the title: autograph date, date of the first copy (when this is not the identifying feature of
  a group) with name of patron or identification of a large manuscript collection in which a copy survives.
- for the few cantatas where this is known, the author of the text is given after the chronological information.
- voice category is provided for cantatas not written for solo soprano and for
  all duets, as this provides evidence for grouping.
- HWV numbers are given only when it is necessary to identify the specific
  version.

Moons 1706 group (Florence and/or Venice)

Chi rapì la pace? (Ruspoli: 31 August 1709)
Fra tante pene
Lucrezia ("O numi eterni") (Ruspoli: 31 August 1709)
Sarai contenta un dì
Udite il mio consiglio (Ruspoli: 16 May 1707)
***
Abdolonymus ("Figlio d'alte speranze")
Sonata a 5
Tacete ohimè (SB)
Caro autor di mia doglia (ST)

1. This entire set is composed on Moons paper of Venetian manufacture;
Burrows/Ronish provide specific identifications: Moons 10, Moons 20, Moons
30, Moons SS10, and Moons SS30. The *Sonata a 5* is included with the group
as the likely overture of *Abdolonymus* (Marx, *Kantaten mit Instrumenten* II,
p. xx). This set comprises the only works that Handel composed completely
on Moons paper of these five subgroups. Handel's first dated Italian autograph, the Latin motet *Dixit Dominus*, bearing the inscription "1707/li [space]
d'aprile/Roma," uses Moons 10, Moons SS10, and Moons AZ10 paper for
the first thirty-five folios (Burrows/Ronish, *Catalogue*), but the last sixteen folios have the Fleur watermark connected with Rome. This partial use of northern Italian (non-Roman) paper implies that Handel either began composing
Dixit Dominus before arriving in Rome or used paper left over from an earlier

visit in northern Italy. A similar situation applies with the autograph of *Rodrigo,* whose overture only is on Moons SS10; the body of the opera is on Roman paper.

2. The set is further identified by the use of a ten-stave rastrum (that is, one that draws ten musical staves at a time). Burrows/Ronish provide measurements of the width of the rastra, which range from 178 mm (*Fra tante pene*) to 193 mm (*Caro autor di mia doglia*).

3. A bill dated 16 May 1707 in the Ruspoli account books for a copy of *Udite il mio consiglio* provides the latest possible date for this group. Although Kirkendale ("Ruspoli," pp. 245 and 249) has argued that all the cantatas copied for Ruspoli were composed for him, there is no firm evidence to support this conclusion, and source evidence would seem to disprove it. This is especially the case for cantatas copied in 1711 when Handel was certainly no longer in residence in Rome, which probably holds for the 1709 copies as well (see below, Moons 1709 group: 3–4). That *Lucrezia* and *Chi rapì la pace?* were copied for Ruspoli on 31 August 1709 only indicates that these works were available in Rome at that time and of interest to Ruspoli.

4. Only in this early Moons group of Italian works does Handel sign his autographs with the German form of his name (Händel); this signature appears in *Lucrezia* and *Sarai contenta un dì,* as well as in *Tacete ohimè* (Watanabe ["Music-Paper," pp. 203, 205–206] concurs, but Burrows/Ronish [*Catalogue,* p. 104] disagree, interpreting the signature on *Lucrezia* and *Sarai contenta un dì* as "Handel" without the umlaut). By the time of *Dixit Dominus,* Handel had italianized his signature to [Giorgio Federico] Hendel (as in England he anglicized it to George Frideric Handel). In sum, all evidence points to this set as a cohesive group that may represent Handel's earliest Italian work and can be dated before his arrival in Rome in January 1707. Although the paper is of Venetian manufacture, its wide distribution across northern Italy makes a specific identification of provenance impossible without further evidence; both Florence and Venice are likely locations. The relation of this paper to Handel's Roman compositions of 1707 strongly supports a date of late 1706.

Pamphili 1707 (Rome)

Sarei troppo felice (Ruspoli: 22 September 1707) Pamphili
Hendel, non può mia musa (Ruspoli: 9 August 1708) Pamphili
***

Delirio amoroso (Pamphili: 12 February 1707) Pamphili
Tra le fiamme (Pamphili: 6 July 1707) Pamphili
Il trionfo del tempo (Pamphili: 14 May 1707) Pamphili

1. *Sarei troppo felice* and *Delirio amoroso* are without surviving autograph. The other three works are composed on Roman (Fleur) paper; Burrows/Ronish identify *Tra le fiamme* and *Il trionfo del tempo* as Fleur 10, *Hendel, non può mia musa* as Fleur 20.

2. The three autographs are ruled with ten staves using five-stave rastra about 82 mm in width (Burrows/Ronish, *Catalogue*).

3. All three of the instrumental cantatas were copied for Pamphili in 1707, between February and July (Marx, "Händel in Rom," pp. 111, 113–115). The copying bills in the Ruspoli ledgers for the continuo cantatas *Sarei troppo felice* in September 1707 and for *Hendel, non può mia musa* in August 1708 are probably copies made for Ruspoli of earlier work.

4. Watanabe ("Music-Paper," p. 203) specifically links the handwriting in *Hendel, non può mia musa* and *Tra le fiamme* and places *Hendel, non può mia musa* in his chronological listing among the compositions of June 1707 ("Music-Paper," p. 213). All three instrumental cantatas have texts by the cardinal, as does *Hendel, non può mia musa*. The textual refrain of *Sarei troppo felice* is also known to be by Pamphili, making it likely that the entire text of this cantata may also be by the cardinal (Pamphili is identified as the author of a cantata by Alessandro Scarlatti [30 April 1701?] with the identical text refrain; see Edwin Hanley, "Alessandro Scarlatti's *Cantate da Camera:* A Bibliographic Study" [Ph.D. dissertation, Yale University, 1963], p. 437). These five works from Pamphili's pen can probably be associated with Handel's first year in Rome, where—on the basis in part of Handel's performance in January on the organ of St. John Lateran, where Pamphili was archpriest—Pamphili seems to have been his first patron.

Ruspoli 16 May 1707 (Rome)

Aure soavi
Del bel idolo mio (Ruspoli: 31 August 1709; paired with *Se per fatal destino?*)
Nella stagion
Poiché giuraro amore
Sei pur bella
Se per fatal destino
***

Diana cacciatrice ("Alla caccia")
Tu fedel? tu costante?

1. *Sei pur bella* is without autograph. *Tu fedel? tu costante?* contains four folios written on Bird AR; the remainder of this cantata is on Fleur 10. The

other works are all composed on Fleur 10 or Fleur 20 (Burrows/Ronish, *Catalogue*).

2. The overture to *Tu fedel? tu costante?* is written on nine staves ruled with a three-stave rastrum about 49 mm in width. As Handel's orchestration for this movement falls into three three-stave brackets, this layout fits perfectly. The score thereafter reverts to ten staves: the four folios on Bird AR are ruled with a ten-stave rastrum of 189.5 mm, and the final seven folios on Fleur 10 adhere to the standard pattern of ten staves ruled with a five-stave rastrum between 81 mm and 82 mm in width. Even though a stave or two is sometimes left blank, the layout of ten staves provides maximum flexibility for the variable scoring of this cantata. Although there is no practical reason for the use of the nine-stave layout in continuo cantatas that demand multiples of two-stave groups, two such cantatas from this group, *Nella stagion* and *Poiché giuraro amore,* also use the nine-stave layout. This arrangement appears in only two further compositions: in the entire instrumental cantata *Un'alma innamorata,* from the immediately following Ruspoli group, where the layout fits the scoring of violin, voice, and continuo; and in what appears to be a leftover bi-folio in *Laudate pueri* (8 July 1707). This specific nine-stave layout is unique in Handel's Italian sojourn—but confirms the supposition that Handel used lined paper in batches: the cantatas with this combination of paper and format only appear in two closely connected copying bills in the Ruspoli documents (16 May and 30 June 1707). A single sheet of Fleur 20 in *Diana cacciatrice* ruled in nine staves in the pattern 4, 4, 1 represents an extremely rare layout (but it can also be found in the overture of *Arresta il passo;* see Ruspoli August/September 1708). The rastrum used in *Del bel idolo mio* matches exactly that of *Se per fatal destino* (all measurements from Burrows/Ronish, *Catalogue*).

3. The keystone for this chronological grouping is the bill dated 16 May 1707 in the Ruspoli account books. However, on the evidence of its paper and layout, *Udite il mio consiglio,* also copied at this time, has been identified as originating earlier in the pre-Roman group of compositions; on the basis of its rastrum, *Del bel idolo mio* has been added to this group.

4. The manuscripts copied for Ruspoli are preserved at the Diözesan-Bibliothek, Münster, in a collection named for its subsequent owner, Fortunato Santini (Ewerhart, "Santini"). These manuscripts assist in various ways to clarify the Ruspoli documents. For example, *Sei pur bella* exists in three versions (HWV 160a, b, c), one of which (HWV 160a) Chrysander believed was not by Handel; however, it is this version that survives in the Santini Collection, even though not in autograph, proving it to be Handel's original setting (Mayo, "Italian Cantatas," pp. 160–162). Of the forty-seven works listed by name in the Ruspoli documents, only four are missing from the Santini Collection. From

this chronological set, only *Diana cacciatrice* does not survive in the Santini Collection.

Ruspoli 30 June 1707 (Rome)

***

Un'alma innamorata
Armida abbandonata ("Dietro l'orme fugaci")
Salve regina
Coelestis dum spirat aura
O qualis de coelo sonus

1. *Coelestis dum spirat aura* does not exist in autograph. *Un'alma innamorata* uses Fleur 10; the remaining works use Fleur 20 (Burrows/Ronish, *Catalogue*).

2. As discussed above (Ruspoli 16 May 1707: 2), *Un'alma innamorata* has nine staves ruled with a three-stave rastrum; it may, therefore, have been composed marginally earlier than the works in this set. The other three autographs all have ten staves ruled with standard five-stave rastra of 81–82 mm (Burrows/Ronish, *Catalogue*).

3. Kirkendale ("Ruspoli," p. 230) identifies *O qualis de coelo sonus* as a motet for Pentecost Sunday (12 June 1707) and *Coelestis dum spirat aura* as having been composed for the feast of Sant'Antonio (13 June 1707). They are listed in the Ruspoli documents as "due Mottetti" and were performed at Ruspoli's country estate in Vignanello. Burrows (*Handel,* p. 27) suggests that the *Salve regina* was performed on Trinity Sunday (19 June 1707). Kirkendale also associates *Armida abbandonata* with this excursion, as well as *Diana cacciatrice* from the May group.

4. From this chronological set, only *Salve regina* does not survive in the Santini Collection (see Ruspoli 16 May 1707: 4).

?Spring 1707 (Rome)

Filli adorata e cara (Ruspoli: 31 August 1709)
Ninfe e pastori (Ruspoli: 28 February 1709)
Stelle, perfide stelle!

1–2. *Filli adorata e cara* is on Fleur 20, the other two cantatas on Fleur 10. All three are identically ruled with ten staves using a five-stave rastrum of about 89–89.5 mm (Burrows/Ronish, *Catalogue*).

3. *Partenza di G. B. Cantata* is Handel's autograph heading for *Stelle, perfide stelle!*. A canceled heading "Partenza di B Cantata di G. F. Hendel" appears on

fol. 73 of the autograph of *Rodrigo* (Burrows/Ronish, *Catalogue*, p. 65), indicating Handel's use of a discarded folio that had originally been intended for a copy of his cantata (Dean/Knapp, *Operas*, p. 110). As *Rodrigo* was largely written in Rome 1707 for performance in October 1707 in Florence, the use of this discarded page in the *Rodrigo* score demonstrates that the cantata must have been written in Rome 1707. *Ninfe e pastori* was copied for Ruspoli on 28 February 1709 in a group of three cantatas; the other two, *Poiché giuraro amore* and *Armida abbandonata,* originate from Ruspoli's household in May and June 1707. *Filli adorata e cara* appears in the Ruspoli account books for 31 August 1709, when twenty-one works (or partial works) by Handel were copied for Ruspoli. Of these, ten are continuo cantatas that were copied previously (sometimes twice), the majority of these (seven) from 1707.

4. Watanabe ("Music-Paper," p. 208) associates *Ninfe e pastori* and *Stelle, perfide stelle!* with *Se per fatal destino* (Ruspoli 16 May 1707) on the basis of handwriting, placing them all in 1707. He associates the handwriting of *Filli adorata e cara* with other 1707 works, including *Un'alma innamorata* (30 June) and *Diana cacciatrice* (16 May) ("Music-Paper," p. 203).

Colonna 1707 (Rome)

***

Donna che in ciel (February?)
Dixit Dominus (April)
Laudate pueri (8 July)
Nisi Dominus (13 July)
Saeviat tellus
Te decus virginum
Haec est regina virginum

1. In this group only *Dixit Dominus* and *Laudate pueri* exist in autograph. *Dixit Dominus* begins with thirty-five folios on Moons paper identified by Burrows/Ronish as Moons 10, Moons SS10, and Moons AZ10, indicating that this work was either begun before Handel arrived in Rome or composed on paper left over from an earlier period (see Moons 1706 group). The last seventeen folios of *Dixit Dominus* include a bi-folio on the unique Fleur V, but otherwise it and *Laudate pueri* are on standard Roman paper (Fleur 10 and Fleur 20).

2. The Moons paper is ruled with ten-stave rastra of between 188 mm and 192.5 mm in width (Burrows/Ronish, *Catalogue*). Both the watermark subgroups and the rastra identify this paper with the pre-Roman 1706 group. The Fleur paper is ruled with ten staves using a five-stave rastrum of 82–83 mm

(Burrows/Ronish, *Catalogue*). *Laudate pueri* contains a single bi-folio ruled in nine staves with a three-stave rastrum associated with the Ruspoli May group.

3. Handel dated his autograph of *Dixit Dominus* April 1707, Rome. *Laudate pueri* is signed 8 July, and *Nisi Dominus*, whose autograph was destroyed by fire in 1860, was dated 13 July. The text of *Saeviat tellus* honors the Carmelite Order, and a nineteenth-century note on the copy in the British Library (Egerton MS 2458) identifies the work as having been composed for the Festival of Our Lady of Mount Carmel on 16 July [1707] at the church of the Madonna di Monte Santo in the Piazza del Popolo, Rome, "at the expense of the Colonna family." With the exception of *Donna che in ciel*, whose text refers to "the deliverance of Rome from an earthquake on 2 February 1703" (Burrows, *Handel*, p. 35), all the Latin church music in this group could be related to a Vespers service mounted by Cardinal Colonna in honor of the Carmelite festival.[1]

4. No specific composition or performance date is known for *Donna che in ciel*. It is likely to have been performed on 2 February, the anniversary of an earthquake that struck Rome in 1703. Although performance dates in 1708 and 1709 have been tendered, 1707 seems most likely on the basis of musical style (Hicks, "Musical Development," p. 87). Burrows (*Handel*, p. 35, n. 26) suggests that, like the Vespers service, this composition may have been commissioned by Colonna.

8-stave group 1707 (?Ottoboni, Rome)

Dimmi, O mio cor
E partirai, mia vita?
Occhi miei
Venne voglia (A) (*Amore uccellatore*)
Vedendo Amor (A)
Sans y penser (Ruspoli: 22 September 1707)
***

Spande ancor (B)
No se emenderá jamás (Ruspoli: 22 September 1707)
Ero e Leandro ("Qual ti riveggio")

1–2. This chronological set has a mixed assortment of watermarks largely unified by a layout of only eight staves, using either eight- or four-stave rastra (see Burrows/Ronish, *Catalogue*, for the following details). There are four watermark-layout groups. *Occhi miei* and *Ero e Leandro* share the Bird AR paper and the use of an eight-stave rastrum about 168 mm in width. The eight staves of *Venne voglia* and *Vedendo Amor* (on A30) are drawn with a four-stave rastrum of 81 mm. Those of *Dimmi, O mio cor*, *E partirai, mia vita?* and *Spande ancor* (on

A20) are drawn with a four-stave rastrum of 76.5 mm. *Sans y penser* (on Fleur 10 and Fleur 20) and the last two folios of *No se emenderá jamás* (on Fleur 10) use a four-stave rastrum of about 71 mm; the first four folios of *No se emenderá jamás* have ten staves and use the standard five-stave rastrum (81–82 mm). There has been some fluctuation in the identification of provenance and date for the three A20 cantatas: *Dimmi, O mio cor, E partirai, mia vita?* and *Spande ancor.* Burrows/Ronish (*Catalogue,* p. xxiv) identify "A10–A30" exclusively with Italian paper. In an earlier work, however, Burrows ("Hanover," p. 53) conflated A20 and A40 paper, placing works on both types in Hanover, 1710, and Marx (*Kantaten mit Instrumenten* I, p. xvi) recently has followed this earlier conclusion, placing *Spande ancor* in Hanover. Of course, Handel could have carried Italian paper to Hanover, but, in fact, it seems he rarely carried blank music paper from one city to another. In contrast, the use of Bird AR paper in four folios of *Tu fedel? tu costante?* (see Ruspoli: 16 May 1707, above) demonstrates the (maddening, but not surprising) exchange of paper among Handel's closely associated Roman patrons.

3. *Ero e Leandro* is the only composition by Handel that has been identified with Cardinal Pietro Ottoboni's patronage. A note on the autograph written by a former owner in 1837 describes the cantata as having been written in Rome 1707 for Ottoboni (Marx, "Ottoboniana," pp. 71–72). The specific period of Ottoboni's patronage in 1707 may possibly be identified in a letter of 24 September 1707 to Prince Ferdinand from his Roman correspondent Annibale Merlini describing a virtuoso archlute player who had performed at the palaces of both Ottoboni and Colonna and whose skill could be attested by "the famous Saxon" (Deutsch, *Handel,* pp. 19–20), undoubtedly Handel, who would shortly be returning to Florence for the preparations for his opera *Rodrigo.* The 22 September 1707 copying bill for *Sans y penser* and *No se emenderá jamás* in the Ruspoli accounts connect these works with the same time period.

4. The grouping of this set of works follows from the consistent use of eight staves in the general layout of the page. Its chronological placement derives from the association of *Ero e Leandro* with Ottoboni, the placement of Handel at Ottoboni's in September (following similarly important groups of works for Pamphili, Ruspoli, and Colonna), and the confirmation of eight-stave layout in autographs of this exact period in the Ruspoli accounts. Although eight-stave layout drawn with a four-stave rastrum is common in Roman copies (Watanabe, "Music-Paper, pp. 222–225, "rastra D"), it is largely limited in autographs to this set (but see *Se tu non lasci amore* below, Naples 1708). Further, two cantatas from the A20 group that have sometimes been placed in Hanover, 1710 (*E partirai, mia vita?* and *Dimmi, O mio cor*) were revised in London as part of the pedagogical group of cantatas (see below, English revised cantatas), and a comparison of the musical style in the earlier versions with the revisions

strongly supports an original composition date not later than 1707 (see Chapter 2). Watanabe chronologically links this entire set of works with other compositions from 1707: he connects the handwriting of *Sans y penser* and *No se emenderá jamás* with *Menzognere speranze* (all copied for Ruspoli, 22 September 1707) ("Music-Paper," p. 214) and associates all the other works in this group by handwriting ("Music-Paper," pp. 200, 206–207), placing them in his chronological list even earlier than I would, around April 1707.

Ruspoli autumn 1707 (Rome)

Menzognere speranze
Ne' tuoi lumi
Qualor l'egre pupille
***

Cor fedele (SSA)
Ah! crudel (Ruspoli: 10 October 1711)

1–2. *Qualor l'egre pupille* and *Ne' tuoi lumi* do not survive in autograph. The remaining three cantatas are written on Fleur 10 and Fleur 20 paper with ten staves drawn with five-stave rastra of 81–82 mm (Burrows/Ronish, *Catalogue*). A single sheet of Deer paper in *Cor fedele* may indicate that this work was revised for performance in Naples (Marx, *Kantaten mit Instrumenten* I, p. xviii); see below (Naples 1708).

3. The three continuo cantatas all appear in a Ruspoli copying bill dated 22 September 1707 and are apparently new works. Also copied at this time were Pamphili's *Sarei troppo felice,* and the *Cantata Francese* and *Cantata Spagniola* (*Sans y penser* and *No se emenderá jamás*), both tentatively associated with Ottoboni. Kirkendale ("Ruspoli," pp. 230–231) suggests that the "cantata a tre" listed for 14 October is *Cor fedele*. Marx (*Kantaten mit Instrumenten* I, p. xviii) places this cantata instead with *Il trionfo del tempo* (May 1707) because the designation *Monsù Hendel* is used only on the bindings of *Il trionfo del tempo, Cor fedele,* and *Arresta il passo* (see below, Ruspoli August/September 1708). However, Handel repeatedly appears as *Monsù Hendel* in Ruspoli's account books until the end of 1708 (see, for example, Kirkendale, "Ruspoli," p. 267, showing bills for September 1708), indicating that this designation was more widely used than just during one month of 1707.

4. *Ah! crudel* was copied for Ruspoli on 10 October 1711, long after Handel had left Italy, but its autograph bears the title "Qual Ti riveggio" in a scribal hand. In making use of this discarded sheet, Handel merely crosses out the one cantata title and replaces it with the other—"A Crudel" (Burrows/Ronish, *Catalogue*, p. 282). As Marx (*Kantaten mit Instrumenten* I, p. xvi) argues, this may in-

dicate that *Ah! crudel* was written at the same time as *Qual ti riveggio* (*Ero e Leandro*), placing it around September 1707. Its paper and layout associate it with the Ruspoli rather than the Ottoboni group.

Autumn 1707 (Florence)

***

Rodrigo (November?)

1–4. The overture is on Moons SS10 paper lined with a ten-stave rastrum, connecting its composition with the pre-Roman group, and suggesting, unusually, that Handel composed the overture first. The remainder of the opera is written on Fleur 10 and Fleur 20 paper with ten staves ruled with five-stave rastra of about 81 mm or 89.5 mm (Burrows/Ronish, *Catalogue,* pp. 64–65), indicating that Handel composed this work in Rome. The date and place of performance were discovered and have been discussed by Strohm ("Händel in Italia," pp. 156–160) and Weaver/Weaver (*Florentine Theater,* p. 210).

Spring 1708 (Rome: Ruspoli)

Lungi dal mio bel nume (3 March 1708; Ruspoli: 31 August 1709)
***
La resurrezione (Ruspoli: performed 8/10 April)

1–4. *Lungi dal mio bel nume* is composed on Fleur 10; *La resurrezione* on Fleur 10 and Fleur 20. Both are ruled with ten staves using a five-stave rastrum of 81 mm to 81.5 mm (Burrows/Ronish, *Catalogue*). *Lungi dal mio bel nume* is dated by Handel 3 March 1708; *La resurrezione* was performed 8/10 April 1708. These works mark the return of Handel to Rome after an absence of about four months, during which time he was certainly in Florence for the performance of *Rodrigo,* probably in Venice for the the opera season, but possibly in Hamburg for the performance of his opera(s) *Florindo* and *Daphne* in January 1708 (see Chapter 1). Handel apparently spent only about two months in Rome, leaving on 1 May, probably for Naples; according to Ruspoli's accounts, his bed and other necessities, which were rented in March, were returned after 1 May (Kirkendale, "Ruspoli," p. 239).

Naples 1708

Mentre il tutto è in furore (Ruspoli: 28 August 1708)
Nel dolce tempo (A)

Nell'africane selve (B)
Quando sperasti (Ruspoli: 9 August 1709)
Sento là che ristretto (A) (Ruspoli: 31 August 1709)
***

Cuopre tal volta (B)
Se tu non lasci amore (SAB)
Quel fior che all'alba ride (SAB)
Aci, Galatea e Polifemo (SAB) Nicola Giuvo

1. The autograph of *Aci, Galatea e Polifemo* (except for a single sheet of Fleur 10) is written on two types of paper that are distinctive: Fleur VC and Deer AP. The only other compositions of Handel on these papers are the instrumental cantata for bass *Cuopre tal volta* on Fleur VC and the continuo cantatas *Sento là che ristretto* for alto and *Mentre il tutto è in furore* for soprano on Deer AP. *Nell'africane selve* for bass and *Quando sperasti* for soprano are the only compositions on closely related Deer paper (only lacking the initials AP). The trio *Se tu non lasci amore* is composed on the standard Roman Fleur 10 and Fleur 20. *Nel dolce tempo* for alto and the trio *Quel fior che all'alba ride* are without autograph (see Burrows/Ronish, *Catalogue,* for details).

2. The Deer AP paper in *Aci, Galatea e Polifemo* and *Mentre il tutto è in furore* is ruled in ten staves with a five-stave rastrum measuring 86 mm. The Deer AP paper in *Sento là che ristretto,* the Fleur VC paper in *Aci, Galatea e Polifemo,* and the related Deer paper are ruled in ten staves with a five-stave rastrum measuring about 88.5 mm. *Se tu non lasci amore* is ruled like the "Ottoboni" group, with eight staves using a four-stave rastrum of about 70–71 mm. *Cuopre tal volta* is uniquely ruled with sixteen staves using a four-stave rastrum of about 46 mm (see Burrows/Ronish, *Catalogue,* for details).

3. *Aci, Galatea e Polifemo* is signed by Handel "Napoli li 16 di Giugno. 1708. d'Alvito," connecting the work definitively with the wedding of Beatrice Tocco and Tolomeo Saverio Gallio, Duke of Alvito, which took place on 19 July 1708 (Vitali/Furnari,"Händels Italienreise," p. 54). *Se tu non lasci amore* is signed "G. F. Hendel/ li 12 di luglio/ 1708/ Napoli," but "probably" not in Handel's hand (Burrows/Ronish, *Catalogue,* p. 267); the paper and rastrum do not match the other Neapolitan works, but the two SAB trios, unless documentary evidence arises to contradict their placement here, fit neatly with *Aci, Galatea e Polifemo* and the two sets of solo cantatas for the same voice ranges. If *Se tu non lasci amore* was composed with the other works on eight-stave paper (8-stave group 1707; ?Ottoboni, Rome), it was surely revived for Naples, which is what the date on the manuscript may indicate.

4. This group fits together on a number of grounds. *Aci, Galatea e Polifemo* can definitely be associated with Naples. The three cantatas on the same papers

as the serenata (Fleur VC and Deer AP) replicate the voices required for it: *Cuopre tal volta* (bass), *Sento là che ristretto* (alto), and *Mentre il tutto è in furore* (soprano). The two cantatas on the related Deer paper add a second solo cantata for two of the voice ranges: *Nell'africane selve* (bass) and *Quando sperasti* (soprano). A cantata for alto can be added to complete this second set: *Nel dolce tempo,* which lacks a surviving autograph, has been associated with the Neapolitan area because of its textual reference to the river Volturno (Strohm, "Händel in Italia," p. 169, n. 77). Vitali/Furnari ("Händels Italienreise," pp. 58–59) have shown that Handel's primary patrons in the Neapolitan area were the Duke Gaetani d'Aragona and his wife Aurora Sanseverino, whose primary residence in Piedimonte d'Alife lies particularly near the Volturno. Mainwaring places Handel in Naples immediately after *La resurrezione;* he identifies a "Donna Laura" (that is, Donn'Aurora) as Handel's patroness; and he speaks of "invitations from most of the principal persons who lived within reach of that capital" (*Memoirs,* pp. 66–67). The documents largely confirm these statements. Burrows (*Handel,* p. 35) associates *Mentre il tutto è in furore* with Ruspoli because it contains warlike imagery similar to that in the later 1708 trio cantata *Oh, come chiare,* not only written for Ruspoli, but including him as one of the characters. The paper evidence indicates otherwise and implies that Handel's two "warlike" cantatas were written for opposite sides in the War of Spanish Succession.

Ruspoli August/September 1708 (Rome)

Clori, vezzosa Clori
Ditemi, O piante
Lungi da voi (A; Santini version for soprano)
Lungi n'andò Fileno
Manca pur quanto sai
Se pari è la tua fé (second version)
Stanco di più soffrire (A; Santini version for soprano)
***
Clori, mia bella Clori (?)
Arresta il passo (SS) (revised from 1707?)
Amarilli vezzosa (*Il duello amoroso*) (SA)
Oh, come chiare (SSA)

1. *Ditemi, O piante, Lungi da voi, Clori vezzosa, Stanco di più soffrire, Se pari è la tua fé,* and *Amarilli vezzosa* are without surviving autograph. The rest are on standard Roman paper: *Manca pur quanto sai,*[2] *Lungi n'andò Fileno,* and *Clori, mia bella Clori* on Fleur 10, *Arresta il passo* on Fleur 20, and *Oh, come chiare* on a mixture of Fleur 10 and Fleur 20 (Burrows/Ronish, *Catalogue*).

2. The typical Roman layout of ten staves ruled with a five-stave rastrum also dominates. *Manca pur quanto sai*, *Lungi n'andò*, *Clori, mia bella Clori*, and *Oh, come chiare* use a five-stave rastrum of between 81 mm and 82 mm. *Arresta il passo* uses a slightly larger rastrum between 82 mm and 83 mm; further, its overture uses the rare 4, 4, 1 layout identical to the single sheet in *Diana cacciatrice* from the Ruspoli May 1707 group.

3. This set consists largely of cantatas that appear by name in the Ruspoli accounts for copying between 9 August 1708 and 10 September 1708. *Arresta il passo* (whose second aria begins "Fiamma bella che al ciel s'invia") seems to be represented in the ledgers by a payment to two violinists for playing "Cantata Fiamma bella di Monsù Hendel" on 14 July 1708 (Kirkendale, "Ruspoli," p. 240). Whether the whole cantata was performed is not certain; Kirkendale has "no doubt" that the entire cantata "crowned" the first general meeting of the Arcadians in 1708 ("Ruspoli," p. 241) when Ruspoli took over as host, but Marx (*Kantaten mit Instrumenten* I, p. xvii) argues, in part on the basis of borrowings from Keiser's operas, that this cantata was written "probably in the spring or summer of 1707" and that only "the aria 'Fiamma bella' (no. 2) was sung again [for Ruspoli] in July 1708." Although borrowings from Keiser prove little about chronology, as Handel continued to borrow from this composer for years, Kirkendale, who "doubt[s] that Ruspoli [at his first meeting as host] would have presented a work that was not new" ("Ruspoli," p. 241, n. 71), allows (on the basis that she can find "no bill for copies of the parts") that this could be an "older work" ("Ruspoli," p. 240 and p. 241, n. 71). In fact, the different five-stave rastrum for *Arresta il passo*, as compared with other works in this group, and the use of the rare 4, 4, 1 layout for its overture suggest an earlier date. Moreover, the surviving copy in the Santini Collection demonstrates that the cantata was revised at some point by the addition of two arias and two recitatives (Ewerhart, "Santini," pp. 127–128). Given all the evidence, it seems likely that this work was composed or revised ahead of time for a complete performance in July 1708, with advance knowledge that Handel would be away from Rome for a period. Kirkendale suggests that the "sizable bill for food" consumed by Handel at Ruspoli's in July demonstrates that he must have returned by mid-month ("Ruspoli," p. 239). A third instrumental cantata listed without title ("Cantata à voce sola con VV") may refer to *Clori, mia bella Clori* (Marx, *Kantaten mit Instrumenten* I, p. xvii). Kirkendale ("Ruspoli," p. 248) had suggested that the unnamed cantata could be *Ah! crudel;* but this cantata is now tentatively dated a year earlier based on Handel's use of a discarded sheet with a title from the cantata *Ero e Leandro*. Nevertheless, the placement of *Clori, mia bella Clori* in this group must remain speculative for lack of additional supporting evidence.

4. If *Arresta il passo* dates from an earlier period, it would not be the only cantata to appear in the account books during summer 1708 for which this is the

case. In addition to those cantatas listed here, the Ruspoli account books for August and September also include *Hendel, non può mia musa,* which has been dated to 1707; both *Quando sperasti* and *Mentre il tutto è in furore* can be placed in Naples. The five continuo cantatas in this set without surviving autograph thus demand further scrutiny. The Santini copy of *Stanco di più soffrire* contains the note that the original was a third lower. Similarly, the Santini Collection copy of *Lungi da voi* provides a unique soprano version; the other multiple copies of this cantata are in the alto range. Both of these transpositions point to Ruspoli's one regularly paid singer, the soprano Margarita Durastante. The close parity between the cantatas listed in the account books and the cantatas that survive in the Santini Collection indicates that we have a near-complete picture of which cantatas were performed for Ruspoli; significantly, all of these were copied in the soprano range (undoubtedly for Durastante). This raises the question of origin not just for *Stanco di più soffrire* and *Lungi da voi,* but for all those (soprano) cantatas in the Ruspoli documents known to exist primarily in a range other than soprano. For example, the two alto cantatas from Naples both appear transcribed for soprano in the Santini Collection: *Sento là che ristretto* (whose autograph is for alto) and *Nel dolce tempo* (which is for alto in ten of fourteen surviving copies). Of the three remaining cantatas from the 1708 Ruspoli group that do not survive in autograph, the soprano Santini copy of *Ditemi, O piante* is one of a large number of similar copies; the Santini version of *Clori, vezzosa Clori* is the sole surviving copy; and the Santini version of *Se pari è la tua fé,* which is unique, has been shown to be a revision.[3] It may be, therefore, that, of the cantatas copied for Ruspoli in August of 1708, *Arresta il passo* is a revision of a 1707 work and *Hendel, non può mia musa, Quando sperasti, Mentre il tutto è in furore, Lungi da voi,* and *Stanco di più soffrire* are all copies of earlier works, perhaps composed for another patron. The textual revision of *Se pari è la tua fé* supports a similar hypothesis for this work as well: the first version of the recitative is in blank verse throughout (a characteristic of Handel's very early cantatas), while the revised Italian version is rhymed throughout (see Chapter 3 on the relation of text and chronology). Subtracting these cantatas leaves only four of the ten continuo cantatas listed in the Ruspoli documents for August 1708 as potentially new compositions written at that time: *Manca pur quanto sai, Ditemi, O piante, Clori, vezzosa Clori,* and *Lungi n'andò Fileno.*

Moons 1709 group (Florence and/or Venice)

Ah, che pur troppo è vero
Clori, degli occhi miei

Non sospirar
Un sospir
***

Alpestre monte
Giù nei Tartarei regni (SB)
Che vai pensando (SB)
Amor gioie mi porge (SS)
Va, speme infida (SS)

1–2. No autograph survives for *Va, speme infida.* The other cantatas and duets in this set are all written on Moons G paper and ruled with a twelve-stave rastrum measuring 188.5–189 mm (Burrows/Ronish, *Catalogue*).

3–4. The lack of any Roman copies of the works in this group suggests they were composed after Handel left Rome for the last time. Although the Ruspoli accounts contain bills in 1709 for copying cantatas by Handel, it is to be doubted that he was in residence. That is, if questions can be raised about the provenance of the cantatas listed in the Ruspoli documents for August 1708, when Handel was certainly in residence, then those same questions are intensified for those cantatas listed in 1709, when Handel's presence cannot be confirmed. Three cantatas are listed for 28 February 1709; two of these, however, are second copies of works from 1707: *Poiché giuraro amore* and *Armida abbandonata.* The third, *Ninfe e pastori,* can also be associated with Rome by its paper (Fleur 10) and dated to 1707 by its rastrum (five-stave, 80–89.5 mm) (Burrows/Ronish, *Catalogue*, p. 101). In March 1709, Antonio Caldara was engaged as Ruspoli's *maestro di cappella,* and Handel's presence after this time is still further to be doubted. In August 1709, twenty-one works (or partial works) by Handel were copied for Ruspoli. Of these, nine are continuo cantatas that were copied previously (sometimes twice) for Ruspoli, the majority of these (seven) from 1707. Of the remaining twelve works, three belong to the Moons 1706 group (*Chi rapì la pace?, Lucrezia,* and *Fra tante pene*); one has an autograph date of 1708, Rome (*Lungi dal mio bel nume*); one is associated through its autograph for alto with Naples and transposed in the Santini Collection (*Sento là che ristretto*); the autograph of *Del bel idolo mio* matches the rastrum of *Se per fatal destino* (Ruspoli: 16 May 1707) and may be paired with it; and the autograph of *Filli adorata e cara* uses the rastrum of *Stelle, perfide stelle!* and *Ninfe e pastori* (Ruspoli: 28 February 1709 and 31 August 1709), all of which can tentatively be dated to 1707. The remaining four cantatas, *Dalla guerra amorosa, Lungi da me, pensier tiranno!, Da sete ardente afflitto,* and *Zeffiretto,* are discussed below (Italian with autograph before 1709 and Italian without autograph before 1709).

Kirkendale dates Handel's departure from Rome in autumn 1708 to 12 September, on the basis of a final food bill for Handel that is limited to the first eleven days of the month ("Ruspoli," p. 243). Between this date and the Venetian performance of *Agrippina* in December 1709, Handel's whereabouts cannot be securely documented. The specific date and provenance of these cantatas thus remain a question, but it is likely that the set was written in Florence or Venice between October 1708 and October 1709.

Agrippina Moons group (Florence and/or Venice)

***

Agrippina condotta a morire
Apollo e Dafne (SB)
Quando in calma ride (SB)
Agrippina

1–2. This set is dominated by the opera *Agrippina,* whose autograph is entirely on Moons SS20 ruled with twelve-stave rastra of two distinct widths, 189 mm and 193–193.5 mm (the aria "Pur ch'io ti stringa" appears on a single sheet of GVH paper—see below, Hanover—separate from the main manuscript). The other three works are placed in this set by their association with *Agrippina*. *Agrippina condotta a morire* begins on Moons SS20 ruled with a twelve-stave rastrum of about 193 mm; it concludes on Moons FS (unique in Handel's autographs) ruled with a ten-stave rastrum of about 182.5 mm. *Quando in calma ride* is entirely on Moons SS20 ruled with a ten-stave rastrum of about 185 mm. The primary paper group of *Apollo e Dafne* is Moons SS20 ruled with a ten-stave rastrum of about 184 mm. Thus, this set is defined by two Moons papers unique to it: Moons SS20 and Moons FS. The twelve-stave rastrum, very like that used in the Moons 1709 group, is limited to the opera and the opening of *Agrippina condotta a morire;* the other works use a ten-stave rastrum similar to, but distinctively smaller than, those used in the Moons 1706 group. *Apollo e Dafne* requires special consideration because it presents a particularly complex autograph. In addition to the main thread of Moons SS20 paper for the first twenty-four folios, the score is interrupted with insertions on three different papers: CV, A40, and Unicorn. Further, in the final thirteen folios the Unicorn paper becomes dominant and is interrupted with an insertion on yet a fourth type of paper: DS. The A40 paper contains one of the standard Italian layouts, with ten staves ruled with a five-stave rastrum of 82.5 mm. However, CV, Unicorn, and DS are ruled in eight or ten staves with a single-stave rastrum of about 11 mm. Unicorn and DS appear nowhere else in Handel's autographs, but Unicorn is used briefly in a set of library copies of Steffani's operas made at Hanover around 1709, CV is used for one of Handel's "Hanover" duets (see below), and paper ruled with a single-stave rastrum was standard in Hanover (Burrows, "Hanover," p. 48). Thus it seems likely that *Apollo e Dafne* was either unfinished when Handel left Italy or underwent a thorough revision in Hanover (see also Burrows/Ronish, *Catalogue*).

3–4. Mainwaring obliquely seems to associate *Apollo e Dafne* with the opera *Agrippina* and with Venice: "At *Agrippina* [Vittoria's] inclinations gave new lustre to her talents. Handel seemed almost as great and majestic as *Apollo*, and it was far from the lady's intention to be so cruel and obstinate as *Daphne*" (Mainwaring, *Memoirs*, p. 54). Marx questions the possibility that this cantata was written for performance in Italy because of its use of solo bassoon, which he describes as "hardly known in Italian orchestras before 1710" (Marx, "Zur Kompositionsgeschichte von Händels Pastoralkantate 'Apollo e Dafne' [HWV 122]," *GHB*, 1 [1984]: 70; see also pp. 82–83). However, Harris Saunders has shown that bassoons were certainly known in Venetian opera as early as 1693 in Perti's *Nerone fatto Cesare*, but also—chronologically more to the point—in Mancia's *Alessandro in Susa* of 1708 (Harris Sheridan Saunders, Jr., "The Teatro Grimani di San Giovanni Grisostomo: The interaction of family interests and opera in Venice [1678–1714]," paper given at the American Musicological Society Annual Meeting [New Orleans, 1987]). Furthermore, *Apollo e Dafne* seems to be closely related to the three soprano-bass duets written at the same time: *Giù nei Tartarei regni, Che vai pensando,* and *Quando in calma ride.* As already seen in regard to Handel's Neapolitan works and those compositions copied for Ruspoli, the prevalence of a single voice type or combination suggests specific singers at the houses or courts at which Handel was composing and is a good marker for tentatively determining provenance and date where there is some question. That is, the two trios for soprano, alto, and bass were probably associated with and possibly composed for Naples, and the transpositions for soprano in the Santini Collection were undoubtedly copied for Durastante. The Hanoverian duets (see below, Hanover group) are all composed for soprano and alto, and these represent the only duets by Handel for this vocal combination written before 1720. All other duet combinations, including soprano-tenor, soprano-soprano, and soprano-bass, are exclusively related to Moons paper and, therefore, to northern Italy. The dominant duet combination in 1709 was soprano-bass, including three duets and, most likely, *Apollo e Dafne.*

Italian (with autograph) before 1709

Allor ch'io dissi addio
Care selve
Zeffiretto (Ruspoli: 31 August 1709)
***

Ah, che troppo ineguali
Nel dolce dell'oblio (*Pensieri notturni*)

1–2. All five works are ruled in ten staves with a five-stave rastrum. *Allor ch'io dissi addio* and *Zeffiretto* are both on A10 and use a rastrum of about 83 mm. *Care selve* is on Fleur 10 and uses a rastrum of about 81 mm. *Ah, che troppo ineguali* and *Nel dolce dell'oblio* are both on Fleur 20, with rastra measuring about 81 mm and 82 mm, respectively (Burrows/Ronish, *Catalogue*).

3–4. The aria "Aurette vezzose" from *Zeffiretto* appears in a bill for copying in the Ruspoli account books for 31 August 1709, thus placing it definitively in Italy before that date. *Allor ch'io dissi addio* can be paired with it on the basis of the A10 paper, not found elsewhere in Handel's autographs, and an identical rastrum. The autographs of *Care selve*, *Ah, che troppo ineguali* (a sacred work), and *Pensieri notturni* are written on standard Roman paper, certainly allowing their placement in Italy. Marx (*Kantaten mit Instrumenten* II, pp. xxi) further connects the autograph of *Pensieri notturni* in paper and handwriting with *Dixit Dominus*, which would indicate a 1707 date for this work. In his chronological list, Watanabe places *Care selve* among the Roman 1708 works ("Music-Paper," p. 216, no. 100) and all the others in 1707 ("Music-Paper," pp. 207–208, 212, nos. 27, 28, 43, and 70).

Italian (without autograph) before 1709

Dalla guerra amorosa (B: Ruspoli: 31 August 1709)
Lungi da me, pensier tiranno! (Ruspoli: 31 August 1709)
Da sete ardente afflitto (Ruspoli: 31 August 1709)
Irene, idolo mio (Santini Collection)
O lucenti, O sereni occhi (Santini Collection)
Torna il core (Santini Collection)
Figli del mesto cor
***

Notte placida (Santini Collection)

1–4. With the exception of *Figli del mesto cor*, all these works can be placed in Italy by reason of their appearance in the Ruspoli account books by 1709 and/or in the Santini Collection. *Dalla guerra amorosa* survives in the Santini Collection in a unique soprano copy. Burrows suggests that this cantata was composed in the soprano range for Ruspoli and transposed for bass in Hanover ("Hanover," p. 53, note "e," where "this cantata" refers to *Dalla guerra amorosa*), but stylistic evidence and the Santini copy itself argue against this. In the bass version, two significant cadences proceed by unison between the voice and continuo, a common procedure in bass continuo arias but not in other voice ranges. In the soprano copy in the Santini Collection, one of these cadences is preserved, now in octaves, creating a contrapuntal anomaly. The other is first written out as an exact transposition of the bass version and then altered to avoid the succession of parallel octaves (Ex. A.1). These alterations argue for the primacy of the bass version, which must, therefore, precede the Ruspoli copy (31 August 1709) in the Santini Collection, and, like other copies, was probably transposed for Durastante to sing. *Lungi da me, pensier tiranno!* and *Irene, idolo mio,* like *Nel dolce tempo* (see above, Naples 1708) survive primarily in alto copies, suggesting that they too were transposed for Ruspoli's household. Further, both *Dalla guerra amorosa* and *Lungi da me, pensier tiranno!* contain textual and musical refrains. Two other cantatas with refrains, *Sarei troppo felice* and *Occhi miei,* can be dated to 1707, suggesting that refrains might be a stylistic trait related to a specific time frame. *Solitudini care* (see below, Undocumented cantatas) may perhaps be added to this group of refrain cantatas (see Chapter 3). Finally, the manuscript copy of *Dalla guerra amorosa* for bass that Burrows associates with Hanover (RM 19.e.7 on A40 paper) also contains *Figli del mesto cor,* whose musical style strongly argues for a 1707 date (see Chapter 5). A Hanoverian manuscript could, of course, contain Italian cantatas, but this specific manuscript may also be of Italian rather than Hanoverian provenance; Burrows describes the copyist's hand as "rather Italianate and, indeed, rather reminiscent of the general style of the Ruspoli copyists" (Burrows, "Hanover," p. 52).

Example A.1a *Dalla guerra amorosa,* "Non v'alletti un occhio nero," cadence from the bass and soprano versions.

Example A.1b *Dalla guerra amorosa,* "Fuggite, sì fuggite," cadence from the bass and soprano versions.

Hanover group

Nice, che fa?
Venus and Adonis ("Behold where weeping Venus stands") Hughes
***

Languia di bocca (possibly for London)
Sono liete, fortunate (SA)
A mirarvi io son intento (SA)
Conservate, raddoppiate (SA)
Tanti strali al sen mi scocchi (SA)
Troppo cruda, troppo fiera (SA)

1. *Sono liete, fortunate* and *Conservate, raddoppiate* are on A50, *Languia di bocca* on IV; both are papers otherwise unknown in Handel's autographs. *A mirarvi io son intento* is on GVH, only found elsewhere in Handel's autographs in a single sheet added to *Agrippina* before performance (see above, *Agrippina* Moons group), and thus can be definitely associated with Italy (Burrows, "Hanover," p. 49). *Tanti strali al sen mi scocchi* is composed on CV, found also in *Apollo e Dafne*. *Nice, che fa?* appears on A40, found also in a set of three sonatas and in *Apollo e Dafne* (Burrows, "Hanover," p. 52, where the paper is identified as "watermark (3)"). *Troppo cruda, troppo fiera* is without autograph.

2. This group can be connected with Hanover through its use of paper associated with the Hanover "revision" of *Apollo e Dafne* and with the specific use of a single-stave rastrum. *Languia di bocca* and the four chamber duets that survive in autograph all are ruled with single-stave rastra in different formats. *Nice, che fa?*, in contrast, is ruled in the standard Roman pattern of ten staves with a five-stave rastrum measuring 83–83.5 mm (Burrows/Ronish, *Catalogue*), leaving open the possibility of an Italian provenance for this work. Watanabe ("Music-Paper," p. 207) places *Nice, che fa?* around the time of the eight-stave Italian group, which he dates to about May 1707.

3. Handel must have left Italy shortly after the performances of his opera *Agrippina*, which ran in Venice from 26 December 1709 to around the end of January; the next opera opened in the same theater on 8 February 1710 (Saunders, "Handel's *Agrippina*," p. 98). Handel carried with him letters of introduction from Prince Ferdinand and passed through Innsbruck, as a letter of 9 March 1710 from Duke Karl Philipp to Prince Ferdinand attests. By early June Handel was in Hanover, where he was appointed *maestro di cappella* on 16 June 1710. According to Mainwaring, Handel accepted the position with the understanding that he could absent himself almost immediately. He visited Düsseldorf in September and by the end of the year was in London. He did not return to Hanover until summer 1711 at the earliest, and little more than a year later, by

October 1712, Handel was back in London for good. Mainwaring writes that during his year in Hanover, Handel composed twelve duets and a "variety of other things for voices and instruments" (Mainwaring, *Memoirs,* p. 85).

4. Burrows has identified a surviving volume, entitled "Duetti del Sigr. Giorgio Federico Handel" on GVH paper and bound in a typical Hanoverian style, that contains ten duets and the two trios: *Quel fior che all'alba ride* and *Se tu non lasci amore.* Given a collection whose Hanoverian provenance seems clear, Burrows suggests that these twelve works, despite the inclusion of two trios, represent the Hanoverian "duettos" mentioned by Mainwaring ("Hanover," p. 55). The ten duets and two trios have differing provenance. The trios were composed in Naples or earlier. The soprano-bass duets *Tacete ohimè* (Moons 1706), *Che vai pensando* (Moons 1709), and *Quando in calma ride* (*Agrippina* Moons), and the two soprano duets, *Amor gioie mi porge* (Moons 1709) and *Va, speme infida* (without autograph, but possibly paired with *Amor gioie mi porge,* as both are for two sopranos), were probably composed in northern Italy. The duets that were likely composed in Hanover include: *Sono liete, fortunate, A mirarvi io son intento, Conservate, raddoppiate,* and *Tanti strali al sen mi scocchi,* on the basis of paper evidence, and *Troppo cruda, troppo fiera,* which is paired with *Sono liete, fortunate* in an early copy (Burrows, "Hanover," p. 56). Notably, all the Hanoverian duets are for soprano and alto. *Venus and Adonis* is associated with Hanover by a letter written by Handel from Hanover to a friend in London asking if John Hughes will send him an English text (Deutsch, *Handel,* p. 44); the text of *Venus and Adonis* is by John Hughes (see Chapters 5 and 6).

London (1710–1716)

Bella ma ritrosetta
Dolc'è pur d'amor l'affanno (A) (HWV 109a) Paolo Rolli?
Siete rose (A)
Son gelsomino (A) (HWV 164b) Paolo Rolli
***

Splenda l'alba (A)
Mi palpita il cor (A) (HWV 132c) with flute
Echeggiate, festeggiate (SSSAB)

1. Unlike the apparent interchange of paper between Hanover and Italy, the paper Handel used in England is distinct. Although this paper was imported from the Netherlands, its association with Handel in London permits the phrase "English paper." *Echeggiate, festeggiate, Splenda l'alba,* and *Siete rose* are composed on C10, also associated with the operas *Rinaldo* (1711), *Il pastor fido*

(1712), and *Silla* (1713?) and largely limited to those years. *Bella ma ritrosetta* is on B20, associated with *Silla* and with the Utrecht Jubilate (1713) of the same period. *Dolc'è pur d'amor l'affanno* and *Son gelsomino* are on D10, paper that was also used in *Rinaldo* and the Utrecht Te Deum. *Mi palpita il cor* (HWV 132c) is on IV2, unique in Handel's autographs (see Burrows/Ronish, *Catalogue*).

2. The rastra confirm the period 1710–1716 for the cantatas. *Bella ma ritrosetta, Dolc'è pur d'amor l'affanno, Siete rose, Son gelsomino, Echeggiate, festeggiate,* and *Splenda l'alba* are all laid out with ten staves in the rastral pattern of 4, 4, 2. The specific measurements of these in *Siete rose* and *Splenda l'alba* (67 mm, 67 mm, 29.5–30 mm) are unique in Handel's works; *Mi palpita il cor* uses the unique pattern of twelve staves drawn with a four-stave rastrum of the same size (67 mm). The other cantatas use two distinct patterns of 4, 4, 2 that closely parallel those found in *Rinaldo* (approximately 73− mm, 73− mm, 31+ mm and 68 mm, 68 mm, 28.5 mm; see Burrows/Ronish, *Catalogue*).

3. The large serenata *Echeggiate, festeggiate* (formerly known in misordered and fragmentary form as *Io languisco*) celebrates the expected accession of the Hapsburg archduke Charles to the Spanish throne as Charles III. Like the later Utrecht Te Deum, this work is closely tied to the political situation surrounding the War of Spanish Succession and can, therefore, be dated within a very narrow time frame. It is written on English paper, making autumn 1710 its earliest possible date. Charles III, who is named in the serenata text, was proclaimed Emperor Charles VI on 17 April 1711, providing the latest possible date.

4. *Bella ma ritrosetta,* the only solo cantata for soprano in this set, is also on different paper from other cantatas in this group. All the other solo cantatas are for alto (or mezzo-soprano) voice, and may be grouped with the two alto continuo cantatas in the next group. Not surprisingly, this London alto set contains many stylistic similarities (Harris, "London Cantatas," pp. 86–102). At least four of these have texts by Paolo Rolli, who was to become a principal librettist for the soon-to-be-established Royal Academy of Music: *Son gelsomino* and *Dolc'è pur d'amor l'affanno*[4] from this group and *Deh! lasciate* and *Ho fuggito,* immediately following. Rolli arrived in London early in 1716.

London (1717–1723)

Deh! lasciate (A) Paolo Rolli
Ho fuggito (A) Paolo Rolli
L'aure grate (A) (HWV 121b)
***

Crudel tiranno Amor
Langue, geme (SA)
Se tu non lasci amore (SA)
***

Acis and Galatea (Cannons)
Esther (Cannons)

1. The two continuo cantatas and two duets are written on C20, as are *Acis and Galatea* (on B50 and C20) and *Esther,* which papers can be connected in Handel's autographs with compositions over a very wide span, from 1715 to 1731 (Burrows/Ronish, *Catalogue*). This setting of *L'aure grate* does not survive in autograph (an autograph fragment based on the same text [HWV 121a] contains a discarded version). *Crudel tiranno Amor* does not exist in autograph.

2. *Acis and Galatea* has ten staves drawn with a single-stave rastrum of about 9 mm, associated with the anthems for Cannons (1717–1718) and *Il pastor fido* and *Teseo. Esther* has ten staves drawn with a two-stave rastrum of about 30 to 31 mm, which cannot be found earlier but continues into the early Academy Opera period in such works as *Floridante* from 1721 (see Burrows/Ronish, *Catalogue*). The two continuo cantatas and the two duets are ruled in ten staves with a two-stave rastrum of about 28 mm, associated by Burrows/Ronish with the period 1722 to 1726 on the basis of its use in such Academy operas as *Ottone, Flavio, Giulio Cesare,* and *Tamerlano.*

3. In 1715 Elizabeth Legh (c. 1694–1734) of Adlington Hall in Cheshire began to acquire one of the most important collections of Handel's music in manuscript.[5] Most of the volumes are dated, and those from between 1715 and 1720 offer a capsule summary of Handel's achievements in his first decade in London. The copies of *Acis and Galatea* and *Esther* are both dated 1718, corroborating the performance dates of these two Cannons compositions. The two volumes of cantatas, dated respectively 1718 and 1720, are also of great interest, for just as the cantatas preserved in the Santini Collection from the Ruspoli library provide a good survey of the works written in Italy, the Legh volumes illustrate the state of Handel's cantata corpus at the end of the period in his life when writing "house music" was a regular occupation.[6] These volumes contain all the new, alto continuo cantatas associated with London, including *Deh! lasciate* and *Ho fuggito* in the 1720 volume, suggesting that they were composed in that year or before. However, the dates on these volumes bear closer investigation. Donald Burrows has shown that both *Clori, ove sei?* (1718 volume) and *Del bel idolo mio* (1720 volume) were added in the hand of Philip Hayes (1738–1797), illustrating that the volumes were originally bound with blank pages that were filled in later (Donald Burrows, "Sources, Resources, and Handel Studies," in *Handel Tercentenary Collection,* p. 30). The date on each volume may indicate the year in which the volumes were begun, with additions continuing for many years. However, *Deh! lasciate* and *Ho fuggito* seem to be a part of the original collection, and can probably be dated close to 1720. *L'aure grate* survives in a manuscript preserved in Cardiff dated 1718, indicating composition in that year or earlier.

4. *Crudel tiranno Amor* appears as the last cantata in the Legh 1718 volume, but Burrows has shown that this paper is of a somewhat later date and must have been added to the original collection before binding (or rebinding). Hicks suggests that it represents the "new cantata" performed by Durastante, who had come to London to sing with Handel and the Royal Academy, at her benefit concert on 5 July 1721 (Anthony Hicks, "Record Reviews," *MT,* 112 [1971]: 867). It makes a particularly apt ending to Handel's cantata period: on the one hand, it looks back to the significant compositions for Ruspoli in Rome and, on the other, it moves out of the private sphere onto the public stage.

English revised (pedagogical) cantatas (1714–1724)

Dolc'è pur d'amor l'affanno (HWV 109b)
E partirai, mia vita? (HWV 111b)
Lungi dal mio bel nume (HWV 127c)[7]
Mi palpita il cor (HWV 132a; revision of *Dimmi, O mio cor* [HWV 106])
Ninfe e pastori (HWV 139c)
Sei pur bella (HWV 160c)
Sento là che ristretto (HWV 161c)
Se pari è la tua fé (HWV 158c)[8]
Son gelsomino (HWV 164a)
***

Mi palpita il cor (HWV 132b) with oboe

1. *Dolc'è pur d'amor l'affanno* (HWV 109b) and *Mi palpita il cor* (HWV 132a) are without autograph. All the other continuo cantatas in this group survive on C20; *Mi palpita il cor* (HWV 132b) is on B20. Burrows/Ronish associate C20 with a wide period, from 1715 to 1731; B20 is found in works from around 1713, such as *Silla* and the Utrecht Jubilate, and also in the anthems from Cannons of 1717–1718.

2. The continuo cantatas are ruled in ten staves with two-stave rastra ranging from 29 mm to 30.5 mm in width (Burrows/Ronish, *Catalogue*). *Mi palpita il cor* (HWV 132b) has a unique layout in Handel's autographs of eight staves ruled 3, 3, 2.

3–4. John Mayo has identified seven of these cantatas as a group on the basis of a shared watermark, layout, and handwriting and by the prodigious use of bass figures: *E partirai, mia vita?, Lungi dal mio bel nume, Ninfe e pastori, Sei pur bella, Sento là che ristretto, Se pari è la tua fé,* and *Son gelsomino.* He suggests that these were written by Handel for his use in teaching keyboard realization to Princess Anne in the mid-1720s (Mayo, "Kantatenrevisionen," pp. 63–77). However, there is reason to allow some chronological flexibility, for a copy of

Sento là che ristretto appears in the Cannons inventory dated 1720, and the manuscript copy (GB-Lbl add. ms. 62102) identified by Graydon Beeks ("The Chandos Collection," in *Handel Collections,* p. 154) demonstrates that the Cannons listing represents the English revision (*Sento là che ristretto* was written for alto in Naples, transposed for soprano in Rome, and revised for soprano in England). Furthermore, Brydges recollects in a letter of 1724 that about ten years previously he had overseen the musical education of his former servant George Monroe by having him study with "Mr. Handell and Dr. Pepusch," and that as a result he had become "a perfect master both for composition and performance on the organ & harpsichord" (C. H. Collins Baker and Muriel I. Baker, *The Life and Circumstances of James Brydges—First Duke of Chandos* [Oxford, 1949], p. 130). Handel may have used this cantata to teach Monroe as many as ten years before he taught Princess Anne. However, the dated Cannons copy does not prove that the autograph was written earlier, for Handel may have continued to revise his teaching material for years. Specifically, the Cannons copy lacks some of the figures found in the autograph version, and may represent an earlier stage.

Mayo points out that Roman numerals in these autographs (VIII in *Ninfe e pastori* and X in *Son gelsomino*) imply a collection of at least ten cantatas. Because the text of *Son gelsomino* is by Paolo Rolli, Mayo adds the late pair of cantatas, *Ho fuggito* and *Deh! lasciate,* also with texts by Rolli, as well as *Mi palpita il cor* (with oboe) to make ten (Mayo, "Kantatenrevisionen," pp. 64–65). However, there may be a better way to identify a group of ten "pedagogical" cantatas. All seven of the "original" group are for soprano, and all are revisions: *E partirai, mia vita?* (?Ottoboni, 1707), *Lungi dal mio bel nume* (Ruspoli, 1708), *Ninfe e pastori* (Ruspoli, 1707?), *Sei pur bella* (Ruspoli, 1707), *Sento là che ristretto* (Naples, 1708, for alto), *Se pari è la tua fé* (Ruspoli, before 1708), and *Son gelsomino* (London, c. 1713). Moreover, four of these were revised from or through alto versions; that is, *Sento là che ristretto* and *Son gelsomino* were originally written for alto, and *Lungi dal mio bel nume* and *Ninfe e pastori* were both revised for alto early in Handel's London tenure. On the assumption that this "pedagogical" group contains cantatas for soprano, revised from earlier works often in the alto range, *Mi palpita il cor* (revised from the earlier English version for alto with flute) fits the profile, but *Ho fuggito* and *Deh! lasciate,* both for alto and both unrevised, do not. However, there are two other cantatas that do: *Dolc'è pur d'amor l'affanno* (HWV 109b, a revision, like *Son gelsomino,* of an English alto cantata) and *Mi palpita il cor* (HWV 132a), a revision of the 1707 alto cantata *Dimmi, O mio cor,* neither of which survives in autograph. These ten cantatas, perhaps compiled over a period of years with a pedagogical purpose, may stretch just beyond the period of Handel's private patronage. Handel was appointed music teacher to the royal princesses by 9 June 1723 (Burrows, *Handel,*

p. 387), and he moved into his own house in July. However, none of these cantatas is new, and they do not represent continuing composition of private music. Rather, as works revised for a different purpose, they may be placed into a similar category as Handel's continued borrowings from the cantatas into his operas and oratorios.

Undocumented cantatas

Clori, ove sei? (Legh Collection)
Fra pensieri (A; Legh Collection)
Partì, l'idolo mio
Qualor crudele (A; Legh Collection)
Solitudini care

1–2. None of these cantatas survives in autograph.

3–4. *Clori, ove sei, Fra pensieri,* and *Qualor crudele* appear in the Legh manuscripts (see above, London 1717–1723: 3); the latter two for alto are among the significant number of alto cantatas preserved in this collection, which includes, in addition, all the new London alto cantatas, six known Italian cantatas for alto, and two Italian soprano cantatas transposed for alto, just as the Santini Collection preserves alto cantatas transposed for soprano (see above, Ruspoli August/September 1708: 4). Perhaps Elizabeth Legh had an alto voice. Two Italian copies of *Fra pensieri,* one associated with the Santini Collection, suggest an Italian provenance, which seems confirmed by Handel's borrowing of the setting of the aria "Fra pensieri" into the opera *Rodrigo* (1707); see Chapter 3. *Qualor crudele* is also without autograph, but can be identified as Italian in origin on the basis of style analysis (Harris, "Paper, Performing Practice," pp. 71–72). *Solitudini care* contains a musical and textual refrain, which may place it with the other refrain cantatas in Rome 1707 (see Chapter 3).

Cantatas for which Handel's authorship is doubtful

Che mi consiglio Amor (Legh Collection)
Clori, sì, ch'io t'adoro
Dal fatale momento
Dolce mio ben, s'io taccio
Qual sento io non conosciuto
Vi conosco occhi bugiardo (Legh Collection)
Vuo morir (Legh Collection)

1–2. None of these cantatas survives in autograph.

3–4. *Clori, sì, ch'io t'adoro, Dolce mio ben, s'io taccio,* and *Qual sento io non conosciuto* survive in one or two copies in large collections of Handel's cantatas. *Dal fatale momento* survives in a number of sources, and is attributed variously to Handel and Mancini. *Vi conosco occhi bugiardo* is attributed to Bononcini in three other copies. None can be documented, and most contain stylistic elements that argue against Handel's authorship.

Notes to Appendix 1

1. For information on the Latin Church music, see Anthony Hicks, "Handel's Vespers?" in "Letters to the Editor," *MT,* 126 (1985): 201; H. Watkins Shaw, "Handel's Vesper Music: Some MS Sources Rediscovered," *MT,* 126 (1985): 392–393; Graham Dixon, "Handel's Vesper Music: Towards a Liturgical Reconstruction," *MT,* 126 (1985): 393–397; Graham Dixon, "Handel's Music for the Carmelites: A Study in Liturgy and Some Observations," *EM,* 15 (1987): 16–29; J. Merrill Knapp, "Handel's Roman Church Music," in *Händel e gli Scarlatti a Roma,* ed. Nino Pirrotta and Agostino Ziino (Florence: Leo S. Olschki, 1987), pp. 15–27; and Graham Dixon, "Handel's Music for the Feast of Our Lady of Mount Carmel," in *Händel e gli Scarlatti a Roma,* pp. 29–48.

2. Kirkendale lists this cantata as "Manca pur d'amor l'affanno" ("Ruspoli," p. 272), which does not reflect the listing in the Ruspoli account books (which she provides in facsimile in fig. 1, following p. 240) where the title given is simply "Manca pur." The error seems to be an accidental conflation of two titles: *Manca pur quanto sai* and *Dolc'è pur d'amor l'affanno,* although the latter does not appear in the Ruspoli accounts at all.

3. For further discussion of the Santini version (HWV 158a) of *Se pari è la tua fé,* see Mayo, "Italian Cantatas," p. 166, and Mayo, "Kantatenrevisionen," p. 66. Reinhard Strohm, in "A Book of Cantatas and Arias bought in Florence, 1723," *The British Library Journal,* 21 (1995): 184–201, argues that the copy in BL add. ms. 71535 (and add. ms. 14212) represents the original version (no HWV number). The version listed as HWV 158b is a garbled version of the original and does not have compositional authority. HWV 158c is a later English revision; see English revised (pedagogical) cantatas (1714–1724).

4. Anthony Hicks identifies the text of the first aria of *Dolc'è pur d'amor l'affanno* as the first aria of a cantata text by Paolo Rolli beginning with the recitative "Soffri mio caro Alcino." This text was set by Antonio Caldara, who was appointed Ruspoli's *maestro di cappella* in 1709; the manuscript is dated 14 October 1715 (Anthony Hicks, "Paolo Rolli's Canzonets and Cantatas," unpublished paper presented at the Durham Conference on Baroque Music [July 1992]). I am very grateful to Mr. Hicks for sharing his research with me before publication.

5. See Winton Dean, "The Malmesbury Collection," in *Handel Collections,* pp. 29–38. See also Donald Burrows and Terence Best, "Guide to the Volumes of the Malmesbury Collection," unpublished typescript available at the Hampshire Record Office where microfilms of this collection are available for study. After Legh's death, the collection was passed first to John Robartes (later Earl of Radnor) and then in 1741 to James Harris, father of the first Earl of Malmesbury. The collection has remained in the family

(hence its name) and is still preserved by the current Earl of Malmesbury. I am grateful to the Earl of Malmesbury for making copies of these manuscripts available at the Hampshire Record Office.

6. The cantata volumes were separated from the main Legh collection before it was passed on to James Harris. They are now preserved in the Bodleian Library, Ms Mus.d. 61–62. See Donald Burrows, "Sources, Resources and Handel Studies," in *Tercentenary Collection,* pp. 19–42, and Harris, "Paper, Performing Practice," pp. 53–78.

7. The HWV number according to HHB II; Burrows/Ronish (mistakenly?) label this cantata HWV 127b (*Catalogue,* p. 104).

8. The HWV number according to HHB II; Burrows/Ronish label this cantata HWV 158b (*Catalogue,* p. 114).

APPENDIX 2

Texts and Translations of the Continuo Cantatas

This appendix provides the texts of the sixty-seven continuo cantatas securely attributed to Handel. Of these, sixty-five are in Italian, one is in French, and one in English. For the Italian and French texts, I provide parallel English translations that aim for accuracy over elegance. The syntax of the Italian poetry is often difficult. Sometimes this has necessitated awkward word order in English, and sometimes the only solution has been to alter the line order of the English translation, but a literal line-by-line translation was the overall goal.

The majority of the texts survive only in the cantata manuscripts and, therefore, present a number of hurdles to the would-be translator. Verse length needs to be determined from internal rhythmic and rhyme patterns, and spelling and orthography are complicated both by eighteenth-century usage and by scribal error; an effort has been made to modernize and correct the text throughout. The layout follows a typical eighteenth-century format: recitative is given in Roman type, arias in italic; and every line begins with a capital letter. Handel's adaptations of the text, including the use of arioso, are not indicated, except in *Sei pur bella, Udite il mio consiglio,* and the very complicated *Lucrezia.* Punctuation is largely editorial.

A handful of the cantatas have been previously translated, and in some cases these translations have provided models from which my own are adapted. I would like especially to acknowledge the translations of Judith Purnell James in A. V. Jones, ed., *G. F. Handel: 10 Solo Cantatas for Soprano and Basso Continuo,* vols. 1 and 2 (London: Faber Music, 1985); in particular, my translation of *Manca pur quanto sai* is based on hers. The translations of *Nell'africane selve* and *Nella stagion* are adapted from those of Avril Bardoni in *Handel: Italian Cantatas* (L'Oiseau-Lyre 430282-2, 1991). The few translations reproduced in their entirety are cited at the end of the cantata text. I am deeply indebted to Daniele Benati (Lecturer in Italian at MIT) and Terence Best for reading the texts and translations and offering important corrections.

The cantatas are presented here alphabetically; however, each is identified chronologically to facilitate cross-referencing to Appendix 1.

Ah, che pur troppo è vero (Florence/Venice 1709)

Ah, che pur troppo è vero	Ah, it is only too true
Che del Nume d'amor son prigioniero;	That I am a prisoner of the god of love;
Finché dolci catene	As long as sweet chains
Mi strinsero al mio bene,	Bound me to my love,
Vissi felice, e non conobbi affanno:	I lived happily, and knew not anguish:
Or che destin crudele	Now that cruel destiny
M'invola l'idol mio	Steals from me my idol,
Provo ch'il cieco Dio	I find that the blind god
È un Dio tiranno.	Is a tyrant god.
Quando del tuo partir,	When the fatal hour,
Clori adorata,	Adored Clori,
Giunse l'ora fatale,	Of your departure came,
Ahi! con qual pena	Alas! with what pain
La sofferse il mio core!	My heart suffered it!
Clori, pensalo tu, tel' dica amore.	Clori, think of this, let love speak to you of it.
Col partir la bella Clori,	*With the departure of the beautiful Clori,*
Si partì dall'alma mia	*Every joy, every pleasure*
Ogni gioia, ogni piacer.	*Parted from my soul.*
Ma che fido io non l'adori,	*But that I not adore her faithfully,*
Non farà la sorte ria	*Wicked fate cannot make happen,*
Se mi niega di goder.	*Even if it prevents me enjoying [her].*
In solitaria parte	In secluded places
Volgo sempre le piante,	I turn always my steps,
Afflitto e solo,	Tormented and alone,
E sol pensando a Clori	And only by thinking of Clori
Tempro il mio duolo:	Do I moderate my grief:
All'adorata mia	To my adored one
Spesso rivolgo i lumi,	I often turn my eyes,
Che le lacrime a fiumi	Which then shed
Versan allor,	Rivers of tears,
Poiché vedove e sole	Since, bereft and alone,
Le miro del mio ben,	I see [the tears] of my beloved,
Del mio bel sole.	Of my beautiful sun.
Care mura! in voi d'intorno	*Dear walls! Since around you*
Già ch'in van raggiro il piede,	*Now I wander in vain,*

Se accoglieste Clori un giorno,	*If once you received Clori,*
Accogliete or la mia fede.	*Receive now my faith.*

Numi ingiusti, spietati, amor tiranno,	Unjust pitiless gods, tyrant love,
Perché donaste a Clori	Why did you give to Clori
Tanta beltà, tal senno e tanta fede?	So much beauty, such wisdom and so much faith?

E a me giacché voleste	And since you wanted
Di sì raro tesor rendermi amante,	To make me love such a rare treasure,
Perché non concedeste,	Why did you not grant to me
O virtude maggiore e maggior sorte,	Either greater strength and a better fate,
O togliendomi Clori almen la morte?	Or, taking Clori away from me, at least [grant me] death?

Da che perso ho la mia Clori,	*Since I have lost my Clori,*
Altro oggetto che d'orrori	*My eyes see nothing*
L'occhio mio non sa mirar.	*But horrible things.*
Di morir nemmen ho sorte,	*I do not even have the fortune to die,*
Perché mora in doppia morte,	*Because I would die a double death,*
E di Clori in lontananza,	*And with Clori far away,*
La mia fé, la mia costanza,	*My faith, my constancy,*
Mi dà vita e fa sperar.	*Gives me life and makes me hope.*

Allor ch'io dissi addio (Italian autograph, before 1709)

Allor ch'io dissi addio e ch'io lasciai	When I said good-bye and left
Quel memorabil loco	That unforgettable place
Dove nacque il mio foco,	Where my passion was born,
Pensò folle il cor mio	My foolish heart thought
Tutti gli ardori suoi render di gelo,	To render all its ardor into ice,
E fortuna cangiar per cangiar cielo.	And to change fortune by changing my surroundings.

Ahi lassa! che mi segue	Ah me, alas, love follows me
In ogni tempo, in ogni parte amore,	At all times, and in every place,
E di notte e di giorno, a tutte l'ore,	And renders, night and day, at all hours,
All'occhio della mente,	To my mind's eye,
Rende l'amato oggetto ognor presente.	The beloved object always present.

Son qual cerva ferita che fugge,	*I am like the wounded doe that flees*
Dalla man che l'ancide e l'impiaga.	*From the hand that kills and wounds it.*
Ma se meco è lo stral che mi strugge	*But if the arrow that afflicts me is [lodged] in me,*
Lontananza non salda la piaga.	*Distance will not heal the wound.*

Anzi se nacque il mio amoroso desio	Indeed, since my amorous desire was born
D'una bella virtù figlio innocente,	The innocent child of a beautiful virtue,
Sia lontano o presente,	Whether far or near,
Sempre fisso è nel cor	Always is set in my heart
L'amato oggetto,	The beloved object,
Né a così giusto affetto	Nor to such a just love
Resiste di ragion l'alto consiglio,	Does the high counsel of reason resist,
Ch'anzi a seguir m'esorta	Which rather urges me to follow
Un bell'amor che di virtude è figlio.	A beautiful love that is the child of of virtue.

Il dolce foco mio,	*My sweet passion,*
Ch'accende un bel desio,	*That is lit by a beautiful desire,*
Amor lusinga.	*Love encourages.*
Ma nasce un rio timor,	*But a nagging fear is born,*
Onde languisce il cor,	*Wherefore my heart languishes,*
Ch'egli non finga.	*That he [Love/the beloved] might be pretending.*

Aure soavi (Rome, 1707; Ruspoli: 16 May 1707)

Aure soavi e liete,	Soft and delightful breezes,
Ombre notturne e chete,	Hushed evening shadows,
Voi dall'estivo ardore	From summer heat
Dolci ne difendete.	You give us sweet relief.
Ma non trova il mio core,	But my heart cannot find,
Nel suo cocente ognor loco amoroso,	In its ever-burning, loving core,
Chi lo difenda o chi gli dia riposo;	The one who will defend it or give it rest;
Onde fra voi solingo,	Wherefore alone among you,
Di parlar a colei	I imagine speaking to her,
Che pur non m'ode,	Who does not hear me,
Aure soavi, ombre notturne io fingo.	Soft breezes, evening shadows.

Care luci, che l'alba rendete	*Dear eyes, that bring the dawn*
Quand'a me così belle apparite	*When so beautiful you appear to me,*
Voi nel cor mille fiamme accendete,	*You light a thousand flames in my heart,*
Ma pietà dell'ardor non sentite.	*But you do not feel pity for the burning.*

Pietà, Clori, pietà	Pity, Clori, pity,
Se quel che pietà sia	If that which is pity
Dentro al tuo cor si sa.	Is known inside your heart.
Deh! fa che l'alma mia	Pray! make my soul
Veda e conosca a prova,	See and experience the proof
Che la pietà nel tuo bel cor si trova.	That pity exists in your beautiful heart.

Un'aura flebile,
Un'ombra mobile,
Sperar me fa
Che Clori amabile,
Nell'alma nobile
Senta pietà.

A gentle breeze,
A passing shadow,
Makes me hope
That lovely Clori
In [her] noble soul
Feels pity.

Bella ma ritrosetta (London, 1710–1716)

Bella ma ritrosetta,
Fissar il guardo si
Posso nei tuoi sembianti
Senza penar per te.
Ne già la ritrosetta
Potesse far così
Se tanti folli amanti
Fosser eguali a me.

Beautiful but coy lady,
I am able to fix my gaze
On your features
Without yearning for you.
But the coy lady
Would not be able to act this way
If all the foolish lovers
Were like me.

Oh, quanto godo in rimirarti spesso
De tuoi soggetti, fra lo stuol seguace.

Oh, I rejoice greatly in often gazing at you,
One of your subjects, among the following
   throng.

A chi giri uno sguardo
Che menzognero alletta,
A chi dal cor mendace
Volgi una paroletta,
A chi un riso,
A chi un gesto,
Tra lascivo e modesto,
e a tutti piace,
La vana esca fallace.
Io sol che ti conosco
E che non t'amo
Mi rido dell'inganno
E non m'appresso all'amo.

To this one you throw a look
That, false, ensnares,
To that one, from a lying heart,
You toss [pretty,] little word[s],
To this one a laugh,
To that one a gesture,
Part vulgar and part modest,
And it is pleasing to all,
The vain, deceptive bait.
Only I, who knows you
And does not love you,
Laugh at the deception
And do not come near to the hook.

Mi rido di veder,
Per l'esca del piacer,
Tutti in tormento.
Ma riderò più ancor,
Quand'uno vincitor
Sarà contento.

I laugh to see,
For the bait of pleasure,
All in torment.
But I will laugh still more,
When a victor
Will be content.

Care selve (Italian autograph, before 1709)

Cara selve, aure grate,	Dear woods, welcome breezes,
Erbette e fiori,	Grasses and flowers,
Che l'aspre mie querele,	Who, companions of my sorrow,
Compagne al dolor mio,	So often hear
Sì spesso udite,	My harsh complaints,
Tutti a Clori ridite,	All of you, say to Clori,
Se d'altro che di lei parlo e ragiono,	Whether I speak and think of anything other than her,
E quanto all'amor suo fedel io sono.	And how much I am faithful to her love.

Ridite, a Clori,	*Say to Clori,*
Erbette e fiori	*Grasses and flowers,*
Se altro mai sento	*Whether I ever feel*
Foco al mio cor.	*Another fire in my heart.*
Se lei non miro,	*If I do not gaze on her,*
Piango e sospiro,	*I weep and sigh,*
E'l mio lamento	*And my lament*
Figlio è d'amor.	*Is the child of love.*

Se cangiarsi potesse	If it was possible to change
L'antica forma usata,	One's old, customary form,
Oh! quante volte, oh! quante	Oh! how many times, oh! how often
In fronda, in sasso, in fior mi cangerei,	Into a branch, a stone, a flower, would I change myself,
Almen baciar potrei	At least, although trampled underfoot,
Calpestato talor sue vaghe piante;	I would be able to kiss her beautiful feet;
E nelle belle mani,	And into her beautiful hands,
Cangiato in fronda o fiore,	Changed into a branch or flower,
Mi porterebbe amore.	Love would carry me.

Non ha forza nel mio petto	*No other affection, no other beauty,*
Altro affetto, altra beltà.	*Has power in my breast.*
Non conosce l'alma amante	*The loving soul knows nothing*
L'incostante infedeltà.	*Of fickle inconstancy.*

Chi rapì la pace? (Florence/Venice, 1706)

Chi rapì la pace al core?	*Who stole peace from my heart?*
Chi dal sen l'alma rubò?	*Who robbed the soul from my breast?*
Ah! lo so,	*Ah! I know,*

Con un guardo fatto dardo,
Nume cieco mi piagò.

With a dart-like glance
The blind god wounded me.

Figlio d'un fabbro e amore
Col ner d'una pupilla
Segnò la morte al core,
E perché suoi trionfi
Soffero più superbi e crudeli,
Quell'occhio che fu strale
Cangiò Cupido in face funerale.

The son of a blacksmith and love,
With those dark eye[s]
Dealt death to my heart,
And because I suffer
His proudest and cruelest triumphs,
That eye that became an arrow
Cupid changed into a funeral torch.

Pupilla lucente
In stella funesta,
Amore cangiò.
Così *quel* splendore,
Con empio rigore
La morte additò.

The shining eye[s]
Love changed
Into a fatal star.
Thus that splendor
With pitiless severity
Pointed to death.

Clori, degli occhi miei (Florence/Venice, 1709)

Clori, degli occhi miei, del cuore,
Gran piacer, gran tormento.
Perché in tanta beltà tanto rigore?
Vedi chiaro argomento
Della tua crudeltade?
A te d'intorno
Parlano notte e giorno
Della fierezza tua l'acque ed i venti,

E pur tu non intendi, e tu non senti.

Clori, the great joy and torment
Of my eyes and heart,
Why in such beauty such hardness?
Do you see any good reason
For your cruelty?
All around you
Night and day
The winds and the waters speak of your
    disdain,
And yet you do not understand, and you do
    not hear.

Quel bel rio ch'a duro scoglio
Frange intorno i chiari umori
Sai che dice in sua favella?

That beautiful stream that on a hard rock
Breaks up its clear waters,
Do you know what it is saying in its own
    language?

Dice ogn'or col mio cordoglio,
Questo sasso è il cor di Clori,
Clori, ahi, cruda ancor che bella.

It speaks every hour with my grief,
"This rock is the heart of Clori,
Clori, alas, cruel yet beautiful."

Ma d'un scoglio peggiore
È'l sasso del tuo cor.
Quello si frange

But worse than a rock
Is the stone of your heart.
That one breaks up

Allo spesso cader d'onda stillante;   At the frequent fall of dripping water;
Te rendono più cruda e più costante,   But the streams from my ever-weeping eyes
L'onde del ciglio mio che sempre piange.   Render you more cruel and unmoving.

Quella che miri   *That playful breeze*
Aura scherzosa   *That you see*
Muover le fronde   *Move the leafy branches*
Di querce annosa,   *Of an ancient oak,*
Sai ciò ch'intanto   *Do you know meanwhile*
Dicendo va.   *What it is saying?*
Co' miei sospiri   *With my sighs:*
Dice di Clori: *It says of Clori:*
Qui si nasconde   *"Here hides*
Alma ritrosa   *A reluctant soul*
Che tien per vanto   *That makes a boast*
La crudeltà.   *Of its cruelty."*

Clori, ove sei? (undocumented; Italian?)

Clori, Clori, ove sei?   Clori, Clori, where are you?
Lungi dagli occhi miei,   Far from my eyes,
Dimmi dove t'aggiri,   Tell me where you wander,
Perché possano almeno   So that at least the last sighs of my breast
Giungere al tuo bel seno,   Will be able
Del seno mio quest'ultimi sospiri.   To arrive at your lovely bosom.

Se gli ascolti ti diranno,   *If you listen to them they will say to you,*
Che non io ma sol affanno   *That not I but only anguish*
Oggi vive e spira in me.   *Today lives and dies in me.*
Ti diranno ch'il dolore   *They will say to you that sadness*
Fa le parti in me del core,   *Took the place of my heart,*
Da ch'il cor è ardor con te.   *Since my heart burns with you.*

Né creder giacché finto   And do not think that imagined
Sia questo mal ch'oggi mi vuol estinto,   Is this pain that today wishes me dead,
Che se morte si chiama   For if absence is called
Dell'anima e del sen la lontananza,   The death of the soul and breast,
È morte a chi ben ama,   It is death to one who loves well,
E più che nel suo petto   And whose soul, more than in his own
                                                           breast;
Ha l'alma sua nell'adorato oggetto.   Lives in his adored object.

Dell'idol mio,   *I can no longer,*

Più non poss'io,	Without the beautiful rays
Senza i bei rai,	Of my idol,
Godere il dì.	Enjoy the day.
Come fia mai	How will it be
Ch'io qui respiri	That I breathe here
L'aura gradita,	The welcome breeze,
Se la mia vita	If my life
Non è più qui.	Is no longer here.

Clori, vezzosa Clori (Rome, 1708; Ruspoli: 9 August 1708)

Clori, vezzosa Clori,	Clori, charming Clori,
Lontan dal tuo sembiante	Far from your countenance,
Fra i taciturni orrori	Among the silent terrors
Di boscareccie piante,	Of the [dark] woods,
Fra le pompe del prato,	Among the splendor of the fields,
E il mororar del rio,	And the murmur of the river,
Ho sempre dinanzi	I always have before me
Il tuo bel volto amato.	Your beautiful, loved image.

Il bosco, il prato, il rio,	The wood, the field, the river,
Di te, caro ben mio	My dear beloved,
L'imagine adorata	Carry back the adored image
Riportano al pensier.	Of you to my thoughts.
E se zampilla il fonte	And if the fountain gushes forth,
Mi par di star à fronte	I seem to stand in front of
De lumi tuoi vivaci	Your sparkling eyes
E del tuo guardo arcier.	And your dart-like glance.

Se l'usignol canoro,	If the singing nightingale,
Dolcemente si lagna	Sweetly complaining
Dell'infida compagna,	Of his unfaithful companion,
Mi vi-chiama nel seno	Calls up in my breast
Quel geloso veleno	That jealous poison
Che lontano da te	That, far from you,
M'opprime il core:	Oppresses my heart:
In somma a tutte l'ore,	[Then] in sum, at all hours,
E dovunque vi-volgo il piede errante	And wherever I wander,
Sempre fido e costante	Always faithful and constant,
Mi si fa scorta amore,	Love escorts me,
Quel caro amor che servo tuo mi rese,	That dear love that made me your servant,
E di fiamma si bella il cor m'accese.	And with a beautiful flame fires my heart.

Non è possibile,	*It is not possible,*
O Clori amabile	*O lovely Clori,*
Che di te scordesi	*For the loving heart*
L'amante cor.	*To forget you.*
Non è credibile	*It is not believable*
Quanto durabile	*That burning ardor*
Sarà nell'anima	*Will be so lasting*
L'acceso ardor.	*In the soul.*

Dalla guerra amorosa (Italian, without autograph; Ruspoli: 31 August 1709)

Dalla guerra amorosa,	From the war of love,
Or che ragion mi chiama,	Now that reason calls me,
O miei pensieri,	O my thoughts,
Fuggite pur, fuggite,	Fly indeed, fly,
Vergognosa non è	Flight is not inglorious
In amor la fuga,	In love,
Che sol fuggendo un'alma	For only by fleeing
Del crudo amor può riportar la palma.	Is a soul able to win the palm [of victory] from cruel love.

Non v'alletti un occhio nero,	*Do not be charmed by any dark eye[s]*
Con suoi sguardi lusinghiero	*Alluring with their glances*
Che da voi chieda pietà.	*That may beg pity from you.*
Che per far le sue vendette,	*For in order to take revenge,*
E con arco e con saette,	*With both bow and arrow,*
Ivi amor nascoso sta.	*Love stands hidden there.*

Fuggite, sì fuggite!	Fly, yes, fly!
Ahi! di quanto veleno,	Ah! how much poison
Amore asperge i suoi piaceri,	Love sprinkles over his pleasures,
Ah! quanto [som]ministra duol, e pianto,	Ah! how much sadness and crying he gives to
A chi lo segue e le sue leggi adora.	The one who follows him and worships his laws.

Se un volto v'innamora,	If a [beautiful] face makes you fall in love,
Sappiate, O pensieri miei,	Know, O my thoughts,
Che ciò che piace	That that which pleases
In brev'ora svanisce, e poi dispiace.	In a short while vanishes, and then brings sorrow.

La bellezza è com'un fiore,	*Beauty is like a flower,*
Sul matin vivace e bello,	*In the morning lively and lovely,*

Sul matin di primavera,
Che la sera langue e more,
Si scolora e non par quello.

Fuggite, sì fuggite!
A chi servo d'amor vive in catena,
È dubbioso il gioir, certa la pena.

In the morning of springtime,
Which in the evening languishes and dies,
It fades and no longer seems what it was.

Fly, yes fly!
To one who, a servant of love, lives in chains,
Joy is doubtful, pain certain.

Da sete ardente afflitto (Italian, without autograph; Ruspoli: 31 August 1709)

Da sete ardente afflitto,
Un fonte agli occhi miei fingo presente,
All'alma mia dolente,
Mentre già par che passi
Refrigerio si dolce e sì soave;

Cura molesta e grave
Riscuote il mio pensiero,

Onde il cor più s'affanna e si confonde,

E sospirando esclama:
Dov'è l'amico rio? Dove son le onde?

Suffering from a burning thirst,
I imagine a spring before my eyes,
And to my sorrowful soul,
It already seems that
A cooling so sweet and so gentle is passing
    by;

Troubling and grave care
Rouses my thought [brings me back to
    reality],

Wherefore my heart is more distressed and
    confused,

And sighing it exclaims:
Where is the friendly stream? Where are the
    waves?

Penso al rio, ma penso insieme
Che deluso dal pensiero,
Più s'affanna il mesto core.
E nel sen ch'acceso geme,
Più si avanza un duol sereno
Più si fa grave l'ardore.

I think of the stream, but at the same time
I think that deluded by the thought,
My sad heart is more distressed.
And in my breast that, inflamed, groans,
The more a steady sorrow grows
The more intense the burning becomes.

Amanti, ecco vi svelo
Qual sia l'ardor che sento,
E del fonte ideato
Il bel ristoro;
E il ruscel che presente
In sì ria lontananza
Me figura il pensiero
Del mio tesoro,
E la sete ch'avanza
Di Tantalo il martoro

Lovers, behold, I reveal to you
What is the burning that I feel,
And of the imagined spring
[What is] the beautiful relief;
The stream that appears
In such hateful distance
For me shapes the thought
Of my beloved,
And the thirst that exceeds
The martyrdom of Tantalus

È il caro, il dolce, il tenero desio
Solo di riveder l'idolo mio.
Or pensate qual soffra
Il povero mio cor duolo inumano,
Quando per duolo rio
Crede che sia vicino ed è lontano.

Quando non son presente
All'idolo ch'adoro,
Sento ch'allor dolente
Il cor mancando va.
E pur fiero destino
Spesso al mio bel tesoro
Non vuol ch'io sia vicino
E sospirar mi fa.

Is the dear, sweet tender desire
Only to see again my idol.
Now consider how much
My poor heart suffers inhuman grief,
When through desperate sadness
It believes that s/he is near when s/he is far.

When I am not near
To the idol that I adore,
I feel then that, sorrowful,
My heart grows faint.
And yet fierce destiny
Often does not wish me to be near
My beautiful treasure
And makes me sigh.

Deh! lasciate (London, c. 1720)
By Paolo Rolli

Deh! lasciate e vita e volo
All'amabile usignuolo,
Cacciatori, per pietà.
Col suo flebile lamento,
Ei ridice il mio tormento
All'ingrata che lo fa.

Ah! leave both life and flight
To the sweet nightingale,
O hunters, for pity's sake.
With his plaintive song,
He tells of my torment over and over
To the ungrateful one who causes it.

Crudele, impara almen dalla compagna
Di quel dolce usignuolo innamorato
A render a chi t'ama
Amore per amore.
Scaccia il vano timore,
Che, come altrui, me ti dipinge ancora
Menzognero e incostante.
Amabil troppo è tua beltà divina,
E troppo la conosce il core amante.

Cruel one, learn at least from the partner
Of that sweet, loving nightingale
To return to him who loves you
Love for love.
Chase away the vain fear,
That still, like others, depicts me to you
As untrue and fickle.
Too pleasing is your divine beauty,
And too well the loving heart knows it.

Lascia la dolce brama
Di riamar chi t'ama
Venir nel tuo bel cor.
La vera gioia intende
Quell'anima, che rende
Amore per amor.

Let the sweet longing
To return the love of him who loves you
Enter your beautiful heart.
That soul which renders
Love for love
Knows true joy.

Del bel idolo mio (Rome, with Ruspoli spring 1707 group?; Ruspoli: 31 August 1709)

Del bel idolo mio	This is the fragile, earthly corpse
Quest'è la fragil sua terrena salma.	Of my beautiful idol.
Per rintracciar quell'alma	In order to track down her soul
Scenderò d'Acheronte	I will descend
Al tenebroso lago;	To the gloomy lake of Acheronte;
Quell'adorato imago	That beloved image
Mi sarà cinosura infra gl'abissi.	Will be my guiding light among the abysses.
Corri, corri a morir, misero amante,	Run, run to die, miserable lover,
Che la mortal sentenza	Since the deadly decision I have already
Io già la fulminai, e già la scrissi.	Made, and already written.
Formidabil gondoliero,	*Formidable gondolier,*
Io ti bramo, approda alla riva.	*I want you, approach the shore.*
Nel varcare il temuto sentiero,	*While crossing the fearful border,*
Un certo diletto	*A certain delight*
Mi nasce nel petto,	*Is born in my breast,*
Che l'alma ravviva.	*That revives my spirit.*
Ma se non la rinvengo	But if I do not find her again
Là nello stigio regno,	There in the stygian kingdom,
Misero, oh! che farò?	Miserable one, oh! what will I do?
Piangerò, ma le mie lacrime	*I will weep, but my tears*
Saran simboli di fé.	*Will be symbols of faith.*
Quando piange un'alma forte,	*When a strong soul cries,*
Sol nel regno della morte,	*Even in the kingdom of death,*
Si lusinga aver mercè.	*It hopes to find mercy.*
Fra quell'orride soglie,	Over those horrid thresholds,
Tutto festante,	Completely jubilant,
Ti raggira il piede	One wanders into
Olocausto d'amor, e della fede.	A conflagration of love and of faith.
Su rendetemi colei,	*Give her back to me,*
Consolate un infelice,	*Console an unhappy soul,*
Cari numi, amati dei,	*Dear spirits, beloved gods,*
Voglio Nice.	*I want Nice.*
Date tregua al duol interno!	*Give peace to my inward grief!*
Dalle fiamme dell'inferno	*From the flames of the inferno*
Sorgerò nova fenice.	*I will rise a new phoenix.*
Voglio Nice.	*I want Nice.*

Dimmi, O mio cor (?Ottoboni: Rome, 1707)

Dimmi, O mio cor, che brami,
Se con sì fieri, e insoliti risalti,
Agitando il mio petto
Ognor m'affliggi!
Tu che solo ricetto
Di delizie e contento esser dovresti,
Mentre quel ben ch'adori
Arde con doppie fiamme,
E pur tu pien d'affanni
Ognor gemi e sospiri?
Sento ch'il cor dolente
A me così risponde:
È ver, che sono amato,
Ma ti sovvenga al fin,
Che son piagato.

Mi piagò d'amor lo strale,
E fatale la saetta in me vibrò.
Che sebbene il mio Fileno
Per me porti acceso il seno,
Pure il fato rio spietato,
A penar mi destinò.

Dunque se il rio destino,
E'l crudo fato vuol
Ch'io viva penando,
Di che fare poss'io?
Se fu sola tua colpa,
Quando per gli occhi al core
Portasti la cagion, del mio dolore?
Ah! mio core infelice!
Quanto, ahi! quanto t'inganni,
Se tu pensi
Che io sia ministra de' tuoi affanni,
Poi che il nume d'amore
Dagli occhi di Fileno
Ti tramandò l'ardore!
Ma non temer, mio core,
Armati di costanza
Che anch'io contenta e paga di mia sorte,

Tell me, O my heart, what you desire,
If with such cruel, and unusual vividness,
Agitating my breast
You always torment me!
[My heart], you ought only to be
A receptacle of delight and content,
While that love that you adore
Burns with a double flame,
And yet full of anguish
Do you always groan and sigh?
I hear the miserable heart
Respond thus to me:
It is true that I am loved,
But remember in the end,
That I am wounded.

The dart of love wounded me,
And the fatal arrow struck me.
For even though my Fileno
Feels his breast burning for me,
Still a pitiless, evil fate
Destined me to suffer.

Therefore if evil destiny,
And [if] cruel fate wishes
That I should live suffering,
What can I do about that?
If it was your fault alone,
When through the eyes to the heart
You carried the cause of my sadness?
Ah! my unhappy heart! how much, alas!
How much you deceive yourself,
If you think
That I am the cause of your anguish,
Since the god of love
From the eyes of Fileno
Passed the ardor to you!
But do not fear, my heart,
Arm yourself with constancy,
For I, content and satisfied with my fate,

Purché m'ami il mio ben, sprezzo la
   morte.

Provided my beloved loves me, scorn even
   death.

Cari lacci, amate pene,
Pene grate e dolce affanno!
Per quel caro amato bene
Non son crudele catene,
No, ch'amor non è tiranno.

Sweet chains, loving pains,
Pleasing pain and dear affliction!
For such a dear loving beloved,
They are not cruel chains,
No, for love is not a tyrant.

Ditemi, O piante (Rome, 1708; Ruspoli: 9 August 1708)

Ditemi, O piante, O fiori voi,
Che da Eurilla mia beltà prendete,
Dite, vedeste mai
Più risplendenti rai,
Ninfa di lei più vaga o più gentile?
Ah no, ch'altra simile
A lei darsi non puote,
Se tutto il vago, e il bello,
Che si mira in altrui sparso e diviso,

Tutto raccolse amor nel suo bel viso.

Tell me, O plants, O you flowers,
You who mirror my beautiful Eurilla,
Tell me, have you ever viewed
More resplendent rays,
A nymph more lovely or more kind than she?
Ah no, another like her
There cannot be,
Since all the charm, and the beauty,
That one gazes at scattered and divided in
   others,
Love has gathered together in her beautiful
   face.

Il candore tolse al giglio,
Alla rosa il bel vermiglio,
Quando amore la formò.
Al suo petto diè il candore,
Della rosa il bel cinabro,
E alle sue pupille ardenti
Tutti i rai del sol donò.

The brilliant white he took from the lily,
From the rose the beautiful vermilion,
When love formed her.
To her breast he gave the brilliant white,
From the rose the beautiful red lips,
And to her ardent eyes
He bestowed all the rays of the sun.

Ma la beltà del volto
Non è il pregio maggiore
Ch'in lei si celi
Se nel suo nobil core
Tutto lo stuol delle virtudi è accolto,
E con tal lume in seno
Tanti sparge d'intorno
Raggi dal viso adorno
Ch'abbagliato riman,
Chi la rimira

But the beauty of her face
Is not the most precious gift
Hidden within her,
Since in her noble heart
All the host of virtues is collected,
And with so much light in her breast
She scatters around
So many rays from her beautiful face
That they remain dazzled
Who gaze again at her,

Come rimaner suole
Chi le pupille sue fissa nel sole.

As one is wont to remain
Who fixes his eyes on the sun.

Per formar sì vaga e bella
Pastorella
Con virtude amor s'unì.
Tutto il bel che appar di fuore
Diele amore
E virtù l'alma abbellì.

In order to create such a lovely
And beautiful shepherdess
Love united with virtue.
All external beauty
Love gave her in abundance
And virtue adorned her soul.

Dolc'è pur d'amor l'affanno (London, 1710–1716)
By Paolo Rolli?

Dolc'è pur d'amor l'affanno,
Se compagno del tormento,
Il contento viene ancor.
Se le pene unite vanno,
Con la speme e con l'affetto,
Il diletto è poi maggior.

Even the anguish of love is sweet,
If, along with the pain,
Pleasure comes too.
If the sufferings go together
With hope and tenderness,
Then the pleasure is even greater.

Il viver sempre in pene
Stanca i desir d'amore,
E il viver lieto sempre
Piace ma sazia il core.
Dolci ripulse e graziosi sdegni,
Certe sventure inaspettate e lievi,
Danno tormento, è ver,
Ma fan talora più soavi i piacer,
Quanto più brevi.

Living always in pain
Wearies the desires of love,
And living always happy
Pleases but satiates the heart.
Sweet denials and gracious disdain,
Certain unexpected and slight misfortunes,
Give torment, it is true,
But sometimes make the pleasures sweeter
Although briefer.

Se più non t'amo,
Non ti doler,
Ch'amarti, O bella,
Io più non so.
Ma da te bramo
Caro piacer,
Se tu sei quella
Che mi piagò.

If I no longer love you,
Do not grieve,
For to love you, O beauteous one,
I no longer know how.
But from you I crave
Sweet pleasure,
If you are that one
Who wounded me.

E partirai, mia vita? (?Ottoboni: Rome, 1707)

E partirai, mia vita?
Né in quel del tuo partir crudo momento

And will you leave me, O my life?
And will not my soul leave me

Farà l'anima mia da me partita?	In that cruel moment of your departing?
Ah! se un duro tormento	Ah! if merely thinking of a harsh torment
Nel ripensarvi sol quasi m'uccide,	Almost kills me,
Che farà quel dolore,	What will be the effect of that grief,
Che allora (ahimè) per gli occhi miei	Which (alas!) will pierce my eyes
Con tutti gli strali suoi	And with all of its darts
Mi scenderà sul core?	Fall on my heart?
Vedrò teco ogni gioia, ogni bene,	*I shall see all joy, all pleasure,*
Da me lungi rivolgere il piè,	*Go with you far away from me,*
E gli affanni, gli strazi, le pene,	*And grief, torture and pain*
Tutti insieme restarsi con me.	*Remain all together with me.*
Vedrò d'ombre infelici,	I shall see the day,
Privo dei lumi tuoi,	Deprived of the light of your eyes,
Cingersi il giorno;	Plunged into unhappy shadows;
Scorgerò d'ogni intorno	I shall see myself surrounded
Aggirarmisi orror, mestizia, e pianto;	On all sides by horror, sadness and tears;
E congiurati intanto	And meanwhile will conspire
Un desir disperato	Desperate desire
Ed un sovra d'ogn'altro aspro martire	And suffering more bitter than any other
Faranno il mio morir più che morire.	To make my dying worse than death.
Pria che spunti un dì sì fiero,	*Before such a dreadful day dawns,*
Togli a me la vita, O Amor.	*Take my life, O God of Love;*
Onde men l'anima afflitta,	*So that my soul, less afflicted,*
Né dal duol tanto traffitta,	*And not so pierced with grief,*
Nel da lui preso sentiero	*May go after my heart*
Possa gir dietro al suo cor.	*Along the path it has taken.*

Translation by Terence Best (slightly amended) in Donald Burrows, ed., *G. F. Handel: Songs and Cantatas* (Oxford: Oxford University Press, 1988).

Figli del mesto cor (Italian: without autograph)

Figli del mesto cor,	Offspring of the mournful heart,
Pianti e sospiri,	You tears and sighs,
Voi, nell'uscir dal seno,	In escaping the breast,
Turbate il bel sereno	You disturb the beautiful serenity
Del ciel d'amore.	Of the heaven of love.
E su le ree pupille	And in the unkind eyes
Della crudel mia Fille,	Of my cruel Fille,
Schierate a stuolo a stuolo	You line up rank upon rank
I nemici guerrier de' miei respiri.	The enemy warriors of my sighs.

E l'ingrata mi vede e dice poi:
Deh! vogliono di più gli oltraggi tuoi.

Son pur le lacrime
Il cibo misero
Ch'io prendo ognor.
Sempre tra gemiti
Non spiro altr'aere
Che del dolor.

Così mia dura sorte,
Senza sperar pietà,
Mi guida a morte.

Cruda legge d'un alma costante,
Che non puote non esser amante
D'un bel volto, ma volto infedel.
Ma più cruda è la tempra d'un core,
Che sprezzando i comandi d'amore,
Vuol il vanto sol d'esser crudel.

Volea seguir, quand'ecco,
Crescendo col dolor del pianto l'acque,
Si svenne affranto, e nel svenir si tacque.

And the ungrateful one sees me and says:
Ah! Your outrages deserve still more.

Tears are still
The wretched food
That I always take.
Always groaning,
I breathe no other air
Than that of sorrow.

Thus my hard fate
Without hope of pity
Leads me to death.

Cruel law for a constant soul,
Who cannot but love
A beautiful but unfaithful face.
But more cruel still is the temper of a heart,
Which scorning the commands of love,
Wants only the boast of being cruel.

He wished to go on, when suddenly,
His tears of grief welling up with sorrow,
He fainted exhausted, and in fainting was
    silent.

Filli adorata e cara (Rome, spring 1707?; Ruspoli: 31 August 1709)

Filli adorata e cara,
Filli che fosti e sei l'anima mia,
Se lontananza ria
Mi divide da te,
Svelse il mio core
Da questo amante petto,
Sallo il ciel, sallo amore.
Quanto dolente, ahi! quanto,
Porto ramingo e solitario il passo,
Ove aspergo di pianto
Ogni riva, ogni fiore, ed ogni sasso.

Se non giunge quel momento,
Che ritorni a me, mia bella,
Sempre mesto piangerò.

Filli, adored and dear,
Filli, you who have been and are my soul,
If evil distance
Divides me from you,
My heart is ripped
From my loving breast,
[As] heaven knows, love knows.
How sadly, alas! how sadly
I drag my wandering and solitary steps,
Where I spread tears over
Every river, every flower and every stone.

If that moment does not arrive,
In which you return to me, my love,
Always sad I will weep.

Pur mi dice il mio tormento,	*However my torment tells me,*
Per voler di cruda stella	*Because of the desire of a cruel star,*
Non sì presto io ti vedrò.	*I shall not so soon see you.*

Ma se volesse mai mia cruda sorte,   But if my cruel fate ever wished,
Che pria di riveder tue luci amate,   That before seeing again your loving eyes,
Il rio dolore mi chiamasse a morte,   An evil sadness would call me to death,
Sappi, O Filli, mio Nume,   Know, O Filli, my goddess,
Che estinto ancor t'adorerà costante   That even dead my loving spirit,
La fredda salma mia,   My cold corpse,
Lo spirto amante.   Would adore you constantly.

Lungi da te, mia speme,   *Far from you, my hope,*
Langue, sospira, e geme,   *This faithful heart*
Fedele questo cor.   *Languishes, sighs and groans.*
Da te lontan, mia vita,   *Far from you, my life,*
La morte m'è gradita   *Death is welcome to me,*
E sola bramo ognor.   *And I long for [it] only and always.*

Fra pensieri (undocumented: Rome, 1707?)

Fra pensieri quel pensiero,   *Among my thoughts, the one thought*
Che d'ogn'altro più leggiero,   *That is lighter than all the others,*
Primo a Clori giungerà,   *And will get to Clori first,*
Dal mio core il premio avrà.   *Will receive the reward from my heart.*
Ma compagni nel ardire,   *But equal in boldness,*
Nella brama, nel desire,   *Longing and desire,*
So che a gara voleranno,   *I know that they will vie with one another as they fly,*

So che insieme giungeranno,   *I know that they will arrive together,*
Né distinguersi potrà   *Nor will it be possible to distinguish*
Chi di lor primo sarà.   *Which of them will be first.*

E se fia che volando   And if it be that as they fly
Con ostinato nobile valore,   With continued noble determination,
Non sia fra miei pensieri   There will not be among my thoughts
Chi si possa vantar per vincitore,   One that can claim to be the winner,
Ciascuno dal mio core il premio speri.   Let each one still hope for the prize from my heart.

Per risvegliar in lor gara ambiziosa   To awaken in them ambitious rivalry
Di giunger più spediti a trovar Clori,   To reach Clori more quickly,
Io lor prometto   I promise never to disturb
Di non turbar mai quel sicuro piacere,   That certain pleasure in them

Che proveranno in sempre raggirarsi
Intorno a sì perfetto
Ed amoroso oggetto.
Né di questo maggiore
Premio può darvi, O miei pensieri, il core.

That they will always feel in circling
Around such a perfect
And lovable object.
Nor can the heart give you
A greater prize than this, O my thoughts.

Pronti l'ale dispiegate,
Miei pensieri, ratti volate,
A trovar la bella Clori.
E, fissandovi in costei,
Dite pur che al par di lei
Non v'è oggetto che innamori.

Quickly, spread your wings,
Quickly fly, O my thoughts,
And find the beautiful Clori.
And clinging to her,
Say that compared to her,
There is no other object that can inspire love.

Fra tante pene (Florence/Venice, 1706)

Fra tante pene e tante
Che il cieco Nume a' servi suoi comparte,

Non sapeva il mio core
Qual fosse la più fiera e la maggiore,
Pure al fin la distingue, ed abbastanza

Provò che la più fiera é lontananza.

Among so many, many afflictions
That the blind god apportions to his
    followers,

My heart did not know
Which was the fiercest and greatest,
Yet in the end it distinguished, and
    sufficiently

Experienced that the fiercest is distance.

Se avvien che sia infedele,
La bella mia crudele,
Mentre la miran gli occhi,
Respira questo cor.
Se gelosia m'affanna
Quando la mia tiranna
Dolce favella,
Allor pur mi ristora,
Ma il farà al fin ch'io mora;
Giunge la lontananza,
Che privo di speranza,
Mi strugge nel dolor.

If it happens that she is unfaithful,
My beautiful cruel one,
While my eyes gaze on her,
my heart breathes [is content].
If jealousy vexes me
When my tyrant
Speaks sweetly,
Then, however, she restores me,
But will in the end cause me to die;
But if absence is added,
Then, devoid of hope,
It destroys me in grief.

Torna, torna, mio bene,
Lascia per me quelle delizie amene,
Che l'acque del mio pianto,
L'aure de' miei sospiri,
Ti doneranno ancor qualche conforto;

Return, return, my beloved,
For me abandon those pleasant delights,
For the waters of my weeping,
The breezes of my sighs,
Will again bring you some comfort;

Altra speme di aita or non m'avanza,
Che la pena più fiera è lontananza.

No other hope of aid is now left to me,
Because the cruelest pain is absence.

A sanar le ferite d'un core,
Lontananza bastante non è.
Che tiranno più accrese il dolore,
È un dolor che maggiore non v'è.

To heal the wounds of a heart,
Absence is not enough.
That tyrant increases the sadness more,
[And] is a grief greater than which there is
    none.

Hendel, non può mia musa (?Pamphili: Rome, 1707; Ruspoli: 9 August 1708)
By Benedetto Pamphili

Hendel, non può mia musa
Cantare in un istante
Versi, che degni sian
Della tua lira,
Ma sento che in me spira
Sì soave armonia
Che ai tuoi concenti
Son costretto cantare in questi accenti:

Handel, my muse cannot
Sing in an instant
Verses which are worthy of your lyre,
But I feel that in me
There breathes
Such sweet harmony
That I am compelled to sing
In praise of your music in these words:

Poté Orfeo col dolce suono
Arrestar d'augelli il volo
E fermar di belva al pié;
Si muovero a un sì bel suono
Tronchi, e sassi ancor dal suolo,
Ma giammai cantar li fé.

Orpheus with his sweet sounds
Could stop birds in their flight
And the wild beast in its tracks;
Trees were moved by such beautiful sounds,
And rocks were even lifted from the ground,
But he never made them sing.

Dunque maggior d'Orfeo
Tu sforzi al canto
La mia musa all'ora
Che il plettro appeso avea
A un tronco annoso, e immobile giacea.

So you, greater than Orpheus,
Force my muse into song,
Just when it had
Hung the plectrum
On a hoary tree, and lay motionless.

Ognun canti, e all'armonia
Di novello Orfeo si dia
Alla destra il moto

Let everyone sing, and inspired
By the harmony of the new Orpheus,
Let the hand move again on the lyre
Let there be motion to the hand

Al canto voce

And the voice find such song
And voice to the song such

Tal che mai s'udì.
E in sì grata melodia

As was never heard before.
And in such pleasing melody

Tutto gioia l'alma sia,	*Let the soul be all joy, and so,*
Ingannando il tempo intanto	*Whiling away the time,*
Passi lieto e l'ore, e il dì.	*Let it happily pass the hours and the day.*

Translation (with alternate readings in Roman type added to the final aria) by Terence Best, in Donald Burrows, ed., *G. F. Handel: Songs and Cantatas* (Oxford: Oxford University Press, 1988).

Ho fuggito (London, c. 1720)
By Paolo Rolli

Ho fuggito Amor anch'io,	*I too have fled from Love,*
Ho spezzato i lacci suoi:	*I have broken its bonds:*
Ma che poi?	*But what then?*
Son tornato in servitù.	*I have returned into bondage.*
E che pensi far, cor mio?	*And what do you think you are doing, O my heart?*
I passati tuoi tormenti,	*Do you not remember*
Non rammenti?	*Your past torments?*
No, non li rammenti più.	*No, you remember them no longer.*
La dolce libertà,	Does sweet liberty,
Tanto bramata un tempo,	Once so longed for,
Or non t'aggrada più,	No longer please you,
Folle mio core?	My foolish heart?
Sai pur quanto periglio,	Do you know how much danger,
Quante amarezze	How much bitterness
Ad incontrar tu vai?	You are going to meet?
Povero cor, lo sai?	Poor heart, do you know?
Delle false speranze,	Of the false hopes,
Della tradita fede,	Of the betrayed trust,
Ancor non hai	Do you not yet have
Prova certa o bastante?	Certain and sufficient proof?
Parlo in van; tu rispondi:	I speak in vain; you respond:
Ahi! sono amante.	Alas, I am in love.
È troppo bella,	*She is too beautiful,*
Troppo amorosa,	*Too loving,*
La pastorella,	*The shepherdess,*
Che t'invaghì.	*Who has charmed you.*
Mio cor, sì, sì,	*Yes, yes, my heart,*
Torna ad amare.	*Return again to love.*

Di quelle vaghe
Pupille nere,
Le dolci piaghe,
Fuggir chi può?
Tu non puoi, no, no,
Son troppo care.

Who can flee
The sweet wounds
Of those lovely
Dark eyes?
You cannot, no, no,
They are too dear.

The following translation appears in GB-Lbl Zweig ms 36:

Most beautiful,
Most loving
Shepherdess,
Who with desire
Inflames my heart,
Return again and love.
Who can flee
The sweet wounds
Made by
Those black roving eyes?
Thou canst not,
No, they are too dear.

Irene, idolo mio (Italian, without autograph; Santini Collection)

Irene, idolo mio,
Crudele Irene!
Invan tento fuggire il mio destin.
Se meco porto impressa
Della tua crudeltà,
Del mio sprezzato amor,
L'imago istessa,
Io t'amo, e tu non credi,
Io peno, e pur non hai pietà
De' miei sospir,
Delle mie pene,
Ch'io penerei contento,
Se pietà avesti almen del mio tormento.

Irene, my idol,
Cruel Irene!
In vain I try to flee my destiny.
Since I carry imprinted within me
The very image
Of your cruelty,
And of my rejected love,
I love you, and you do not believe me,
I suffer, and still you do not have pity
For my sighs,
Or my anguish,
For I should suffer gladly,
If you at least had pity for my torment.

Tormento maggiore
Di quel del mio core,
Dar, no, non si può.
S'io parlo d'Irene,

Greater suffering
Than that of my heart,
There cannot be, no.
If I speak of Irene,

S'accrescon le pene,
E pace non ho.

Talor che cerco, O Irene,
Spiegar col labbro,
I sensi del mio core,
Irene, ah! non rispondi,
E con ingiusti sensi,
Infido chiami il puro affetto mio.
Se ver te volgo il ciglio,
Altrove allor volgi gli sguardi tuoi,
Onde sempre per te, prova il mio core

Cagion di nova pena, e di dolore.

In tanti affanni
È immerso il core,
Pace non trova
Quest'alma mia.
Pria fu lo sdegno,
Poi fu il rigore,
Or la tormenta
La gelosia.

Contro forza fatale
Del dio bendato
È ver che nulla vale;
Ma ben può fedeltade
Ammollir d'un sen lo sprezzo rio;
Onde spera il mio core
Vincer con la costanza il tuo rigore.

Quanto più rigida
Si mostra Irene,
Sempre più fervida
La fiamma è in me.
Mia bella, sprezzami,
Ch'io pur t'adoro,
E più costante
Sarò per te.

The anguish grows,
And I have no peace.

Sometimes when I try, O Irene,
To explain with my lips,
The feelings of my heart,
Irene, ah! you answer not,
And with unjust feelings,
You call my pure affection unfaithful.
If I turn my eyes toward you,
You then turn your glance elsewhere,
Wherefore because of you, my heart always
    finds
Reason for new pain, and for suffering.

In such pangs
My heart is immersed,
This soul of mine
Finds no peace.
First there was scorn,
Then severity,
And now jealousy
Torments it.

Against the fatal strength
Of the blindfolded god,
It is true that nothing avails;
But faithfulness is well able
To soften the cruel disdain of a breast;
Wherefore my heart hopes
To conquer with constancy, your severity.

The more harsh
Irene shows herself,
Always the more fervid
The flame is within me.
My beauty, disdain me,
For I still adore you,
And the more constant
I will be to you.

L'aure grate (*La Solitudine*) (London, c. 1718)

L'aure grate, il fresco rio,	The welcome breezes, the cool river,
L'ombre tacite del bosco,	The quiet shade of the wood,
Fan più dolce, al pensier mio,	Make sweeter to my mind
La soave libertà.	Sweet liberty.
Se son priva del contento	If I am deprived of the happiness
D'altro ben che non conosco,	Of another joy that I know not,
Nemmen provo alcun tormento	Neither do I experience any of the pain
Che con quello sempre va.	That always goes with it.
Non v'è delizia umana,	There is no human delight
Soave più d'una tranquilla vita.	Sweeter than a quiet life.
In queste solitudini remote,	In this remote solitude,
Dalle cure lontana,	I live my happy days
Vivo lieti i miei giorni;	Far from cares;
E le verdi campagne,	The green countryside,
Gl'ameni boschi,	The pleasant woods,
I limpidi ruscelli,	The clear streams,
Vagheggio;	I observe fondly;
E i frutti e i fiori,	The fruits and flowers,
Or colgo or gusto or miro;	Now I gather, now taste, now gaze at;
E la piena d'odori aura respiro.	And I breathe the air full of fragrances.
No, che piacer non v'è	No, there is no pleasure
Più amabile di te,	More pleasing than you,
Placida libertà.	Sweet liberty.
Se non t'apprezza un cor,	Even if a heart treasures you not,
Quanto ti piange allor,	How it weeps for you then,
Allor che più non t'ha.	Then when it no longer has you.

Lucrezia ("O numi eterni!") (Florence/Venice, 1706?)

(recitative)

O numi eterni! O stelle, stelle!	O eternal gods! O stars, stars!
Che fulminate empii tiranni,	You who strike down wicked tyrants,
Impugnate a' miei voti orridi strali.	Take up at my bidding your terrible darts.
Voi con fochi tonanti	With your thundering flames
Incenerite il reo Tarquinio e Roma;	Reduce to ashes the evil Tarquin and Rome itself;
Dalla sua superba chioma	From his proud brow
Omai trabocchi il vacillante alloro:	May the trembling laurel fall;
S'apra il suolo in voragini,	May the earth open an abyss at his feet

Si celi, con memorando esempio,

Nelle viscere sue l'indegno e l'empio.

(aria)
Già superbo del mio affanno,
Traditor dell'onor mio,
Parte l'empio, lo sleal.
Tu punisci il fiero inganno
Del fellon, del mostro rio,
Giusto ciel, Parca fatal.

(recitative)
Ma voi forse nel cielo
Per castigo maggior del mio delitto,
State oziosi, O provocati numi
Se son sorde le stelle,
Se non mi odon le sfere,
A voi, tremende deità,
Del abisso, mi volgo a voi s'aspetta
Del tradito onor mio far la vendetta.

(aria)
Il suol(o) che preme, l'aura che spira
L'empio Romano, s'apra, s'infetti.
Se il passo move, se il guardo gira,
Incontri larve, ruine aspetti.

(recitative)
Ah! che ancor nell'abisso
Dormon le furie,
I sdegni e le vendette.
Giove dunque per me non ha saette,
È pietoso l'inferno?
Ah! Ch'io già sono in odio al cielo!
Ah dite!
E se la pena non piomba sul mio capo,
A' miei rimorsi è rimorso il poter
Di castigarmi.

(arioso)
Questi la disperata anima mia puniscan,
sì,

And, making of him an example none will
forget,
Hide the impious miscreant in its bowels.

Already exulting in my suffering,
The betrayer of my honour,
Wicked and faithless, takes his leave.
Oh, punish the arrogant deceit
Of this traitor, this evil monster,
Just heaven, O deadly Fate!

Perhaps in order to mete out in heaven
Greater punishment for my injury,
You remain idle, O provoked gods!
If the stars are unheeding,
If the spheres are deaf to my pleas,
To you, fearful gods
Of the abyss, I turn, [and] wait for you
To avenge my betrayed honour.

May the ground beneath his feet open up,
And the air the evil Roman breathes grow foul!
Wherever his step leads him, or his eyes turn,
May he meet ghosts, and expect destruction.

Ah! In the abyss
The Furies remain dormant,
Their indignation and their vengeance mute.
Has Jove no thunderbolts for me?
Has the Underworld become merciful?
Ah! am I already a thing of hatred to heaven?
Ah, tell!
If punishment does not fall on my head,
To my griefs is added the remorse of having
The power to punish myself.

May this remorse punish my despairing soul,
yes,

(recitative)
Ma il ferro che già intrepida stringo

And may the sword which, fearlessly, I
    already hold

(arioso)
Alla salma infedel porga la pena.

Do justice to my faithless body.

(recitative)
A voi, a voi, padre, consorte,
A Roma, al mondo presento il mio morir;
Mi si perdoni il delitto esecrando,
Ond'io macchiai involontaria il nostro
    onor.
Un'altra più detestabil colpa,
Di non m'aver uccisa pria del misfatto,
Mi si perdoni.

To you, to you, father, husband,
To Rome, to the world I offer my death;
May I be forgiven the hateful crime,
By which, against my will, I tainted our
    honour.
May another, more hateful crime,
Not killing myself before the evil act,
Be forgiven me.

(arioso)
Già nel seno comincia
A compir questo ferro i duri uffizii.
Sento ch'il cor si scuote più dal dolor
Di questa caduta invendicata
Che dal furor della vicina morte.

Now in my breast this blade
Begins to accomplish its cruel task.
My heart is more deeply hurt by the pain
Of this unavenged wrong
Than by the fury of approaching death.

Ma se qui non m'è dato
Castigar il tiranno,
Opprimer l'empio,
Con più barbaro esempio,
Per ch'ei sen cada estinto;
Stringerò a' danni suoi mortal saetta,
E furibonda e cruda,
Nell'inferno farò la mia vendetta.

But if it be not my destiny here on earth
To punish the tyrant,
And overcome him for his impiety,
With a more savage example,
So that he falls lifeless;
I will take up my deadly shafts against him,
And, furious and cruel,
Will wreak my vengeance in the Underworld!

Translation (slightly amended) from Abba Caspar in *Händel—Lucrezia: Cantates pour alto solo* (Virgin Classics 791480-2, 1991).

Lungi dal mio bel nume (Rome, 3 March 1708; Ruspoli: 31 August 1709)

Lungi dal mio bel nume,
Dal bell'idolo mio,
Per me sereno il lume
Non diffonde per l'etra il biondo Dio.

Far from my guiding spirit,
From my beautiful idol,
It is not for me that the sun god
Diffuses serene light through the air.

L'aura, ch'intorno spira,
È figlia del mio cor, ch'ognor sospira;

E del ruscello son l'onde correnti
Parto degli occhi miei sempre piangenti.

Lontano dal mio tesoro
Struggo l'amante cor,
In pena ardente.
Né trova mai ristoro,
Al fiero suo dolor,
L'afflitta mente.

Senza la vaga Clori,
Non ho pace un momento,
E sol porge alimento
La speranza e il desire a' miei dolori.
La speme a tutte l'ore
Mi dice: tornerà l'amato bene,

Ma risponde il desire:
E quando, quando viene?

Son come navicella
Esposta in mezzo al mar,
De 'venti al rio furor.
Scorre fra la procella,
Né può lido trovar,
Immersa nel timor.

Lungi da te, ben mio,
Entro un ammasso d'affanni,
Combattuto son io.
Lusingano i miei danni
Ancor del tempo fuggitivo l'ore,
Che non portano al cor quel caro istante,

In cui poss'io mirare il tuo sembiante.

Torna, vieni, non tardare,
Bella Clori, amato bene!
Corri, vola a consolare
Del mio cor tutte le pene.

The air that blows around
Is the daughter of my heart, who is always sighing,
And the ripples of the stream
Are the offspring of my ever-weeping eyes.

Far from my treasure,
I consume my loving heart,
In ardent pain.
The afflicted mind
Finds no respite
For its fierce sorrow.

Without the lovely Clori,
I have not a moment's peace,
And hope and desire
Only offer nourishment to my sorrows.
Hope is constantly
Saying to me: the beloved dear one will return,
But desire replies:
and when, when is she coming?

I am like a small boat
Exposed in the middle of the sea,
To the terrible fury of the winds.
It runs before the storm,
And cannot find the shore,
Immersed in fear.

Far from you, my beloved,
By a multitude of afflictions,
I am assailed.
My sufferings are deluded by
The hours of passing time
Which do not bring to my heart that dear moment,
When I can gaze upon your face.

Return, come, do not delay,
Beautiful Clori, my dear beloved!
Run, fly to console
All the sorrows of my heart.

Lungi da me, pensier tiranno! (Italian, without autograph; Ruspoli: 31 August 1709)

Lungi da me, pensier tiranno!
Tu mi vorresti rendere infelice
Col farmi credere Tirsi un traditore.
Ma sento, ch'il mio core mi dice
Che non può l'alma sì bella
Esser a me rubella.
Dunque da questo sen fugga l'affanno!
Lungi da me, pensier tiranno!

Away from me, tyrannous thought!
You would like to make me unhappy
By making me believe Tirsi a traitor.
But I feel that my heart tells me
That it is not possible for a soul so beautiful
To be untrue to me.
So from this breast let anguish flee!
Away from me, tyrannous thought!

Pensier crudele, se vuoi ch'io creda
Ch'il mio bel Tirsi sia ingannator,
Fa ch'il mio amore teco l'unisca,
Poi lo bandisca da questo cor.

Cruel thought—if you wish me to believe
That my handsome Tirsi is a traitor,
Grant that my love may connect him with you,
Then banish him from my heart.

Ma se amor ciò contrasta
E'l cor ripugna,
La sua virtù mel vieta,
E la sincerità del suo bel genio;

But if love opposes that
And the heart resists,
Then his own virtue forbids it to me
Along with the sincerity of his beautiful
  spirit;

Non vogliono ch'io creda
Che sia Tirsi ingrato.
Lungi dunque da me, pensier spietato!

They do not wish me to believe
That Tirsi is ungrateful.
Away then from me, cruel thought!

Fuggi da questo sen,
O barbaro pensier,
Lasciami in pace!
Sebben m'aduli amor
Per te consente il cor,
Perché ti piace.

Fly from this breast,
O barbarous thought,
Leave me in peace!
Although love flatters me,
My heart consents for your sake
Because it pleases you.

Non sa il mio cor sincero
Creder d'error capace un'alma grande.
Dunque torna, O pensiero,
Coi sogni a funestar la mente oppressa,
E lascia a me la libertade intiera
Di credere Tirsi mio d'alma sincera.

My sincere heart cannot
Believe a great soul capable of error.
So turn back, O thought,
With visions to afflict my oppressed spirit,
And leave me the complete freedom
To believe my Tirsi a sincere soul.

Tirsi amato, adorato mio Nume!
Vieni, O caro, ritornami in sen.
Farfalletta son io, che le piume
Ardo al lume del caro mio ben.

Beloved Tirsi, my adored god!
Come, my love, come back to my breast.
A butterfly am I, whose wings
I burn at the light of my dear beloved.

Lungi da voi (Rome, 1708; Ruspoli: 9 August 1708)

Lungi da voi, che siete
Poli del mio pensier,
Languidi lumi,
Come ognor mi consumi
Fiero dolor tiranno,
Amor! lo spieghi, amore,
Che di crudele affana,
A l'ultime agonie
Spinge il mio core.
Pallido nel sembiante,
Tratto fuor di me stesso,
Talor doglioso amante
Esclamo sospirando:
E quando, O Cieli, e quando
A goder tornerò luci sì belle?

Ma il duol par che responda:
Soffri sì rie procelle
Senza speme di calma,
Se lontane da te son le mie stelle.

Un affanno più tiranno
Di crudele lontananza,
Non si trova e non si dà.
E il mio core, che si muore,
Può ridir, quanto s'avanza
La sua fiera crudeltà.

Ah! languide pupille,
Ah! labbri pallidetti,
Di teneri diletti,
Incapace son io, da voi lontano,
E con furore insano,
Qualor penso che a voi
Mi tolse averso fatto,
Misero e disperato,
Vorrei morir per vagheggiarvi almeno,
Ombra di amor felice,
A cari lacci, a lieti ardori in seno;

Ma perché spero un giorno
Tornarvi a riveder, d'alta costanza

Far from you, who are
The poles [full extent] of my thought,
Languid eyes,
How he always consumes me,
The fierce, sad tyrant, Love!
Let Love himself explain it,
Who to the last agony
Of cruel anguish
Pushes my heart.
Pallid of feature,
Dragged outside myself,
Sometimes sorrowfully loving,
I exclaim, sighing:
When, O heavens, when
Will I once more enjoy [those] eyes so
     beautiful?

But it seems that the sadness responds:
You suffer such terrible storms
Without hope of calm,
If you are far from my stars [the eyes].

An anguish more tyrannical
Than cruel distance,
Cannot be found and does not exist.
And my heart, that dies away,
Can say again, how much her fierce cruelty
Increases it.

Ah! languid eyes,
Ah! pale little lips,
Of tender delights,
I am incapacitated, far from you,
And with mad frenzy,
Whenever I reflect that
An adverse fate took me from you,
Miserable and desperate,
I would die only to gaze upon you,
Shadow of a happy love,
With dear chains, with pleasant passions in
     the breast;

But because I hope one day
To see you again, I remain

Sono esempio penoso in lontananza.

A painful example of true fidelity in
  separation.

Chi sa? vi rivedrò,
Il cor così mi dice,
Ed io meno infelice,
Così voglio sperar.
E se non troverò
Fallace la speranza
Vedrete la costanza
Di chi vi seppe amar.

Who knows? I will see you again,
So says my heart to me,
And I, less unhappy,
Thus wish to hope.
And if I do not find
That hope is false,
You [the eyes] will see the constancy
Of one who knew how to love you.

Lungi n'andò Fileno (Rome, 1708; Ruspoli: 28 August 1708)

Lungi, lungi n'andò Fileno,
Filen, del viver mio parte migliore,
Alma dell'alma mia,
Cor del mio core!
O Dio! sapessi almeno,
Dov'ei lasciandomi rivolse il piede,
Che, in segno di mia fede,
Al caro ben volar vorrei d'appresso,
Ma giacché tanto a me non è concesso,
Ah! disfatevi intanto
Mie dolenti pupille in mesto pianto.

Far, far Fileno has gone,
Fileno, the better part of my life,
Soul of my soul,
Heart of my heart!
O God! if at least I knew
Where, leaving me, he directed his steps,
For, as a sign of my faith,
I would fly close to my dear beloved,
But since that much is not granted to me,
Ah! dissolve meanwhile
My grieving eyes in bitter tears.

Sì, piangete, O mie pupille,
Ed al suon di vostre stille
Coi sospir risponda il cor.
E risuoni in flebil eco,
In ogn'antro, in ogni speco,
La mia pena, il mio dolor.

Yes, weep, O my eyes,
And at the sound of your tears
Let my heart respond with sighs.
And let resound in plaintive echo,
In every cave, in every cavern,
My suffering and my sorrow.

Ahi! m'inganno, infelice,
Se in così rio tormento,
Spero trovar pietà del mio martire!
No, non basta il soffrire,
Se sperar non mi lice
In così fiera sorte,
Se non la tirannia di cruda morte.
Né giova il pianger sempre
A franger del destin le dure tempre.

Ah! I deceive myself, unhappy me,
If in such cruel torment
I hope to find pity for my torture!
No, the suffering is not enough,
If it is not permitted for me to hope
In such a cruel fate,
Except for the tyranny of a cruel death.
Nor does the endless weeping help
To break the harsh grip of destiny.

Dunque se il tanto piangere	*Thus, if so much weeping*
Non basta il fato a frangere,	*Is not enough to crush fate,*
Vivere io più non vuò,	*I wish to live no longer,*
Ch'il misero mio cor,	*Since my miserable heart,*
A così rio dolor,	*Such cruel pain,*
(Al fiero suo dolor,)	*(Its own fierce pain,)*
Resistere non può.	*Can no longer withstand.*

N.B.: The additional text in parentheses near the end of the last aria is a textual variation included with the original in Handel's setting.

Manca pur quanto sai (Rome, 1708; Ruspoli, 9 August 1708)

Manca pur quanto sai	Fail as much as you know how,
Tirsi incostante alla costanza mia,	Inconstant Tirsi, to respond to my constancy,
Che far già non potrai	You will never make me
Che, fedel quanto io fui, fedel non sia.	Less faithful than I was.
Spesso tradita io sono,	I am often betrayed,
E mi spiace, nol niego, il tradimento:	And I do not like, I deny it not, the treachery:
Ma taccio e ti perdono,	Yet I am silent and forgive you,
Perché so ch'il tradirmi è tuo contento:	For I know that betraying me is your delight:
Ne sarà mai ch'io voglia	Nor will it ever be that I should wish
Turbar le gioje tue con la mia doglia.	To disturb your joys with my pain.
Benché tradita io sia,	*Although I am betrayed,*
Sempre fedel sarò.	*I shall always be faithful.*
Moro di gelosia;	*I die of jealousy;*
Eppur, O mio tiranno,	*And yet, O my tyrant,*
Inganno per inganno	*Deception for deception*
Giammai ti renderò.	*Shall I never render you.*
Inventa nuove frodi,	Find new frauds,
S'ancor sazio non sei,	If you are not yet sated,
E degli affanni miei	And triumph over and enjoy
Trionfa e godi.	My sufferings.
Saprà l'alta mia fede	My great faith will know
Mostrarsi invitta ad ogni grave offesa,	How to show itself unconquered by every grave offense,
E otterrà la vitoria in tanta impresa.	And will obtain victory in so great an undertaking.

All'amor mio,	*To my love,*
Lo so ben io,	*I know it well,*
Ritornerai	*You will return*
Pentito, un dì.	*Penitent one day.*
E allor vedrai,	*And then you will see*
Se mai si diede	*If ever existed*
Un'altra fede,	*Another faith,*
Bella così!	*As beautiful!*

Mentre il tutto è in furore (Naples, 1708; Ruspoli: 28 August 1708)

Mentre il tutto è in furore, ed ogni intorno	While everything is in a rage, and all around
Di timpani e di trombe il rauco suono,	The raucous sound of the timpani and trumpet
Strepitosi ne fan la notte, e il giorno,	Fills the night and day with uproar,
Mentre i boschi e le valli,	While the woods and valleys,
Al nitrìr de' cavalli,	At the neighing of the horses,
Rendon eco guerriera,	Return a warlike echo,
Tu sol, forte Filen,	You only, brave Fileno,
Ten stai pensando	Remain thinking
Nel sen di molle amore.	In your breast of soft love.
Ah! no, risveglia il core,	Ah, no! awaken your courage,
Impugna il brando.	Grasp the sword.
Dove, in mezzo alle stragi, rimbomba	*Wherever, in the middle of the slaughter, resounds*
La bellica tromba,	*The warlike trumpet,*
Corri, invitto mio bene, a pugnar.	*Run, my invincible love, to fight.*
E la fama, perfino alle sfere,	*And let fame, when*
Vinte già le nemiche schiere,	*You have conquered the enemy battalions,*
Poi si senta tuo nome portar.	*Then hear your name carried even to the stars.*
Vanne, sì, vedi e vinci,	Go, yes, see and conquer,
E poi ritorna a me carco di palme,	And then return to me laden with palms,
E di trionfi onusto,	And with triumphs,
Cinto d'allor, O augusto!	Crowned with laurel, O august one!
Torna a goder che anch'io godrò,	Return to happiness for I also shall be happy,
Se potrò dire, amante io sono	If I am able to say, that I am loved
D'un, che in campo sembrò	By one who on the battlefield seemed like
Fulmine e tuono.	Thunder and lightning.

Combatti e poi ritorna
A innamorare il cor.
E allor lieto dirai,
Che non provasti mai
Più dolce amor.

Fight and then return
To inspire the heart with love.
And then, happy, you will say,
That you have never tasted
A sweeter love.

Menzognere speranze (Rome, 1707; Ruspoli: 22 September 1707)

Menzognere speranze,
Itene in bando
Lungi da questo petto,
Che con sincero affetto,
Vi credé, vi diè fede,
Ed or pentito,
La sua propria follia,
Piange tradito.
Legge del voler mio
Furon, finché cercai
D'amore mercede,
Speranza, amore e fede;
Or che delusa sono,
Speme, fede ed amor,
Pongo in obblio.

Deceitful hopes,
Be banished
Far from this heart which,
With sincere affection,
Believed you, trusted you,
And now penitent,
Bewails its own folly,
Betrayed.
The rulers of my will,
While I sought
Love's reward,
Were hope, love and faith;
Now that I am disappointed,
Hope, faith and love
I cast into oblivion.

Lascia di più sperar
Se non vuoi lacrimar,
Povero core!
Non usar fedeltà,
Vanta sol crudeltà,
Se brami trionfar
Del Dio d'amore.

Leave off hoping
If you do not want to weep,
Poor heart!
Do not practice fidelity,
Value only cruelty,
If you desire to triumph over
The god of love.

Ai vezzi d'un sembiante
Di vaga garzoncella,
Alle lusinghe, non credea quest'alma.

In the charming countenance
Of a lovely maid,
In her enticements, my soul does not
    believe.

Spezzerò d'ogni amante
I simulati affetti,
E se talun costante
Vedrò piagato, lacrimar d'amore,
Sarà suo maggior vanto
Ch'io non rida al suo pianto,

I shall shatter every lover's
False sentiments,
And if I see wounded
Such a constant one, crying of love,
It will be his greatest glory
If I mock not his tears,

O pur sua maggior sorte,	Or his greatest fortune
Trovar in me pietà della sua morte.	To find in me pity for his death.
Altra speme or non alletta	*No other hope now lures*
Questo cor che la vendetta	*This heart than revenge,*
E lo star in libertà:	*And to remain free:*
Rider vuò quando gli amanti	*I shall want to laugh when lovers*
Genuflessi a me davanti,	*Kneel before me,*
Chiederan invan pietà.	*Asking in vain for mercy.*

Mi palpita il cor (London, c. 1722; revision of *Dimmi, O mio cor*)

Mi palpita il cor né intendo perché.	My heart flutters, but I know not why.
Agitata è l'alma mia, né so cos'è.	My soul is agitated, but I know not what it is.
Dimmi, O mio cor, che brami,	Tell me, O my heart, what you desire,
Se con sì fieri, e insoliti risalti,	If with such cruel, and unusual vividness,
Agitando il mio petto,	Agitating my breast,
Ognor m'affliggi!	You always torment me!
Tu che solo ricetto	[My heart], you ought only to be
Di delizie e contento esser dovresti,	A receptacle of delight and content,
Mentre quel ben ch'adori	While that love that you adore
Arde con doppie fiamme,	Burns with a double flame,
E pur tu pien d'affanni	And yet full of anguish
Ognor gemi e sospiri?	Do you always groan and sigh?
Sento ch'il cor dolente	I hear the miserable heart
A me così risponde:	Respond thus to me:
È ver, che sono amato,	It is true that I am loved,
Ma ti sovvenga al fin,	But remember in the end,
Che son piagato.	That I am wounded.
Mi piagò d'amor lo strale,	*The dart of love wounded me,*
E fatale la saetta in me vibrò.	*And the fatal arrow struck me.*
Che sebbene il mio Fileno	*For even if my Fileno*
Per me porti acceso il seno,	*Would feel his breast burning for me,*
Pure il fato rio spietato,	*Still a pitiless, evil fate*
A penar mi destinò.	*Destined me to suffer.*
Ma non temer, mio core,	But do not fear, my heart,
Armati di costanza	Arm yourself with constancy,
Che anch'io contenta e paga di mia sorte,	For I, content and satisfied with my fate,

Purché m'ami il mio ben, sprezzo la
    morte.

Cari lacci, amate pene,
Pene grate e dolce affanno!
Per quel caro amato bene
Non son crudele catene,
No, ch'amor non è tiranno.

Provided my beloved loves me, scorn even
    death.

Sweet chains, loving pains,
Pleasing pain and dear affliction!
For such a dear loving beloved,
They are not cruel chains,
No, for love is not a tyrant.

Nel dolce tempo (Naples, 1708)

Nel dolce tempo,
In cui ritorna a noi,
Di novello colore
Adorna e piena,
La bella età fiorita,
Che a' diletti d'amor
Ne chiama e invita,
Leggiadra Ninfa e vaga,
Al bel Volturno in riva,
Là dove un alto pin l'erba copriva,
Vidi da lunge starsi,
E di rose e viole il petto ornarsi
Onde ratto ivi giunto, O Dio! mirai

Due lumi, un labbro, un seno, crin sì
    vago,
Che n'arsi a un tratto e del mio ardor son
    pago.
Quindi volto a colei ch'ho sempre al core,

Dissi così, pietà chiedendo e amore:

Pastorella, coi bei lumi,
Erbe e fiori anch'innamori,
Pastorella del mio cor.
E quest'aure, e questi fiumi,
Sussurando, mormorando,
Per te sol parlan d'amor.

Di pallido color,
La Ninfa intanto
Coprì il bel viso,

In the sweet time,
When returns to us,
With new color
Adorned and full,
The beautiful flowery season,
Which to the delights of love
Calls and invites us,
A graceful and charming nymph,
On the bank of the Volturno,
Where a tall pine tree shaded the grass,
I saw seated from afar
With roses and violets adorning her breast,
So that I rushed there quickly, O God! and I
    beheld

Two eyes, a mouth, a breast, and hair so
    lovely,
That I suddenly caught fire and am
    contented with my ardor.
Therefore I turned to her whom I always
    have in my heart,
And I spoke thus, asking for mercy and love:

Shepherdess, with your beautiful eyes,
You inflame even the grasses and flowers,
Shepherdess of my heart.
And these breezes and streams
Whispering, murmuring,
For you alone they speak of love.

A pallid color
Meanwhile covered
The Nymph's beautiful face,

Ed ostro poscia il tinse,
Qual chi, temendo
E vergognando,
Suole mostrare in volto
Or rose ed or viole.
Pur sorridendo alfine onestamente,
A me rivolta disse:
Pastor, tua nobil alma,
Tuo costume gentil,
Tuo vago viso,
Dolce fiamma d'amor
Destano al core,
Ma dell'amore
È l'onestà maggiore!
Ond'io risposi allora:
Piacemi, bella, il tuo leggiadro aspetto,

Ma più dell'alma ancor la virtù rara.
Onesta t'amo più, più mi sei cara.

And then crimson colored it,
Like one who, shy
And bashful,
Is accustomed to show in her face
Now roses, now violets.
Then at last smiling openly,
She turned to me and said:
Shepherd, your noble soul,
Your gentle manner,
Your pleasing face,
Awaken a sweet flame
Of love in my heart,
But honesty is
Greater than love!
So I then responded:
Your charming appearance pleases me, lovely
    one,
But still more the rare virtue of your soul.
The more I love you because you are honest,
    the more you are dear to me.

Senti, di te, ben mio:
Cantar, dal bosco al rio,
L'augelli ancora,
In questa piaggia e in quella,
Lodar di te, mia bella,
I lumi, i labbri, il cor,
L'onesto e fido amor,
S'ascolta ognora.

Listen, my beloved:
The birds singing of you
From the wood to the stream,
On this bank and that,
Praising, my beautiful one,
Your eyes, your lips, your heart,
And your honest and faithful love,
One hears continually.

Nell'africane selve (Naples, 1708)

Nell'africane selve,
Ove rei spaventi,
O cada o sorga il giorno,
S'odono sempre intorno—
Ululati di belve,
Sibili di serpenti
E d'augelli rapaci orride strida—
Fiero leon s'annida,
Ed audace e maestoso,
Non soggiace al timor fra l'altre fiere;

In the forests of Africa
Where fearsome monsters,
Whether at dawn or sunset,
Are heard all around—
The howling of beasts,
The hissing of serpents
And the eerie screams of birds of prey—
The proud lion has his den,
And, bold and majestic,
He does not succumb to fear among the
    other animals;

Stampa nei boschi, altiere,
L'orme del passo errante,
Ma se mai, fra le piante,
Un raggio lo ferisce
D'insidiosa e lucida facella,
L'audacia del leon non è più quella.

Langue, trema, e prigioniero
Fra le reti allora inciampa,
Quando stampa l'orme sicure.
E del suo valor primiero
Perde tutta la costanza,
E con misera sembianza
Piange pur le sue sventure.

Nice, là fra confine di valli incolte

E boscarecci orrori,
Scevro' da quei timori
Di perder mai la libertà gradita,
E superbo e discolto
Trassi, come leon, l'ore di vita.
Ma quando de' tuoi lumi
Mi ferì poi la geminata face,
Piagato e senza pace,
Tuo prigionier me fe l'arciero Dio!
Dunque, bell'idol mio,
Se fida l'alma mia te solo brama,
Con esempio di fede ama chi t'ama.

Chiedo amore,
Altro non bramo,
Io che t'amo
E serbo fé.
E pietà
L'anima mia
Sol desia
Se vive in te.

Proudly he prints
His wandering footsteps in the forest,
But if ever through the branches
He is struck by a ray [of light]
From an insidious bright torch,
The lion's audacity is not what it was.

Pining, trembling and a prisoner
In the nets, he stumbles now,
When he would confidently tread.
And of his former strength
He loses all the firmness,
And with sad mien
He weeps for his fate.

There, Nice, among the confines of valleys
    wild
And awe-inspiring forests,
Free from those fears
Of ever losing my desired liberty,
I, proud and unfettered,
Passed, like the lion, my days.
But when your [eyes']
Twin shafts [of light] struck me,
Wounded and no longer at peace,
The archer-god made me your prisoner!
Therefore, my beloved,
Since my faithful spirit longs for you alone,
With the example of faithfulness, love him
    who loves you.

I ask for love,
Naught else beside,
I who love you
And keep faith.
And pity
Is all my soul
Would seek,
If [pity] lives in you.

Nella stagion (Rome, 1707; Ruspoli: 16 May 1707)

Nella stagion che, di viole e rose
Il giardin si riveste,

In the season when violets and roses
Bedeck the garden anew,

Per mitigar le fiamme sue amorose,	To assuage the flames of passion,
Amarilli vezzosa,	Pretty Amarilli,
Assisa in piaggia erbosa	Seated on a grassy bank
D'un mirto all'ombra, con dogliosi accenti,	In the shade of a myrtle tree, with mournful voice,
Spiegò, mesta e piangente,	Unfolded, sad and weeping,
Al bel idolo suo questi lamenti:	These laments to her beloved idol:

Ride il fiore in seno al prato	*The flowers smile in the meadow*
A tornar la primavera	*At the return of spring,*
E con soffio delicato	*And with gentle breath*
Spira l'aura lusinghiera.	*The caressing breeze blows.*
Solo tu, crudele ingrato,	*You alone, cruel and unkind,*
Sdegni ognor la fé sincera	*Do ever scorn the loyalty*
Del mio petto innamorato	*Within my loving breast,*
Con sì barbara maniera.	*In such a heartless fashion.*

Così la ninfa al bel garzon dicea,	Thus spoke the nymph to the handsome boy,
E co' tepidi fiumi	And with the warm tears
Che versava dai lumi,	That flowed from her eyes,
E nell'erba e ne' fior pietà movea;	Moved the very grass and flowers to pity;
Tal che vinto il meschino	So was the rascal vanquished,
Da quelle note armoniche e dogliose,	And, his heart softened
Fatto pietoso alfin così rispose:	By that sweet, sad song, at last replied:

Tergi il ciglio lagrimoso,	*Dry those tears,*
Acciò torni più vezzoso	*So that the loveliness of your face*
Del tuo volto il bel seren.	*Returns more beautiful.*
Io per te languisco e moro,	*I yearn for you, I die for you,*
Caro e dolce mio tesoro,	*Dear and sweet love.*
E si strugge il cor in sen.	*And my heart melts away in my breast.*

Ne' tuoi lumi (Rome, 1707; Ruspoli: 22 September 1707)

Ne' tuoi lumi, O bella Clori,	*Within your eyes, O beautiful Clori,*
Si nascose il mio destino.	*Is hidden my destiny.*
Così facile si rese	*So easily my heart yielded,*
Il mio cor, ne si difese	*Not defending itself*
Dallo stral d'un Dio bambino.	*From the arrow of the child god.*

Credi che quanto dolci	Know that your glances
Eran gli sguardi tuoi,	Were as sweet as
Soave tanto fosse il piacer	The pleasure of desiring them
Di vagheggiarli amante.	As a lover was gentle.

Ma qual fallace incanto,   But like a false enchantment,
Sparì la speme;   Hope disappeared;
E fosco, in un instante,   And, in an instant,
M'appare il ciel d'amore,   The heaven of love appears dark to me,
Pria sì giocondo e luminoso al core.   Once so entertaining and bright to my heart.

Superbetti occhi amorosi,   *Proud, loving eyes,*
Sì crudeli, sì vezzosi,   *So cruel, so charming,*
Perché siete, O Dio, con me?   *Why are you, O God, with me?*
Se già vostra è l'alma mia,   *If my soul is now yours,*
Vantar seco tirannia,   *Boasting that tyranny sides with you*
Vostra gloria alfin non è.   *Is not in the end your [greatest] glory.*

Sul pallido mio volto,   In my pale visage,
Spiega le meste insegne   My sorrow reveals
Dell'estinta mia pace,   The sad signs
Il mio dolore;   Of my lost peace;
E il trionfante amore   Triumphant love
Le addita il core,   Points out my heart to her,
Ed ella,   While she,
Dal piacer del mio dolore,   From pleasure at my pain,
Appar più bella.   Seems more beautiful.

La mia piaga se v'appaga,   *If my wound satisfies you,*
Cari lumi, io son contento.   *Dear eyes, I am content.*
V'amo tanto, che, nel pianto,   *I love you so much, that, in weeping,*
Mi par dolce anche il tormento.   *Even torment seems sweet to me.*

Nice, che fa? (?Hanover, 1710)

Nice, che fa? che pensa?   What is Nice doing? What is she thinking?
Rispondi, alato Dio,   Answer, winged god,
Or che solo son io da lei lontano,   Now that I am alone, far from her,
So, che dir me potresti   I know that you could tell me,
Che non l'agita vano   That the desire to see me again
Desio di revedermi, e che sospira   Does not trouble her in vain, and that she
                                              sighs,

Dove il suo piè raggira;   As her feet wander;
Che con dolce favella   That with sweet language
Vorebbe la mia bella   My beloved would like
Darmi fede maggior di mia costanza,   To render me a faith [even] greater than my
                                              [own] constancy,

Che soave speranza   That the sweet hope

D'esser mia la conforta,	Of being mine comforts her,
E quasi ascolto	And I almost hear
Che ragiona così, ma non è molto.	That she reasons thus, but only faintly.

Se pensate che mi moro,	*If you think that I am dying,*
Allor sì che dir potrei,	*Then in that case I could indeed say,*
Nice mia, non pensa poco.	*My Nice thinks [of me] a lot.*
E contento nel martoro,	*And content with martyrdom,*
Forte allora morirei,	*I could die then bravely,*
Tutto affanni e tutto foco.	*All anguish and desire.*

Ah! per maggior mio duolo	Ah! for my greater grief,
Lungi da gli occhi suoi	Far from her eyes,
Misero, afflitto, e sola	Wretched, afflicted, and alone,
Mi conduce a morir la pena ria:	An evil torment leads me to death:
E moro quando meno	And I die when
La bell'anima mia	My beautiful beloved
Pensa che in un baleno	Thinks [of me] less, so that in a flash
Son da fiero dolor condotto a morte.	I am brought to death by fierce grief.
Dunque se son già corte	So if they are now brief,
L'ore del viver mio,	The hours of my life,
Vanne bendato Dio	Go blind god,
Al caro ben intorno;	Back to be with my dear;
Digli: muore chi t'ama,	Tell her: he who loves you is dying,
E morendo ancor brama	And dying, still craves
Spirar l'ultimo fiato al tuo ritorno.	To breathe his last at your return.

Verrà, sì, verrà chi adoro, sì,	*She will come, yes, she will come whom I adore,*
Se così gli parlerai,	*If you will speak to her thus,*
A dar pace al duolo mio.	*To give peace to my pain.*
Ma so ben ch'il mio tesoro	*But I know well that my treasure*
Lacrimar poi rivedrai,	*You will see then weeping,*
Se ridir mi sentirà;	*If she hears me saying again:*
Io ti lascio, io moro, addio.	*I leave you, I die, farewell.*

Ninfe e pastori (Rome, spring 1707?; Ruspoli: 26 February 1709)

Ninfe e pastori che nel cor nudrite	Nymphs and shepherds, who nourish in your hearts
Dolce amorosi ardori,	Sweet, ardent loves,
Deh! per pietà mi dite,	Oh, for pity's sake! tell me,
Dove si aggira la mia bella Clori;	Where my beautiful Clori wanders;
E se saper volete	And if you wish to know

I suoi pregi, i suoi vanti, i suoi costumi,	Her merits, her reputation [or] her habits,
Io vel dirò, ma poi,	I will tell you, but then,
Non fissate lo sguardo ai lumi suoi.	Do not gaze upon her eyes.
È una tiranna la ninfa bella,	*She is a tyrant, the beautiful nymph*
Che m'innamora;	*Who enchants me;*
Sempre rubella,	*Always stubborn,*
Fugge ed inganna	*She flees and deceives*
Chi più l'adora.	*The one who loves her most.*
Vince la ninfa mia,	My nymph surpasses
Coi suoi bei lumi,	With her beautiful eyes,
Del sole i rai lucenti,	The shining rays of the sun,
E sono i labbri suoi rubini ardenti;	And her lips are like blazing rubies;
Nella guancia vezzosa	In her lovely cheek
Pompeggia gentilmente e giglio e rosa;	She gently displays both lilies and roses;
La fronte è un ciel sereno;	Her brow is a heaven serene;
Cede il candido avorio al bianco seno.	The purest ivory yields to her white breast.
La vaga ninfa mia	My lovely nymph
È un misto di bellezza e leggiadria.	Is a combination of beauty and elegance.
Ha nel volto un certo brio,	*She has in her face a certain liveliness,*
L'idol mio,	*My idol,*
Che diletta e spira ardor.	*That delights and inspires love.*
Le sue vaghe pupillette	*Her lovely little eyes*
Son saette	*Are arrows*
Che dan palme al Dio d'amor.	*That give the victory to the god of love.*
Questo oggetto sì vago e sì vezzoso,	That object [of beauty] so lovely and so
	charming,
Sempre crudo e ritroso,	Always cruel and reluctant,
Sprezza della mia fé gli alteri vanti,	Scorns the proud pledges of my faithfulness,
Sorda ai sospiri, alle querele, ai pianti.	Is deaf to my sighs, my complaints, my tears.
Deh! per pietà, pastori,	Oh! For pity's sake, shepherds,
Se mai vedete Clori, —	If you ever see Clori, —
Ditele che il mio core	*Tell her that my heart*
Arde per lei d'amor tutto fedele.	*Burns for her with a totally faithful love.*
E se niega mercè,	*And if she refuses mercy,*
Ditele voi per me, bella crudele.	*Say to her for me, "[You are a] cruel beauty."*

Non sospirar (Florence/Venice, 1709)

Non sospirar, non piangere,	*Sigh not, cry not,*
Mio cor, che sono i gemiti	*My heart, for groans are*
Indegni del tuo duol.	*Unworthy of your sadness.*
Chi non desia né spera	*Who neither desires nor hopes*
Si pasce della pena,	*Feeds on pain,*
E conservarla intiera	*And wishes to keep it*
Tutt'in sé stesso vuol.	*Inside himself completely.*
Sol potrai co' respiri	You can only with breathing
Porger qualche alimento	Bring some sustenance,
Alla vita non già	Not indeed to the life
Ch'in altro loco	That in another place
Vive fuori di te,	Lives outside you,
Ma al tuo bel foco.	But to your beautiful desire.
Sì bel foco è quel che t'arde,	*Such beautiful desire is that which enflames you,*
Che non puoi dolerti, O cor.	*So that you cannot be sad, O heart.*
Soffri pur che alla costanza	*Yet you suffer because hope*
È svantaggio la speranza	*Is a detriment to constancy*
Quando è gloria un vago ardor.	*When a beautiful passion is glorious.*

Occhi miei (?Ottoboni: Rome, 1707)

Occhi miei, che faceste?	My eyes, what have you done?
Nel contemplar curiosi	By curiously contemplating
Quel vivo fuoco che dalle pupille	The lively fire that from her eyes
Vibra la vaga Fille,	The lovely Fille shoots,
Il cuor tradiste, che ogni sua difesa,	You betrayed my heart, whose every defense,
Ogni sua speme in voi riposto avea.	Whose every hope had rested in you.
Da quell'ora pungenti e velenosi a ferirlo	From that hour, sharp and dangerous,
Per voi passaro i dardi.	The darts passed through you to wound it.
E nel fatale incontro di due sguardi	And in the fatal encounter of two glances
E libertade e vita al cuor toglieste.	You took both liberty and life from my heart.
Occhi miei, che faceste?	My eyes, what have you done?
Ve lo dissi, e nol credeste:	*I said this to you, and you did not believe it:*
Che negli occhi di costei,	*That in those eyes of hers,*
Solo inteso a danni miei,	*Only intended for hurting me,*
S'ascondeva il Dio d'amor.	*The god of love hid himself.*
Troppo tardi v'accorgeste	*You realized too late*

Ch'il mirar que' lusinghieri
Occhi neri
Gran periglio era del cor.

That gazing into those enticing
Black eyes
Was a great danger for the heart.

Il misero innocente
D'un delitto non suo
La pena e il danno sente.
Del suo grave dolor voi siete rei.
Che faceste, occhi miei?

The miserable one [the heart],
Innocent of a crime not its own,
Suffers the pain and injury.
For its grave sorrow you are guilty.
What have you done, my eyes?

Troppo caro costa al core.
Quel piacere che prendeste
Da quegli occhi tutti ardor.
E sospira, langue e more,
Quando soli voi dovreste
Sentir tutto il suo dolor.

It costs the heart too much,
That pleasure that you took
From those eyes which are all passion.
And it sighs, languishes and dies,
When you [eyes] alone ought
To suffer all of its pain.

O lucenti, O sereni occhi (Italian, without autograph; Santini Collection)

O lucenti, O sereni
Occhi, luci fatali,
Ben vi scorgo quai tremoli baleni;
Che fulmini d'amore
Presagite crudeli a questo core?

O shining, O serene
Eyes, fatal lights,
I see you as quivering lightning flashes;
What cruel thunderbolts of love
Do you presage to this heart?

Per voi languisco e moro,
Luci belle e pur godete.
Voi, negandomi ristoro,
Dispettose m'uccidete.

For you I languish and die,
Beautiful lights, and yet you rejoice.
You, denying me relief,
Scornful, kill me.

Messaggiero verace,
Or la guerra bramate,
Or la tregua vi piace,
E per tormento all'alma innamorata
Siete qual acri demoni d'averno,
E nel ciel di beltà lampi d'inferno.

True messengers,
Now you desire war,
Now a truce pleases you,
And to the torment of a loving soul
You are like savage demons of Hades,
And in a heaven of beauty, flashes of hell.

In voi, pupille ardenti,
Ritrovo il mio piacer,
Trovo la pena.
Per voi, luci splendenti,
Quel faretrato amor,
Il mio dolente cor
Stringe in catena.

In you, burning eyes,
I rediscover my pleasure,
[And] I find pain.
Because of you, splendid lights,
Love, with his arrows,
My sad heart
Binds in chains.

Partì, l'idolo mio (undocumented; Italian?)

Partì, l'idolo mio,	He left, my idol,
L'adorato mio bene,	My well-adored one,
Ed io restai,	And I remained,
Ma con qual core, O Dio!	But with what heart, O god!
Su, dillo, anima mia, tu che sai,	Tell it, my soul, you that know,
Se pure hai lingua ed hai virtù che basti	If indeed you have a tongue and enough strength
A dir come partì come restasti.	To relate how he left as you stayed behind.

La bella vita mia,	*My very life,*
So che m'abbandonò,	*I know has abandoned me,*
Ma poi ridir qual sia	*But to express*
Il mio dolor non so.	*My sadness, I know not how.*

Oh, voi che m'ascoltate,	Oh, you that hear me,
Se vedeste il tormento	If you understood the torment
Onde sospiro,	For which I sigh,
Mossi tutti a pietate	All having been moved to pity
Del mio grave martiro,	For my great suffering,
O piangereste, o pur direste al meno:	Either would weep, or say at least:
Povera Clori,	Poor Clori,
Oh, quanti affanni ha in seno!	Oh, how much anguish she has in her breast!

Tormentosa crudele partita,	*Agonizingly cruel parting,*
Tu m'uccidi e ancor non moro.	*You kill me, but still I do not die.*
Pria dovevi privarmi di vita,	*You ought rather to have deprived me of life,*
Che privarmi dell'idol ch'adoro.	*Than to deprive me of the idol that I adore.*

Poiché giuraro amore (Rome, 1707; Ruspoli: 16 May 1707)

Poiché giuraro amore	Since Love
E Clori infida,	And unfaithful Clori
Di farmi eterna guerra	Swore to make such eternal war on me,
Tale, e tanta si serra,	So much that clamped
Intorno al mesto core	Around my sad heart is
Densa importuna nebbia di dolore,	A thick, festering fog of pain
Che dissipa e disperde	That fragments and disperses
D'ogni mia speme il verde,	The beginning of my every hope,
D'alte, confuse, dolorose strida	I make high, confused, sad cries
Fo risuonar la più reposta selva,	That resound in the most remote forest,
Sì che ne teme e fugge	So that in fear flees
Ogni augello, ogni belva,	Every bird, every beast,

Ed io, smarrito e solo,	And I, lost and alone,
All'aure, a' tronchi, a' sassi	To the winds, the trees and rocks,
Così narro piangendo il mio gran duolo.	Thus, weeping, narrate my great sorrow.

Figli di rupe alpestra,	*Offspring of the rugged cliff,*
Duri sassi,	*Hard stones,*
Cangerassi	*Your fate will change*
Forse un dì la vostra sorte.	*Perhaps one day.*
Vi darà mano maestra,	*A divine hand will give you*
Forza spirto e valore	*Strength, spirit and valor*
Ch'al furore	*That will release you from*
Vi torranno del tempo e della morte.	*The fury of time and death.*

Io senza speme di cangiar mai tempre	I, without hope of ever changing the nature
Nel mio dolor sarò l'istesso sempre,	Of my sadness, will be always the same,
Sol nel mesto mio core.	Alone in the sadness of my heart.
Col tempo il duol diverrà maggiore.	With time the sadness will only become greater.

Ahi che a sì dura sorte	Ah, from such a hard fate
Non può sottrarmi altro che morte.	Nothing but death can save me.
Ahi che a miei danni intenta,	Ah, but intent on my suffering,
Per me solo la morte, è pigra e lenta.	Death, for me alone, is lazy and slow.

Basterebbe a tor di vita	*The sadness that I feel*
Mille cori, il duol ch'io sento,	*Would suffice to take from life a thousand hearts,*
Né sì fiero aspro tormento	*[But] such fierce, bitter torment,*
Al mio cor morte non dà.	*Does not give death to my heart.*
Che la morte, in lega unita	*For death, in league united*
Co' nemici del mio core,	*With the enemies of my heart,*
Vuol di Clori, vuol d'amore	*Wants to emulate*
Adular la crudeltà.	*The cruelty of Clori and of Love.*

Qualor crudele (undocumented; Italian?)

Qualor crudele, sì, ma vaga Dori,	Whenever cruel, yes, but lovely Dori,
A tue rare bellezze fisso le luci,	I gaze at your rare charms,
E a tuoi ridenti lumi,	And at your laughing eyes,
Veggio ed ammiro quanto	I see and admire how much
San far per nostra meraviglia i numi.	The gods are able to achieve for our astonishment.
Indi ascolto un pensiero	Then I hear a thought

Dirmi: tu peni è vero,
Ma per celeste oggetto;
Onde crescon del pari
Lo stupore e l'affetto;
E la speranza, lor fida compagna,
Con sue lusinghe più dilette e care,
Raddolcisce al desio le pene amare.

Nel pensar che sei l'oggetto
Del desio dell'alma ardente,
Per diletto dell'affetto
È men fiero il mio dolor.
Son com'aquila ch'al sole
Fissa il guardo, ma non sente
La pupilla che le duole,
Perché gode al suo splendor.

Ma poi qualor dalla soave bocca
Sciogli, in note dolcissime e canore,
Parolette d'amore,
Nei modulati accenti,
Sì graziose e care,
Che fermi in aria ad ascoltarle i venti,

Nel verno renderian la calma al mare,
Fuor di sé l'alma mia,
Tutte le pene obblia,
E lieta, mentre tacita respira,
Tutta negli occhi e nell'orecchie accolta,
Null'altro fuor che i tuoi bei labbri mira,

Null'altro fuor ch'il tuo bel canto ascolta.

Nell'incanto del tuo canto,
Mi tormenti, mi contenti,
Cara del Dio d'amor,
Bella sirena.
Sei ritrosa ma vezzosa,
Superbetta ma diletta,
Dai pena ma puoi far
Dolce la pena.

Tell me: you suffer, it is true,
But for a heavenly object;
Thus grow equally
Marvel and affection;
And hope, their faithful companion,
With its dearest and most flattering illusions,
Makes sweeter the bitter pains of desire.

In thinking you are the object
Of desire of my burning soul,
Because of the delight of love,
My grief is less cruel.
I am like the eagle that at the sun
Fixes its gaze, but does not feel
The pain in his eye,
Because he enjoys the splendor.

But then whenever from that sweet mouth
You give forth, in sweetest singing notes,
Little words of love,
In varied accents,
So dear and charming,
That you stop the winds in the air to listen to
    them,
And in the winter render calm to the sea,
My soul transported,
Forgets all its troubles,
And gladly, while silently breathing,
All gathered in the eyes and ears,
It gazes at nothing other than your lovely
    lips,
And listens to nothing other than your sweet
    singing.

In the enchantment of your singing,
You torment me, you delight me,
Darling of the god of love,
Beautiful siren.
You are coy but charming,
Haughty but beloved,
You give pain, but can make
The pain sweet.

Qualor l'egre pupille (Rome, 1707; Ruspoli: 22 September 1707)

Qualor l'egre pupille,
Stanco di più pensar,
Chiudo alla luce,
Il pensier mi conduce
A ripensar ciò ch'obbliar vorrei,

E in pensier sì profondo,
L'un coll'altro pensiervia più confondo.

Discaccia dalla mente
La memoria dolente
Del mio perduto ben,
Del volto vago,
Che se lungi è dall'occhio
Nel core e nel pensier sempre ho l'imago.

È il pensier nella mia mente
Come nave in mar fremente,
Duro scoglio è la mia fè.
Io'l nocchier son infelice,
Cui non lice
Por di speme in porto il piè.

Lungi del caro oggetto,
Volsi ardito le piante,
Ma ancor l'anima amante,
Serba l'istessa amor, l'istessa fede,
E mai pace il pensiero al cor concede.

S'altri gode pensando al suo bene,
Io pensando m'accresco il dolore.
Nel pensier s'altri pasce l'amore
Col pensier io nudrisco le pene.

Chi chiama amor tiranno,
È folle, è un grand'inganno;
Il tiranno più fiero,
Che tormenta quest'alma è il mio
    pensiero.

Whenever, my languishing eyes,
Tired of thinking any more,
I close to the light,
A thought leads me
To remember that which I would like to
    forget,
And in thought so intense,
The one stream of thought I confuse more
    and more with the other.

[The confusion] drives out of my mind
The sad memory
Of my lost beloved,
[And] of the lovely face,
Which if it is far from my eyes,
I always have the image of it in my heart and
    in my thoughts.

The thought in my mind is
Like a ship tossing in the middle of the sea,
My faith is a hard rock.
I am the unhappy seafarer,
Who is not allowed
With hope to place a foot in the harbor.

Far from the dear object,
I courageous(ly) turned my steps away,
But still the loving soul
Keeps the same love, the same faith,
And the thought never grants peace to the
    heart.

If another rejoices in thinking of his beloved,
I increase my sadness by thinking.
If another in thinking feeds love,
With thinking I nourish pain.

Whoever calls love tyrannical,
Is foolish, it is a great error;
The most fierce tyrant,
That torments this soul is my thoughts.

Quando sperasti (Naples, 1708; Ruspoli: 9 August 1709)

Quando sperasti, O core,
Così dolce alimento
Al tuo fiero tormento,
Al tuo dolore?
Torna, Fille, e ritorna
La cara pace all'alma,
E da tempeste il sen torna alla calma.

Non brilla tanto il fior,
Quando che riede il sol
A dargli vita,
Quanto che gode il cor,
Se riede a torgli il duol
Fille gradita.

Gode, festeggia e ride,

Tortorella che vede,
Tutt'amor tutta fede,
Tornar la cara sua compagna al nido;
E giunta a quella intorno,
Con mille baci e vezzi,
Lieta vola e s'aggira;
E se pria per dolore sospirò,
Per piacer dopo sospira.
Così a Fille, se torna,
Vuò ne' labbri vivaci,
Stampar l'anima in baci,
E'l suo volto adorato,
Voglio incensar de' miei sospir col fiato.

Voglio darti a mille a mille
Dolci baci, O cara Fille,
Perché servan di catene,
A restar sempre con me.
E vuò darti a cento a cento
Tali vezzi in un momento,
Che soffrir dovrai ben pene,
Se lontan ne porti il piè.

When did you ever hope, O heart,
Such sweet succor
For your fierce suffering,
For your grief?
Return, Fille, and bring back
Sweet peace to my soul,
And from storms return calm to my breast.

The flower does not shine as much,
When the sun returns
To give it life,
As the heart rejoices,
If to take away its sorrow
Welcome Fille returns.

The turtle dove rejoices, celebrates and
    laughs,
When he sees,
Full of love and faith,
His dear companion return to the nest;
And joining her,
With a thousand kisses and caresses,
He lightly flies and spins about;
And if previously he sighed with sorrow,
Afterwards he sighs with pleasure.
Thus, if she returns,
I wish on Fille's lively lips,
To press my soul with kisses,
And her beloved face,
I wish to perfume with the breath of my
    sighs.

I wish to give you thousands and thousands
Of sweet kisses, O dear Fille,
So that they serve as chains,
To keep you always with me.
And I want to give you hundreds and hundreds
Of such caresses in a moment,
That you will have to suffer much pain,
If you carry yourself far away.

Sans y penser (*Cantate française*) (Rome, 1707; Ruspoli: 22 September 1707)

Silvie:

Sans y penser	*Without thinking about it*
À Tirsis j'ay su plaire.	*I made Thyrsis fall in love with me.*
Sans y penser	*Without thinking about it*
Aussi Tirsis m'a su charmer.	*Thyrsis also claimed my heart.*
Amour prend soin,	*Love has taken charge*
Prend soin de cette affaire.	*Of this affair.*
Il pourrait bien se	*He [also] might withdraw from it*
Dégager sans y penser.	*Without thinking about it.*

Tirsis:

Si'l ne falloit que bien aimer	If loving well were all that were required
Pour attendrir ma bergère,	To soften the heart of my shepherdess,
Tous mes rivaux	All my rivals
Ne sçauroient	Could not
M'alarmer.	Excite my fears.
Mais, hélas! ce n'est point l'amant	But, alas! it is not the lover
Le plus fidèle qui doit espérer	Who is most constant who can hope to be
D'être heureux.	Rewarded with joy.
C'est toujours celui	It is always the one
Qui sait plaire	Who knows how to charm
Et que l'on croit	And who is thought to be
Le plus amoureux.	The most loving.

Petite fleur brunette,	*O tiny, dark flower,*
Aimable violette,	*O violet so winsome,*
Que ne puis je avec	*Why cannot I exchange my*
Vous changer mon triste sort!	*Sad fate with you!*
Vous languissez dans	*Your petals wilt*
Le sein de Silvie.	*On Sylvia's bosom.*
Je trouverais	*I would find life where*
La vie où vous trouvez la mort.	*You find death.*

Vous, qui m'aviez procuré	You, who aroused in me a love
Une amour éternelle	That could last forever,
Vous, qui j'aimais si tendrement,	You, whom I loved so tenderly,
Pouvez vous bien être infidèle	Can it be so that you are unfaithful
À votre plus fidèle amant?	To your most faithful lover?
Je devrois vous rendre le change,	I ought to pay you back in your own coin,
je devrois vous haïr ou changer.	I ought to hate you or change.

Mais si c'est par là qu'on se venge,	But if that is how one gets revenge,
Je ne veux jamais me venger.	I never want to do so.

Silvie:

Nos plaisirs seront	*Our pleasures will*
Peu durables,	*Only be fleeting,*
Le destin a comté nos jours.	*For Fate has counted our days.*
Ne songeons	*Let us not think*
Qu'à les rendre aimables,	*Only of how to make them happy,*
Puis qui'l les a rendus si courts.	*Since it has made them so short.*
Aimons nous, l'amour nous convie	*Let us love, for love invites us,*
Livrons nous à tous nos désirs,	*And give way to all our desires,*
Sans compter les jours de la vie.	*Without counting the days of our life.*
Cherchons à goûter ses plaisirs.	*Let us seek to enjoy its pleasures.*
Aimons nous.	*Let us love.*

Vous ne sauriez flatter ma peine,	You cannot assuage my sorrow,
Doux ruisseaux, paisible fontaine.	Soft waters, peaceful fountain.
Mon Tirsis va quitter ce lieu.	My Thyrsis is about to go from here.
Hélas! Hélas! Ma douleur est extrême	Alas! Alas! My distress knows no limits,
Quand je pense qu'il faut	When I think that it is necessary
Recevoir adieux	To receive farewells
De ce charmant berger que j'aime.	From this charming shepherd whom I cherished.

Tirsis:

Non, non je ne puis plus souffrir	*No, no, I can no longer bear*
Les infidélités	*The faithlessness*
D'une ingrate bergère	*Of an ungrateful shepherdess.*
Ma bouteille sera	*Now this bottle will*
Désormais mon plaisir.	*Henceforth be my pleasure.*
Si quelquefois elle devient légère	*And if perchance it gets light,*
J'en suis quitte pour la remplir.	*All I need to do is refill it.*

I am grateful to Terence Best for providing this translation. A free translation (for singing) can be found in George Frideric Handel, *Airs français,* ed. Percy M. Young (Kassel: Bärenreiter-Verlag, 1972).

Sarai contenta un dì (Florence/Venice 1706)

Sarai contenta un dì,	*You will one day be happy,*
Nice, mi partirò.	*Nice, I shall leave.*

Giacché tu vuoi così,   Since you wish it thus,
T'ubbirdirò.   I will obey you.

Ma con qual pena, O Dio!   But with what pain, O god!
Perché ingrata mi sei,   Because you are ungrateful to me,
M'offendi in guisa che me forzi al partir,   You offend me so that you force me to part,
E del partir io avrò la colpa   And for the parting I shall have the blame
E soffrirò il martire.   And suffer the torment.

Benché io sia che m'allontani,   Although I am the one that you send away,
Tu sei quella che mi lasci.   You are the one who leaves me.
Tu rendendo i voti vani,   You, rendering your vows vain,
Fai perfin ch'io li tralasci.   Even make me give mine up.

Sarei troppo felice (Rome, 1707; Ruspoli: 22 September 1707)
By Benedetto Pamphili?

Sarei troppo felice,   I would be very happy,
S'io potessi dar legge   If I were able to give laws
Al mio pensiero.   To my thoughts.
Che val bellezza e senno,   What avails beauty and judgment,
Amor, fede, costanza,   Love, faith, constancy,
Arte o consiglio,   Cleverness or wisdom,
Nel mio grave periglio?   In my grave danger?
Se poi forte abbastanza,   If strong enough then,
Sopra i pensieri miei,   Over my thoughts,
Non ho possanza?   Have I no power?
Quando men givo altera   Once, I went around
Ch'ogni mio sguardo incatenasse un core. Proud that my every glance enchained a
                                             heart.

Fileno il traditore,   Fileno, the traitor,
Con più dura catena   With even stronger chain
Il core ed il pensier mi stringe e frena.   My heart and thoughts binds and restrains.
E pur l'amo spergiuro;   And yet I love him, the perjurer;
Benché infido l'adoro a mio dispetto.   Although unfaithful, in spite of myself, I
                                             adore him.

Gran contrasto ho nel petto,   I have great conflict in my breast,
E fra l'ira e l'amor pace non spero.   And between hate and love I do not hope for
                                             peace.

Sarei troppo felice,
s'io potessi dar legge   [as above]
al mio pensiero.

Se al pensier dar mai potrò,	If I can ever give to my thoughts,
Come al piè, legge e misura,	As I do to my feet, law and measure,
Il mio cor pace godrà.	My heart will enjoy peace.
Dall'infido lungi andrò,	I will go far from the unfaithful one,
Ma la pena allor più dura	But then worse pain
Temo, O Dio! ch'ancor sarà.	I fear, O God! will ensue.

Clori, schernita Clori,	Clori, scorned Clori,
Mi rammento l'offesa,	I remember the offense,
E l'offensor no(n) sò scacciar dal core,	And I do not know how to drive the offender from my heart,

Che pur troppo è dolore,	For it is only too painful,
Amar riamata	To love, having been loved in return,
Ma non gradita;	But not accepted [as a beloved];
Il sospirar d'amore	Love's sigh
È vergogna e dolor	Is a shame and a pain,
Molto più fiero	Even more fierce.
Sarei troppo felice,	
S'io potessi dar legge	*[as above]*
Al mio pensiero.	

Giusto Ciel se non ho sorte	Just heavens, if it is not my fate
Di tornar in libertà,	To return to liberty,
Il pensier mi dà la morte	The thought [itself] brings me death
Se tal forza il duol non ha.	If sadness lacks such strength.
(Il pensier mi dia la morte)	(Let the thought bring me death)
(Se tal forza il cor non ha.)	(If the heart lacks the strength.)

Ah! che un cieco ho per guida	Ah! I have a blind one for a guide
E un dio tiranno	And a tyrannical god
Ha del mio cor l'impero,	Has command of my heart.
Sarei troppo felice	
S'io potessi dar legge	*[as above]*
Al mio pensiero.	

N.B.: The additional text in parentheses at the end of the second aria is a textual variation included with the original in Handel's setting.

Sei pur bella (Rome, 1707; Ruspoli: 16 May 1707)

Sei pur bella, pur vezzosa	You are so beautiful, so lovely,
Bianca Rosa in mezzo ai fior.	White rose in the midst of the flowers.

I colori lor son tanti	*Their colors are too many*
Tu sol vanti il tuo candor.	*[While] you display only your innocence.*

Version 1 continuation

Candida Rosa, inosservata e lieta,	Innocent rose, unobserved and happy,
Con soave fragranza	With sweet fragrance
Alzi fra gli altri fior fronte modesta,	You raise a modest brow among the other flowers,
Bella senza baldanza,	Beautiful without boldness,
Armata per difesa e non molesta;	Armed for defense and not for injury;
Ferendo il molle piè di Citerea	Wounding the soft feet of Venus
Sdegnasti esser regina, essendo rea.	You disdained to be queen, being guilty.
L'altra dunque di porpora vestita,	Let the other [rose] of purple dressed,
Forse sangue o vergogna,	Perhaps with blood or shame,
Vada or superba per l'altrui ferita,	Be proud now of that one's injury,
Che se l'amor di regno non rampogna	For if a desire to reign does not put off
Turba d'amanti o tributarii fiori,	The crowd of lovers or lesser flowers, [then]
Cortese senza fasto e senza amori	Courteous without pomp and without passions
Fuor dell'invidia stessa,	Other than envy itself,
(arioso)	
Vivi alla pace tua, vivi a te stessa.	Live in your peace, live in yourself.

Nascermi sento al core	*I feel born in my heart*
Dal candor di tua presenza	*From the innocence of your being*
Bel desio di libertà.	*The beautiful desire of liberty.*
Mi rinfaccia il tuo colore	*[But] your color taunts me*
Che perduto ho l'innocenza,	*That I have lost my innocence,*
Che più pace il sen non ha.	*That my breast has no more peace.*

Version 2 continuation

Se vien l'ape ingegnosa	If a clever bee comes
Per involarne il ruggiadoso umore,	To steal the dewy nectar,
Volando appena tocca	It, flying, hardly touches
Ogn'altro fiore	Every other flower,
Ma per diletto sovra te si posa.	But for delight over you it alights.
Se vien Ninfa vezzosa	If a lovely nymph comes
A far ghirlande	To make a garland
Spoglia degli altri fiori il prato ameno,	She strips the pleasant meadow of the other flowers,
Ma solo tu, fra le tue verdi foglie	But only you, among your green leaves
Posta vicino al cor;	She places near her heart;
Le adorni il seno.	You adorn her breast.

E certo allor	*And certainly then*
La Regina d'ogn'altro fior	*[You are] the queen of every other flower*
Se adorni la beltà, O vaga rosa.	*If you adorn beauty herself, O graceful rose.*
Ma il tuo candor	*But your innocence*
Pungente spina difende ancor	*Is still defended by prickly thorns*
Ed a ragion ti fa tanto orgogliosa.	*And rightly makes you very proud.*

Sento là che ristretto (Naples, 1708; Ruspoli: 31 August 1709)

Sento là che ristretto	I hear that restricted there
Nell'angusto confin di sterpi e sassi	In the narrow confine of stumps and rocks
Degli argentei suoi passi	The clear little brook
Limpido ruscelletto	Sighs for the now lost liberty
La già perduta libertà sospira;	Of its silvery steps;
Vedo come s'aggira	I see how it swirls
Per l'innalzate sponde	Through high banks
Con l'impeto dell'onde,	With the force of waves,
Devastando i recinti	Ravaging the walls
Per giungere ad unirsi	In order to succeed in uniting itself
Al mare che freme;	With the raging sea;
Ascolto alfin che geme	I hear at last that it groans
Quasi dicesse allora,	As if it then says
Con lento mormorio:	With slow murmur:
Belle arene del mare	Beautiful shore of the sea,
Non vi posso baciare	I cannot kiss you
Come vorrei, se prigionier son io.	As I would like, if I am a prisoner.

Mormorando esclaman l'onde	*Murmuring, the waves exclaim*
Vi sospiro, O belle arene.	*I sigh for you, O beautiful shore.*
Ma innalzando più le sponde	*But raising the banks higher,*
Il villan qui mi trattiene.	*The farmer holds me here.*

Son io Nice il ruscello,	Nice, I am the brook,
E di bellezza il mare	And the sea of beauty
È il tenero tuo seno	Is your soft breast
Ove, tra vivi scogli	Where, among living rocks,
Va del mio core a naufragar il pino.	The ship of my heart goes to be wrecked.
Or se fiero destino	Now if a cruel fate
Misero al par di quello,	As pitiful as that one there
Mi vieta il ribaciar	Forbids me from kissing once more
Di sì placido mar	The far shores
Le sponde estreme,	Of the very serene sea,
Pensa il cor quanto geme,	Imagine how much my heart groans,

E come in vario loco,	How in a different place,
Vittima troppo fida, ardo nel foco.	A too faithful victim, I burn in the fire.

Se un sol momento	*If for a single moment*
Non ti rimiro,	*I do not gaze at you,*
Peno e sospiro,	*I suffer and sigh,*
Caro mio ben.	*My beloved.*
E quell'affanno	*And this anguish*
Che per te sento	*That I feel for you*
Si fa tiranno	*Becomes the tyrant*
Del fido sen.	*Of my faithful heart.*

Se pari è la tua fé (Rome, 1708; Ruspoli: 28 August 1708)

Se pari è la tua fé	*If your faithfulness is equal*
Al foco che ho nel sen,	*To the fire I have in my breast,*
Ardo contento.	*I burn contented.*
Perché egual mercè	*Because my torment*
Avrà da te, mio ben,	*Will have from you, my love,*
Il mio tormento.	*Equal reward.*

Il penar per chi s'ama,	The pain for whom one loves,
Se gradito a colei per cui si pena,	If pleasing to that one for whom one is in pain,
Penar non è.	Is not painful.
Cupido, al par degli altri numi,	Cupid, like the other gods,
L'olocausto desia.	Requires sacrifice.
E questo è il core, e in premio	And this is my heart, and in reward
A tanto sacrificio,	For such a sacrifice,
Poi d'una bellezza	He gives us then
Dona il core a noi.	The heart of a beautiful woman.

Non s'afferra d'amor il porto	*The port of love is never gained*
Senza mai patir procelle.	*Without ever suffering storms.*
Dopo i nembi e le tempeste	*After the clouds and tempests*
Son più bel lume, le stelle.	*The stars are more beautiful lights.*

Alternate middle recitative (Roman type = abbreviated London version)

Sì, sì, questa sia solo	Yes, yes, let this alone be
La mercè del mio duolo,	The reward for my sadness,
E gema pur l'anima mia fra pene,	*And let my spirit groan indeed amid pains,*
Fra ferite e catene;	*Among wounds and chains;*
Che se fedel mi sei,	For if you are faithful to me,

Son piaceri del cor,
Gli affanni miei,
E se pur colla fé mi giuri amore,

Vedrà l'alma e i martiri, in porto, il core.

My afflictions
Are the pleasures of my heart,
And if indeed with faithfulness you pledge me love,

My heart will see my soul and [its] agonies into port.

Se per fatal destino (Rome, 1707; Ruspoli: 16 May 1707)

Se per fatal destino
Del faretrato arcier, vuol la mia sorte
Che muta sia ed amante,
Troppo crudel destino a un cor ch'adora,
Come potrò infelice
Occultar quelle fiamme?
Se una lingua che tace,
Antidoto al suo mal sdegna né brama

Sollievi alle sue doglie,
Parlar dunque dovrò?
No vuò che sia
Taciturna a penar la morte mia.

If, through fatal destiny
Of the armed god, my fate wishes
That I be silent and loving,
Too cruel a fate for a heart that loves,
How will I be able, unhappy one,
To hide my passion?
If a tongue that is silent
Disdains an antidote for its sickness, and does not desire

Relief for its sorrow,
Then should I speak?
No, I want to be
Silent in suffering my death.

Crude stelle! Astri tiranni!
Consigliatemi a morire,
Toglietemi amorose
S'ostinato è il mio timor.
Insegnate al core amante,
La ragion d'un bell'ardire,
O narrate almen pietose,
Al mio ben il mio dolor.

Cruel stars! tyrannical planets!
Counsel me to die,
Or lead me gently away
If persistent is my fear.
Teach the loving heart
The reason for a noble courage,
Or at least in pity, tell
My beloved of my pain.

Ma come incauta
Arridi al tuo mal se tu puoi,
Ora che sola sei,
Ne alcun ti sente, dir il bel nome?
O Dio! troppo pavento
Ch'eco il ridica, e poi
L'aure, che qui d'intorno
Spirano vezzosette,
Co' lor lievi sussurri
Portin, con mio rossore,
Altrove la cagion dei miei martiri.

But how, imprudent one,
Can you smile at your pain, if you are able,
Now that you are alone,
And no one hears you, to say the fair name?
O god! I am too afraid
That Echo will say it again, and then
The graceful breezes,
That around here breathe
With their soft whisperings
Will carry, with my blushes,
Elsewhere the reason for my sufferings.

Dunque misera godi de' guardi sol!

Chi sa che fatto accorto l'idolo tuo
Del tuo penoso foco,
A un reciproco amor non presti loco.

Con voi mi lagnerò,
Occhi, se non trovate
Rimedio a un tanto ardor.
Un guardo, ben sapete,
Può l'amorosa sete
Estinguer del mio cor.

So then, miserable one, be satisfied with
glances alone!
Who knows, having made your idol aware
Of your painful fire,
You may not find a place for reciprocal love.

With you I will lament,
Eyes, if you do not find
A remedy for so much burning.
One look, you well know,
Is able the ardent thirst
Of my heart to quench.

Siete rose (London, 1710–1716)

Siete rose rugiadose,
Belle labbra del mio ben.
Sempre care se ridete,
Se parlate, se tacete,
Accendete questo sen.

Dolce bocca soave,
In te nasce il bel riso lusinghiero,
Che accende amore
In ogni cuor più fiero.
I dolci tuoi sospiri
Fanno obliare all'alma
I suoi martiri;
Ed io, che per te peno,
Cara, se ti riveggio
Allor che taci,
Se le tue parolette
S'un tuo sospir io sento,
Mi scordo ogni tormento.

Per involarmi al duolo
Mi basta solo,
Solo un dolce tuo sospir,
Bocca vezzosa.
Ne' tuoi soavi accenti,
Nei vezzi tuoi ridenti,
Perde ogni suo martir,
L'alma amorosa.

You are dewy roses,
You lovely lips of my dear one.
Always dear, whether you laugh,
Speak, or are silent,
You set my heart aflame.

Soft sweet mouth,
In you is born the sweet, alluring smile,
That awakens love
In even the proudest heart.
Your sweet sighs
Make the soul forget
Its sufferings;
And I, who yearn for you,
Dear one, if I see you again
When you are silent,
If I hear your sweet words
Or one of your sighs,
I forget every torment.

In order to free myself from suffering,
I need only,
Only a sweet sigh of yours,
Pretty mouth.
In your soft words,
In your charming laughter,
The loving soul
Forgets all of its pain.

Solitudini care (undocumented; Italian?)

Solitudini care,
Amata libertà,
Quanto v'adoro.
Rinunzio ogni tesoro,
Ogni pompa, ogni onore;
Cerco pace a quest'alma, e fuggo amore;
Mia gioia e mio diletto
Sarai, bel ruscelletto,
Che mormorando passi
Fra l'erbette e fra sassi;
Il canto degli augelli,
I bei fiori del prato
Mi renderan beato;
Qui di cure noiose
Non sentirò l'affanno;
Di malediche, inique, insidiose,
Di mille frodi e mille,
Qui sottrarrommi al danno.
Così spero passar l'ore tranquille
E sol dal ciel tanta fortuna imploro:

Solitudini care,
Amata libertà,
Quanto v'adoro.

Sei bugiarda, umana speme,
Secca il rio, languisce il fiore,
L'augelletto fugge e muore
Col diletto in un baleno.
Non è gioia senza pene,
Né piacer senza dolore;
Chi più brama gode meno.

Gloria di bella fama
Ingombra il petto del mortale in terra,
Con la penna o con l'armi
In virtude o in valor chiaro si rende,

E se in vita non lice,
Dopo la morte almen sarà felice.
Io sventurato, a tutt'il mondo ascoso
Tanto a sperar non oso;
Ma può del fato ad onta

Sweet solitude,
Beloved liberty,
How much I adore you.
I renounce every treasure,
All pomp and honor;
I seek peace for this soul, and flee love;
My joy and my delight
You will be, beautiful stream,
As you pass murmuring
Among the grasses and stones;
The song of the birds,
The beautiful flowers of the meadow
Will render me blessed;
Here I will not feel the anguish
Of bothersome cares;
Of slanderous, evil, [and] insidious,
Frauds in the thousands,
I will escape here from harm.
Thus I hope to pass the tranquil hours
And only from heaven such fortune I
    implore:

[as above]

You are false, human hope,
The river dries up, the flower wilts,
The bird flies away and dies,
As does delight in a flash.
There is no joy without pain,
No pleasure without sorrow;
Who desires more, enjoys less.

The glory of great fame
Oppresses the breast of mortal man on earth,
[Whether] with the pen or with arms,
In virtue or in valor he makes himself
    famous,

And if it is not allowed in this life,
After death at least he will be happy.
I, unfortunate, to all the world unknown,
I dare not hope so much,
But it is possible in spite of fate

Vincer me stesso,
E de' pensieri miei
(Già ch'infelice fui dal mio natale)

Col saper trionfar, farmi inmortale.

Bella gloria in campo armato,
Trionfar d'invitte schiere
Debellar chi v'ingannò.
Più glorioso e fortunato,
Chi fa guerra al suo pensiero,
E i suoi sensi raffrenò.

To conquer myself,
And over my thoughts
(As I have been unhappy from the day of my birth)

To triumph with knowledge, to make myself immortal.

There is great glory in armed battle,
To triumph over unvanquished troops,
To conquer the one who deceived you.
More glorious and fortunate,
He who makes war on his thoughts,
And has tamed his emotions.

Son gelsomino (London, 1710–1716)
By Paolo Rolli

Son gelsomino, son picciol fiore,
Ma più del giglio son amorose
Le ninfe belle del mio candor.
Han le mie foglie sì grato odore,
Che più soave non han le rose,
Benché regine degli altri fior.

I am a jasmine, I am a tiny flower,
But even more than the lily
The lovely nymphs love my whiteness.
My leaves have such a sweet fragrance,
That even the roses are not more sweet,
Although they are queens among the other flowers.

Tremolante e leggiero,
Fra strette verdi e ben disposte fronde,

Bel vedermi ornamento a un vago crine,

E lievemente ver la guancia inflesso,
Dar e prender bellezza a un tempo istesso.
Quand'uno stuol di fior meco abbellisce

Una brillante testa o un molle seno,
Fassi di me più stima,
E la candida man di chi l'adorna,
Mi pon' com' in trionfo agli altri in cima.

Trembling and light,
Among tightly intertwined, green and well-arranged leaves,

It is lovely to see myself a beautiful ornament on charming tresses,

And softly bending toward the cheek,
Giving and taking beauty at the same time.
When a bunch of flowers together with me beautifies

A shining head or soft bosom,
I am held in greater esteem,
And the fair hand of the one who adorns it,
Places me as if in triumph on top of all the others.

Spesso mi sento dir
Da vezzosetta bocca:
Sei bello, grato e amabile,

Often I hear myself addressed
By a charming mouth:
You are beautiful, agreeable and loveable,

O caro gelsomin!
E spesso in un sospir,
Che passa e che mi tocca,
Godo sentir che invidiano
Gli amanti il mio destin.

O dear, dear jasmine!
And often in a sigh,
Which passes and touches me,
I enjoy feeling that lovers
Envy my destiny.

Stanco di più soffrire (Rome, 1708; Ruspoli: 9 August 1708)

Stanco di più soffrire
Mille barbare pene intorno al core,
Con misero tenore,
Piangendo e sospirando,
Fatto guanciale a miei riposi un sasso,
Giacqui fra l'erbe, affatigato e lasso.
Chiusi al fin le pupille,
E mi parea, sognando,
Dell'adorata bocca
Fortunato goder le vive rose,
E mentre men ritrose
Invitavan con vezzo alle rapine,
Placido non temea
Di barbaro timor l'acute spine.

Tired of suffering any more
A thousand cruel torments around my heart,
With wretched bearing,
Weeping and sighing,
Having made a stone a pillow for my rest,
I lay down on the grass tired and worn out.
I closed my eyes at last,
And it seemed to me, dreaming,
That of the adored mouth,
I was favored to enjoy the bright roses,
And while, less bashful,
They were coyly inviting their ravishment,
I was calm and not afraid
Of the sharp thorns of barbarous fear.

Era in sogno almen contento,
Se vegliando io non ho pace,
E parea ch'in quel momento,
Si rendesse a poco a poco,
Il mio foco
più cocente e più vivace.

In the dream at least there was contentment,
If waking I have no peace,
And it seemed that in that moment,
Little by little,
My ardor became
More intense and lively.

Quando mi parve allora,
Che vi girasse intorno,
Vagabonda e leggiera,
A goder quelle rose ape straniera.
A l'improvviso arrivo,
Più velenosa e ria,
Mi destò gelosia.
Indi proruppi ancora:
Ah! chi sa ch'altro amante
Dolce desio non punga,
Di goder quei cinabri,
E ch'ad unir non giunga
A' labbri del mio ben, gli accesi labbri.

When it then appeared,
That there flew around,
Wandering and light,
To enjoy those roses a rival bee.
At its sudden arrival,
Jealousy, more poisonous and cruel,
Awoke me.
Thereafter I again burst out:
Ah! who knows if another lover
Is not goaded by sweet desire,
To enjoy those red lips,
And does not succeed in joining with
The lips of my beloved, those ardent lips.

Or pensa quanto io t'amo,
Adorato mio bene,
Ch'un sogno ancor mi dà tormenti e
    pene.

Now think how much I love you,
My adored beloved,
That a dream still gives me torment and
    pain.

Se più non t'amo,
Non ti doler,
Ch'amarti, O bella,
Io più non so.
Ma da te bramo
Caro piacer,
Se tu sei quella
Che mi piagò.

If I no longer love you,
Do not grieve,
For to love you, O beauteous one,
I no longer know how.
But from you I crave
Sweet pleasure,
If you are that one
Who wounded me.

Stelle, perfide stelle! (Rome, spring 1707?)

Stelle, perfide stelle!
Iniquo fato!
Ecco giunta quell'ora
Prefissa al mio partire
O pure al mio morire.
V'abbandono del Tebro
Spiaggie fiorite e belle,
Care mura vi lascio,
Sassi amati vi perdo;
Ma se lungi va il piede,
Resta eterna con voi la mia gran fede.

Stars, treacherous stars!
Evil fate!
Now arrives that hour
Predestined for my departure
Or rather for my death.
I forsake you, flowered and beautiful
Banks of the Tiber,
Dear walls, I leave you,
Beloved stones, I desert you;
But if my feet go far away,
My abiding faith remains forever with you.

Se vedrà l'amena sponda
Crescer l'onde,
Dite pur ch'è il pianto mio.
S'udiran la selva o'l prato,
Zeffir grato,
Son sospir ch'al Tebro invio.

If the pleasant shore
Sees the waves grow bigger,
Say then that it is my tears.
If the wood or meadow hear
A pleasant breeze,
They are sighs I am sending to the Tiber.

Dove rivolga il passo.
Lo sa il Ciel,
Ma ogni sasso,
Bagnato dal mio pianto,
V'additerà il sentiero;
Il mio dolor più fiero
Mi dice e fa temer ch'al mio ritorno,

Where my steps should turn,
Heaven knows,
But every stone,
Bathed by my tears,
Will reveal to you the pathway;
My most intense sorrow
Tells me and makes me fear that at my
    return,

Il mio sol più non splenda al Tebro
    intorno.

Taci, mia lingua, taci,
L'ardor che ti consuma,
Giacché nell'ore estreme all'idolo mio
Non devo con un bacio
Scoprir l'amore e dar l'ultimo addio.

Quando ritornerò,
Se in voi ritroverò
L'amato mio tesor,
Sarò felice.
Sperando soffrirò,
Tacendo l'amerò,
Ma di scoprir l'ardor
Mio cor non lice.

My sun will no longer shine upon the Tiber.

Quiet, my tongue, hush,
About the ardor that consumes you,
Since now in the final hours to my beloved
I should not with a kiss
Reveal my love and give a final goodbye.

When I return,
If I find in you
My loving treasure,
I will be happy.
I will suffer with hope,
I will love [her/him] in silence,
But to reveal my love
My heart is not allowed.

Torna il core (Italian, without autograph; Santini Collection)

Torna il core al suo diletto,
Mentre torna a te, mio ben.
(Il cor ritorna a te, ritorna al suo diletto
Mentre torna.)
Dagli, O cara, quel ricetto,
Che ti chiede nel tuo sen.

Volsi appena le piante
Da te, Clori adorata,
Che fuggì dal mio petto
La gioia in un istante,
E ad ogni passo
Sentia (=sentiva) dolente e lasso
Una fiera trafitta,
Un gelido rigor, un foco rio;
Onde ardendo e gelando,
Il piagato cor mio
Già languido cedea al crudo affanno.

Or sì vado disciolto
Dai martir che provai,
Se vagheggio i tuoi rai,
E il lume ancor ch'è nelle stelle accolto;
Or sì che se stemprai,
Qual aurora, le luci in pianti amari,

The heart returns to its delight,
When it returns to you, my beloved.
(The heart returns to you, returns to
Its delight, when it returns.)
Give it, O dear one, that shelter,
That it asks for in your breast.

As soon as I went away
From you, adored Clori,
Joy fled from my breast
In an instant,
And at every step,
Sad and weary, it felt
A fiery, stabbing hurt,
A freezing cold stiffness, a terrible fire;
Wherefore, burning and freezing,
My wounded heart
Now succumbed, already weak, to the cruel
    anguish.

So now I am released
From the suffering that I felt,
If I gaze upon your rays
And the light that is contained in the stars;
So that now if I dissolved,
As the dawn does, the light in bitter tears,

Vicini ho del mio sole,
Per succhiar quelle stille, i raggi chiari.

I have nearby the clear rays
Of my sun [your eyes], in order to dry those
tears.

Mai più da te, mio ben,
Andrà lontano il cor.
Unito nel tuo sen
L'avrai finché vivrà,
E unito in te starà,
Dopo la morte ancor.

My heart will never again
Go far from you, my beloved.
You will have it united in your breast
While it lives,
And united in you will it remain,
Even after death.

N.B.: The text in parentheses in the first aria is a variation included with the original in Handel's setting.

Udite il mio consiglio (Florence/Venice 1706)

Udite il mio consiglio,
Inesperti d'amor pastori, udite;
Se inconstraste giammai
Qui dove suole
Guidar l'errante greggia
Dal colle al piano, o dalla selva al fonte,
Picciola pastorella,
Di membra agili e pronte,
D'atti languidi e schivi,
Che ha nero ciglio in bianco volto,
E fregia della guancia
Il pallor labbro vermiglio,
Fuggite, ah! sì fuggite,
Que' suoi furtivi sguardi,
E quelle sue semplicità mentite.

Listen to my advice,
You shepherds inexperienced in love, listen;
If you ever encounter
Here where she is used to
Guiding the wandering flock
From hills to valley, or from wood to spring,
A little shepherdess,
With quick and agile limbs,
Gestures languid and bashful,
Who has black eyes in a white face,
And, decorating a pale cheek,
Red lips,
Flee, ah! yes, flee,
Those furtive glances of hers,
And her misleading simplicity.

(arioso)
Innocente rassembra, e pur niun'altra
È al par di lei cruda fallace e scaltra.

She appears innocent, and yet no one else
Is as cruel as she is false and cunning.

Non le scherzate intorno,
Ch'il cor v'accenderà.
E in chiederle pietà
Del concepito ardore,
Dirà che nel suo core
Stilla d'amor non ha.

Do not joke around her,
Because she will set your heart on fire.
And when you ask for pity
For your engendered passion,
She will say that in her heart
She has not a droplet of love.

Al verderla sovente,	Seeing her frequently,
Non curante e negletta,	Nonchalant and unaffected,
Abbassar gli occhi in sua maniera onesta,	Lowering her eyes in her virtuous way,
O pur vergognosetta,	Or even gracefully bashful,
Piegar sul collo la leggiadra testa,	Bowing her lovely head on her neck,
E ognor pargoleggiar quando favella;	And always childlike when she speaks;
Ognun diria che semplicetta è quella:	Everyone would say that she is a simple girl:
Semplice è ben ch'il crede.	Simple indeed is the one who believes it.
Poiché qualor si vede	For whenever she seems
Semplice più, più di far preda è vaga,	Most simple, she is most eager for catching prey,
E per ogni suo vezzo apre un piaga.	And with every one of her charms she opens a wound.

Non esce un guardo mai	*Never does a look depart*
Da quegli arcieri rai,	*From those shooting rays,*
Che non saetti un cor.	*That does not wound a heart.*
E'l cor che vien colpito,	*And the heart that is hit,*
Si sente già ferito	*Already feels wounded*
Che non lo crede ancor.	*When it still believes it not.*

Volea più dir, ma tacque	He wished to say more, but
Il misero Fileno,	The miserable Fileno was silent,
E quel che trasse	And what dragged
Doloroso sospir fuori del petto	A sorrowful sigh out of his breast—

(arioso)

Non fu già per amor,	Was not for love,
No, fu per dispetto.	No, it was for spite.

N.B.: The aria "Allor che sorge" printed at the end of this cantata in Chrysander's edition is not part of the cantata (see Harris, *Pastoral,* p. 163, n. 34.)

Un sospir (Florence/Venice, 1709)

Un sospir a chi si muore,	*One sigh to one who dies,*
Per pietà, labbra vezzose,	*For pity's sake, O lovely lips,*
Renderà di questo core	*Will give this heart*
L'agonie meno penose.	*An agony less painful.*

Un tuo sospiro, O cara,	One of your sighs, O dear one,
Disarmerà la morte mia d'orrore,	Will disarm my death of horror,

Del mio fato il rigore	The harshness of my fate
Renderà meno acerbo;	It will render less sharp;
E in dolce obblio	And with sweet oblivion
Chiudendo i mesti lumi,	Closing my sad eyes
Fia men grave la terra al cener mio.	Will make less hard the earth to my ashes.

Se nel punto ch'io moro, ch'io spiro,	*If in the moment that I die, that I expire,*
Dal bel petto tu getti un sospiro,	*From that beautiful breast you breathe a sigh,*
Prende morte d'amor la sembianza,	*Death [will] take on the semblance of love.*
E ingannando l'acceso desire,	*And deceiving the strong desire,*
Penso amore, non penso morire,	*I think of love and not of dying,*
Ch'il mio fato diventa speranza.	*For my fate changes into hope.*

Vedendo Amor (?Ottoboni: Rome, 1707)

Vedendo Amor che per me tesse invano	Love seeing that he had woven
Aveva le sue reti,	His nets in vain for me,
E che, fuggito a caso di sua mano,	And that, having fled by chance from his grasp,

Passavo i giorni miei contenti e lieti,	I was passing my days contented and happy,
Tanto dietro mi stette,	He chased me so closely,
Che suo schiavo mi rese,	That he made me his slave,
E, quando nol pensavo, al fin mi prese.	And, when I least expected it, at last captured me.

In un folto bosco ombroso,	*In a dense, shady wood,*
Io prendea dolce riposo,	*I was taking a sweet rest,*
Una notte fredda e scura.	*On a cool, dark night.*
A un tempo così strano,	*At such an unusual time,*
Io credea Amor lontano,	*I thought Love far away,*
Ma la mia libertà non fu sicura.	*But my freedom was not secure.*

In quel bosco sen venne cheto,	Into that wood he crept softly,
E acciò nol conoscessi,	And so that I could not recognize him,
Mutò l'arco in balestra,	He changed his bow into a catapult,
In sporta la faretra	His quiver into a basket
Ove teneva, in vece de saette,	Where he was holding, instead of arrows,
Più picciole pallette	Many little pellets
Di terra assai tenace,	Of hard clay,
E d'Imeneo la face	And the torch of Hymen
Accesa in un frugnolo.	He lit in a lantern.
Egli non era solo.	He was not alone.

Eurilla aveva seco,	Eurilla was with him,
Che lui guidava, in apparenza cieco.	And guided him who seemed blind.

Camminando lei pian piano,	*Treading very softly,*
Con frugnolo acceso in mano,	*With the lit lantern in her hand,*
Finalmente mi scuoprì.	*Finally she spied me.*
Disse allor: il semplicetto	*Then she said: the simpleton,*
Su quel picciolo rametto	*On that little branch*
Egli dorme, vello lì.	*He sleeps, just look at him.*

Caricò, scaricò subito amore,	Suddenly Love loaded and fired,
E dove appunto il colpo avea diretto	And just where he aimed his shot
Mi colpì sotto il petto,	He hit me, under my breast,
In terra io caddi allora	Then I fell to the ground,
Più per timor smarrito,	More overcome with fear
Che per esser ferito;	Than from having been wounded;
Cercai di liberarmi	I tried to free myself
E da loro salvarmi.	And save myself from them.
Ma sì presto ebbi addosso, e lui, e lei	But so quickly were he and she on top of me,
Che fuggir non potei	That I could not flee.

Rise Eurilla, rise Amore,	*Eurilla laughed, Love laughed*
Che di già mio vincitore	*That already my conqueror*
Mi teniva in servitù.	*Held me in servitude.*
Ed io misero non spero,	*And I, miserable, do not hope,*
Or ch'io son lor prigioniero	*Now that I am their prisoner,*
Di goder pace mai più.	*To enjoy peace ever again.*

Fra tanto sono in gabbia,	Meanwhile I am encaged,
Dove la notte e il giorno,	Where night and day,
Io canto per amor,	I sing for love,
Ma più per rabbia.	But more for rage.

Venne voglia (*Amore ucellatore*) (?Ottoboni: Rome, 1707)

Venne voglia ad Amore	The desire came to Love
Di far l'uccellatore,	To become a birdcatcher,
Di capelli castagni	[And] out of chestnut brown,
Biondi e neri tessè	Blond, and black hair he wove
Di rete un paio;	A pair of nets;
Di poi sul verde colle di speranze	And then on a green hill of hope
Aggiustò il paretaio;	He set up his hiding place (blind/screen);

Vi fece il bosco e la sua cappanetta;	He made there a wood and his little house;
Di fresca mortelletta	Out of fresh myrtle
Tagliò d'intorno tutti i posatoi,	All around he cut perches [for the birds],
Provedè le centine, i tiratoi	He provided all the bows, the pulls (strings)
E tutti gl'altri arnesi,	And all the other equipment,
Né stentò per trovar i contrappesi.	Nor was it hard to find the counterweights (fletchings).

Pose Clori ed Amarilli,	*He put Clori, Amarilli,*
Eurilla, Iole e Filli.	*Eurilla, Iole and Filli*
Nelle gabbie per uccelli.	*In the birdcage.*
Occhi, guance, labbra e petti,	*Eyes, cheeks, lips and breasts*
A un fuscel legati e stretti,	*To a twig tightly bound,*
Gli servivan di zimbelli.	*Served him as decoys.*

Amor gli maneggiava così bene,	Love managed them so well,
Che gli uccelli per forza	That the birds being unable to avoid
Calando nelle sue reti nascose,	Falling into his hidden nets,
Retate ne facea maravigliose.	He made a wonderful catch.
Un giorno anch'io entrai	One day I also entered
Ma per mia buona sorte,	But through my good fortune,
Per una maglia rotta, scapolai.	Escaped through a ripped stitch.

Or ch'io sono accivettato,	*Now that I have been ensnared,*
Ei zimbella, io me la rido.	*He sets out the decoys, and I just laugh.*
Chiama Iole, chiama Filli,	*Iole calls, Filli calls,*
Canta Clori ed Amarilli,	*Clori and Amarilli sing,*
Io sto sodo al macchio ne e non me fido.	*I stay hidden in the bush and trust them not.*

Talora con speranza di scappare,	Sometimes with the hope of escape,
Io vorrei rientrare;	I would like to reenter;
Ma poi meglio pensando,	But then thinking better,
E me stesso sgridando,	And scolding myself,
Io dico che per me saria finita,	I say that it would be the end of me,
Se trovassi la maglia ricucita.	If I found the netting repaired.

Venus and Adonis ("Behold where weeping Venus stands") (Hanover, ?1711)

Behold where weeping *Venus* stands!
What more than Mortal Grief can move
The bright th'Immortal Queen of Love?
She beats her Breast, She wrings her Hands;

And hark, She mourns, but mourns in vain,
Her Beauteous, Lov'd *Adonis,* slain.
The Hills and Woods her Loss deplore:
The *Naids* [sic] hear, and flock around;
And *Echo* sighs, with mimick Sound,
     Adonis is no more!
Again the Goddess raves, and tears her Hair;
Then vents her Grief, her Love, and her Despair.
Dear Adonis, *Beauty's Treasure,*
Now my Sorrow, once my Pleasure;
    O[h] return to Venus' *arms!*
Venus *never will forsake thee;*
Let the Voice of Love o'ertake thee,
    And revive thy drooping Charms.
Thus, Queen of Beauty, as thy Poets feign,
    While thou didst call the Lovely Swain;
        Transform'd by Heav'nly Power,
    The Lovely Swain arose a Flow'r,
        And smiling, grac'd the Plain.
    And now he blooms, and now he fades;
    Venus and gloomy *Proserpine*
    Alternate claim his Charms Divine;
By turns restor'd to Light, by turns he seeks the Shades.
    Transporting Joy,
    Tormenting Fears,
    Reviving Smiles,
    Succeeding Tears,
Are Cupid's *various Train.*
    The Tyrant Boy
    Prepares his Darts,
    With soothing Wiles,
    With cruel Arts,
And Pleasure blends with Pain.

Text taken from John Hughes, Poems on Several occasions. With some Select Essays in Prose (1735), vol. 2.

Zeffiretto (Italian autograph; Ruspoli: 31 August 1709)

Zeffiretto, arresta il volo	*Little breeze, stop your flight*
E rimira il mio martir.	*And behold my martyrdom.*
Puoi volare ov'è il mio bene,	*You who can fly where my beloved is,*

Vanne e di' che s'ei non viene   *Go and say that if he does not come*
A temprar dell'alma il duol,   *To assuage the pain in my soul,*
Già vicino è il mio morir.   *Now near is my death.*

Vanne all'idolo mio,   Go to my beloved,
Digli ch'io qui m'aggiro   Say to him that here I wander
Abbandonata e sola;   Abandoned and alone;
Di' ch'io piango e sospiro   Say that I weep and sigh
Quello degli occhi suoi vago splendor,   For the lovely splendor of his eyes,
Che me sostiene in vita;   That sustains me in life;
Che afflitta e smarrita vive colei,   That afflicted and lost she lives
Che un tempo fu   Who once was
Dell'anima sua fiamma e desio;   The flame and desire of his soul;
E che quella son io,   And that one is I,
Da cui lungi dicea   Far from whom, he once said,
Che viver non potea,   He was not able to live,
E dov'ei può soffrire   And where can he suffer
Viver da me lontano e non morire.   To live far from me and not die.

Auretta vezzosa,   *Lovely little breeze,*
Favella pietosa   *Speak piteously*
Al vago mio sol.   *To my wandering love.*
E digli ch'un giorno   *And tell him that one day*
Ei faccia ritorno   *He should return*
Avanti ch'io mora,   *Before I die,*
Uccisa del duol.   *Killed by grief.*

Bibliographic Abbreviations

It is in the nature of this book that a vast bibliography needed to be referenced, but many citations appear only in a single chapter, some only once. A complete listing of all of these, either undifferentiated in one very long alphabetical list or in a series of lists, still long, with the added problem of overlapping categories, seemed unwieldy at best. I hope the bibliographic system I have chosen will reduce repetitive references while still offering the reader a relatively easy path to full bibliographic citation. Frequently cited journals and reference works are abbreviated, as shown below. In addition, frequently cited articles and books are always given in abbreviated form, also listed below. Every work not listed here is given a complete reference on its first occurrence in every chapter.

Journals and Reference Works

EM	*Early Music*
18cL	*Eighteenth-Century Life*
18cS	*Eighteenth-Century Studies*
18cTI	*Eighteenth Century: Theory and Interpretation*
GHB	*Göttinger Händel-Beiträge*
HHA	*Hallische Händel-Ausgabe*
HHB	*Händel-Handbuch*
HJb	*Händel-Jahrbuch*
HJMW	*Hamburger Jahrbuch für Musikwissenschaft*
HW	*History Workshop: Journal of Socialist and Feminist Historians*
JAMS	*Journal of the American Musicological Society*
JH	*Journal of Homosexuality*
JHC	*Journal of the History of Collections*
JHS	*Journal of the History of Sexuality*
JM	*Journal of Musicology*

JMR	*Journal of Musicological Research*
JSH	*Journal of Social History*
Mf	*Musikforschung*
ML	*Music & Letters*
MQ	*Musical Quarterly*
MR	*Music Review*
MT	*Musical Times*
19cM	*Nineteenth-Century Music*
OG	*Ongaku Gaku: Journal of the Japanese Musicological Society*
PRMA	*Proceedings of the Royal Musical Association*
RIM	*Rivista Italiana di Musicologia*
SJ	*Sculpture Journal*
SdA	*Storia dell'Arte*
SM	*Studi Musicali*
WI	*Word & Image*
WM	*Women and Music*

Bibliographic Citations

Acton, *Medici*	Acton, Harold M. *The Last Medici*. London: Faber and Faber, 1932; repr. London: Thames and Hudson, 1980.
Bach, Handel, Scarlatti	*Bach, Handel, Scarlatti: Tercentenary Essays*, ed. Peter Williams. Cambridge: Cambridge University Press, 1985.
Bray, *Homosexuality*	Alan Bray. *Homosexuality in Renaissance England*. New York: Columbia University Press, 1982; repr. 1995.
Burrows, *Handel*	Burrows, Donald. *Handel*. New York: Schirmer, 1994.
Burrows, "Hanover"	Burrows, Donald. "Handel and Hanover," *Bach, Handel, Scarlatti: Tercentenary Essays*, ed. Peter Williams. Cambridge: Cambridge University Press, 1985, pp. 35–59.
Burrows/Ronish, *Catalogue*	Burrows, Donald, and Martha J. Ronish. *A Catalogue of Handel's Musical Autographs*. Oxford: Clarendon Press, 1994.
Cambridge Companion	*The Cambridge Companion to Handel*, ed. Donald Burrows. Cambridge: Cambridge University Press, 1997.
Catullus, *Poems*, ed. Whigham	*The Poems of Catullus*, ed. and trans. Peter Whigham. London: Penguin Books, 1966.
Catullus, *Poems*, ed. Lee	*The Poems of Catullus*, ed. and trans. Guy Lee. Oxford: Oxford University Press, 1990.
Celebration	*Handel: A Celebration of his Life and Times*, ed. Jacob Simon. London: National Portrait Gallery, 1985.

Crompton, *Byron and Greek Love* — Crompton, Louis. *Byron and Greek Love: Homophobia in Nineteenth-Century England.* Berkeley: University of California Press, 1985.

Dean, *Oratorios* — Dean, Winton. *Handel's Dramatic Oratorios and Masques.* London: Oxford University Press, 1959.

Dean/Knapp, *Operas* — Dean, Winton, and J. Merrill Knapp. *Handel's Operas: 1704–1726.* Oxford: Clarendon Press, 1987.

Dent, *Handel* — Dent, Edward. *Handel.* London: Duckworth, 1934.

Deutsch, *Handel* — Deutsch, Otto Erich. *Handel: A Documentary Biography.* New York: Da Capo Press, 1974.

Doniger, *Implied Spider* — Doniger, Wendy. *The Implied Spider: Politics and Theology in Myth.* New York: Columbia University Press, 1998.

Ewerhart, "Santini" — Ewerhart, Rudolf. "Die Händel-Handschriften der Santini-Bibliothek in Münster," *HJb,* 6 (1960): 111–150.

Guardian — *The Guardian,* ed. John Calhoun Stephens. Lexington, Kentucky: University Press of Kentucky, 1982.

Haggerty, *Men in Love* — Haggerty, George. *Men in Love: Masculinity and Sexuality in the Eighteenth Century.* New York: Columbia University Press, 1999.

Handel Collections — *Handel Collections and their History,* ed. Terence Best. Oxford: Oxford University Press, 1993.

Händel e gli Scarlatti — *Händel e gli Scarlatti a Roma,* ed. Nino Pirrotta and Agostino Ziino. Florence: Leo S. Olschki, 1987.

Harris, *Librettos* — Harris, Ellen T., ed. *The Librettos of Handel's Operas,* 13 vols. New York: Garland, 1989.

Harris, "London Cantatas" — Harris, Ellen T. "Handel's London Cantatas." *GHB,* 1 (1984): 86–102.

Harris, "Paper, Performing Practice" — Harris, Ellen T. "Paper, Performing Practice, and Patronage: Handel's Alto Cantatas in the Bodleian Library MS Mus. d. 61–62." *Festa Musicologica: Essays in Honor of George J. Buelow,* ed. Thomas J. Mathieson and Benito V. Rivera. New York: Pendragon Press, 1995, pp. 53–78.

Hawkins, *History* — Hawkins, Sir John. *General History of the Science and Practice of Music,* vol. 2. London: Novello, 1835.

Heller, "Chastity, Heroism, and Allure" — Heller, Wendy. "Chastity, Heroism, and Allure: Women in Opera of Seventeenth-Century Venice." Ph.D. dissertation, Brandeis University, 1995.

Hicks, "Musical Development" — Hicks, Anthony. "Handel's Early Musical Development," *PRMA,* 103 (1976–1977): 80–90.

Hidden from History   *Hidden from History: Reclaiming the Gay and Lesbian Past,* ed.
                               Martin Duberman, Martha Vicinus, and George Chauncey,
                               Jr. New York: New American Library, 1989.

Hogwood, *Handel*   Hogwood, Christopher. *Handel.* London: Thames and
                               Hudson, 1984.

Illicit Sex   *Illicit Sex: Identity Politics in Early Modern Culture,* ed.
                               Thomas DiPiero and Pat Gill. Athens: University of Georgia
                               Press, 1997.

Keates, *Handel*   Keates, Jonathan. *Handel: The Man and his Music.* New York:
                               St. Martin's Press, 1985.

Kirkendale, "Ruspoli"   Kirkendale, Ursula. "The Ruspoli Documents on Handel."
                               JAMS, 20 (1967): 222–273.

Lang, *Handel*   Lang, Paul Henry. *George Frideric Handel.* New York: W. W.
                               Norton, 1966.

Lord Burlington: *Lord Burlington: Architecture, Art and Life.* London: The
  Architecture   Hambledon Press, 1995.

Lord Burlington—The   *Lord Burlington—The Man and His Politics,* ed. Edward
  Man   Corp. Lewiston: The Edward Mellen Press, 1998.

Mainwaring, *Memoirs*   Mainwaring, John. *Memoirs of the Life of the Late George
                               Frederic Handel.* London: R. and J. Dodsley, 1760.

Marx, "Händel im Rom"   Marx, Hans Joachim. "Händel im Rom—Seine Beziehung zu
                               Benedetto Card. Pamphilj," HJb, 29 (1983): 107–118.

Marx, *Kantaten mit*   Marx, Hans Joachim, ed. *Kantaten mit Instrumenten,* I–III,
  Instrumenten   *HHA,* series 5, vols. 3–5. Kassel: Bärenreiter, 1994, 1995, 1999.

Marx, "Ottoboniana"   Marx, Hans Joachim. "Ein Beitrag Händels zur Accademia
                               Ottoboniana in Rom." *HJMW,* 1 (1974): 69–86.

Mattheson, *Grundlage*   Mattheson, Johann. *Grundlage einer Ehrenpforte* (Hamburg,
                               1740), ed. Max Schneider. Kassel: Bärenreiter, 1969.

Mayo, "Italian Cantatas"   Mayo, John. "Handel's Italian Cantatas." Ph.D. dissertation,
                               University of Toronto, 1977.

Mayo,   Mayo, John. "Einige Kantatenrevisionen Händels." *HJb,* 27
  "Kantatenrevisionen"   (1981): 63–77.

Montalto, *Pamphilj*   Montalto, Lina. *Un mecenate in Roma barocca: Il Cardinale
                               Benedetto Pamphilj (1653–1730).* Florence: Sansoni, 1955.

Music and Theatre   *Music and Theatre: Essays in Honour of Winton Dean,* ed.
                               Nigel Fortune. Cambridge: Cambridge University Press, 1987.

Musicology and Difference   *Musicology and Difference: Gender and Sexuality in Music
                               Scholarship,* ed. Ruth A. Solie. Berkeley: University of
                               California Press, 1993.

New Grove   *The New Grove Dictionary of Music and Musicians,* vol. 16, ed.
                               Stanley Sadie. London: Macmillan, 1980.

Norton, *Molly House* — Norton, Rictor. *Mother Clap's Molly House: The Gay Subculture in England 1700–1830.* London: GMP, 1992.

Ovid, *Metamorphoses,* trans. Watts — *The Metamorphoses of Ovid,* trans. A. E. Watts. San Francisco: North Point Press, 1980.

Ovid, *Metamorphoses,* trans. Melville — Ovid, *Metamorphoses,* trans. A. D. Melville. Oxford: Oxford University Press, 1986.

Petrarch, *Lyric Poems,* ed. Durling — Petrarch. *Petrarch's Lyric Poems: The "Rime sparse" and Other Lyrics,* ed. Robert M. Durling. Cambridge, Mass.: Harvard University Press, 1976.

Pope, *Correspondence* — George Sherburn, ed., *The Correspondence of Alexander Pope.* Oxford: Clarendon Press, 1956.

Pope, *Dunciad* — Pope, Alexander. *The Dunciad,* ed. James Sutherland. *The Twickenham Edition of the Poems of Alexander Pope,* ed. John Butt, vol. 5. New Haven: Yale University Press, 1963.

Pope, *Imitations* — Alexander Pope, *Imitations of Horace, with An Epistle to Dr. Arbuthnot and the Epilogue to the Satires,* ed. John Butt. *The Twickenham Edition of the Poems of Alexander Pope,* ed. John Butt, vol. 4. New Haven: Yale University Press, 1953.

Pope, *Minor Poems* — Pope, Alexander. *Minor Poems,* ed. Norman Ault. *The Twickenham Edition of the Poems of Alexander Pope,* ed. John Butt, vol. 6. New Haven: Yale University Press, 1954.

Pope, *Other Poems* — Pope, Alexander. *The Rape of the Lock and Other Poems,* ed. Geoffrey Tillotson. *The Twickenham Edition of the Poems of Alexander Pope,* ed. John Butt, vol. 2. New Haven: Yale University Press, 1954.

Pope, *Pastoral Poetry* — Pope, Alexander. *Pastoral Poetry and an Essay on Criticism,* ed. E. Audra and Aubrey Williams. *The Twickenham Edition of the Poems of Alexander Pope,* ed. John Butt, vol. 1. New Haven: Yale University Press, 1961.

Pope, *Scriblerus* — Pope, Alexander. *The Memoirs of the Extraordinary Life, Works, and Discoveries of Martinus Scriblerus,* ed. Charles Kerby-Miller. New Haven: Yale University Press, 1950.

Pursuit of Sodomy — *The Pursuit of Sodomy: Male Homosexuality in Renaissance and Enlightenment Europe,* ed. Kent Gerard and Gert Hekma. *Journal of Homosexuality,* 16 (1988).

Queering the Pitch — *Queering the Pitch: The New Gay and Lesbian Musicology,* ed. Philip Brett, Elizabeth Wood, and Gary C. Thomas. New York: Routledge, 1994.

Saunders, "Handel's *Agrippina*" — Harris Sheridan Saunders, "Handel's *Agrippina:* The Venetian Perspective," *GHB,* 3 (1987): 87–98.

Smith, *Oratorios*   Smith, Ruth. *Handel's Oratorios and Eighteenth-Century Thought.* Cambridge: Cambridge University Press, 1995.

Sodomy Trials   *Sodomy Trials: Seven Documents,* ed. Randolph Trumbach. New York: Garland, 1986.

Streatfeild, *Handel*   Streatfeild, R. A. *Handel.* London: Methuen, 1910.

Strohm, "Händel in Italia"   Strohm, Reinhard. "Händel in Italia." *RIM,* 9 (1974): 152–174.

Symposium   *Handel: A Symposium,* ed. Gerald Abraham. London: Oxford University Press, 1954.

Tercentenary Collection   *Handel Tercentenary Collection,* ed. Stanley Sadie and Anthony Hicks. Ann Arbor: UMI Research Press, 1987.

Theocritus, *Poems,* trans. Rist   *The Poems of Theocritus,* trans. Anna Rist. Chapel Hill: University of North Carolina Press, 1978.

'Tis Nature's Fault   *'Tis Nature's Fault: Unauthorized Sexuality during the Enlightenment,* ed. Robert P. Maccubbin. Cambridge and New York: Cambridge University Press, 1987.

Virgil, *Aeneid,* trans. Lewis   Virgil, *Aeneid,* trans. C. Day Lewis. New York: Doubleday, 1953.

Virgil, *Eclogues,* trans. Alpers   *The Singer of the Eclogues: A Study of Virgilian Pastoral,* trans. Paul Alpers. Berkeley: University of California Press, 1979.

Virgil, *Eclogues,* trans. Johnson   *The Pastorals of Vergil: A Verse Translation of the Eclogues,* trans. Geoffrey Johnson. Lawrence: University of Kansas Press, 1960.

Vitali/Funari, "Händels Italienreise" Vitali, Carlo, and Antonello Furnari, "Händels Italienreise—neue Dokumente, Hypothesen und Interpretationen," *GHB,* 4 (1991): 41–66.

Watanabe, "Music-Paper"   Watanabe, Keiichiro. "The Music-Paper used by Handel and his Copyists in Italy, 1706–1710." *Handel Collections and their History,* ed. Terence Best. Oxford: Oxford University Press, 1993, pp. 198–226.

Weaver/Weaver, *Florentine Theater*   Weaver, Robert L., and Norma W. Weaver. *A Chronology of Music in the Florentine Theater, 1590–1750.* Detroit: Information Coordinators, 1978.

Notes

Prologue: "The Ways of the World"

1. My previously published work on the cantatas includes the following: "The Italian in Handel," *JAMS*, 33 (1980): 468–500; "Händel in Florence," *HJb*, 27 (1981): 41–61; "Le cantate romane di Handel," in *Le muse galanti: La musica a Roma nel settecento* (Rome: Enciclopedia Italiana, 1985), pp. 59–76; "Handel's London Cantatas," *GHB*, 1 (1984): 86–102; "Paper, Performing Practice and Patronage: Handel's Alto Cantatas in the Bodleian Library Ms Mus. d. 61–62," in Thomas J. Mathiesen and Benito V. Rivera, eds., *Festa Musicologica: Essays in Honor of George J. Buelow* (New York: Pendragon Press, 1995), pp. 53–78; "Editing Musical Measure: Standardization versus Flexibility," in *Georg Friedrich Händel—ein Lebensinhalt: Gedankschrift für Bernd Baselt (1934–1993)* (Halle: Händel-Haus Halle, 1995), pp. 139–150; and the edition *G. F. Handel: Cantatas for Alto and Continuo* (Oxford: Oxford University Press, 2001).

2. Handel scholars owe a particular debt to Burrows/Ronish, *Catalogue*, which provides a comprehensive and detailed study of all of Handel's autographs.

3. Marx, *Kantaten mit Instrumenten* I–III, with English translations by Terence Best.

4. *The Works of Handel in Score*, 180 nos. (London: Longman and Co., 1787–1797); four accompanied cantatas appeared in nos. 174–176 and twelve continuo cantatas in nos. 176–177.

5. *Georg Friedrich Händels Werke* (Leipzig: Breitkopf & Hartel, 1858–1894, 1902); vols. 50–51 contain seventy-two continuo cantatas and vols. 52A and 52B contain twenty-eight instrumentally accompanied cantatas. The sources on which Chrysander based his edition were in a number of cases incomplete or corrupt.

6. "Handel's Cantatas," *PRMA*, 58 (1931–1932): 33.

7. Abbreviated throughout as *Symposium*.

8. "The Ruspoli Documents on Handel," *JAMS*, 20 (1967): 222–273.

9. It is impossible here to list all the relevant articles; what follows is a selection.

10. Reinhard Strohm, "Händel in Italia: Nuovi contributi," *RIM*, 9 (1974): 152–174: discovery of the libretto of *Rodrigo*, firmly placing this opera in Florence in 1707.

11. Hans Joachim Marx, "Ein Beitrag Händels zur Accademia Ottoboniana in

Rom," *HJMW,* 1 (1974): 69–86, discusses the autograph of *Ero e Leandro* and places this cantata at the academy hosted by Ottoboni.

12. Hans Joachim Marx, "Händel in Rom—seine Beziehung zu Benedetto Card. Pamphilj," *HJb,* 29 (1983): 107–118, identifies cantatas written for Pamphili's household through copyists' bills in the account books.

13. Burrows, "Hanover," pp. 35–59, presents newly discovered documents.

14. Graydon Beeks, "Handel and Music for the Earl of Carnarvon," in *Bach, Handel, Scarlatti,* pp. 1–20, discusses, among other things, the cantata *Sento là che ristretto;* see also Patrick Rogers, "Dating *Acis and Galatea:* A Newly Discovered Letter," *MT,* 114 (1973): 792, dating the work to 1718.

15. Mayo, "Italian Cantatas."

16. In an early trio of articles, I used the autographs as the basis for placing the cantatas geographically and identifying works written for specific patrons; see note 1 above. In the same period a detailed study of Handel's Italian watermarks was published by Keiichiro Watanabe, "The Paper Used by Handel and his Copyists during the Time of 1706–1710," *OG,* 27 (1981): 129–171; revised and reprinted as "The Music-Paper used by Handel and his Copyists in Italy, 1706–1710," in *Handel Collections,* pp. 198–226. The definitive source study of all Handel's autographs was published in 1994: Burrows/ Ronish, *Catalogue.*

17. Keiichiro Watanabe, "Die Kopisten der Handschriften von den Werken G. F. Händels in der Santini-Bibliothek Münster," *OG,* 16 (1970): 225–262; Winton Dean, "Handel's Early London Copyists," in *Bach, Handel, Scarlatti,* pp. 75–97.

18. Marx, *Kantaten mit Instrumenten* I–III.

19. "The Oratorios," in *Symposium,* p. 74.

20. *Baroque Music* (Englewood Cliffs: Prentice-Hall, 1968), p. 188.

21. *Handel and the Opera Seria* (Berkeley: University of California Press, 1969), p. 153.

22. *Rodrigo* (Florence, 1707), *Agrippina* (Venice, 1708), and in London, *Rinaldo* (1711), *Il pastor fido* (1712), *Silla* (1713), *Teseo* (1713), *Amadigi* (1715).

23. However critical to his development as a composer, the Italian years did not, as sometimes is exaggeratedly argued, turn Handel into an Italian composer; see my article, "The Italian in Handel."

24. After 1723 Handel composed very little secular chamber vocal music of note; this repertory primarily includes the chamber duets of the 1740s, some of which were used with such profit in the composition of *Messiah,* and the instrumental cantata *Cecilia volgi un sguardo,* based in part on *Splenda l'alba* of 1710 and performed as an "extra song" in *Alexander's Feast* (1736); see Burrows/Ronish, *Catalogue,* p. 112, for a description of the manuscript containing this work and a later revision *(Carco sempre di gloria),* often listed as separate compositions. Handel apparently revised a group of cantatas as continuo exercises for Princess Anne in the mid-1720s, but none represents a newly composed work; see John Mayo, "Einige Kantatenrevisionen Händels," *HJb,* 27 (1981): 63–77.

25. Handel never published his Chandos Anthems, but he did publish anthems, including the Coronation anthems and the funeral anthem for Queen Caroline.

26. Although cantatas often were not published, the existence of published editions by his close colleagues in London, as well as the publication of a few of Alessandro Scarlatti's cantatas by Estienne Roger in Amsterdam, makes the lack of any published cantatas by Handel all the more remarkable. If Walsh or Roger, both publishers who printed Handel's works, had had an opportunity to publish cantatas by Handel, with or without his permission, they probably would have done so. See John Christopher Pepusch, *Six English Cantatas*, bk. 1 (London: Walsh, Randall & Hare, 1710), bk. 2 (Walsh & Hare, 1720); Giovanni Bononcini, *Cantate e duetti* (London: n.p., 1721); Alessandro Scarlatti, *Cantate à una e due voci col basso continuo, opera prima* (Amsterdam: Estienne Roger, [1701]). See also the publication of cantatas by Bononcini's father, published as Op. 10 and Op. 13: Giovanni Maria Bononcini, *Cantate per camera a voce sola*, libro primo (Bologna: Giacomo Monti, 1677), libro secondo (1678).

27. Colin Timms, "Gregorio Piva and Steffani's Principal Copyist," in Ian Bent, ed., *Source Materials and the Interpretation of Music: A Memorial Volume to Thurston Dart* (London: Stainer & Bell, 1981), p. 170.

28. John Arbuthnot, *The History of John Bull*, ed. Alan W. Bower and Robert A. Erickson (Oxford: Clarendon Press, 1976), pp. xxii–xxiii.

29. Flavia Matitti, "Il cardinale Pietro Ottoboni mecenate delle arti. Cronache e documenti (1689–1740)," *SdA*, 84 (1995): 164, n. 18. Ottoboni's name in the Accademia dei Disuniti, which became the Accademia Ottoboniana, was Crateo Pradelini, an anagram of "Cardinale Pietro." I have found no explanation for his chosen name in the Arcadian Academy.

30. Montalto, *Pamphilj*, p. 193; Montalto suggests that the choice of this name referred to Queen Christina as "the symbolic phoenix [*fenice*] under whose influence Pamphili had spent his youth."

31. On Ruspoli's Arcadian name, see Kirkendale, "Ruspoli," p. 242; and Hans Joachim Marx, "Ruspoli, Francesco Maria," in *New Grove*, vol. 16, p. 334.

32. Reinhard Strohm, "Scarlattiana at Yale," in *Händel e gli Scarlatti*, pp. 113–152, reference to p. 131.

33. Arbuthnot, *John Bull*, pp. xvii and cii.

34. Jonathan Swift, *Gulliver's Travels*, ed. Christopher Fox (Boston: Bedford Books, 1995), p. 269.

35. Ibid., p. 270.

36. Mrs. Delany was born Mary Granville. Her first (arranged) marriage to Alexander Pendarves in 1717, when she was but seventeen years old, ended with his death in 1724. She married the Reverend Dr. Patrick Delany by choice in 1743. I will refer to her throughout this book as Mrs. Delany, as her letters are published under this name.

37. *Mrs. Delany at Court and Among the Wits Being the Record of a Great Lady of Genius in the Art of Living*, ed. R. Brimley Johnson (London: Stanley Paul & Co., 1925), pp. xlii–xliv.

38. Jane Clark, "'Lord Burlington is here,'" in *Lord Burlington: Architecture*, pp. 251–310, reference on p. 252.

39. For a survey of possible political allegory in all of Handel's operas, see especially

Reinhard Strohm, "Handel and His Italian Opera Texts," in *Essays on Handel and Italian Opera* (Cambridge: Cambridge University Press, 1985), pp. 34–79.

40. Smith, *Oratorios.*

41. See Alan Bray, "Homosexuality and the Signs of Male Friendship in Elizabethan England," *HW,* 29 (1990): 1–19, and Haggerty, *Men in Love,* for analyses of the ways in which these two views of same-sex love overlapped.

42. "The blasphemy of talking about politics during the Bach Year," in Richard Leppert and Susan McClary, eds., *Music and Society: The Politics of Composition, Performance and Reception* (Cambridge: Cambridge University Press, 1987), p. 14. I am indebted to the work of McClary, first for shocking me and then for making me think more deeply about these issues. The work of McClary and later that of Michael Marissen, *The Social and Religious Designs of J. S. Bach's Brandenburg Concertos* (Princeton: Princeton University Press, 1995), to name only two scholars, has shown definitively that context has a place in Bach's music, as one might have thought.

43. Michael Linton, "America's Messiah," in *First Things,* no. 78 (December 1997), p. 18; see also Lang, *Handel,* p. 543, and Dean, *Oratorios,* pp. 39–42. Dean writes of Handel: "He found little inspiration in Christianity" (p. 39).

44. Mainwaring, *Memoirs,* pp. 50–51; Burrows, "Handel and Hanover," pp. 35–60.

45. Keates, *Handel,* p. 22, suggests that Handel was "attracted to" Margarita Durastante, Anna Strada, Kitty Clive, and Susannah Cibber, among others.

46. Newman Flower, *George Frideric Handel, His Personality and His Times* (London: Cassel, 1959), pp. 84–85; Tarquini married Farinel in 1689, which would probably make her about fifteen to twenty years older than Handel.

47. Streatfeild, *Handel,* p. 305.

48. Later revised and published in *Queering the Pitch,* pp. 155–203.

49. Keates, *Handel,* p. 22.

50. Burrows, *Handel,* p. 9.

51. Ibid., p. 374, n. 51.

52. The literature on homosexuality in the seventeenth and eighteenth centuries is huge and rich. Throughout this study, I have tried to indicate my indebtedness to those scholars whose work has informed my own. The work of Randolph Trumbach, in particular, has helped to define the field of gay studies in eighteenth-century Britain. In addition, two books that frame this period offer significant additional material: Bray, *Homosexuality,* and Crompton, *Byron and Greek Love.* Finally, Haggerty, *Men in Love,* offers an exemplary study of homoeroticism in the work of three eighteenth-century men of letters, emphasizing the critical point that sexuality cannot be defined solely by genital acts but encompasses love and desire.

53. Joseph Cady, "'Masculine Love,' Renaissance Writing, and the 'New Invention' of Homosexuality," *JH,* 23 (1992): 9–40; citation on p. 9.

54. Michel Foucault, *The History of Sexuality,* trans. Robert Hurley (New York: Random House, 1978; Vintage Book edition, 1990), vol. 1, p. 43 and passim.

55. For example, onanism is the eighteenth-century term for any spilling of the seed outside of intercourse, whether that is effected by self-manipulation or by another. See *Onania; or, the Heinous Sin of Self-Pollution* (8th ed., London: Elizabeth Rumball

for Thomas Crouch, 1723) and *Onanism Display'd* (London: printed for E. Curll, 1719). This practice was strongly discouraged (it was thought to have dire consequences, including madness) but not illegal, and was not considered directly relevant to contemporary discussions of sodomy.

56. See Giovanni Dall'Orto, "'Socratic Love' as a Disguise for Same-Sex Love in the Italian Renaissance," in *Pursuit of Sodomy*, pp. 33–65; Bray, "Homosexuality and the Signs of Male Friendship"; and Raymond Stephanson, "'Epicoene Friendship': Understanding Male Friendship in the Early Eighteenth Century with Some Speculations about Pope," *18cTI*, 38 (1997): 151–170.

57. See Maynard Solomon, *Beethoven* (New York: Schirmer Books, 1998).

58. These terms are now in general use; see G. S. Rousseau, "'In the House of Madam Vander Tasse, on the Long Bridge': A Homosocial University Club in Early Modern Europe," in *Pursuit of Sodomy*, p. 311, n. 1, where Rousseau defines the terms sodomy, homosexuality, homoerotic, homosocial, and homocentric.

59. See Bray, *Homosexuality*, chap. 4: "Molly," pp. 81–114. The molly clubs were first described (probably with irony and exaggeration) in 1709 by Edward Ward in *The History of the London Club[s]*; see Craig Patterson, "The Rage of Caliban: Eighteenth-Century Molly Houses and the Twentieth-Century Search for Sexual Identity," in *Illicit Sex*, pp. 256–269, for a discussion of the veracity of Ward's account.

60. *Select Trials at the Sessions-House in the Old Bailey for Murders, Robberies, Rapes, Sodomy, Coining, Frauds, Bigamy, and Other Offences . . . in Four volumes. From the Year 1720, to this Time* (Dublin: W. Smith, 1742). See also Norton, *Molly House*, p.93.

61. Facsimile published in *Sodomy Trials*.

62. Randolph Trumbach, "London's Sodomites: Homosexual Behavior and Western Culture in the Eighteenth Century," *JSH*, 11 (1977): 1–33, states that the figure is 35 percent. Similar percentages have been recorded for France (Michel Rey, "Parisian Homosexuals Create a Lifestyle, 1700–1750: The Police Archives," *18cL*, n.s. 9 [1985]: 179–191) and Holland (Arend H. Huusen, Jr., "Sodomy in the Dutch Republic during the Eighteenth Century," *18cL*, n.s. 9 [1985]: 169–178). Of the fifteen cases I have read from April 1726 to December 1730, six were of married men.

63. Facsimile published in *Sodomy Trials*, p. 11.

64. Bray, *Homosexuality*, writes, "'Molly' in the homosexual sense of the molly houses etc. was taken over from Molly, a form of the female name Mary: it was part of the effeminate conventions of the homosexual subculture" (p. 137, n. 5). However, since the French "mollesse" means soft or effeminate and "mollicies" was "a common medieval term for effeminacy or sodomy," the etymology of molly in the homosexual sense would seem to derive directly from the Latin "mollis," which means unmanly and effeminate as well as soft. See Vernon A. Rosario, *The Erotic Imagination: French Histories of Perversity* (New York: Oxford University Press, 1997), pp. 15, 20, and 183 (n. 5) for the use of the words "mollesse" and "mollicies." For an analysis of effeminacy as an identifying feature of the eighteenth-century sodomite, see Randolph Trumbach, "The Birth of the Queen: Sodomy and the Emergence of Gender Equality in Modern Culture, 1660–1750," in *Hidden from History*, pp. 129–140, and Patterson, "The Rage of Caliban," in *Illicit Sex*.

65. Norton, *Molly House,* p. 93.

66. Ibid., p. 93; Norton's comments are based on Holloway, *The Phoenix of Sodom* (1813).

67. See Laurence Senelick, "Mollies or Men of Mode? Sodomy and the Eighteenth-Century London Stage," *JHS,* 1 (1990): 33–67; on Bickerstaff, see pp. 58–64. See also Peter A. Tasch, *The Dramatic Cobbler: The Life and Works of Isaac Bickerstaff* (Lewisburg, Pa.: Bucknell Unversity Press, 1971).

68. *The Recantation and Confession of Doctor Kenrick LL.D* (London: printed for Gallen, 1772), p. 9.

69. Ms. papers (c. 1814), quoted in Crompton, *Byron and Greek Love,* p. 46.

70. See Crompton, *Byron and Greek Love,* pp. 118–119 and passim. Beckford's estate of Fonthill previously had belonged to the Earl of Castlehaven, who was executed for sodomy in the seventeenth century; the boy he was accused of abusing, William Courtenay, became an "inveterate homosexual" and never married (H. Montgomery Hyde, *The Love that Dared not Speak its Name: A Candid History of Homosexuality in Britain* [Boston: Little Brown, 1970], pp. 72–75). Beckford married in 1783, which union produced two daughters before his wife's death in 1786. See also Haggerty, *Men in Love,* chap. 5: "Beckford's Paederasty," pp. 136–151.

71. 27 June 1786: *Thraliana: The Diary of Mrs. Hester Lynch Thrale, 1776–1809,* ed. Katharine C. Balderston, 2nd ed. (Oxford: Clarendon Press, 1951), vol. 2, p. 640, as quoted in Crompton, *Byron and Greek Love,* p. 56.

72. Crompton, *Byron and Greek Love,* pp. 52ff.

73. *The True-Born Englishman,* in Walter Scott, ed., *The Novels and Miscellaneous Works of Daniel De Foe* (Oxford: Thomas Tegg, 1841), vol. 20, p. 12, as quoted in Crompton, *Byron and Greek Love,* p. 54.

74. London: A. Dodd and E. Nutt, c. 1730, p. 12.

75. The conviction and execution of the Earl of Castlehaven are discussed in Hyde, *The Love that Dared not Speak,* pp. 44–57; for a seventeenth-century publication, see Anon., *The Tryal and Condemnation of Mervin, Lord Audley Earl of Castle-Haven* (1699), in *Sodomy Trials.* See also on Castlehaven, David F. Greenberg, *The Construction of Homosexuality* (Chicago: University of Chicago Press, 1988), p. 324, and Tim Hitchcock, *English Sexualities 1700–1800* (London: Macmillan Press, 1997), pp. 15 and 66. See Bray, "Homosexuality and the Signs of Male Friendship," for an analysis of the political use of sodomy accusations in the seventeenth century.

76. Bray, *Homosexuality,* pp. 66, 69–70.

77. Louis Crompton, "Gay Genocide: From Leviticus to Hitler," in Louie Crew, ed., *The Gay Academic* (Palm Springs, Calif.: ETC Publications, 1978), pp. 67–91, provides details of this pogrom in Holland; see also the Epilogue.

78. *Plain Reasons for the Growth of Sodomy,* p. 18.

79. This pamphlet is discussed and transcribed in William C. Smith, "'Do you know what you are about?' A Rare Handelian Pamphlet," *MR,* 25 (1964): 114–119.

80. Autograph letters of Mrs. Delany, Newport Public Library, vol. 2, fol. 105; this and other passages concerning the sexual mores of the times were omitted from Lady Llanover (Augusta Hall), ed., *The Autobiography and Correspondence of Mary Granville,*

Mrs. Delany . . . (London: Richard Bentley, 1861), series 1, vols. 1–3; (London: Richard Bentley, 1862), series 2, vols. 1–3; the six Llanover volumes are continuous and are referred to here as 1–6, as they are in the index in vol. 6.

81. Mrs. Delany's description of Lord Bateman as an active homosexual is confirmed by other contemporary sources; see, for example, *The Yale Edition of Horace Walpole's Correspondence,* ed. W. S. Lewis (New Haven: Yale University Press, 1961), pp. xxx, 307–310, where the line "Another Bateman shall debauch the boys" occurs in the bawdy poem "Little Peggy." See also [Richard] Romney Sedgwick, *House of Commons 1715–1754* (London: His Majesty's Stationery Office, 1970), vol. 1, p. 444, wherein it is clearly stated: "Towards the end of 1738 Bateman was separated from his wife for homosexual practices."

82. I am assuming here that Mrs. Delany is actually referring to a Bishop; one of her code names is "Cardinal," but I have found no evidence that Bishop was used in this way (and the more modern use of Bishop to mean penis is irrevelant here).

83. Llanover, vol. 2, p. 453; that Lady Llanover includes this paragraph implies she did not understand it. The play and the character of Fribble are discussed by Senelick, "Mollies or Men of Mode."

84. The issue of "essentialism" has been eloquently discussed by Diana Fuss, *Essentially Speaking: Feminism, Nature and Difference* (New York: Routledge, 1989).

85. Lang, *Handel,* p. 682.

86. From *Common Sense,* as quoted in Keates, *Handel,* p. 268.

87. See Ruth A. Solie, "Introduction: On Difference," in *Musicology and Difference,* pp. 1–22, which provides an excellent introduction to essentialism and other interpretive quandaries.

88. See Maynard Solomon, "Franz Schubert and the Peacocks of Benvenuto Cellini," *19cM,* 12 (1989): 193–206; and among a host of responses see the collection of essays entitled *Schubert: Music, Sexuality, Culture,* ed. Lawrence Kramer, *19cM,* 17/1 (1993).

89. See Philip Brett, "Britten's Dream," in *Musicology and Difference,* pp. 259–280, which begins with the question: "How can a minor third be gay?" See also Susan McClary, "Constructions of Subjectivity in Schubert's Music," in *Queering the Pitch,* pp. 205–233; an example of the controversy surrounding the reading of homosexuality into Schubert's music can be found in Cori Ellison, "A Woman's Work Well Done" [an article on Amy Beach and whether there is such a thing as "women's music"], in *The New York Times,* 7 May 1995, sec. 2, p. 29.

90. See, for example, Marc A. Weiner, *Richard Wagner and the Anti-Semitic Imagination* (Lincoln: University of Nebraska Press, 1995), especially pp. 390–391 ("Afterword," n. 1) for a discussion of the ban on Wagner's music in Israel.

91. See Michael Baxandall, *Patterns of Intention* (New Haven: Yale University Press, 1985); see also the original statement of the "intentional fallacy" in W. K. Wimsatt, Jr., and Monroe C. Beardsley, "The Intentional Fallacy," *Sewanee Review* (1946): 468–488. The question of the composer's emotion begs the question of whether music can be sad or happy in itself. For a discussion of this point see, for example, Peter Kivy, *The Corded Shell: Reflections on Musical Expression* (Princeton: Princeton University Press, 1980), and

Leonard Meyer, *Emotion and Meaning in Music* (Chicago: University of Chicago Press, 1956).

92. Wolfgang Hildesheimer, *Mozart,* trans. Marion Faber (New York: Vintage Books, 1983), p. 191.

93. On the role of the author, see Michael Foucault, "What Is an Author?" in *Textual Strategies: Perspectives in Post-Structuralist Criticism,* ed. Josué V. Harari (Ithaca, N.Y.: Cornell University Press, 1979), pp. 141–160. On listener theory, see Stanley Fish, *Is There a Text in This Class? The Authority of Interpretive Communities* (Cambridge, Mass.: Harvard University Press, 1980). On changing meanings over time and listener theory, see Marcia Citron, *Gender and the Musical Canon* (Cambridge: Cambridge University Press, 1993), especially chap. 5: "Reception"; see also the bibliography she lists in n. 2, p. 266.

94. For an elegant and informed discussion of psychoanalytic approaches to music, see Stuart Feder, "'Promissory Notes': Method in Music and Applied Psychoanalysis," in Stuart Feder, Richard L. Karmel, and George H. Pollack, eds., *Psychoanalytic Explorations in Music,* Second Series (Madison: International Universities Press, 1993), pp. 3–20.

95. For example, the discovery that Leoš Janáček wrote a program for his mammoth *Glagolitic Mass* associating its composition with his extramarital love for Kamila Stosslova does not determine the meaning of the mass. See Leoš Janáček, *Intimate Letters, Leoš Janáček to Kamila Stosslova,* ed. and trans. John Tyrrell (Princeton: Princeton University Press, 1994).

96. Dent, *Handel,* p. 100, as quoted in John H. Roberts, "Why Did Handel Borrow?" in *Tercentenary Collection,* p. 85.

97. Burrows, *Handel,* p. 9.

98. The work of Stuart Feder on Ives and Mahler and that of Maynard Solomon on Mozart and Beethoven offer models of psychoanalytic biography in music.

99. Shakespeare's Sonnet 116, "Let me not to the marriage of true minds," is one of a large group written to an unnamed young man. The loves of David and Jonathan may be found in 2 Samuel 1.26.

100. Smith, *Oratorios.*

101. Ibid., p. 39.

102. Donald Burrows, "Handel: His Life and Work," in *Celebration,* p. 9.

103. See, for example, Deutsch, *Handel,* pp. 114, 115, and 250.

104. Lang, *Handel,* p. 679.

1. Code Names and Assumed Identities

1. Because a bill for a copy of this cantata appears in the account books of the Marquis Ruspoli for 9 August 1708, Kirkendale, "Ruspoli," p. 241, assumes the cantata was composed in 1708, but recent research has shown the greater likelihood of a 1707 date during Handel's first Roman visit; see Donald Burrows, ed., *G. F. Handel: Songs and Cantatas* (Oxford: Oxford University Press, 1988), p. x, and Keiichiro Watanabe, "The Music-Paper used by Handel and his Copyists in Italy 1706–1710," in *Handel Col-*

lections, p. 203, where the work is placed in a group from early autumn 1707 on the basis of handwriting. Further, this date connects the cantata with a group of works from 1707 composed by Handel to texts by Pamphili; see Appendix 1 for evidence and arguments underlying the chronological placement of this and other cantatas throughout this book. Carlo Vitali, "Italy—political, religious and musical contexts," in *Cambridge Companion,* p. 42, continues to give the date 1708, but this date lacks support and seems unlikely.

2. Mainwaring, *Memoirs,* pp. 62–64.

3. Winton Dean, "Charles Jennens's Marginalia to Mainwaring's Life of Handel," *ML,* 53 (1972): 164.

4. Kirkendale, "Ruspoli," p. 241.

5. Mayo, "Italian Cantatas," p. 41.

6. Burrows, ed., *Songs and Cantatas,* p. x.

7. See Chapter 5 for a discussion of rests as a form of musical word-painting.

8. *Cambridge Companion,* in the section "Handel's Works," erroneously lists *Del bel idolo mio* as a cantata for bass, p. 335; like most of the cantatas, it is written for soprano (autograph: British Library RM20.d.12, fols. 40r–42v).

9. See Nino Pirrotta, *Li due Orfei: da Poliziano a Monteverdi* (Turin: ERI, 1969; reprinted 1975; trans. Karen Eales, *Music and Theatre from Poliziano to Monteverdi* [Cambridge: Cambridge University Press, 1982]).

10. *The Birth of Opera* (Oxford: Clarendon Press, 1993), p. 2.

11. Myth and history locate the power of music not just in Orpheus, but also in Apollo and the musician Timotheus of the court of Alexander the Great. John Dryden's *Alexander's Feast,* subtitled "The Power of Music," depicts Timotheus; it was set by Handel in 1736.

12. Facsimile in Harris, *Librettos,* vol. 2, p. 9; Joseph Addison took up this claim in *The Spectator* (6 March 1711): see Deutsch, *Handel,* pp. 35–36.

13. Deutsch, *Handel,* pp. 158–159.

14. Prévost, *Le pour et contre* (Paris, [June?] 1735): see Deutsch, *Handel,* p. 390.

15. Mr. Blythe, *London Magazine* (April 1738): see Deutsch, *Handel,* p. 458.

16. See the poems attributed to John Lockman in *London Magazine* (May 1738): reprinted in Deutsch, *Handel,* pp. 462–463. For an explanation of Lockman's role as a publicist for Vauxhall see David Bindman, "Roubiliac's statue of Handel and the keeping of order in Vauxhall Gardens in the early eighteenth century," *SJ,* 1 (1997): 22–31. Jacob Simon, *Celebration,* pp. 39–40, states that the statue represents Timotheus or Apollo despite contemporary popular belief that it was Orpheus, but Bindman illustrates that, despite a modern tendency to associate the statue with Apollo, a contextual examination proves it to be of Orpheus. See also Malcolm Baker, "Tyer, Roubiliac and a sculpture's fame: a poem about the commissioning of the Handel statue at Vauxhall," *SJ,* 2 (1998): 41–45.

17. See *Celebration,* p. 171, for a description. The quotation comes from Horace, *Odes,* bk. I, no. 24, in which Horace urges Virgil not to be overcome with grief over the death of a friend. In context, the phrase *blandius Orpheo* comes as part of a question alluding to Orpheus's failure: "Even if you should sing more enchantingly than Orpheus,

would the dead return to life?" The comparative *blandius* derives from *blandus,* meaning "flattering, fondling, caressing." I am very grateful to Professor Richard Tarrant for his help with this translation.

18. See, for example, Deutsch, *Handel,* pp. 511 and 727.

19. Thus Horace (*De Arte Poetica*), Thomas Aquinas (*In Aristotelis librum De anima commentarium*), and Dante (*Convivio*). See Don Harrán, "Orpheus as Poet, Musician and Educator," in Richard Charteris, ed., *Essays on Italian Music in the Cinquecento* (Sydney: Frederick May Foundation for Italian Studies, 1990), p. 269.

20. See, for example, Robert A. Skeris, *"Chroma theou": On the Origins and Theological Interpretation of the Musical Imagery Used by the Ecclesiastical Writers of the First Three Centuries, with Special Reference to the Image of Orpheus* (Altotting: Coppenrath, 1976).

21. On Orpheus as a failure, see Emmet Robbins, "Famous Orpheus," and W. S. Anderson, "The Orpheus of Virgil and Ovid," in John Warden, ed., *Orpheus: The Metamorphoses of a Myth* (Toronto: University of Toronto Press, 1982). Robbins discusses especially Plato's *Symposium,* where Orpheus is found "reprehensible as being insufficiently heroic" (p. 17); Anderson identifies Virgil's view of Orpheus as guilty though pathetic (p. 48).

22. John Block Friedman, *Orpheus in the Middle Ages* (Cambridge, Mass.: Harvard University Press, 1970), pp. 8–9. The Phanocles fragments are published in Neil Hopkinson, *A Hellenistic Anthology* (Cambridge: Cambridge University Press, 1988), pp. 45–46, with commentary, pp. 177–181. Phanocles reports that Orpheus's death was the specific result of his love for Calais, a fellow-Argonaut.

23. Orpheus's homosexuality has rarely been discussed in musicological writings. Two exceptions are Ellen Rosand, "L'Ovidio trasformato," in Aurelio Aureli and Antonio Sartorio, *L'Orfeo,* ed. Ellen Rosand, Drammaturgia musicale Veneta 6 (Milan: Ricordi, 1983), who acknowledges it, and Sternfeld, *The Birth of Opera,* pp. 18–21.

24. Robbins, "Famous Orpheus," p. 44 (Ovid, bk. 10, l. 83).

25. Ibid., p. 14.

26. W. K. C. Guthrie, *Orpheus and Greek Religion: A Study of the Orphic Movement* (London: Methuen, 1935), p. 33. See *Lexicon Iconographicum Mythologiae Classicae (LIMC)* (Zurich and Munich: Artemis Verlag, 1994), vol. 7, no.1, pp. 81–105, for a listing and description of vases depicting Orpheus; see pp. 84–88 for images related specifically to the death of Orpheus. Many of the vases with Orpheus imagery are pictured in *LIMC,* vol. 7, no. 2, pp. 57–77, the death of Orpheus especially, pp. 57–65.

27. Angelo Poliziano, *L'Orfeo* (Venice, 1776), ed. Ireneo Affò, trans. Louis E. Lord (London: Oxford University Press, 1931; reprinted Westport, Conn.: Greenwood Press, 1986), p. 100.

28. *Shakespeare's Ovid: Being Arthur Golding's Translation of the Metamorphoses,* ed. W. H. D. Rouse (Carbondale: Southern Illinois University Press, 1961), p. 202; Samuel Johnson defines "stewes" as brothels; *Dictionary of the English Language . . .* (London: Thomas Tegg, 1831 [originally 1755]), vol. 2, p. 741.

29. *Ovid's Metamorphoses in Fifteen Books. Translated by the most Eminent Hands* (London: printed for Jacob Tonson, 1717), p. 335. For the history of this edition, see the Preface to Ovid, *Metamorphoses,* trans. Watts; Watts's translation of the same passage

adds the word "perverse" to Ovid's text, a liberty not taken by Golding: "'Twas he that first in Thrace the example showed / Of love perverse on budding youths bestowed."

30. [William Kenrick], *Love in the Suds; A Town Eclogue* . . . (London: printed for J. Wheble, 1772), pp. 5–6: "Lest female Bacchanals, when flush'd with wine, / Serve thee, like Orpheus, for thy song divine; / . . . / On Hebrus' banks so tuneful Orpheus died; / His limbs the fields receiv'd, his head the tide. / . . . / Oh, horrour, horrour! NYKY back return; / Nor more for grenadiers imprudent burn." NYKY is Kenrick's pseudonym for Bickerstaff.

31. The quotation continues: ". . . the inconceivable appetite which dishonoured the Greeks and Persians of antiquity, [which] constitute[s] the delight, or, to use a juster term, the infamy of the Egyptians. It is not for the women that their amorous ditties are composed: it is not on them that tender caresses are lavished; far different objects inflame them." Charles Nicolas Sonnini, *Travels in Upper and Lower Egypt,* trans. Henry Hunter (London: printed for J. Stockdale, 1799), vol. 1, p. 251–252, cited in Crompton, *Byron and Greek Love,* pp. 117–118.

32. "Critique on Lord Byron's 'Romaunt of Childe Harold's Pilgrimage,'" *La Belle Assemblée,* 2nd series, 6 (supplement for 1812), p. 349, cited in Crompton, *Byron and Greek Love,* p. 194.

33. Curtis Price, "English Traditions in Handel's *Rinaldo,*" in *Tercentenary Collection,* p. 128: "The Orpheus of Flether, Settle, Davenant and D'Urfey is mad, musically deficient and probably homosexual."

34. Mainwaring, *Memoirs,* p. 14.

35. Johann Mattheson, *Georg Friedrich Händel Lebensbeschreibung* (Leipzig: Deutscher Verlag für Musik, VEB, 1978), p. 128, n. 8; Burrows, *Handel,* pp. 11–12; John Butt, "Germany—education and apprenticeship," in *Cambridge Companion,* p. 21, infers from Mainwaring's account that there were probably two visits to Berlin, one in 1698 and one in 1702.

36. Mainwaring, *Memoirs,* pp. 23–24, 26–27.

37. Mattheson, *Grundlage,* p. 93, as translated in Burrows, *Handel,* p. 17.

38. Mainwaring, *Memoirs,* p. 29.

39. Mattheson, *Grundlage,* pp. 93–94, as translated in Burrows, *Handel,* p. 17.

40. Mattheson, *Lebensbeschreibung,* p. 56; in *Grundlage* he gives July 9.

41. Mattheson, *Grundlage,* p. 93n.

42. Ibid., p. 28, as translated in Hogwood, *Handel,* p. 23.

43. Johann Mattheson, *Critica Musica* (Hamburg: Auf Unkosten des Autoris, 1722; Amsterdam: F.A.M. Knuf, 1964), vol. I, p. 243, as quoted (without reference) in Hogwood, *Handel,* p. 24; see also Burrows, *Handel,* p. 19.

44. Mattheson, *Grundlage,* p. 93, as quoted and translated in Burrows, *Handel,* p. 17; Hogwood, *Handel,* p. 23.

45. Friedrich Chrysander, ed., *G. F. Händels Werke,* vol. 38 [Latin Church Music], places the work in Halle, and Mary Ann Parker-Hale agrees ("Die frühe Fassung von Händels *Laudate pueri:* Fragen der stilistischen und chronologischen Einordnung," *HJb,* 30 [1984]: 11–19). Burrows rejects Halle and considers Hamburg the likely provenance, but also allows for the possibility of an early Italian identification (*Handel,* p. 42). Werner Braun chooses Hamburg ("Echtheit und Datierungsfragen im vokalen

Frühwerk Georg Friedrich Händels," in *Händel-Ehrung der Deutschen Demokratischen Republik 1959* [Leipzig: VEB Deutscher Verlag für Musik, 1961], pp. 61–71). Other commentators include Anthony Hicks, who discusses this work as pre-Italian in the context of Handel's early musical style ("Handel's Early Musical Development," *PRMA*, 103 [1976–1977]: 80–90), and Bernd Baselt, who suggests it may have been written in Italy ("Händels frühe Kirchenmusik," in *Konferenzbericht Halle (Saale) 1981*, pp. 21–33).

46. Mainwaring, *Memoirs*, p. 39.

47. On Prince Ferdinand's musicianship, see Mario Fabbri, *Alessandro Scarlatti e il Principe Ferdinando de' Medici* (Florence: L. S. Olschski, 1961), chap. 1, "Ferdinando de' Medici nella vita musicale fiorentina e toscana del suo tempo," pp. 15–29; Acton, *Medici*, pp. 258–260.

48. See Pierluigi Farrari and Giuliana Gerrari, "Presenza del pianoforte alla corte del granducato di Toscana, 1700–1859: Uno studio documentario, con referimenti alle vicissitudini di clavicembali, spinette e spinettoni. I: Fino al 1799," in *Recercare: Rivista per lo studio e la pratica della musica antica*, 7 (1995): 163–211.

49. Fabbri, *Alessandro Scarlatti*, p. 21; Weaver/Weaver, *Florentine Theater*, pp. 31–42.

50. Fabbri, *Alessandro Scarlatti*, p. 22, n. 24 and p. 23; Leto Puliti, "Cenni Storici della vita del Serenissimo Ferdinando de' Medici, Granprincipe di Toscana," in *Atti dell' Accademia del R. Instituto Musicale di Firenze* (Florence, 1874), p. 75.

51. Eleanor Selfridge-Field, *The Music of Benedetto and Alessandro Marcello: A Thematic Catalogue with Commentary on the Composers, Repertory, and Sources* (Oxford: Clarendon Press, 1990), p. 433.

52. Mainwaring, *Memoirs*, pp. 39–40.

53. Ibid., p. 39.

54. Carlo Vitali and Antonello Furnari, "Händels Italienreise—neue Dokumente, Hypothesen und Interpretationen," *GHB*, 4 (1991): 60–62; the letter was written by Duke Antonio Maria Salviati, superintendent of the hunt to Prince Ferdinand.

55. Acton, *Medici*, p. 235; see Werner Braun, "Georg Friedrich Händel und Gian Gastone von Toskana," *HJb*, 34 (1988): 109–121, for a detailed examination of the known whereabouts of Handel and Gian Gastone during this period.

56. Eric W. Cochrane, *Florence in the Forgotten Centuries (1527–1800): A History of Florence and the Florentines in the Age of the Grand Dukes* (Chicago: University of Chicago Press, 1973), p. 344; Leibniz's formal appointment was at the court of Hanover, providing an interesting possible link with Handel's later appointment.

57. Burrows flatly states that "Mainwaring incorrectly identifies [the Prince] as Ferdinand de' Medici" (*Handel*, p. 20, n. 20), but as recently as 1997 Vitali privileges Mainwaring's account in which Ferdinand issues Handel's invitation to Italy, and states that "there is no evidence from the Medici archives to support the presence of either [Ferdinand or Gian Gastone] in Hamburg during 1705–6" ("Italy," in *Cambridge Companion*, p. 40 and p. 290, n. 20).

58. Mainwaring, *Memoirs*, p. 41.

59. Ibid., p. 42.

60. Mattheson, *Grundlage*, p. 94, as translated in Deutsch, *Handel*, p. 12; on Keiser, see John H. Roberts, "Keiser and Handel at the Hamburg Opera," *HJb*, 36 (1990): 63–87.

61. Mainwaring, *Memoirs,* p. 49.

62. Acton, *Medici,* p. 239; Braun, "Händel und Gian Gastone," p. 112.

63. John H. Roberts first suggested that Handel might have traveled back and forth between Italy and Hamburg ("A New Handel Aria, or Hamburg Revisited," in *Georg Friedrich Händel—ein Lebensinhalt: Gedenkschrift für Bernd Baselt (1934–1993)* [Kassel: Bärenreiter, 1995], pp. 113–130); he hypothesizes that Handel's peregrinations may be related to Keiser's "comings and goings" from Hamburg. Keiser left Hamburg in 1707, perhaps opening the way for Handel's return in late 1707. Keiser's return to Hamburg later in 1708 may then have blocked further operas from Handel (pp. 127–128). Roberts cites Mattheson's comments, p. 125; see Mattheson, *Grundlage,* p. 95.

64. Acton, *Medici,* pp. 243–245; Christopher Hibbert, *The House of Medici: Its Rise and Fall* (New York: Morrow, 1975), p. 305.

65. Mainwaring, *Handel,* p. 39.

66. These are chronicled in contemporary sources and discussed in most modern scholarship: see especially Hibbert, *Medici;* Cochrane, *Florence in the Forgotten Centuries;* and Acton, *Medici.* A contemporary manuscript on the life of Gian Gastone has been published as *The Last of the Medici,* intro. Norman Douglas, trans. Harold Acton (Florence: privately printed by G. Orioli, 1930); Acton suggests (p. 30) that the author was Luca Ombrosi.

67. Hibbert, *Medici,* p. 301; Gaetano Pieraccini, *La Stirpe de' Medici di Cafaggiolo: Saggio di ricerche sulla trasmissione ereditaria dei caratteri biologici* 2 (Florence: Vallecchi, 1947), p. 725.

68. Hibbert, *Medici,* p. 301; Pieraccini, *La Stirpe de' Medici,* p. 723.

69. A contemporary biography of the princess Violante Beatrice may be found in *Vita di tre principesse di Casa Medici* (1887 fac. ed., Bologna: Forni, 1967), which is thought also to be by Luca Ombrosi (see note 66).

70. Hibbert, *Medici,* p. 302.

71. Alberto Bruschi has published extensively on Prince Gian Gastone and his circle in works that combine historical fiction with archival documentation: *Gian Gastone: un trono di solitudine nella caligine di un crepuscolo* (Florence: SP/44 Editore, 1995); *Anna Maria Francesca: una principessa boema, una Fiorentina mancata* (Florence: SP/44 Editore, 1995); *Giuliano Dami: aiutante di camera del granduca Gian Gastone de' Medici* (Florence: Opus libri, 1997). Bruschi has also published the funeral orations for Gian Gastone given by Dami and others: *Delle orazioni in morte di S. A. R. Gian Gastone de' Medici, VII granduca di Toscana e delle lodi in vita di Giuliano Dami e compagni: un manoscritto inedito della metà del XVIII secolo* (Florence: A. Falciani, 1997).

72. Acton, *Medici,* p. 245.

73. [Ombrosi], *The Last of the Medici,* lists 371 *ruspanti* by name, pp. 139–159; the list is provided in facsimile in Bruschi, *Giuliano Dami* [taking 26 pages following fig. 71].

74. Hibbert, *Medici,* p. 299.

75. Ibid., pp. 299–300, 304; see *Vita di tre principesse di Casa Medici* for biographies of princess Violante Beatrice, wife of Prince Ferdinand, and princess Eleonora, wife of Francesco Maria.

76. Isabel V. Hull writes, "Cities, such as Hamburg, heavily involved in overseas trade, with transient populations of noncitizens, might simply take perceived sexual license for granted, so long as it was confined to certain areas of the city" (*Sexuality, State, and Civil Society in Germany, 1700–1815* [Ithaca: Cornell University Press, 1996], p. 129, n. 88). For a collection of articles on homosexuality in eighteenth-century Europe, see *Pursuit of Sodomy;* for an overview of the period, see also James M. Saslow, *Pictures and Passions: A History of Homosexuality in the Visual Arts* (New York: Penguin Group, 1999), chap. 3 ("From Renaissance to Reform: Europe and the Globe, 1400–1700") and chap. 5 ("From Winckelmann to Wilde: The Birth of Modernity, 1700–1900").

77. Suetonius, *The Twelve Caesars,* trans. Robert Graves (Baltimore: Penguin Books, 1957), p. 219. Each of these topics relates directly to Nero's life by depicting illicit sex or the murder of a mother or wife. Canace, daughter of the god of the winds, Aeolus, fell in love with her brother and bore his child. Orestes, avenging his mother's sexual license and murder of his father, was, like Nero, a matricide. Oedipus blinded himself after learning he that had committed incest with his mother. Hercules (*Hercules Furens*) is driven mad and murders his wife Megara and their children. I am most grateful to Professor Richard Tarrant for clarifying which story about Hercules was meant by this title.

78. John Dennis, *Essay upon Publick Spirit (1711),* as quoted in Thomas McGeary, "Gendering Opera: Italian opera as the feminine other in Britain 1700–42," *JMR,* 14/1–2 (1994): 24.

79. Wendy Heller has discussed Nero's homosexuality as a subtext of Monteverdi's *L'incoronazione di Poppea,* analyzing the duet between Nero and Lucano (the poet Lucan), "Hor che Seneca è morto," as a musical depiction of a homoerotic sexual release ("Tacitus Incognito: Opera as History in *L'incoronazione di Poppea,*" *JAMS,* 52 [1999]: 39–96). The music for Handel's *Nero* is lost.

80. Dean/Knapp, *Operas,* pp. 68–69.

81. Acton, *Medici,* p. 213.

82. In the autumn of 1708 in Florence, Gian Gastone could have heard yet a third "Nero" opera, Matteo Noris's *Nerone fatto Cesare* set to music by Giacomo Perti (Vitali/Furnari, "Händels Italienreise," p. 52, n. 29).

83. Harris Sheridan Saunders, "Handel's *Agrippina:* The Venetian Perspective," *GHB,* 3 (1987): 89; Reinhard Strohm, "Händel in Italia: Nuovi contributi," *RIM,* 9 (1974): 168–169.

84. Saunders, "Handel's *Agrippina,*" p. 90.

85. Vitali/Furnari, "Händels Italienreise," p. 52, n. 30, point out that compared to other "Agrippina" operas of the period, Handel's "appears the least politically engaged," being rather a "cynical *divertissement* on the superficiality of the theatrical pseudo-Rome." For the alterations to *Agrippina* in 1713, see Dean/Knapp, *Operas,* p. 134. I am grateful to Ellen Rosand for taking the time to examine the 1713 libretto in the New York Public Library and answer my questions.

86. Deutsch, *Handel,* pp. 19–20.

87. The original title of this work is *Vincer se stessa è la maggior vittoria;* in later years (as in Mainwaring) it is referred to as *Rodrigo,* as it will be here as well. For the dis-

covery of the date and place of performance of this opera see Strohm, "Händel in Italia," pp. 156–160, and Weaver/Weaver, *Florentine Theater*, p. 210.

88. Montalto, *Pamphilj*, p. 332. For the sharing of musicians between Ferdinand and Pamphili, see Weaver/Weaver, *Florentine Theater*, p. 65. For the relationship between Ferdinand and his uncle, see Weaver/Weaver, *Florentine Theater*, p. 31.

89. See Flavia Matitti, "Il cardinale Pietro Ottoboni mecenate delle arti. Cronache e documenti (1689–1740)," *SdA*, 84 (1995): 156–243, which offers a documentary biography of Ottoboni; for her discussion of Ottoboni's Florence trip, see p. 159. The position of Protector of France brought disgrace to the Ottoboni family in Venice, which city supported the Austrian claims in the War of Spanish Succession (Edward Olszewski, "Cardinal Pietro Ottoboni (1667–1740) in America," *JHC*, 1 [1989]: 38).

90. For the most recent discussion of Ottoboni's musical patronage, see Stefano La Via, "Il Cardinale Ottoboni e la Musica: Nuovi Documenti (1700–1740), nuove letture e ipotesi," in Albert Dunning, ed., *Intorno a Locatelli* (Lucca: Libreria musicale italiana, 1995), pp. 319–526.

91. Matitti, "Il cardinale Pietro Ottoboni," no. 559, p. 239. Also partially quoted and translated in Gary C. Thomas, "Was George Frideric Handel Gay?" in *Queering the Pitch*, p. 176.

92. Large extracts from these letters are published in Pier Giovanni Baroni, *Un conformista del secolo diciottesimo: Il Cardinale Pietro Ottoboni* (Bologna: Ponte nuovo, 1969).

93. Valesio diary (9 January 1701), reprinted in Matitti, "Il cardinale Pietro Ottoboni," no. 159, p. 201.

94. See Michael M. Ranft, "Petrus Ottoboni," in *Merkwürdige Lebensgeschichte aller Cardinale der Rom. Cathol. Kirche. . . .* (Regensburg: Johann Leopold Montag, 1769), vol. 2, pp. 268–281; p. 271: "Hierbey war er auch dem Frauenzimmer nicht abgeneigt, wie er denn seine Beyschläfferinnen sogar als Heilige soll haben abmahlen und in sein Schlafzimmer setzen lassen."

95. Valesio diary (8 April 1706), in Mattiti, "Il cardinale Pietro Ottoboni," no. 254, p. 210.

96. Mattiti, "Il cardinale Pietro Ottoboni," p. 166, n. 46.

97. Olszewski, "Ottoboni in America," p. 33.

98. Ranft, "Ottoboni," p. 281: "Er liebte Pracht, Verschwendung und Wollüste, war aber dabey leutseelig, dienstfertig und gutthätig."

99. See Montalto, *Pamphilj*, pp. 309–339, "L'orchestra di palazzo"; Hans Joachim Marx, "Die 'Giustificazioni della Casa Pamphilj' als Musikgeschichtliche Quelle," *SM*, 12 (1983): 121–187; Marx, "Händel in Rom."

100. Montalto, *Pamphilj*, p. 325.

101. Deutsch, *Handel*, p. 19.

102. Ursula Kirkendale, "Orgelspiel im Lateran und andere Erinnerungen an Händel: Ein unbeachteter Bericht in 'Voiage historique' von 1737," *Mf*, 41 (1988): 2; see also Montalto, *Pamphilj*, pp. 433–450, "La Colomba Pamphilj della Basilica Lateranense fra il 1699 e il 1730."

103. Kirkendale, "Orgelspiel im Lateran," pp. 1–9, offers the most detailed discus-

sion of this reference. A description of Handel in Rome (published in 1737), including a performance at St. John Lateran, is given here in full transcription; it may also be found in Werner Braun, "Händel und der 'römische Zauberhut' (1707)," *GHB*, 3 (1989): 71–86. It is also worth noting that some years before, during a pilgrimage to Rome, the Grand Duke Cosimo de' Medici had "fulfilled a lifetime's ambition by being appointed a canon of St John in Lateran" (Hibbert, *Medici,* p. 305).

104. Michael M. Ranft, "Bernhardus Pamfili, ein Römer," in *Merkwürdige Lebensgeschichte,* vol. 2, pp. 104–109; p. 109: "Seinem Character nach war er ein sehr gelehrter, staatsklüger und genereuser Herr, der viele gute Eigenschaften hatte, so ihn würdig machten, den Päpstl. Stuhl zu besteigen; was ihn aber daran verhindert, können wir in Ermangelung genauer Nachricht nicht sagen. In der Jugend war er der Eitelkeit sehr ergeben, doch hat er sich, wo möglich, allezeit gehütet, durch ärgerliche Ausschweifungen seinen guten Namen zu verletzen."

105. Armando Marchi, "Obscene Literature in Eighteenth-Century Italy: an Historical and Bibliographical Note," trans. James Coke and David Marsch, in *'Tis Nature's Fault,* pp. 245–246.

106. For a comprehensive discussion of erotic and sexual metaphor in Italian poetry from the fifteenth to seventeenth centuries see Jean Toscan, *Le Carnaval du Langage: Le Lexique Erotique des Poètes de L'Equivoque de Burchiello à Marino: XVe–XVIIe Siècles,* 4 vols. (Lille: Presses Universitaires de Lille, 1981); I am grateful to Christina Fuhrmann for directing me to this extraordinary resource. For discussions of English sexual imagery of the seventeenth century, see Gordon Williams, *A Dictionary of Sexual Language and Imagery in Shakespearean and Stuart Literature* (London: Athlone Press, 1994); and Frankie Rubinstein, *A Dictionary of Shakespeare's Sexual Puns and Their Significance* (Houndmills: Macmillan, 1989).

107. "Stones" has been a metaphor for testicles since at least the twelfth century (Eric Partridge, *A Dictionary of Slang and Unconventional English . . .,* 7th ed. [New York: Macmillan, 1970]). More important, such metaphors can also be documented in erotic Italian baroque poetry. Toscan, *Carnaval du Langage,* identifies "bird" ("uccello" or "ugello"—"augello" being a form of the latter) with the male sexual organ, providing more than forty examples (glossary, p. 1762; discussion and citations, chap. XLII, pp. 1541ff.), and "tree trunk" ("fusto," a synonym for "tronco") as a "métaphore du phallus" (glossary, p. 1699; discussion, pp. 1433–1435).

108. "Voce" is used to mean "penis" by analogy to emission and penetration of sound (see Toscan, *Carnaval du Langage,* glossary, p. 1768). Toscan associates the verb "to sing" ("cantare") specifically with sodomy (*Carnaval du Langage,* glossary, p. 1674).

109. *Il trionfo del tempo* was first performed on 14 May 1707.

110. Poliziano, *L'Orfeo,* p. 100. See the full quotation earlier in this chapter.

111. The translation by George Oldmixon in the wordbook of the 1737 version of Handel's *Triumph of Time and Truth,* although more flowery, misses nothing of the original: "A youth with more than Magic Might / The Soul awakens to Delight, / With his harmonious strains. / And as his Bloom inchants the Eye, / The Hearing, by his Harmony, / Its share of Pleasure gains. / His artful Fingers seem to fly, / So well the Sounds his Touch obey, / 'Tis more than Mortal Harmony." I am most grateful to the

Music Library of the University of California at Berkeley for providing me with a copy of the libretto.

112. Dean/Knapp, *Operas,* p. 72.

113. Ibid., pp. 70–71, where Dean and Knapp also point out that the text was roundly criticized by Friedrich Chrysander in the nineteenth century for its "moral laxity."

114. "The Great Gay Composers," in Dennis Sanders, ed., *Gay Source: A Catalogue for Men* (New York: Coward, McCann & Geoghegan, 1977), pp. 83–84.

115. Mattheson, *Grundlage,* p. 93n; see also Burrows, *Handel,* p. 16, and Hogwood, *Handel,* p. 23.

116. Deutsch, *Handel,* pp. 88, 393, and 488.

117. From the preface to Mattheson, *Grundlage,* p. xxiii; Deutsch, *Handel,* p. 502, translates "wortbrüchig" as having "broken faith."

118. Letter from Jennens to Edward Holdsworth, 15 September 1743, as quoted in Donald Burrows, *Handel: Messiah* (Cambridge: Cambridge University Press, 1991), pp. 32–33.

119. Letter from Jennens to Holdsworth, 5 December 1743, as quoted in Burrows, *Messiah,* p. 33.

120. For Jennens's marginal note see Dean, "Jennens's Marginalia," pp. 160–164.

121. For example, manuscripts in the Fitzwilliam Museum (Mu. MS 51) and the British Library (RM 19.e.7) seem to include Handel's archival copies of cantatas for which autographs are now lacking; see Ellen T. Harris, ed., *G. F. Handel: Cantatas for Alto and Continuo* (Oxford: Oxford University Press, 2001), p. iv.

122. Burrows writes only: "The existence of [three English] copies . . . reveals that some copy of the cantata, independent of [the autograph], accompanied Handel to London" (*Songs and Cantatas,* p. 60).

123. Burrows dates the incomplete and flawed copy c. 1720–1725 (*Songs and Cantatas,* p. 60), thus placing it before Jennens's copy; the later Granville copy (c. 1745) may have used the Jennens cantata volume as its copy text (see Harris, ed., *Cantatas for Alto,* p. vii), which would make the Jennens copy the only complete copy made directly from the lost archival source.

124. I am also unaware of Handel borrowing from this cantata in later years, a typical practice with other cantatas.

2. Women's Voices/Men's Voices

1. The solo instrumental cantatas that Handel composed after leaving Italy, *Languia di bocca lusinghiera, Splenda l'alba, Mi palpita il cor,* and *Crudel tiranno Amor,* are discussed later in Chapter 5.

2. Marx, *Kantaten mit Instrumenten* I–III. See Appendix 1 for more details on chronology.

3. Kirkendale, "Ruspoli," p. 229.

4. Marx, "Ottoboniana," p. 73, suggests that Ottoboni himself may have written the text.

5. Not only do these two cantatas seem to be a pair textually, but they have musical links as well. For example, in the third aria of *Notte placida,* the text setting in mm. 4–5 ("placidette, vezzosette, vezzosette") is motivically related to the recorder line of the second aria of *Nel dolce dell'oblio* (compare mm. 16–18). I am indebted for this comparison to an analysis by John McKay, who worked with me on the instrumental cantatas as an undergraduate at MIT.

6. Marx, *Kantaten mit Instrumenten* I, p. xvii, states that "it is not certain that the arietta . . . belongs to the cantata," and places it in the Appendix. Although the autograph of the arietta appears on a single sheet that may or may not be physically related to the body of the cantata autograph, it is strongly connected by paper type, rastrology, tonality, and instrumentation as well as by the Diana myth itself (as acknowledged by Marx, *Kantaten mit Instrumenten* III, p. 142). The arietta is not likely to have ended the cantata, which is its current manuscript position, and may have been at some point added or deleted, but its origin as part of the Diana cantata seems clear.

7. Edward J. Olszewski, "Cardinal Pietro Ottoboni (1667–1740) in America," *JHC,* 1 (1989): 40–42, facsimile and detail of the collar on p. 43; the painting is now in the Minneapolis Institute of Arts.

8. Flavia Mattiti, "Il cardinale Pietro Ottoboni mecenate delle arti. Cronache e documenti (1689–1740)," *SdA,* 84 (1995): 166, n. 46. Other paintings that Ottoboni chose for Adami contain equally significant subtexts: for example, *Cupid and Psyche* by Benedetto Luti (Rome, National Academy of St. Luca) refers to the story in which Cupid's forbidden love of the mortal Psyche is resolved by raising Psyche to immortality, and *Danae* (U.S.A., private collection), where Jupiter disguises himself as a shower of gold to sleep with the mortal Danae. Ottoboni's gifts to Adami and interventions on his behalf similarly brought (his lover) Adami wealth and position.

9. In the multi-voice cantata *Apollo e Dafne,* Apollo similarly "collapses" from aria to recitative when Daphne is transformed into a laurel, but he then concludes the cantata with a complete and elegiac aria. Throughout Handel's works a movement out of aria into recitative indicates a loss of power or control.

10. All translations from *Abdolonymus* ("Figlio d'alte speranza") are by Terence Best in Marx, *Kantaten mit Instrumenten* II, p. xli.

11. There are classical precedents for Ovid's *Heroides.* Earlier Sappho had spoken with her own voice, and Theocritus had given voice to Simaetha, abandoned by Delphis, in his second *Idyll.* Also, Catullus gives voice to Ariadne (see below), and Ovid's contemporary Propertius wrote a single letter of a woman to her absent husband, but Ovid's is the first collection of women's voices. I am grateful to Professors Robert C. Ketterer and Richard Tarrant for a number of these examples.

12. Giovanni Boccaccio, *Concerning Famous Women,* trans. Guido A. Guarino (New Brunswick: Rutgers University Press, 1963); see also Janet L. Smarr, *Boccaccio and Fiammetta: The Narrator as Lover* (Urbana: University of Illinois Press, 1986).

13. Boccaccio, *Concerning Famous Women,* pp. xxxvii–xxxviii. See Heller, "Chastity, Heroism, and Allure," p. 19. I am indebted to Heller's work for her survey of seventeenth-century catalogues of women, her discussion of "women who lament," and for numerous bibliographical references.

14. Heller, "Chastity, Heroism, and Allure," p. 18. See Glenda McLeod, *Virtue and Venom: Catalogs of Women from Antiquity to the Renaissance* (Ann Arbor: University of Michigan Press, 1991), for a discussion of catalogues of women in an earlier period.

15. Pietro Paolo di Ribera, *Le glorie immortali di trionfi et heroiche impresse d'ottocento quarantacinque donne illustre antiche, e moderne dotate di conditioni e scienze segnalate* (Venice: Evangelista Dericlino, 1609); discussed in Heller, "Chastity, Heroism, and Allure," pp. 54–57, where she raises the possibility that Ribera may have been referring to Agrippina's mother, who had the same name.

16. Pallavicino (Venice: Guerigli, 1642); Malipiero (Venice: Surian, 1642); see Heller, "Chastity, Heroism, and Allure," pp. 127, 237, and 435.

17. Heller, "Chastity, Heroism, and Allure," pp. 128 and 150.

18. Francesco Pona, *La galeria delle donne celebri* (Bologna: Cavalieri, 1633); see Heller, "Chastity, Heroism, and Allure," p. 57.

19. Loredano, *De gli scherzi geniali. Parte prima* (Venice: Guergli, 1654); see Heller, "Chastity, Heroism, and Allure," p. 128.

20. As quoted and translated in Heller, "Chastity, Heroism, and Allure," p. 436, where she retains the Italian spelling of Actaeon as Atteone.

21. Catullus, *Carmine* 64, ll. 192–250, see Catullus, *Poems,* ed. Lee, pp. 90–95.

22. Virgil, *Aeneid,* trans. Lewis, bk. 4, ll. 600–602 and 615–621.

23. Heller, "Chastity, Heroism, and Allure," p. 140.

24. As quoted and translated in ibid., p. 140.

25. As quoted and translated in ibid., p. 253.

26. As quoted and translated in ibid., p. 140.

27. David Hurley, "Dejanira and the Physicians: Aspects of Hysteria in Handel's *Hercules,*" *MQ,* 80 (1996): 548–561.

28. Nicholas Robinson, *A New System of the Spleen, Vapours, and Hypochondriack Melancholy* (1729), as quoted in Hurley, "Dejanira and the Physicians," p. 551.

29. *The Works of Thomas Sydenham, M.D.*, trans. from Latin by R. G. Latham (London: Sydenham Society, 1848–1850), vol. 2, p. 85, as quoted in Hurley, "Dejanira and the Physicians," p. 550.

30. As translated by Terence Best in Marx, *Kantaten mit Instrumenten* II, p. xxxiii, with very slight alteration.

31. Ibid., p. xxxv.

32. Ellen Rosand, *Opera in Seventeenth-Century Venice: The Creation of a Genre* (Berkeley: University of California Press, 1991), pp. 363–364.

33. Boyd, "Form and Style in Scarlatti's Chamber Cantatas," *MR,* 25 (1964): 17–26.

34. Josephine Wright, "The Secular Cantatas of Francesco Mancini (1672–1736)" (Ph.D. dissertation, New York University, 1975), pp. 106–107.

35. The revisions have been discussed by Mayo, "Italian Cantatas," chap. 3, "Alternative versions and revisions," pp. 145–194, and "Einige Kantatenrevisionen Händels," *HJb,* 27 (1981): 63–77. *E partirai, mia vita?* is discussed by Mayo in "Italian Cantatas," pp. 151–155.

36. See Mayo, "Italian Cantatas," p. 153.

37. Mancini's cantata is transcribed from manuscript: London, British Library Add. MS 14213.

38. All translations of *Alpestre monte* are by Terence Best in Marx, *Kantaten mit Instrumenten* I, p. xxvii.

39. Marcello's cantata is transcribed from manuscript: Bologna, Civico Museo Bibliografico Musicale MS GG 144, n. 15, fols. 62–65. The final section, "Nell' inferno," is composed in aria style but not in aria form: despite aria-like word repetition and melismatic writing, its structure is without formal repetitive pattern, and the harmony is open-ended (moving from E-flat major to C minor). Curiously, the manuscript lacks the final C minor chord. Eleanor Selfridge-Field writes that "Handel's completely different setting of the same title . . . is textually different after 'Il suol preme' [the second aria]," but an examination of the two cantatas shows the texts to be identical except for a word or two (*The Music of Benedetto and Alessandro Marcello: A Thematic Index with Commentary* [Oxford: Clarendon Press, 1990], p. 140).

40. Wolff, "Die Lucrezia-Kantaten von Benedetto Marcello und Georg Friedrich Händel," *HJb*, 3 (1957): 74–88.

41. The comparison examples of Marcello's and Handel's settings of *Lucrezia* have previously appeared in Wolff, "Die Lucrezia-Kantaten."

42. Wolff, "Die Lucrezia-Kantaten," p. 79.

43. Lipking, *Abandoned Women and Poetic Tradition* (Chicago: University of Chicago Press, 1988), p. xx and p. 128.

44. Roger North as quoted in Ian Spink, *English Song: Dowland to Purcell* (London: B. T. Batsford, 1986), p. 103.

45. Lipking, *Abandoned Women,* p. xviii, writes: "The stereotype is so firmly established, in fact, that an abandoned man may begin to feel his sexual identity waver. Some cultures exclude the possibility of male abandonment."

46. In some, especially musical, versions of the story, Orpheus is allowed to lament. However, as Susan McClary writes in her discussion of Monteverdi's *Orfeo,* the lamenting Orpheus becomes a feminized hero. She notes that the "mistake" of depicting a lamenting man was "rarely repeated" in the history of opera and associates some coolness in the reception of *Orfeo* to this problem (*Feminine Endings: Music, Gender, and Sexuality* [Minneapolis: University of Minnesota Press, 1991], pp. 46–48).

47. Lipking, *Abandoned Women,* pp. 150–151.

48. Pope, *Correspondence,* vol. 1, p. 338. Lipking writes, "Pope hinted to more than one of his female correspondents that she was the cause of his grief" (*Abandoned Women,* p. 151).

49. Pope, *Correspondence,* vol. 2, p. 189.

50. My categorization is indebted to Lipking, *Abandoned Women,* chap. 1: "Ariadne at the Wedding: Abandoned Women and Poetic Tradition," pp. 1–31.

51. Hurley, "Dejanira and the Physicians," pp. 548–561.

52. "Per punir che m'ha ingannata" was added by Handel to *Agrippina* during its Venetian run (Dean/Knapp, *Operas,* p. 129). Handel also uses this aria for two other women with a different text each time but in similar circumstances. Esilena sings it in *Rodrigo* as she decides to cede her husband to his mistress (a wrenching but generous

decision), and Polissena sings it in *Radamisto* after her husband orders her away (and she threatens wrath and vengeance).

53. Kirkendale, "Ruspoli," p. 246.

54. Ibid., p. 246; this broader popularity is clear in the seventeenth-century depictions of Lucrezia mentioned above (published in Bologna and Venice).

55. Mainwaring, *Memoirs,* p. 200; see Appendix 1.

56. Kirkendale rebuts the argument that the Lucrezia cantata is part of a group written in Florence on the basis of the rarity of Lucrezia depictions in the Grand Duchy, but this provenance has to remain a possibility as long as there is no documentary evidence that excludes it ("Ruspoli," pp. 246–247).

57. The sentiment is not rare in Handel's works, and frequently occurs in similar circumstances; examples include Cleopatra (*Giulio Cesare*) after she is taken prisoner by her brother ("Piangerò") and Ariodante (*Ariodante*) after Polinesso has convinced him (falsely) that his beloved Ginevra is untrue ("Scherza infida"). In both these cases, however, the danger passes. Lucrezia and Bajazet are uniquely related in that both are suicides.

58. Handel alters the vocal line where necessary to accommodate the different text; Roger L. Lustig, "An Unusual Handelian Self-Borrowing and Handel's Dramatic Designs" (unpublished typescript).

59. CD liner notes in *George Frideric Handel (1685–1759): Carmelite Vespers (1707)* (EMI Records, CDS 7497492, 1989); see also Graham Dixon, "Handel's music for the Carmelites: A study in liturgy and some observations on performance," *EM,* 15 (1987): 16–29.

60. See Graydon Beeks, "'A Club of Composers': Handel, Pepusch and Arbuthnot at Cannons," in *Tercentenary Collection,* pp. 215–217.

61. Lipking, *Abandoned Women,* p. 25.

3. Pastoral Lovers

1. Reinhard Strohm, "Scarlattiana at Yale," in *Händel e gli Scarlatti,* pp. 113–152. For the discussion of this manuscript, Misc. Ms. 166, see pp. 125–131.

2. Adami's pastoral name was "Caricle Piseo"; see Strohm, "Scarlattiana," pp. 129–130.

3. Strohm, "Scarlattiana," p. 126 and 131; Strohm provides a description of each miniature, none of which, however, is reproduced.

4. The number of continuo cantatas written in Rome is undoubtedly more than the twenty-eight that can be absolutely identified (see Appendix 1).

5. These versions are given by Chrysander as 54a (first version) and 54 (second version), since he believed that 54a was not by Handel. A third version was completed later in London. See Mayo, "Italian Cantatas," pp. 160–164, where he unravels Chrysander's confusion. The Händel-Werke-Verzeichnis correctly identifies the three versions as HWV 160 a, b, and c.

6. See Ellen T. Harris, "Metastasio and Sonata Form," *HJb,* 45 (1999): 19–36, on the expansion of aria form in the eighteenth century.

7. In D Müs HS 1899, f. 83–89; see Rudolf Ewerhart, "Die Händel-Handschriften der Santini-Bibliothek im Münster," *HJb*, 6 (1960): 140.

8. Although I cannot provide a definitive date for the second non-Roman group, I am willing to accept the probability that it contains the last cantatas Handel wrote in Italy. One musical piece of evidence for the date (later than September 1707) and provenance (not Rome) of this group resides in Handel's borrowing of musical material from the aria "La mia piaga" in the 1707 Ruspoli cantata *Ne' tuoi lumi* (22 September 1707) in the aria "Da che per so ho la mia Clori" from *Ah, che pur troppo è vero,* which provides not only a chronological order but also a geographic distinction: Handel rarely borrowed from his own works in cases where both the original and the borrowed version would be heard in the same city in close succession.

9. I am indebted to Elizabeth Connors for this description.

10. Haskell, *Patrons and Painters: A Study in the Relations Between Italian Art and Society in the Age of the Baroque* (London: Chatto & Windus, 1963), pp. 164–165.

11. Petrarch, Poem 87, ll. 1–8, from Petrarch, *Lyric Poems,* ed. Durling, pp. 190–191.

12. Petrarch, Poem 117, ll. 5–11, from ibid., pp. 224–225. There is even an echo of the incipits of specific poems by Petrarch in some of Handel's cantata titles (incipits), such as *Nel dolce tempo, Nella stagion,* and *Occhi miei.* Although these are not sufficiently unusual phrases to permit an absolute identification, Petrarch himself quoted the title of *Nel dolce tempo* in another of his poems (no. 70), and it seems very likely that the resonance in the cantatas was intended as well.

13. On same-sex pastoral poetry see David M. Halperin, *Before Pastoral: Theocritus and the Ancient Tradition of Bucolic Poetry* (New Haven: Yale University Press, 1983).

14. Ovid, *Metamorphoses,* trans. Melville, pp. 29–32.

15. Theocritus, *Poems,* trans. Rist, p. 120.

16. Thucydides, *History of the Peloponnesian War,* bk. 6.53ff., trans. Richard Crawley, ed. Robert B. Strassler (New York: The Free Press, 1996), p. 390.

17. Theocritus. *Poems,* trans. Rist, pp. 203–204; see also W. M. Clarke, "Achilles and Patroclus in Love," *Hermes,* 106 (1978): 381–396, reprinted in Wayne R. Dynes and Stephen Donaldson, eds., *Homosexuality in the Ancient World* (New York: Garland, 1992), pp. 95–110.

18. Virgil, *Aeneid,* trans. Lewis, bk. 9, p. 207.

19. Virgil, *Eclogues,* trans. Alpers, p. 15.

20. Virgil, *Eclogues,* trans. Johnson, p. 58.

21. James M. Saslow, *The Poetry of Michelangelo: An Annotated Translation* (New Haven: Yale University Press, 1991), pp. 48–50.

22. Ibid., p. 50; again Saslow can point to early drafts of a finished poem where the sex of the beloved, originally identified as "signor mio," is finally obscured (if not suppressed) by the use of "tu."

23. Hans Joachim Marx, "Händel in Rom—seine Beziehung zu Benedetto Card. Pamphilj," *HJb,* 29 (1983): 108–109.

24. Kirkendale, "Ruspoli," p. 242–243. Durastante's name during her later career in London was "anglicized" to Margherita Durastanti; I have chosen to retain the Italian spelling most common in the Ruspoli accounts.

25. See Ellen T. Harris, ed., *G. F. Handel: Cantatas for Alto and Continuo* (Oxford: Oxford University Press, 2001), p. 159.

26. Translation by Alan Curtis from the liner notes to the complete recording directed by Alan Curtis (1999, Virgin Veritas: CDCB 7243 5 45897 2 0); the aria is lacking in Chrysander's edition.

27. Translation by Mària Steiner in the liner notes to the complete recording directed by Nicholas McGegan (1988, Hungaroton: HCD 12912–12).

28. Translation by Terence Best in Marx, *Kantaten mit Instrumenten* II, p. xl.

29. In regard to Juno's aria in *Semele,* Winton Dean correctly ponders, "Could anything be more pointed than the group of four derisive semiquavers on the first beat of each bar?" (*Oratorios,* p. 389). However, by comparing the *Semele* version only to the earlier (1710) aria also sung by Juno, Dean overlooks how very different the patterns of sixteenth notes sound in each of the different settings.

30. Theocritus, *Poems,* trans. Rist, p. 203.

31. Lesbia represents Clodia Metelli, wife of Q. Metellus Celer. Juventius has not been identified, but as Kenneth Quinn writes, "We need not doubt that the persons talked about or addressed in the homosexual poems exist: if not all historically identifiable, they are too tightly enmeshed in the known facts of Catullus' life to be fictitious" (*Catullus: An Interpretation* [London: Batsford, 1972], p. 246, from the section entitled "The Homosexual Poems," pp. 242–256). In *Catullus and His World: A Reappraisal* (Cambridge: Cambridge University Press, 1985), T. P. Wiseman offers a fine discussion of how Catullus disguises (and reveals) his contemporaries ("*Falso nomine,*" pp. 130–136).

32. See Petrarch, *Lyric Poems,* ed. Durling, poem 10, pp. 44–45 for the first reference to the Colonna family, and pp. 4–7 for a discussion of the existence and identity of "Laura."

33. Robert Coleman, *Vergil: Eclogues* (Cambridge: Cambridge University Press, 1977), pp. 108–109. For more on the relation of Virgil's poetry and life see, in Charles Martindale, ed., *The Cambridge Companion to Virgil* (Cambridge: Cambridge University Press, 1997), Richard J. Tarrant, "Aspects of Virgil's reception in antiquity," pp. 56–72; Tarrant, "Poetry and power: Virgil's poetry in contemporary context," pp. 169–187; and Ellen Oliensis, "Sons and lovers: sexuality and gender in Virgil's poetry," pp. 294–311. I am indebted to Professor Tarrant for referring me to Donatus and to the work of Coleman on Virgil and Quinn on Catullus, as well as for general assistance and advice.

34. See Aelius Donatus, *Life of Virgil,* trans. David Wilson-Okamura *(www.virgil.org/vitae/a-donatus.htm).*

35. Kirkendale, "Ruspoli," p. 242; see the translation and notes by Terence Best in Marx, *Kantaten mit Instrumenten* II, pp. xlix–xliii. The text of this cantata may be compared to Petrarch's Poem 53 ("Spirto gentil") in which he supports the 1347 attempt to reinstate the Roman Republic and refers to Stefano Colonna the Elder as a "marble column" *(marmorea colonna)* of support (see Petrarch, *Lyric Poems,* ed. Durling, pp. 124–131).

36. Burrows, *Handel,* p. 33, n. 20, based on a copying bill for a new "beginning"

(overture?) of the oratorio by the composer Carlo Cesarini; see Marx, "Händel in Rom," pp. 110–111, 115.

37. Deutsch, *Handel,* p. 23; Kirkendale, "Ruspoli," p. 239.

38. Mattheson, *Grundlage,* p. 95.

39. Kirkendale, "Ruspoli," p. 239.

40. Mainwaring, *Memoirs,* pp. 65–67.

41. Burrows/Ronish (*Catalogue,* p. 267) suggest that the notation on the trio is "probably not" in Handel's hand.

42. Antonello Furnari, "I rapporti tra Händel e i Duchi D'Alvito," in *Händel e gli Scarlatti,* pp. 73–78, and Carlo Vitali and Antonello Furnari, "Händels Italienreise— neue Dokumente, Hypothesen und Interpretationen," *GHB,* 4 (1991): 54. The author of the libretto was Nicola Giuvo, who joined the Arcadian Academy in 1711 with the name Eupidio Siriano. Indeed, there seems to be a strong connection between the Roman Academy and Handel's Neapolitan trip and commission. In 1708 a celebratory collection of poems was published in Rome in honor of the wedding of Tolomeo Gallio and Beatrice [Tocco] Sanseverino, including work by Paolo Rolli, who would later become one of Handel's primary librettists in London. (See Furnari, "I rapporti," and Vitali/Furnari, "Händels Italienreise.")

43. Vitali/Furnari, "Händels Italienreise," pp. 54–55; Donn'Aurora (which when spoken sounds very similar to what an English speaker might hear as "Donna Laura") was the wife of the Duke of Laurenzano. The phonetic mistranscription may be evidence that Mainwaring was taking notes from an oral recounting.

44. Strohm, "Händel in Italia," pp. 152–174; Vitali/Furnari, "Händels Italienreise," pp. 58–59.

45. Handel's setting of this text demonstrates his apparent lack of concern for the political views of his patrons; in the War of Spanish Succession the Duke of Alvito supported the Austrian forces, whereas Ruspoli opposed them. These compositions on both sides of the political issue preview Handel's composition of a Te Deum and Jubilate in London for Queen Anne celebrating the Peace of Utrecht, which ended the War of Spanish Succession; Handel's employer, the Hanoverian Elector, was opposed to this settlement, and, shortly after composing the Te Deum, Handel was fired. See Chapter 5 for further details and references.

46. Dean/Knapp, *Operas,* p. 110.

47. Friedrich Chrysander introduced this interpretation in his biography of Handel (*G. F. Händel* [Leipzig, 1858–1867; reprinted Hildesheim: Breitkopf & Härtel, 1966], vol. 1, p. 231); the subsequent history of this explication of the heading, with its assumption that it was Handel who was departing, is provided by Rita Steblin, "Did Handel meet Bononcini in Rome?" *MR,* 45 (1984): 179–183.

48. This manuscript is preserved in Vienna: A Wn 17750; see Steblin, "Did Handel meet Bononcini?"

49. Bernd Baselt, *HHB,* vol. 2, p. 594; Baselt gives no source for the first name of von Binitz, which does not appear in Mattheson's commentary. Perhaps the parentheses indicate a supposition.

50. Friedrich Chrysander, *Georg Friedrich Händels Werke,* vol. 51, "Preface."

4. Cantata Couples and Love Triangles

1. Marx, *Kantaten mit Instrumenten* I, p. xviii.

2. Haskell, *Patrons and Painters: A Study in the Relations Between Italian Art and Society in the Age of the Baroque* (London: Chatto & Windus, 1963), pp. 164–165; see also Chapter 3 above.

3. The duet in *Poro*, "Cara/Caro," both precedes and forms part of the finale. The duet was also at one point a part of *Agrippina* (1709) as a love duet between Ottone and Poppea.

4. Edward J. Kenney, "Introduction," in Ovid, *Metamorphoses*, trans. Melville, p. xviii.

5. Translation by Terence Best in Marx, *Kantaten mit Instrumenten* II, pp. xxxvi–xxxvii.

6. Claude Lévi-Strauss, "The Structural Study of Myth," in *Structural Anthropology*, trans. Claire Jacobson and Brooke Grundfest Schoepf (New York: Basic Books, 1963), pp. 206–301; see p. 208.

7. Campbell, *The Hero with a Thousand Faces* (Princeton: Princeton University Press, 1949/1973), p. 30; Campbell identifies the source of the word "monomyth" as James Joyce's *Finnegans Wake* (New York: Viking Press, 1939), p. 581.

8. Doniger, *Implied Spider*, pp. 64, 88, and 93.

9. For example, Doniger speaks of multiforms in *Siva, The Erotic Aesthetic* (New York: Oxford University Press, 1981), p. 37; see also Joseph Nagy, "The Sign of the Outlaw: Multiformity in Fenian Narrative," in John M. Foley, ed., *Comparative Research on Oral Traditions: A Memorial for Milman Parry* (Columbus: Slavica Press, 1987), pp. 465–492.

10. Doniger derives her term from Mikhail Bakhtin: "Bakhtin has taught us to recognize competing voices in the novel and different interpretive communities within the same text; we can, with profit, use Bakhtinian concepts of multivocality not only to bring women's voices into texts written by men but also to bring the voices of texts composed in one culture into texts composed in other cultures" (*Implied Spider*, p. 85).

11. *Aci, Galatea e Polifemo* lacks an overture. On the admittedly slim chance that the overture to *Agrippina* (Venice, 1709), previously used in *Donna che in ciel* (Rome, 1707?, 1708?, 1709?), was originally composed for *Aci, Galatea e Polifemo* (Naples, 1708), it is possible that this cantata, too, opens with a chase of sorts. As Anthony Hicks states in the program for the 1985 performance of *Aci, Galatea e Polifemo* at the Eighth London Handel Festival, the *Agrippina* overture was chosen for inclusion in that performance because it is "in a suitable key" and is scored unusually, as is *Aci*, for a single oboe. Although Hicks does not suggest that the *Agrippina* overture originated with *Aci*, this possibility is strengthened by the number of other borrowings from *Aci* into *Agrippina*, and also by the musical content of the overture itself. The rushing upward scales in combination with the shaking repeated-note motive can be found in Polyphemus's arrival aria, "Sibilar l'angui d'Aletto," and the triplet motion with which it alternates could represent not only the pastoral environment but Galatea specifically, as in her aria, "S'agita in mezzo all'onde," which depicts the sea. That is, the overture might

depict Polyphemus chasing the water nymph Galatea back to the sea, leaving the Cyclops alone in the final *adagio*—foreshadowing the events of the cantata itself. A chase is also audible in the *Ouverture* to *Cor fedele.*

12. See Robert M. Durling, "Preface," in Petrarch, *Lyric Poems,* ed. Durling, especially pp. 2 and 27.

13. Theocritus, *Poems,* trans. Rist.

14. Virgil, *Eclogues,* trans. Alpers.

15. Ovid, *Metamorphoses,* trans. Melville, p. 320.

16. See Virgil, *Eclogues,* trans. Alpers, p. 121.

17. Theocritus, *Poems,* trans. Rist, p. 101.

18. The complexity of these multiple maskings is described in detail in Virgil, *Eclogues,* trans. Alpers, p. 124.

19. Ibid., p. 125; see Chapter 3 above for a discussion of the eighteenth-century interpretation of *Eclogue* II as autobiographical.

20. Theocritus, *Poems,* trans. Rist, p. 76.

21. Ibid., p. 77.

22. "Introduction," in Ovid, *Metamorphoses,* trans. Melville, p. xxv.

23. Translations of the libretto of *Aci, Galatea e Polifemo* are by Anthony Hicks in the program of the Eighth London Handel Festival (20–27 April 1985).

24. Vitali and Furnari have shown that the librettist of Handel's *Aci, Galatea e Polifemo* was the Abbate Nicola Giuvo ("Händels Italienreise," pp. 41–66).

25. Handel borrowed this accompanimental idea from Reinhard Keiser's aria "Wallet nicht so laut" from his opera *Octavia* (Hamburg, 1705); see John H. Roberts, "Handel's Borrowings from Keiser," *GHB,* 2 (1986): 68–69, 75.

26. Dean, *Oratorios,* p. 18, compares the formal plan and affect of Clori's "Barbaro, tu non credi" to Dejanira's mad scene in Hercules. Of course, Dejanira kills her husband Hercules.

27. Dean/Knapp, *Operas,* p. 500. Because Handel associated sharp keys with pain, he frequently set arias of political victims in keys of one or two sharps while having their conquerors sing in flat keys (Ellen T. Harris, "Harmonic Patterns in Handel's Operas," in Mary Ann Parker, ed., *Eighteenth-Century Music in Theory and Practice: Essays in Honor of Alfred Mann* [Stuyvesant, N.Y.: Pendragon Press, 1994], pp. 97 and 115). For his seductresses, Handel moves out further to the extremes (keys with three and four sharps).

28. Translations of *Cor fedele* are by Terence Best in Marx, *Kantaten mit Instrumenten* I, pp. xxxviii–xliv.

29. Eve Kosofsky Sedgwick, *Between Men: English Literature and Male Homosocial Desire* (New York: Columbia University Press, 1985).

30. Haggerty, *Men in Love,* p. 35. Lee's play, which was one of the models for Handel's *Alessandro* (1726), depicts the love of Alexander the Great and his "favorite" Hephestion, which influences Alexander's decision to give a woman in marriage to Hephestion rather than to her beloved. The gift of the woman is meant to strengthen the homosocial bond between the two men.

31. Liner notes, *George Frideric Handel: Clori, Tirsi e Fileno,* Nicholas McGegan, conductor (Harmonia Mundi 907045).

32. Marx, *Kantaten mit Instrumenten* I, p. xviii.

33. The personal context for *Il trionfo del tempo* was Pamphili's homoerotic desire for Handel; that of *Agrippina* might have been the association of one of the Medici with Nero. The personal context for *Cor fedele* is unknown.

34. A. Pigler (*Barockthemen: Eine Auswahl von Verzeichnissen zur Ikonographie des 17. und 18. Jahrhunderts* [Budapest: Verlag der Ungarischen Akademie der Wissenschafter, 1956], vol. 2, pp. 117–118) lists 39 examples of this image. In England it was a favorite subject of Anthony Ashley Cooper, third Earl of Shaftesbury, chosen by him as the example by which to illustrate the proper methods of iconography (see Ronald Paulson, *Emblem and Expression: Meaning in English Art of the Eighteenth Century* [Cambridge, Mass.: Harvard University Press, 1975], pp. 38–43) and "constantly replicated, echoed—and parodied—in later works, including those of Hogarth" (Jenny Uglow, *Hogarth: A Life and a Work* [New York: Farrar, Straus and Giroux, 1997], p. 74).

35. The word *l'opre* in the last line literally reads "my works" or "my deeds." As a subtext (for Pamphili the author), *l'opre* could mean "artistic work," as in *opus* or *opera*.

36. Kirkendale, "Ruspoli," p. 240; Ellen T. Harris, *Handel and the Pastoral Tradition* (London: Oxford University Press, 1980), p. 31. See also "L'Accademia d'Arcadia" in Gaetano Compagnino, Guido Nicastro, and Giuseppe Savoca, eds., *Il Settecento: L'Arcadia e l'età della riforme,* in Carlo Muscetta, ed., *La Letteratura Italiana: Storia e Testi* (Laterza: Bari, 1973), vol. 4, no. 1, p. 40.

37. Translation by Terence Best in Marx, *Kantaten mit Instrumenten* I, p. xxxiii (reordered to provide a line-by-line translation).

38. Handel thereafter returned the style to a religious setting by using a variant of this aria in "Die Rosen Krönen" in the *Brockes Passion,* where the Daughter of Zion sings with a mixture of love (for Jesus) and despair (for the crown of thorns on his brow).

39. Handel provides no articulation markings in his autograph. The marking *spizzicato* appears in the Münster copy from the Santini Collection (Ruspoli). Marx (*Kantaten mit Instrumenten* III, p. 124) interprets this to mean, correctly I believe, *pizzicato* and not *spiccato*. I am grateful to Louise K. Stein for looking at this aria in terms of a possible Spanish "heritage" and for referring me to the work of Maurice Esses; she suggests that "Se vago rio" is similar to the "folias ytalianas" of the eighteenth century. Maurice Esses (*Dance and Instrumental Diferencias in Spain during the 17th and early 18th centuries,* 3 vols. [Stuyvesant, N.Y.: Pendragon Press, 1992]) describes the various functions of the *folias,* including a comic spectacle in which "boys dressed as women ride around on the shoulders of men," so that *folias* can refer directly "to the boys in the performance" (vol. 1, pp. 637–638), and stylized aristocratic dance (vol. 1, pp. 646–647). He traces the transfer of Spanish instrumental settings of the *folia* to Italy in the early seventeenth century, citing a strummed guitar book of 1606 as one of the earliest (vol. 1, p. 647). Esses also discusses the importance of flat-7 (and other flatted) chords in the *folia* (vol. 1, pp. 579–580).

40. Campbell, *The Hero,* pp. 60–62.

41. Bernd Baselt, "Wiederentdeckung von Fragmenten aus Händels verschollenen Hamburger Opern," *HJb*, 29 (1983): 7–24; Baselt, *HHB*, vol. 3, pp. 125–126.

42. Translation based on that by Terence Best in Marx, *Kantaten mit Instrumenten II*, p. xlv, rearranged so as to provide a line-by-line translation.

43. The metaphor aria of the moth was so common that it was parodied in *The Beggar's Opera*, when Mrs. Peachum sings of her daughter Polly: "If Love the Virgin's Heart invade, / How like a Moth, the simple Maid / Still plays about the Flame!"

44. Doniger, *Implied Spider*, p. 84.

45. Translation by Samuel Humphreys in the 1732 libretto, in Harris, *Librettos*, vol. 7, p. 49.

5. Silence and Secrecy

1. Mainwaring, *Memoirs*, p. 72.

2. Hawkins, *History*, pp. 790–791.

3. Ibid., p. 806.

4. Ibid., p. 859.

5. It is difficult to place specific works in Hanover other than the chamber duets and a final version of *Apollo e Dafne*. Additional works that may have been composed in Hanover include the continuo cantata *Nice, che fa?*, the English cantata *Venus and Adonis*, and the instrumental "cantata" fragment *Languia di bocca*, which consists only of one recitative-aria pair and may have been intended not as a cantata but as part of an opera.

6. For a discussion of the distinction between Handel's cantatas written in Italy and in England and its use as a chronological tool, see Harris, "Paper, Performing Practice."

7. See Ellen T. Harris, "Harmonic Patterns in Handel's Operas," in Mary Ann Parker, ed., *Eighteenth-Century Music in Theory and Practice: Essays in Honor of Alfred Mann* (Stuyvesant, N.Y.: Pendragon Press, 1994), pp. 77–118. A discarded autograph version of the continuo cantata *L'aure grate* (1718?) illustrates Handel's later practice: he composes the first aria, enters the recitative text into the score without setting it, and begins to write out the second aria. More extensive evidence of this "aria-first" compositional practice can be found in the autograph of *Giulio Cesare*.

8. Handel's operas that relate to earlier Florentine performances are as follows: *Tamerlano* (Alessandro Scarlatti, *Il gran Tamerlano*, 1706), *Sosarme* (Giacomo Antonio Perti, *Dionisio re di Portogallo*, 1707), *Ariodante* (Perti, *Ginevra Principessa di Scozia*, 1708), *Berenice* (Perti, *Berenice Regina di Egitto*, 1709), and *Rodelinda* (Perti, *Rodelinda Regina de' Longobardi*, 1710). The librettos of all of these operas were by Antonio Salvi; however, Handel's *Tamerlano* was actually based on a later libretto on the same subject by Agostin Piovene. There is no evidence that Handel was in Florence in autumn 1710, but he may have had the opportunity to see a score or libretto of *Rodelinda* in Düsseldorf, where the Elector was married to Prince Ferdinand's sister, Anna de' Medici.

9. Burrows, *Handel*, p. 35.

10. Mario Fabbri, *Alessandro Scarlatti e il Principe Ferdinando de' Medici* (Florence: L. S. Olschiski, 1961), p. 24.

11. As Burrows points out, Ferdinand's letter "does not necessarily imply that Handel was then in Florence" (*Handel*, p. 36, n. 27).

12. Reinhard Strohm, "Händel in Italia: Nuovi contributi," *RIM*, 9 (1974): 169, n. 76.

13. Mainwaring, *Memoirs*, p. 52. See also Harris Sheridan Saunders, "Handel's *Agrippina:* the Venetian Perspective," *GHB*, 3 (1987): 87.

14. Burrows, "Hanover," p. 35.

15. As quoted and translated in Burrows, "Hanover," p. 39.

16. Mainwaring, *Memoirs*, pp. 50–51.

17. Ibid., pp. 53–54.

18. Reinhard Strohm, "Handel and his Italian Opera Seria Texts," in *Essays on Handel and Italian Opera* (Cambridge: Cambridge University Press, 1985), p. 278, n. 82; see also Leto Puliti, "Cenni Storici della vita del Serenissimo Ferdinando de' Medici, Gran-principe di Toscana," in *Atti dell' Accademia del R. Istituto Musicale di Firenze* (Florence, 1874), p. 73.

19. Weaver/Weaver, *Florentine Theater*, p. 209.

20. Strohm, "Handel and his Italian Opera Seria Texts," p. 64.

21. Burrows, *Handel*, p. 30, n. 16.

22. This date probably follows the convention by which the new year began on 25 March. Thus the date on the Steffani duets could refer to any period from late 1706 to the end of March 1707, and Handel is known to have arrived in Rome by January 1707.

23. Hawkins, *History*, vol. 2, pp. 857–858; also quoted in Deutsch, *Handel*, p. 28.

24. Through surviving correspondence; see Burrows, "Hanover," p. 38, n. 15.

25. See Colin Timms, "Gregorio Piva and Steffani's Principal Copyist," in Ian Bent, ed., *Source Materials and the Interpretation of Music: A Memorial Volume to Thurston Dart* (London: Stainer & Bell, 1981), pp. 169–170.

26. Carlo Vitali, "Italy—political and musical contexts," in *Cambridge Companion*, p. 43; *HHB*, vol. 4, p. 43.

27. Harris Sheridan Saunders, "Handel's *Agrippina:* the Venetian perspective," *GHB*, 3 (1987): 88 and 94, n. 15.

28. Mainwaring, *Memoirs*, pp. 71–72.

29. Burrows, "Hanover," p. 35, n. 4, reports that "according to Erich Graf von Kielmansegg, *Familien-Chronik* (Vienna, 1910), Kielmansegg offered the kapellmeister-ship [sic] to Handel in Venice in 1710"; however, it is not clear whether this statement offers independent corroboration of Mainwaring's history or in fact derives directly from it.

30. Fabbri, *Alessandro Scarlatti*, p. 26.

31. As part of this service, Steffani spent the period between November 1708 and April 1709 in Rome, where he might have met Handel.

32. Burrows, "Hanover," p. 41.

33. Mainwaring, *Memoirs*, p. 74.

34. Duncan Chisholm ("Handel's 'Lucio Cornelio Silla': its problems and context,"

EM, 14 [1986]: 68) prints a letter from the Hanoverian agent in London to the Elector of 23 May–3 June 1712 forwarding a request from the Duke of Marlborough that Handel be allowed to return to London.

35. Abel Boyer, *The History of the Reign of Queen Anne digested into Annals* (London, 1703–1713), vol. 9, p. 315, as quoted in Burrows, "Hanover," p. 41. Marx suggests that this "dialogue" could have been *Apollo e Dafne* (*Kantaten mit Instrumenten* II, p. xx).

36. Burrows, *Handel*, p. 64.

37. Handel probably taught Wych's son Cyril, who succeeded his father as English resident. It is well to remember that Mattheson himself was on his way to London in 1704 (when Handel urged him to return to Hamburg), and the introductions he must have had with him would probably have come from the Wych family. Burrows suggests that some of Handel's Hamburg music may survive in lute arrangements that passed from the Wych family to Lord Danby (*Handel*, p. 20). See also Tim Crawford, "Lord Danby's Lute Book: A new source of Handel's Hamburg music," *GHB*, 2 (1986): 9–19.

38. Mainwaring, *Memoirs*, p. 84.

39. As quoted and translated in Deutsch, *Handel*, p. 44.

40. Hawkins, *History*, pp. 790–791; Britton died in 1714 (Hawkins, *History*, p. 789).

41. Mainwaring, *Memoirs*, p. 85.

42. Hawkins, *History*, p. 859.

43. Clark, "'Lord Burlington is Here,'" in *Lord Burlington: Architecture*, pp. 251–310. See also in the same volume Howard Colvin, "Introduction," pp. xxiii–xxix. A second volume of essays is devoted entirely to this hypothesis: *Lord Burlington—The Man.*

44. Clark, "'Lord Burlington is Here,'" pp. 274–275, suggests that Jacobitism may have played a role in the "suspension" of the composer Giovanni Bononcini and the librettist Paolo Rolli, both associated with Burlington, from the Academy of Music in 1722 at the time of the Atterbury Plot.

45. "Proper Missionaries: Clergymen in the Household of Lord Burlington during the Period 1715–1753," in *Lord Burlington—The Man*, pp. 91–119.

46. Richard Hewlings, "Chiswick House and Gardens: Appearance and Meaning," in *Lord Burlington: Architecture*, pp. 1–150.

47. Hawkins, *History*, p. 859; italics added.

48. Chisholm, "Handel's 'Lucio Cornelio Silla,'" pp. 64–70; J. Merrill Knapp, "The Libretto of Handel's *Silla*," *ML*, 50 (1969): 68–75; see especially p. 71.

49. Chisholm cites the contemporary historian Abel Boyer as reporting that "the Rabble" greeted the French ambassador in the streets with "a Cry of NO PAPIST, NO PRETENDER" ("Handel's 'Lucio Cornelio Silla," p. 66).

50. Chisholm, "Handel's 'Lucio Cornelio Silla,'" p. 69.

51. See Ragnhild Hatton, *George I: Elector and King* (London: Thames and Hudson, 1978), pp. 60–62 and 134–138.

52. BL add. ms. 47,028, fols. 5v–6r.

53. BL add. ms. 47,028, fol. 7v.

54. Hatton, *George I*, pp. 99–100.

55. Translation of the "Argomento" in the libretto from Chisholm, "Handel's 'Lucio Cornelio Silla,'" pp. 64–65.

56. The phrase is taken from Winton Dean, *Handel and the Opera Seria* (Berkeley: University of California Press, 1969), p. 11.

57. Plutarch, "Sylla," in *The Lives of the Noble Grecians and Romans: The Dryden Translation*, edited and revised by Arthur Hugh Clough [1864] (New York: Random House, 1992) vol. 1, pp. 607–638, especially pp. 608 and 637; see also Robert C. Ketterer, "Senecanism and the 'Sulla' Operas of Handel and Mozart," in Eric Csapo, Robert C. Ketterer, C. W. Marshall, and John Porter, eds., *Crossing the Stages: The Production, Performance and Reception of Ancient Theater: Selected Papers Presented at a Conference held in Saskatoon, Saskatchewan on 22–25 October, 1997*, in *Syllecta Classica*, 10 (1999): 214–233, see especially p. 222.

58. See Clark, "'Lord Burlington is Here,'" p. 293, for an expansion of this idea (in n. 199 she cites an example of this hope as early as 1719).

59. Chisholm, "Handel's 'Lucio Cornelio Silla,'" p. 69.

60. *Amadis of Gaul. An Opera . . .* (London: Jacob Tonson, 1715), p. [v]; facsimile in Harris, *Librettos*, vol. 2, p. 259.

61. Burrows, "Hanover," p. 42–45.

62. Ibid., p. 42.

63. Ibid., p. 44.

64. Ibid.

65. Donald Burrows and Robert D. Hume, "George I, the Haymarket Opera Company and Handel's *Water Music*," *EM*, 19 (1991): 333.

66. Burrows, "Hanover," p. 45.

67. As quoted and translated in Burrows, "Hanover," p. 45.

68. Robert Steensma, *Dr. John Arbuthnot* (Boston: Twayne Publishers, 1979), see especially chap. 3, "*The History of John Bull*," pp. 50–67.

69. Speech to the House of Commons (3 February 1738) in [William Cobbett,] *The Parliamentary History of England, from the earliest period to the year 1803*, vol. 10: 1737–1739 (London: T. C. Hansard, 1812), cols. 400–401, partially quoted by Clark, "Lord Burlington is Here," p. 262.

70. John Harris, *The Palladians* (London: Trefoil Books, 1981), p. 18.

71. Michael I. Wilson, *William Kent: Architect, Designer, Painter, Gardener, 1685–1748* (London: Routledge & Kegan Paul, 1984), p. 37.

72. As Clark writes of Burlington's reputed Jacobitism: "The absence of direct, written proof of Lord Burlington's Jacobitism is a matter of concern to many people. It is possible that some day, somewhere this evidence will surface but those who are familiar with the measures taken by important Jacobites to conceal their identities and their activities will realise that it is naive to expect it. A painstakingly collected accumulation of circumstantial evidence, carefully weighed up, is all that we can hope for to help us understand this mysterious *eminence grise*" ("'His zeal is too furious': Lord Burlington's Agents," in *Lord Burlington—The Man*, p. 181).

73. John Gay, *Trivia, Or, The Art of Walking the Streets of London*, in Vinton A. Dearing, ed., *John Gay, Poetry and Prose* (Oxford: Clarendon Press, 1974), vol. 1, p. 157.

74. (March 1716?) Pope, *Correspondence*, vol. 1, p. 338.

75. (9 July 1716) Pope, *Correspondence*, vol. 1, p. 347.

76. Dearing, ed., *John Gay, Poetry and Prose,* vol. 1, p. 203. The Epistle concerns a "trip to Exeter" in 1716. Although not published until 1720, the poem was circulating by 1717. Gary C. Thomas assumes the "friend" is William Kent, but this cannot be as Kent only arrived in England in 1720 ("Was George Frideric Handel Gay?" in *Queering the Pitch,* p. 178).

77. David Nokes, *John Gay: A Profession of Friendship* (Oxford: Oxford University Press, 1995), pp. 43–44.

78. This is not to say that it was ever typical in early modern Europe to avow homosexual desire, but only that, following a period in the seventeenth century when it had been possible for the aristocracy and some authors to be more open, that window of opportunity was closing. As Joseph Cady points out, "declared 'unmentionableness'" was "a centuries-old code term for homosexuality" ("'Masculine Love,' Renaissance Writing, and the 'New Invention' of Homosexuality," *JH,* 23 [1992]: 14, n. 8).

79. Raymond Bentman, "Thomas Gray and the Poetry of 'Hopeless Love,'" *JHS,* 3 (1992–1993): 212–213.

80. As quoted in Bray, *Homosexuality,* p. 61.

81. *Plain Reasons for the Growth of Sodomy in England* (London: A. Dodd and E. Nutt, c. 1730), p. 23.

82. As quoted in Norton, *Molly House,* p. 107.

83. A cursory survey of English editions published during this period reveals the following publication dates: 1698, 1712, 1724, 1727, 1739, 1752, 1757, 1762, 1766, and 1770. There were, in addition, publications in England of the original Greek and of Latin translations.

84. Longinus, *On the Sublime,* trans. T. S. Dorsch, *Classical Literary Criticism* (Harmondsworth: Penguin Books, 1965), p. 109.

85. Hildebrand Jacob, *Of the Sister Arts; an Essay* (1734), facsimile reproduction in The Augustan Reprint Society, no. 165, Introduction by Niklaus R. Schweizer (Los Angeles: William Andrews Clark Memorial Library, 1974), p. 25.

86. Ronald Paulson, *Emblem and Expression: Meaning in English Art of the Eighteenth Century* (Cambridge, Mass.: Harvard University Press, 1975), p. 51; Paulson also states here that Richardson uses "a white gap on the page" in his earlier novel *Pamela* (1740), but I have not found an early edition that does so.

87. Laurence Sterne, *The Life and Opinions of Tristram Shandy,* ed. Graham Petrie (London: Penguin Books, 1967), vol. 3, p. 192 (chapter 12).

88. See George Winchester Stone, Jr., and George M. Kahrl, *David Garrick: A Critical Biography* (Carbondale, Ill.: Southern Illinois University Press, 1979), pp. 540–548, for contemporary commentary on Garrick's playing of Hamlet.

89. James Boaden, ed., *The Private Correspondence of David Garrick with the Most Celebrated Persons of his Time* (London: H. Colburn and R. Bentley, 1831–1832), vol. 1, p. 109.

90. Ibid., p. 110.

91. Ibid., p. 136.

92. (Saarbrucken: Universität des Saarlandes, 1998); see especially chap. 5, "Silence and Rests in Music," pp. 83–121.

93. Danielewicz-Betz, *Silence and Pauses,* p. 90; she is so startled by the lack of musicological research that she mentions it repeatedly (see, for example, pp. xi and 84). Noteworthy in this regard is the lack of any article on the history or theory of silence in *New Grove.*

94. Danielewicz-Betz, *Silence and Pauses,* p. 84. The expanded definition of silence to include various low-level sounds is typical of most discussion of musical silence. For example, Lewis Jones ("Silence and Music," in *Silence and Music and Other Essays* [Sussex: The Book Guild, 1992], pp. 7–43) also discusses boundary silence ("Emergent Music") as well as music that represents silence ("Silence as part of Music," "Unharmonised Music," and "Music that Describes Silence").

95. Legrand, "Pauses fonctionnelles et silences expressifs: Esquisse d'une typologie des silences dans la musique du baroque tardif," *Les cahiers du CIREM,* no. 32–34 (1994): 28–36.

96. Gaudibert, "Les silences: Essai sur les différentes catégories du silence musical," *Les cahiers du CIREM,* no. 32–34 (1994): 113–120.

97. I am grateful to Fleur de vie Weinstock, who worked with me as a research assistant in 1996 when she was an undergraduate at Harvard University and I was a Fellow at the Bunting Institute at Radcliffe College. Her compilation of silent moments in the cantatas forms the background to this discussion.

98. See the edition of this work in Ellen T. Harris, ed., *G. F. Handel: Cantatas for Alto and Continuo* (Oxford: Oxford University Press, 2001).

99. Translation by Terence Best in Marx, *Kantaten mit Instrumenten* I, p. xlvii.

100. In the modern edition, an editorial question mark is added to this one iteration of "perché," but not to any of the others (Marx, *Kantaten mit Instrumenten* I, p. 276).

101. This was a continuing issue in Handel's compositional practice. When he rewrote the aria "La virtute è un vero nume" from the cantata *Splenda l'alba* (1710) as part of an Ode in honor of St. Cecilia associated with the performance of *Alexander's Feast* (1736), his new version contained grammatical rests throughout the aria. The 1710 version has none.

102. The rest in the bass under the word *solo* three measures before the end heightens this effect; Marx, *Kantaten mit Instrumenten* II, provides an *f* in the bass, which note has been obliterated by Handel and replaced with a rest.

103. As with "Ho fuggito," the rest could easily be eliminated—either by changing the sustained dotted quarter to a quarter note and having the eighth upbeat follow immediately, or by extending the dotted quarter through the rests. In a later revision of this aria (1717–1718), Handel recomposed the ending more thoroughly and eliminated both the fermata and the rests.

104. Translation adapted from Terence Best in Marx, *Kantaten mit Instrumenten* II, p. xlvi.

6. Culmination of the Private

1. Hawkins, *History,* p. 859.

2. On Chandos and his Cannons estate, see C. H. Collins Baker and Muriel I.

Baker, *The Life and Circumstances of James Brydges—First Duke of Chandos* (Oxford: Clarendon Press, 1949); on the Cannons Concert, see pp. 132–133. For more recent research on Chandos's patronage of Handel, see Graydon Beeks, "'A Club of Composers': Handel, Pepusch and Arbuthnot at Cannons," *Tercentenary Collection,* pp. 209–221.

3. Beeks, "'Club of Composers,'" p. 210.

4. Ibid.

5. Patrick Rogers, "Dating 'Acis and Galatea': a Newly Discovered Letter," *MT,* 114 (1973): 792. Dalrymple (d. 1721) had been solicitor general to Queen Anne and from 1709 the queen's advocate in Scotland, placing him close professionally and geographically to the Scotsman Arbuthnot. The letter was written to Hugh Campbell (d. 1731), Third Earl of Loudoun, also a Scottish politician; see also *HHB* IV, p. 76.

6. Beeks, "'Club of Composers,'" p. 211.

7. See Smith, *Oratorios,* p. 276. Not only in the contemporary list of scores in Chandos's library, but in the earliest surviving scores, *Esther* is titled simply "Oratorium." In Chrysander's edition the 1732 adaptation and expansion of *Esther* for public performance is titled *Esther,* but the original Cannons version is titled *Haman and Mordecai.* Given that both Racine's play and Thomas Brereton's translation, the source texts for Handel's work, are titled *Esther* and that this is the title by which the work is commonly known, the *HHA* has also titled the 1718 version *Esther,* as I do here as well.

8. Brian Trowell ("*Acis, Galatea and Polyphemus:* a 'serenata a tre voci'?" in *Music and Theatre,* p. 82) and the Twickenham edition (Pope, *Minor Poems,* p. 434) both cite (Trowell with reservations) the preface to the libretto of Samuel Arnold's *Omnipotence,* based on Handel's music, where the authorship of both *Esther* and *Acis and Galatea* is attributed to the trio of authors; but the same preface also states that *Esther* was originally composed in German and *Acis and Galatea* in Italian, and therefore credits Pope, Arbuthnot, and Gay with an English translation suited to Handel's music. The extensive borrowings in *Esther* from the *Brockes Passion* give a bit of truth to this comment, but the general misconception concerning the origin of the Cannons works and the late date of the statement render it of little merit in a determination of the authorship of either work (*Omnipotence* [London: Printed for W. Griffin, 1773], pp. ii–iii).

9. Trowell, "*Acis, Galatea and Polyphemus,*" pp. 31–93.

10. Graydon Beeks, "Handel and Music for the Earl of Carnarvon," in *Bach, Handel, Scarlatti,* pp. 1–19; Beeks discusses the chronology of the anthems, showing that "the Cannons Concert did not grow steadily in every detail from its inception to its dispersal in 1721" (p. 5); thus the early anthems typically use three-part ensembles, although the "second" of the first four pairs uses four-part ensembles. The last three anthems use four- or five-part ensembles.

11. The additional roles are sung by soprano, alto, and three tenors as opposed to the STTTB distribution of named characters. However, in *Esther* the top choral "tenor" part is (also) labeled "alto," lessening the seeming discrepancy somewhat.

12. Transformed, that is, from rhymed decasyllabic couplets to shorter lines with four strong accents in iambic meter, with the rhyme returning therefore more quickly (see Ellen T. Harris, *Henry Purcell's Dido and Aeneas* [Oxford: Clarendon Press, 1987],

p. 34f., for a discussion of contemporary thought on sung English text). The example in the text is taken from Dean, *Oratorios,* pp. 194–195, where other examples are given.

13. *Ovid's Metamorphoses: in fifteen books. / Translated by Mr. Dryden. Mr. Addison. Dr. Garth. Mr. Mainwaring. Mr. Congreve. Mr. Rowe. Mr. Pope. Mr. Gay. Mr. Eusden. Mr. Croxall. And other eminent hands; publish'd by Sir Samuel Garth* . . . (London: J. Tonson, 1716). See John Winemiller, "Recontextualizing Handel's Borrowings," *JM,* 15/4 (1997): 444–470, for a complete list of the textual and musical borrowings in *Acis and Galatea.*

14. Pope, *Pastoral Poetry,* p. 364.

15. Peter Anthony Motteux and John Eccles, *The Rape of Europa by Jupiter* (1694) and *Acis and Galatea* (1701), Introduction by Lucyle Hook, The Augustan Reprint Society, no. 208 (Los Angeles: William Andrews Clark Memorial Library, 1981).

16. Dean, *Oratorios,* pp. 155, 157, and 160.

17. Ibid., p. 157; in Handel's opera *Orlando* (1732), Zoroastro's counsel to Orlando is a heroic version of Polyphemus's somewhat bumbling instruction to himself to give up feminine wiles and return to heroic glory ("Purgalo ormai da effeminate sensi . . . Di tua Gloria custode ti stimolo a seguirla" / "Purge all effeminate feelings from [your heart] . . . As guardian of your Glory I urge you to follow it"). I discuss other parallels between *Acis and Galatea* and *Orlando* in *Handel and the Pastoral Tradition* (London: Oxford University Press, 1980), but I am indebted to Richard Tarrant for this comparison.

18. Hughes was also close to Pope, who had based his poetic epistle *Eloisa to Abalard* (1717) on Hughes's English prose translation (1713) of a late seventeenth-century French elaboration of the original Latin. "Pope's correspondence with Hughes begins in 1714, and continues intermittently till Hughes's death in 1720" (Pope, *Other Poems,* p. 277, n. 5).

19. See Winemiller, "Recontextualizing Handel's Borrowings," p. 455. Note that "Hush ye pretty warbling choir" can be traced back through Handel's earlier works to an aria by Keiser with exactly the same affect, "Wallet nicht zu laut" from his opera *Octavia.* John H. Roberts, "Handel's Borrowings from Keiser," *GHB,* 2 (1986): 75.

20. See Dean, *Oratorios,* p. 197, and Winemiller, "Recontextualizing Handel's Borrowings," p. 452.

21. Pope, *Minor Poems,* p. 217.

22. Smith, *Oratorios,* chapter 11: "*Esther to Athalia,*" pp. 276–287.

23. Ibid., p. 277.

24. Ibid., p. 284.

25. Ibid., p. 279, citing the chapter on *Esther* in Olivier Lutaud, *Des révolutions d'Angleterre à la révolution française* (The Hague: Martinus Nijhoff, 1973), pp. 119–147.

26. Smith, *Oratorios,* p. 282.

27. *Memoirs of Martin Scriblerus* was mostly written in 1714 and in 1716–1718; other material was added in 1726–1727. For details of the club and an understanding of its goals, I am indebted to the fine edition and detailed commentary of Charles Kerby-Miller (Pope, *Scriblerus*).

28. Pope, *Scriblerus,* p. 171.

29. Ibid., p. 274.

30. The reference to the Esther story in the *Scriblerus* probably necessitates some amendment to Smith's statement that "Pope himself has left no reference to *Esther*" (Smith, *Oratorios,* p. 278).

31. Smith, *Oratorios,* p. 278–279.

32. Ibid., p. 280.

33. Ibid., p. 284.

34. Ibid., p. 280.

35. Gay, Pope, and Arbuthnot, as well as Jonathan Swift, the primary members of the Scriblerian Club, were particularly fond of including multiple subtexts or voices in their writing. Swift's *Gulliver's Travels,* Arbuthnot's "John Bull" pamphlets, Gay's *The Beggar's Opera,* and Pope's *Dunciad* are only the most obvious examples of (social, political, and literary) satire from their pens.

36. The relation of *Acis and Galatea* to the pastoral tradition has been raised often. I offer a musico-pastoral reading in *Handel and the Pastoral Tradition;* Trowell discusses the libretto in terms of Pope's theory of the pastoral in order to argue that the text was completed not by Pope or Gay but by John Hughes ("*Acis, Galatea and Polyphemus,*" pp. 83–93); and Diane Dugaw argues that *Acis and Galatea* depicts the destruction of the pastoral ("Parody, Gender, and Transformation in Gay and Handel's *Acis and Galatea,*" *18cS,* 29 [1996]: 345–367). I am indebted to both Trowell and Dugaw in the following discussion and have tried to highlight their specific contributions throughout. I am also grateful to Michael O'Loughlin for suggesting a comparison between Ambrose Philips and Polyphemus (Aston Magna Academy at Yale University, 1997).

37. John Gay, "The Proeme," in *The Shepherd's Week* (London: Ferd. Burleigh, 1714), p. [iv].

38. John Calhoun Stephens writes of the 27 April 1713 paper: "This *Guardian* is Pope's annoyed response to the praise of Ambrose Philips in the series on pastoral poetry" (*Guardian,* p. 640).

39. *Guardian,* pp. 161–162.

40. Dugaw also associates Acis with pastoral convention and his death with its death ("Parody, Gender, and Transformation," p. 357); she does not make a connection between Polyphemus and Philips.

41. E. J. Kenney, "Introduction," in Ovid, *Metamorphoses,* trans. Melville, p. xxv.

42. Roberts, "Handel's Borrowings," pp. 51–76, and John H. Roberts, ed., *Handel Sources: Materials for the Study of Handel's Borrowings. Reinhard Keiser: 'Adonis and Janus'* (New York: Garland Publishing, 1986), vol. 1.

43. Keiser and Handel first came into contact in Hamburg. The subject of Handel's first opera, *Almira* (1705), had already served Keiser for an opera produced in Weissenfels (1704) and was used again by Keiser in yet another version for Hamburg (1706). Thereafter two different librettos based on the story of Nero were set, probably in direct competition, by Keiser and Handel (with Keiser's seeming to win; Handel's score does not survive). Handel's setting of the *Brockes Passion* was also a competition in which Telemann, Mattheson, and Keiser participated. There can be little doubt that Handel was keenly competitive with his older rival. See John H. Roberts, "Keiser and Handel at

the Hamburg Opera," *HJb,* 36 (1990): 53–87, and Dorothea Schröder, "Zu Entstehung und Aufführüngsgeschichte von Händels Oper *Almira.* Anmerkungen zur Edition des Werkes in der Hallischen Händel-Ausgabe," *HJb,* 36 (1990): 147–153.

44. Roberts, "Handel's Borrowings," pp. 51–76.

45. My thinking on artists' relations to their predecessors is indebted to Harold Bloom, *The Anxiety of Influence: A Theory of Poetry* (London: Oxford University Press, 1973).

46. See note 19 above; see also Roberts, "Keiser and Handel at the Hamburg Opera," for the relationship of Galatea's "Heart the seat of soft delight" to Keiser's aria "Fonte, che stilli" in the opera *Arsinoe.*

47. Dugaw recognizes the centrality of Galatea to the Cannons version of *Acis and Galatea,* but describes her generally as "the poignant, ambivalent, and interiorizing onlooker of a very modern-seeming world" ("Parody, Gender, and Transformation," p. 346).

48. Eve Kosofsky Sedgwick, *The Epistemology of the Closet* (Berkeley: University of California Press, 1990).

49. Marcel Proust, *Remembrance of Things Past: Cities of the Plain,* trans. C. K. Scott Moncrieff (New York: Vintage Books, 1970), p. 49. Proust quotes directly from Racine's *Esther,* Act I, ll. 122–124 and 101–106.

50. Sedgwick, *Epistomology of the Closet,* pp. 75–76.

51. For contemporary, published transcripts of sodomy trials see *Select Trials for Murders, Robberies, Rapes, Sodomy, Coining, Frauds, and other Offences: at the Sessions-House in the Old-Bailey . . .,* vol. 1: 1720–1724 (London: J. Wilford, 1735), vol. 2: 1724–1732 (London: J. Wilford, 1735); see also Bray, *Homosexuality,* chap. 4: "Molly," pp. 81–114.

52. Crompton, *Byron and Greek Love,* p. 30; Crompton provides a detailed discussion of Bentham's unpublished papers on homosexuality, pp. 19–53.

53. A description of the "vast Concourse of People [that] had assumbled upon the Occasion, . . . who had collected dead Dogs, Cats, &c. in great Abundance, which were plentifully thrown at them," and of the death of one of the men convicted for attempted sodomy and the horrible injuries of the other appears in *The Daily Advertiser,* 11 April 1780, p. 1, col. 2. Burke's speech is given in *The Parliamentary History of England from the Earliest Period to the Year 1803* (London: Printed by T. C. Hansard, 1814), vol. 21, cols. 388–389. Both are discussed by Crompton, *Byron and Greek Love,* p. 32.

54. Crompton, *Byron and Greek Love,* p. 27.

55. Bray, *Homosexuality,* p. 114.

56. I am grateful to John Winemiller for pointing out the original text; see his article, "Recontextualizing Handel's Borrowings," pp. 444–470.

57. See, for example, Trowell, *"Acis, Galatea and Polyphemus,"* pp. 86–89; Dugaw writes that "Dean—like other critics—certainly overreads Gay's dependence on Pope's *Autumn* for these lines, [but] there may indeed be a poignant evocation of the polished realm of these early pastorals" ("Parody, Gender, and Transformation," p. 357, n. 35).

58. Pope, *Pastoral Poetry,* p. 46.

59. See Robert H. MacDonald, *William Drummond of Hawthornden: Poems and*

Prose (Edinburgh: Scottish Academic Press, 1976), especially "Poems," bk. 1, Sonnet xlvi and bk. 2, Song 1, and "Sonnets," 1. Bray, *Homosexuality,* associates the name Alexis specifically with homosexuality, making specific reference to Marlowe (p. 64); Bray, however, also writes: "It would be anachronistic and naive to see a validation of homosexual love in the writings of . . . Drummond" (p. 60). The caution is appropriate to relationships involving genital sex, but not to other types of same-sex affection. Whatever the true relationship of Drummond and Sir William may have been, Pope seems to have associated Drummond's poems about Damon and Alexis with Virgil's and his own poetic homoeroticism.

60. David F. Greenberg, *The Construction of Homosexuality* (Chicago: University of Chicago Press, 1988), p. 145.

61. Euripides, *Cyclops,* in David Kovacs, trans., *Euripides: Cyclops, Alcestis, Medea* (Cambridge, Mass.: Harvard University Press, 1994), p. 129, ll. 578–584. The final line of this quotation is sometimes omitted in translation, as in *Three Greek Plays for the Theatre,* trans. Peter D. Arnott (Bloomington: Indiana University Press, 1961), following, presumably, an earlier practice of deleting homosexual sentiments in classical works where possible.

62. Voltaire, *Oeuvres complètes* (1785), vol. 29, p. 323, n. 17; cited in Crompton, *Byron and Greek Love,* p. 22.

63. Dugaw, "Parody, Gender, and Transformation," p. 352. See the introduction of the facsimile edition for a discussion of Eccles's song: Curtis Price, ed., *Don Quixote: The Music in the Three Plays of Thomas Durfey* (Tunbridge Wells: R. Macnutt, 1984). On Purcell's song, see Curtis Price, *Henry Purcell and the London Stage* (Cambridge: Cambridge University Press, 1984), pp. 215–216.

64. William Averell, *A mervailous combat of contrarieties. Malignantlie striuing in the me[m]bers of mans bodie, allegoricallie representing vnto vs the enuied state of our florishing commonwealth: wherin dialogue-wise by the way, are touched the extreame vices of this present time. VVith an earnest and vehement exhortation to all true English harts, couragiously to be readie prepared against the enemie* (Printed by I. C. for Thomas Hacket, 1588), quoted in Simon Shepherd, *Amazons and Warrior Women: Varieties of Feminism in Seventeenth-Century Drama* (Brighton: The Harvester Press, 1981), p. 67.

65. See Lucyle Hook, "Introduction," in Peter Anthony Motteux and John Eccles, *The Rape of Europa by Jupiter (1694) and Acis and Galatea (1701),* The Augustan Reprint Society, no. 208 (Los Angeles: William Andrews Clark Memorial Library, 1981).

66. Curtis Price and Irena Cholij, "Dido's Bass Sorceress," *MT,* 127 (1986): 615–618.

67. Theocritus, *Poems,* trans. Rist, p. 80.

Epilogue: "True Representation"

1. As quoted in [Richard] Romney Sedgwick, *House of Commons 1715–1754* (London: Her Majesty's Stationery Office, 1970), p. 444.

2. Norton, *Molly House,* p. 49.

3. *The Tryal and Condemnation of Mervin, Lord Audley Earl of Castle-Haven at Westminster, April the 5th 1631* (London, 1699), facsimile reproduction in *Sodomy Trials.*

4. *The Women-Haters Lamentation* (London, 1707), quoted in the Prologue.

5. As quoted in Bray, *Homosexuality,* p. 100.

6. *The Fifteenth Account of the Progress made toward suppressing profaneness and debauchery* (London, 1710), as quoted in Norton, *Molly House,* p. 52.

7. Tim Hitchcock, *English Sexualities, 1700–1800* (London: Macmillan Press, 1997), p. 71.

8. The data on sodomy and rape cases were gathered from *Select Trials for Murders, Robberies, Rapes, Sodomy, Coining, Frauds, and other Offences: at the Sessions-House in the Old-Bailey . . .,* vol. 2: 1724–1732 (London: J. Wilford, 1735).

9. *Plain Reasons for the Growth of Sodomy in England* (London: A. Dodd and E. Nutt, c. 1730), p. 22.

10. Louis Crompton, "Gay Genocide: From Leviticus to Hitler," in Louie Crew, ed., *The Gay Academic* (Palm Springs, Calif.: ETC Publications, 1978), pp. 67–91, provides details of this pogrom in Holland, including contemporary prints and a list of those who were executed with their reactions to sentencing; see also, for a brief summary, Norton, *Molly House,* pp. 253–254.

11. *Plain Reasons for the Growth of Sodomy,* pp. 11–12.

12. Facsimile reproduction in *Sodomy Trials.*

13. Bray, *Homosexuality,* p. 90, in reference to the *44th Account of . . . the Societies for Promoting Reformation of Manners,* also discussed in Norton, *Molly House,* p. 69.

14. *Memoirs of the Court of Lilliput* (London: J. Roberts, 1727), attributed by Pope to Eliza Haywood; see J. V. Guerinot, *Pamphlet Attacks on Alexander Pope 1711–1744: A Descriptive Bibliography* (London: Methuen, 1969), p. 99. The use of the word "stature" plays on the dual meaning of physical size (Pope was a very small man) and social significance, and the scene itself is borrowed directly from the episode in Swift's *Gulliver's Travels* when Gulliver is stranded among the giants of Brobdingnag: "That which gave me the most Uneasiness among these Maids of Honour, when my Nurse carried me to visit them, was to see them use me without any Manner of Ceremony, like a Creature who had no Sort of Consequence. For, they would strip themselves to the Skin and put on their Smocks in my Presence, while I was placed on their Toylet directly before their naked Bodies; which, I am sure, to me was very far from being a tempting Sight, or from giving me any other Motions than those of Horror and Disgust." (*Gulliver's Travels,* ed. Christopher Fox [Boston: Bedford Books, 1995], p. 120).

The use of this passage for an attack on Pope carried a number of stings besides alleging impotence with women. It made fun of Pope's physical size, it suggested that he was of no social consequence, it suggested further that he had no interest in women (no "Will . . . of doing any . . . Mischief"), and it used the work of Pope's closest friend, Swift, as its basis.

15. *The Progress of Wit: A Caveat. For The Use of an Eminent Writer* (London: J. Wilford, 1730).

16. Hill was angered by a critical note in the *Dunciad* that he took, probably correctly, to be about him. Hill and Pope carried on a heated correspondence following the publication of *A Caveat,* in which Hill threatened further publications "correcting" Pope. Pope writes (26 January 1731), "But I do know *certainly,* my moral Life is *superior*

to that of most of the *Wits* of these Days," and Hill responds (28 January 1731), "If you had not been in the *Spleen,* when you wrote me this Letter, I persuade myself, you would not, immediately after censuring the *Pride* of Writers, have asserted, that you, *certainly, know* your moral Life, above that of most of the Wits of these Days: At any other Time, you would have remembered, that *Humility* is a moral Virtue." The correspondence seems ultimately to have allowed both men to vent their spleen. Hill never published his *Essay on Propriety, and Impropriety, . . . from the Writings of Mr. Pope,* sending Pope the original manuscript, and Pope omitted the offensive note in the next edition of the *Dunciad.* See Pope, *Correspondence,* vol. 3, pp. 164–177.

17. *Guardian,* no. 40 (27 April 1713), p. 160.

18. Robert Halsband, *Lord Hervey: Eighteenth-Century Courtier* (New York: Oxford University Press, 1974), pp. 109–111; Pope, *Imitations,* p. 119, notes to ll. 321, 325, and 329.

19. See Brian Trowell, "*Acis, Galatea and Polyphemus:* a 'serenata a tre voci'?" in *Music and Theatre* for details of these earlier performances.

20. See Ellen T. Harris, *Handel and the Pastoral Tradition* (Oxford: Oxford University Press, 1980), pp. 212–223 for a detailed discussion of this version, with a chart illustrating the interleaving process on pp. 216–217.

21. See Dean, *Oratorios,* pp. 178–179; Handel also never restored Polyphemus's misogynist aria, "Cease to beauty to be suing," or Galatea's "Must I my Acis still bemoan" with its text about the "lovely charming youth" dying for his "constancy and truth."

22. Charles Nicolas Sonnini, *Travels in Upper and Lower Egypt,* trans. Henry Hunter (London: Printed for J. Stockdale, 1799), vol. 1, pp. 251–252, as quoted in Crompton, *Byron and Greek Love,* pp. 117–118.

23. *Celebration,* pp. 40–41.

24. Laetitia-Matilda Hawkins, *Anecdotes, Biographical Sketches and Memoirs* (London: F. C. and J. Rivington, 1822), vol. 1, pp. 195ff.

25. 19 July 1740, Hampshire Record Office (9M73/G556/6); partially quoted in Rosemary Dunhill, *Handel and the Harris Circle* (Winchester: Hampshire Record Office, 1995), pp. 7–8. I am grateful to Lord Malmesbury for permission to publish material from the Harris family correspondence (see further below). An edition of extensive excerpts from these letters edited by Rosemary Dunhill and Donald Burrows covering all discussions involving music is in the process of publication by Oxford University Press.

26. Richardson, "The Science of a Connoisseur," p. 196, as quoted in Jenny Uglow, *Hogarth: A Life and a World* (New York: Farrar, Straus and Giroux, 1997), p. 73.

27. Uglow, *Hogarth,* p. 58.

28. Cesar Ripa, *Iconologia, or Moral Emblems* (London: Benjamin Motte, 1709), as quoted in Ronald Paulson, *Emblem and Expression: Meaning in English Art of the Eighteenth Century* (Cambridge, Mass.: Harvard University Press, 1975), p. 55.

29. Ernst Kris, "The Psychology of Caricature," in Ernst Kris, ed., *Psychoanalytic Explorations in Art* (New York: International Universities Press, 1952), p. 180.

30. M. Dorothy George, *English Political Caricature to 1792* (Oxford: Clarendon Press, 1959), pp. 11, 85–86.

31. Uglow, *Hogarth,* p. 57.

32. Burrows, "Handel: His Life and Work," in *Celebration,* p. 9.

33. Richard W. Wallace, "Joseph Goupy's Satire of George Frideric Handel," *Apollo,* 117 (1983): 104–105.

34. Edward F. Rimbault, "Goupy's Caricature of Handel," *Notes & Queries,* 5th Series, 5 (1876): 263–265; Wallace, "Goupy's Satire," pp. 104–105.

35. James Hall, *Illustrated Dictionary of Symbols in Eastern and Western Art* (London: J. Murray, 1994), pp. 10 and 200; see also Wallace, "Goupy's Satire," pp. 104–105.

36. *Celebration,* p. 40.

37. Rimbault, "Goupy's Caricature," p. 264.

38. Pope, *Dunciad,* p. 346; see also Deutsch, *Handel,* p. 543. The passage is discussed in Smith, *Oratorios,* pp. 76–77.

39. Ripa, *Iconologia,* p. 39, fig. 153.

40. Ibid., p. 1, fig. 4.

41. Ibid., p. 67, fig. 268.

42. *Metamorphoses,* trans. A. D. Melville (Oxford: Oxford University Press, 1986), p. 75.

43. Rimbault, "Goupy's Caricature," p. 265; the gated wall does resemble in architectural outline the entrance to Burlington House in such Hogarth drawings as *Masquerades and Operas* (1724; see Uglow, *Hogarth,* pp. 99–101) and *Taste* (c. 1732; see Deutsch, *Handel,* illustration V, after p. 64).

44. *The Reminiscences of Henry Angelo I* (1904), p. 316, as cited in *Celebration,* p. 41.

45. See Wallace, "Goupy's Satire," pp. 104–105.

46. Hall, *Illustrated Dictionary,* p. 34.

47. Ripa, *Iconologia,* p. 7, fig. 26.

48. *Celebration,* pp. 40–41.

49. As quoted in Bray, *Homosexuality,* p. 16.

50. Revised Standard Version.

51. Rimbault, "Goupy's Caricature," p. 264.

52. *Celebration,* p. 40; Wallace, "Goupy's Satire," p. 104.

53. Hall, *Illustrated Dictionary,* p. 200.

54. Michael Rocke, *Forbidden Friendships: Homosexuality and Male Culture in Renaissance Florence* (New York: Oxford University Press, 1996), pp. 109 and 223; see also the references in Jean Toscan, *Le Carnaval du Langage: Le Lexique Erotique des Poetes de l'Equivoque de Burchiello à Marino (Xve–XVIIe Siècles)* (Lille: Presses Universitaires de Lille, 1981), under *gufo,* vol. 4, p. 1705.

55. Norton, *Molly House,* p. 135.

56. Lady Llanover (Augusta Hall), ed., *The Autobiography and Correspondence of Mary Granville, Mrs. Delany* . . . (London: Richard Bentley, 1861–1862), vol. 2, p. 267.

57. *Autograph Letters of George Frideric Handel and Charles Jennens* (London: Christie, Manson & Woods, 1973), p. 25, cited in David Hunter, "Margaret Cecil, Lady Brown: 'Persevering Enemy to Handel' but 'Otherwise Unknown to History,'" *WM,* 3 (1999): 49, n. 43.

58. Mainwaring, *Memoirs,* p. 134.

59. The misogynistic attitude associating Handel's enemies solely with women is examined in Hunter, "Lady Brown," pp. 43–58.

60. This poem is discussed in Hunter, "Lady Brown," pp. 48–50, and in Hunter, "Advice to Mr. Handel," *Newsletter of the American Handel Society,* 12/3 (1997): 3 and 6; the poem survives in a single sheet in Houghton Library, Harvard University.

61. Ovid, *Metamorphoses,* trans. Melville, bk. 10, p. 249.

62. The poem is reprinted in Deutsch, *Handel,* pp. 603–605, and in Hunter, "Lady Brown," p. 50 (italics as given).

63. Hunter, "Lady Brown," p. 51.

64. Italics in the original, as reproduced in Hunter, "Lady Brown," pp. 51–52.

65. Hugh Amory, ed., *Miscellanies by Henry Fielding, Esq.* (Oxford: Clarendon Press, 1993), vol. 2, p. 147, n. 6.

66. Modern commentators, typically, see only heterosexual innuendo. For example, on the basis of the third poem, which states that Hecate desired Orpheus to stay in Hell for her own pleasure, Duncan Chisholm adds Lady Brown to the list of women sexually attracted to Handel. His contention that her opposition derived from being personally scorned would, of course, match the situation of the Thracian women. However, Chisholm chooses not to mention Orpheus's preference for Thracian men and boys as the driving force for his rejection of women, nor does he continue the analogy to Handel at this point; see Chisholm, "Handel in Hell?" *Handel Institute Newsletter,* 9/1 (1998): [4].

67. Dunhill, *Handel and the Harris Circle,* pp. 6–7.

68. 19 January 1744, Hampshire Record Office (9M73/G642/31).

69. Hampshire Record Office (G3009/3); the puppet-show would have been given by the puppet-master Mr. [John] Russell, see Hunter, "Lady Brown," p. 54 and n. 65.

70. 28 February [1750?], Hampshire Record Office (9M73/G644/25).

71. 27 January 1752, Hampshire Record Office (G347/50).

72. As described in a letter of Hester Thrale, 27 June 1786; *Thraliana: The Diary of Mrs. Hester Lynch Thrale, 1776–1809,* 2nd ed., ed. Katharine C. Balderston (Oxford: Clarendon Press, 1951), vol. 2, p. 640, quoted in Crompton, *Byron and Greek Love,* p. 56.

73. *The Tryal and Condemnation of Mervin, Lord Audley Earl of Castle-Haven at Westminster, April the 5th 1631* (London, 1699), facsimile reproduction in *Sodomy Trials.*

74. BL add. ms. 47,028, fol. 7v.

75. Sonnini, *Travels in Upper and Lower Egypt,* pp. 251–252, as quoted in Crompton, *Byron and Greek Love,* pp. 117–118.

76. 1638 (2nd ed.), 1665 (3rd ed.), 1667 (4th ed.), 1677, extracted in John Harris, *A compleat collection of voyages and travels . . .* (London: T. Bennet, 1705); for a modern abridgment see Thomas Herbert, *Travels in Persia 1627–1629,* ed. Sir William Foster, C.I.E. (London: George Routledge & Sons, 1928).

77. Herbert, *Travels in Persia,* p. 155; see also p. 78 for a very similar description.

78. Ibid., p. 124.

79. *Catalogue of the Library of The Right Honorable The Earl of Malmesbury at Hurn Court 1815,* preserved at Houghton Library, Harvard University (f MS Eng 1396).

80. 22 April 1738, Hampshire Record Office (9M73/G944/1); 4 May 1738, Hampshire Record Office (9M73/G349/3).

81. Clive T. Probyn, *The Sociable Humanist: The Life and Works of James Harris 1709–1780* (Oxford: Clarendon Press, 1991), p. 141.

82. *Cyropaedia* VII, trans. Walter Miller (Cambridge, Mass.: Harvard University Press, 1947), vol. 2, pp. 287–291.

83. David F. Greenberg, *The Construction of Homosexuality* (Chicago: University of Chicago Press, 1988), p. 123.

84. On 28 July 1743, John Christopher Smith wrote to Anthony Ashley Cooper, Fourth Earl of Shaftesbury, about Handel's refusal to write for the Middlesex company. He says, "I wrote the contents [of the offer] to Mr. Goupy with the desire to communicate it to Mr. Handel (for it seems he has taken an aversion to see me, for having been to[o] much his friend)" (Betty Matthews, "Unpublished letters concerning Handel," *ML,* 40 [1959]: 263).

85. *The Works of James Harris, Esq. With an account of his life and character, by his son The Earl of Malmesbury* (London: F. Wingrave, 1801), p. xi.

86. See, for example, *A Faithful narrative of the Proceedings . . . against Robert Thistlethwayte, late Doctor of Divinity, and Warden of Wadham College for a sodomitical Attempt upon Mr W. French, Commoner of the same College* (London: Sold at the Britannia in the Old-Baily, 1739).

87. "New Handel Biographies," *MT,* 126 (1985): 90.

Title Index of Handel's Cantatas, Duets, and Trios

Page numbers in italics refer to music examples or tables.

General Index

Page numbers in italics refer to illustrations or music examples.